THE APPLICATION OF THE COMPETITION RULES
(ANTITRUST LAW) OF THE EUROPEAN ECONOMIC COMMUNITY
TO ENTERPRISES AND ARRANGEMENTS EXTERNAL
TO THE COMMON MARKET

THE APPLICATION OF THE COMPETITION RULES (ANTITRUST LAW) OF THE EUROPEAN ECONOMIC COMMUNITY TO ENTERPRISES AND ARRANGEMENTS EXTERNAL TO THE COMMON MARKET

BY

BOAZ BARACK

GIRTON COLLEGE

CAMBRIDGE

SPRINGER SCIENCE+BUSINESS MEDIA, LLC 1981

This book was submitted as a dissertation for the degree of Doctor of Philosophy in the University of Cambridge (June 1980).

Library of Congress Cataloging in Publication Data

Barack, Boaz.
The application of the competition rules (antitrust law) of the European Economic Community to enterprises and arrangements external to the Common Market.

Bibliography: p.
1. Antitrust law—European Economic Community countries. I. Title.
Law 343.4'072 81-2816

344.0372 AACR2

ISBN 978-94-017-4484-3 ISBN 978-94-017-4482-9 (eBook)
DOI 10.1007/978-94-017-4482-9

Originally published by Kluwer. Deventer. The Netherlands in 1981
Softcover reprint of the hardcover 1st edition 1981

I

ACKNOWLEDGMENT

This work is dedicated primarily to the late Prof. Jacques Van Damme under whose supervision I worked at the College of Europe, Belgium, where I pursued part of my research. I have benefitted no end from his wide knowledge and experience in the legal field and enjoyed his outstanding personality during our working hours. Professor Van Damme suddenly passed away last summer, and never lived to see this work completed.

To my supervisor at Cambridge, Mr. P.J. Allott, I owe thanks for his cooperation and for patiently bearing with my efforts at writing in a language which is not my mother-tongue. It was with Mr. Allott's recommendation that I benefitted from the immeasurable help of the Commission of the European Communities, which both provided me with documents and arranged personal meetings with Commission officials.

Grateful acknowledgement is due to the following bodies, who provided financial assistance and enabled me to carry out this study: Girton College, Cambridge for their research scholarship; the British Council (Israel), for their studentship; The Leo Baeck Lodge (London) and the Minna-James-Heinemann-Stiftung (West Germany) who came to my help when lack of finance became crucial in the final stage of the research; and to the Belgian Ministry of National Education and Dutch Culture which enabled me to work for a period of time at the College of Europe, Bruges.

ACKNOWLEDGMENT

This work is dedicated primarily to the late Prof. Jacques Van Damme under whose supervision I worked at the College of Europe, Belgium, where I pursued part of my research. I have benefitted no end from his wide knowledge and experience in the legal field and enjoyed his outstanding personality during our working hours. Professor Van Damme suddenly passed away last summer, and never lived to see this work completed.

To my supervisor at Cambridge, Mr. P.J. Allott, I owe thanks for his cooperation and for patiently bearing with my efforts at writing in a language which is not my mother-tongue. It was with Mr. Allott's recommendation that I benefitted from the immeasurable help of the Commission of the European Communities, which both provided me with documents and arranged personal meetings with Commission officials.

Grateful acknowledgement is due to the following bodies, who provided financial assistance and enabled me to carry out this study: Girton College, Cambridge for their research scholarship; the British Council (Israel), for their studentship; The Leo Baeck Lodge (London) and the Minna-James-Heinemann-Stiftung (West Germany) who came to my help when lack of finance became crucial in the final stage of the research; and to the Belgian Ministry of National Education and Dutch Culture which enabled me to work for a period of time at the College of Europe, Bruges.

TABLE OF CONTENTS

Page

Page

VII

Page

TABLE OF CASES

(The method of reference to Community cases dealt with in the text of the thesis is by giving a complete reference only once, when the case is first mentioned (to E.C.R. with regard to the Court's judgments and to C.M.L.R. with regard to Commission decisions). When the same case is again mentioned reference is made only to its name and to the appropriate pages or paragraphs in the publication. The following table of cases also provides references to the C.M.L.R. for the Court's judgments and to the JO. or the O.J., for the Commission decisions).

COURT OF JUSTICE OF THE EUROPEAN COMMUNITIES

ACF Chemiefarma v. Commission (41/69)[1970] E.C.R. 661.

Béguelin Import Co. v. G.L. Import-Export S.A. (22/71)[1971] E.C.R. 949; [1972] C.M.L.R. 81.

Belgische Radio en Televisie (BRT) and Société Belge des Auteurs Compositeurs et Éditeurs v. SV SABAM and NV Fonior (127/73)[1974], E.C.R. 51, 313; [1974] 2 C.M.L.R. 238.

B.M.W. Belgium SA and Others v. Commission (32, 36-82/78)[1979] E.C.R. 2345; [1980] 1 C.M.L.R. 370.

Boehringer Mannheim GmbH v. Commission (45/69)[1970] E.C.R. 769.

Brasserie de Haecht S.A. v. Wilkin (No.1)(23/67)[1967] E.C.R. 407; [1968] C.M.L.R. 26.

Brasserie de Haecht S.A. v. Wilkin (No.2)(48/72)[1973] E.C.R. 77; [1973] C.M.L.R. 287.

Bresciani v. Administrazione Italiana Delle Finanze (87/75)[1976] E.C.R. 129.

Cadillon S.A. v. Firma Höss Maschinenbau KG (1/71)[1971] E.C.R. 351; [1971] C.M.L.R. 420.

Centrafarm BV and de Peijper v. Sterling Drug Inc. (15/74)[1974] E.C.R. 1147; [1974] 2 C.M.L.R. 480.

Centrafarm BV and de Peijper v. Winthrop BV (16/74)[1974] E.C.R. 1183; [1974]2 C.M.L.R. 480.

Cimenteries v. Commission (8-11/66)[1967] E.C.R. 75; [1967] C.M.L.R. 77.

Consten SA and Grundig-Verkaufs GmbH v. Commission (56 & 58/64)[1966] E.C.R. 299; [1966] C.M.L.R. 418.

De Norre and de Clercq v. NV "Brouwerij Concordia" (47/76)[1977] E.C.R. 65; [1977] 1 C.M.L.R. 378.

Deutsche Grammophon Gesellschaft GmbH v. Metro-SB-Grossmärkte GmbH & Co. KG (78/70)[1971] E.C.R. 487; [1971] C.M.L.R. 631.

EMI Records Ltd. v. CBS United Kingdom Ltd. (51/75)[1976] E.C.R. 811; [1976] 2 C.M.L.R. 235.

EMI Records Ltd. v. CBS Grammofon A/S (86/75)[1976] E.C.R. 871; [1976] 2 C.M.L.R. 235.

EMI Records Ltd. v. CBS Schallplatten GmbH (96/75)[1976] E.C.R. 913; [1976] 2 C.M.L.R. 235.

ERTA, E.C. Commission v. EEC Council (22/70)[1971] E.C.R. 263; [1971] C.M.L.R. 335.

Europemballage Corporation and Continental Can Co. Inc. v. Commission (6/72)[1973] E.C.R. 215; [1972] C.M.L.R. 690.

Geigy AG v. Commission (53/69)[1972] E.C.R. 619; [1972] C.M.L.R. 557.

Haegeman Sprl v. Belgium (181/73)[1974] E.C.R. 449; [1975] 1 C.M.L.R. 515.

Hoffmann-La Roche & Co. AG v. Commission (85/76)[1979] E.C.R. 461; [1979] 3 C.M.L.R. 211.

Hugin Kassaregister & Hugin Cash Register Ltd. v. Commission (22/78) [1979] E.C.R. 1869; [1979] 3 C.M.L.R. 345.

I.C.I. v. Commission (48, 49, 51-57/69)[1972] E.C.R. 619; [1972] C.M.L.R. 557.

Istituto Chemioterapico Italiano SpA and Commercial Solvents Corporation v. Commission (6 & 7/73)[1974] E.C.R. 223; [1974] 1 C.M.L.R. 309.

Kramer (3/76)[1976] E.C.R. 1279.

La Technique Minière (LTM) v. Maschinenbau Ulm GmbH (56/65)[1966] E.C.R. 235; [1966] C.M.L.R. 357.

Metro-SB-Grossmärkte GmbH & Co. KG v. Commission (26/76)[1976] E.C.R. 1353.

Miller International Schallplatten GmbH v. Commission (19/77)[1978] E.C.R. 157-158; [1978] 2 C.M.L.R.334.

Nederlandse Vereniging voor de Fruit - en Groentenimporthandel and Nederlandse Bond van Grossiers in Zuiduruchten en ander Geïmporteerd Fruit "Frubo" v. Commission (71/74) [1974] E.C.R. 1031, 1095; [1975] 1 C.M.L.R. 646.

Nold v. Commission (4/73)[1974] E.C.R. 491; [1974] 2 C.M.L.R. 338.

Portelange S.A. v. Smith Corona Marchant International S.A. (10/69) [1969] E.C.R. 309; [1974] 1 C.M.L.R. 397.

Sandoz AG v. Commission (53/69)[1972] E.C.R. 845; [1972] C.M.L.R. 557.

Sirena v. Eda and Others (40/70)[1971] E.C.R. 69; [1971] C.M.L.R. 260.

"Suiker Unie" (Coöperative Vereniging) UA and Others v. Commission (40-48, 50, 54-56, 111, 113 & 114/73)[1975] E.C.R. 1663; [1976] 1 C.M.L.R. 295.

Transocean Marine Paint Association v. Commission (17/74)[1974] E.C.R. 1063; [1974] 2 C.M.L.R. 459.

United Brands Co. and United Brands Continental BV v. Commission (27/76) [1976] E.C.R. 425; [1978] 3 C.M.L.R. 83.

Van Zuylen Frères v. Hag AG (192/73)[1974] E.C.R. 731; [1974] 2 C.M.L.R. 127.

Völk v. Vervaecke (5/69)[1969] E.C.R. 295; [1969] C.M.L.R. 273.

Wilhelm v. Bundeskartellamt (14/68)[1969] E.C.R.1; [1969] C.M.L.R. 100.

COMMISSION DECISIONS

ABG Oil Companies Operating in the Netherlands, O.J. 1977, L117/1; [1977] 2 C.M.L.R. D1.

Alliance de Constructeurs Français de Machines-outils, J.O. 1968, L201/1; [1968] C.M.L.R. D23.

Aniline dyes cartel, J.O. 1969, L195/11; [1969] C.M.L.R. D23.

BMW Belgium NV and Belgian Dealers, O.J. 1978, L45/33; [1978] 2 C.M.L.R. 126.

Bulloch A. & Co. and Others v. The Distillers Company Ltd., O.J. 1978 L50/16; [1978] 1 C.M.L.R. 400.

Business Records of Fides SpA, O.J. 1979, L57/33; [1979] 1 C.M.L.R. 650.

Business Records of Vereininqung Deutscher Freiform-Schmieden, Re, O.J. 1978, L10/52; [1978] 1 C.M.L.R. D63.

CFA, J.O. 1968, L276/29; [1968] C.M.L.R. D57.

Christiani and Nielsen, J.O. 1969, L165/12; [1969] C.M.L.R. D36.

Cimbel, J.O. 1972, L303/24; [1973] C.M.L.R. D167.

Cobelaz (No.1)(Usines de Synthèse), J.O. 1968, L276/13; [1968] C.M.L.R. D45.

Cobelaz (No.1)(Cokeries), J.O. 1968, L276/19; [1968] C.M.L.R. D60.

Community v. Members of the Genuine Vegetable Parchment Association O.J. 1978, L70/54; [1978] 1 C.M.L.R. 534.

Continental Can Co. Inc., J.O. 1972, L7/25; [1972] C.M.L.R. D11.

CSV, O.J. 1976, L192/27.

Davide Campari-Milano Spa, O.J. 1978, L70/69; [1978] 2 C.M.L.R. 397.

DECA, J.O. 1964, 2761; [1965] C.M.L.R. 50.

DRU/Blondel, J.O. 1965, 2194; [1965] C.M.L.R. 180.

De Laval/Stork, O.J. 1977, L215/11.

Duro-Dyne/Europair, O.J. 1975, L29/11; [1975] 1 C.M.L.R. D62.

Franco-Japanese Ballbearings Agreement, O.J. 1974, L343/19; [1975] 1 C.M.L.R. D8.

French Producers of Fine Papers, O.J. 1972, L182/24.

French and Taiwanese Mushroom Packers, Re, O.J. 1975, L29/26; [1975] C.M.L.R. D83.

FRUBO, O.J. 1974, L237/16; [1974] 2 C.M.L.R. D89.

Gema (No.1) J.O. 1971, L134/15; [1971] C.M.L.R. D35.

Grundig/Consten, J.O. 1964, 2545; [1964] C.M.L.R. 489.

Henkel/Colgate, J.O. 1972, L14/14.

Hoffmann-La Roche & Co. AG., O.J. 1976, L223/27; [1976] 2 C.M.L.R. D25.

IFTRA Rules for Producers of Virgin Aluminium, O.J. 1975, L228/3; [1975] 2 C.M.L.R. D20.

Investigation at AM & S. Europe Ltd., O.J. 1979, L199/31; [1979] 3 C.M.L.R. 345.

Jallatte-Voss and Jallatte-Vandeputte, J.O. 1965, 37; [1966] C.M.L.R. D1.

Junghans, O.J. 1977, L30/10; [1977] 1 C.M.L.R. D82.

Kabelmetal/Luchaire, O.J. 1975, L222/34; [1975] 2 C.M.L.R. D40.

Kodak, J.O. 1970, L147/24; [1970] C.M.L.R. D19.

Lipton Cash Registers and Business Equipment Ltd. v. Hugin Kassaregister AB and Hugin Cash Registers Ltd., O.J. 1978, L22/23; [1978] 1 C.M.L.R. D17.

Miller International Schallplatten GmbH, O.J. 1976, L357/40; [1977] C.M.L.R. D61.

Nicholas Frères/Vitapro, J.O. 1964, 2287; [1964] C.M.L.R. 505.

Omega, J.O. 1970, L242/22; [1970] C.M.L.R. D49.

Pittsburgh CorningEurope, J.O. 1972, L272/35; [1973] C.M.L.R. D2.

Prym/Beka, O.J. 1973, L296/24; [1973] C.M.L.R. D250.

Putz M.V. Kawasaki Motors (UK) Ltd.; The Community v. Kawasaki Motoren GmbH, O.J. 1979, L16/9; [1979] 1 C.M.L.R. 448.

Raymond, J.O. 1972, L143/39; [1972] C.M.L.R. D45.

Rieckermann, J.O. 1968, L276/25; [1968] C.M.L.R. D78.

SABA, O.J. 1976, L28/19; [1976] 1 C.M.L.R. D61.

Sirdar/Phildar, O.J. 1975, L125/27; [1975] 1 C.M.L.R. D93.

Sugar Cartel, O.J. 1973, L140/17; [1973] C.M.L.R. D65.

Supexie, J.O. 1971, L10/12; [1971] C.M.L.R. D1.

Theal/Watts, O.J. 1977, L39/19; [1977] 1 C.M.L.R. D44.

Transocian Marine Paint Association, J.O. 1967, 163; [1967] C.M.L.R. D9; O.J. 1974, L19/18; [1974] 1 C.M.L.R. D11; O.J. 1975, L286/24; [1975] 2 C.M.L.R. D75.

United Brands Co. (Chiquita) O.J. 1976, L95/1; [1976] 1 C.M.L.R. D28.

VVVF, J.O. 1969, L168/22; [1970] C.M.L.R. D1.

Vacuum Interrupters Ltd., O.J. 1977, L48/32; [1977] 1 C.M.L.R. D67.

WEA/Filipacchi, SA, J.O. 1972, L303/52; [1973] C.M.L.R. D43.

Zoja/CSC-ICI, J.O. 1972, L299/51; [1973] C.M.L.R. D50.

SELECTION OF OTHER JUDICIAL DECISIONS

International Courts

Advisory Opinion in the Reparation for Injuries Case I.C.J. Reports (1949), p.174.

Barcelona Traction, Light and Power Co. Ltd. I.C.J. Reports (1970), p.1.

The S.S. "Lotus" P.C.I.J. Ser. A., No.9 (1927), p.1.

United States of America

Alfred Dunhill of London Inc. v. Republic of Cuba 425 U.S. 682 (1976).

American Industrial Contracting Inc. v. Johns-Manville Corp., 326 F. Supp. 879 (W.D.Pa. 1971).

Ampicillin Antitrust Litigation, In re, Civil No.882-870 (D.DC., filed March 19, 1970).

Application of Chase Manhattan Bank, 297, F. 2d 611 (2d Cir. 1962).

Atlantic Refining Co. v. FTC, 381 U.S. 357 (1965).

Baysoy v. Jessop Steel Co., 90F. Supp. 303 (W.D.Pa. 1950).

Burke v. Ford and Kune 389 U.S. 320, ss Sup. Ct. 443, 19L. Ed. 554 (1967).

California Motor Transport Co. v. Trucking Unlimited, 404 U.S. 508, 92 Sup. Ct. 609, 30 L. Ed. 2d 642 (1972).

Continental Ore Co. v. Union Carbide Corp., 370 U.S. 690, 82 Sup. Ct. 1404, 8 L. Ed. 2d 777 (1962).

Dobbins v. Kawasaki Motors Corp., 362 F. Supp. 54 (D. Ore. 1974).

FTC v. Brown Shoe Co., 384 U.S. 316, 86 Sup. Ct. 1501, 16 L. Ed. 2d 587 (1966).

FTC v. Motion Picture Advertising Serv. Co. 344 U.S. 392 (1953).

FTC v. Texaco, Inc. 393 U.S. 223, 89 Sup. Ct. 429, 21 L. Ed. 2d 394 (1968).

Gibbons v. Ogden, 22 U.S. (9 Wheat) 1, 189-190 (1829).

Grand Union Co. v. FTC, 300 F. 2d 92 (2d Cir. 1962).

Hoffman Motors Corp. v. Alfa Romeo S.p.A. 244 F. Supp. 70 (S.D.N.Y. 1965).

Holophane Co. v. United States, 119 F. Supp. 114 (S.D. Ohil 1954).

Ings v. Ferguson, 282 F. 2d 149 (2d Cir. 1960).

Interamerican Ref. Corp. v. Texaco Maracaibo, Inc. 307F. Supp. 1291 (D. Del. 1970).

International Shoe Co. v. Washington, 326 U.S. 310, 66 Sup. Ct. 154, 90 L. Ed. 95 (1945).

Investigation of World Arrangements, In re, 13 F.R.D. 280 (D.D.C. 1952).

McGee v. International Life Insurance Co., 355 U.S. 220, 78 Sup. Ct. 199, 2 L. Ed. 2d 223 (1957).

Manderville Island Farms, Inc. v. American Crystal Sugar Co., 334 U.S. 219, 232, 68 Sup. Ct. 996, 1004, 92 L. Ed. 1328, 1338 (1948).

Occidental Petroleum Corp. v. Buttes Gas & Oil Co., 331 F. Supp. 92 (C.D. Cal. 1971), aff'd per curiam, 461 F. 2c 1261 (9th Cir. 1972) cert. denied, 409 U.S. 950 (October 24, 1972).

Société Internationale, etc. (I.G. Chemie) v. McGranery, 14 F.R.D. 44, 53 (D.D.C. 1953).

Thomsen v. Cayser, 243 U.S. 66, 37 Sup. Ct. 353. 61 L. Ed. 597 (1917).

Timberlane Lumber Co. v. Bank of America, 549 F. 2d 597 (9th Cir. 1976).

Timken Roller Bearing Co. v. United States, 341 U.S. 593, 71 Sup. Ct. 971, 95 L. Ed. 1199 (1962).

United States v. Aluminium Co. of America, Eq. No. 85-73 (S.D.N.Y. 1937), 148 F. 2d 416 (1945).

United States v. American Tobacco Co., 221 U.S. 106, 31 Sup. Ct. 632, 55 L. Ed. 663 (1911).

United States v. Deutsches Kalisyndikat Gesellschaft, 31 F. 2d 199 (S.D.N.Y. 1929).

United States v. First National City Bank, 396 F. 2d 897 (2d Cir. 1968).

United States v. General Electric Co., 82 F. Supp. 753, 884, 885 (D.N.J. 1949).

United States v. General Electric Co., 115 F. Supp 835 (D.N.J. 1953).

United States v. Imperial Chemical Industries Ltd. 100 F. Supp. 504 (S.D.N.Y. 1951), opinion on relief, 105 F. Supp. 215 (S.D.N.Y. 1952).

United States v. National Lead Co., 332 U.S. 319, 67 Sup. Ct. 1634, 91 L. Ed. 2077 (1947).

United States v. Pacific Arctic Ry. & Nav. Co., 228 U.S. 87, 33 Sup. Ct. 443, 57 L. Ed. 742 (1913).

United States v. Scophony Corp. of America, 333 U.S. 795, 68 Sup. Ct. 855, 92 L. Ed. 1091 (1948).

United States v. Sisal Sales Corp., 274 U.S. 268, 47 Sup. Ct. 592, 71 L. Ed. 1042 (1927).

United States v. United States Alkali Export Assn. 325 U.S. 196, 65 Sup. Ct. 1120, 89 L. Ed. 1554 (1945).

United States v. United States Alkali Export Assn. Inc., 86 F. Supp. 59 (S.D.N.Y. 1949).

United States v. The Watchmakers of Switzerland Information Center Inc. 1963 Trade Cases para. 70.600 (S.D.N.Y. 1962).

United States v. Women's Sportswear Mfg. Assn. 336 U.S. 460, 69 Sup. Ct. 714, 93 L. Ed. 805 (1949).

Westinghouse Electric Corp. Uranium Contracts Litigation, 405 F. Supp. 315 (J.P.M.D.L. 1975).

Westinghouse Electric Corp. v. Rio Alson Ltd., Antitrust and Trade Reg. Rep. (BNA) No.786, at A-3 (N.D. 1 Il., filed October 15, 1976).

United Kingdom

Badische Anilin and Soda Fabrik v. Basle Chemical Works, Bindschedler [1898] A.C. 200, H.L.

British Nylon Spinners Ltd. v. Imperial Chemical Industries Ltd. [1953] 1 Ch. 19 (C.A. 1952)(Interlocutory Appeal); British Nylon Spinners Ltd. v. Imperial Industries Ltd. [1954] 3 Weekly L.R. 505 (Ch.)(final appeal).

Smith, Stone and Knight v. Birmingham Corporation [1939] 4 All E.R. 116.

Westinghouse Electric Corp. Uranium Contract Litigation [1978] 2 W.L.R. 81 (H.L. 1977), aff'd [1977] 3 W.L.R. 492 (C.A.) rev'd on add'l facts [1977] 3 W.L.R. 430 (C.A.).

BIBLIOGRAPHY

BOOKS

Barounos, D., Hall, D.F. and James, J.R., EEC Antitrust Law; Principles and Practice (London, 1975).

Baxter, I.F.G., Essays on Private Law: Foreign Law and Foreign Judgments (Toronto, 1966).

Beale, J.H., A Treatise on the Conflict of Laws, Vol. 3,(New York,1935).

Bebr, G., Judicial Control of the European Communities (London,1962).

Bellamy, C.W. and Child, G.D., Common Market Law of Competition (2nd ed., Morris, A.L., Asst., London, 1978).

Blake, H.M. (ed.), Business Regulation in the Common Market Nations, vols. 1, 2, 3,(New York, 1969).

Brewster, K., Antitrust and American Business Abroad (New York, 1958).

Brierly, J.L., The Law of Nations: An Introduction to the International Law of Peace (6th ed., Waldock, H., Oxford, 1963).

Brownlie, I., Principles of Public International Law (2nd ed., Oxford, 1973).

Cheatham, E.E., Griswald, E.N., Reese, W.L.M. and Rosenberg, M., Cases and Materials on Conflict of Laws (5th ed., New York, 1964).

Cheshire, G. and North, P.M., Private International Law (9th ed., London,1974).

Collins, L., European Community Law in the United Kingdom (London,1975).

Common Market Reporter; Doing Business in Europe (CCH ed., New York, loose leaf).

Cross, R. and Johes, P.A., An Introduction to Criminal Law (7th ed., London 1972).

Crotti, A.F., Trading Under EEC and United States Antitrust Laws (London,1977).

Cunningham, J.P., The Fair Trading Act 1973; Consumer Protection and Competition Law (London,1974).

Deringer, A. and Others, The Competition Law of the European Economic Community (CCH ed., Chicago, 1968).

Edwards, C.D., Control of Cartels and Monopolies; An International Comparison (New York, 1967).

EEC Commission, Practical Guide to Articles 85 and 86 of the Treaty of Rome (Brussels, 1962)(reprinted in Campbell, Common Market Law, Vol. 2, sec. 2605 (1969)).

Ehrenzweig, A.A., *A Treatise on the Conflict of Laws* (St. Paul, 1962).

Friedmann, W.G. (ed.), *Antitrust Law; A Comparative Symposium* (London,1956).

Fugate, W.L., *Foreign Commerce and the Antitrust Laws* (2nd ed., Boston, 1973).

George, K.D. and Joll, C. (eds.), *Competition Policy in the United Kingdom and the EEC* (London,1975).

Gijlstra, D.J. and Murphy, D.F. (eds.), *Leading Cases and Materials on the Competition Law of the EEC* (1976).

Goldman, B., *European Commercial Law* (London,1973).

Goodrich, H.F., *Handbook of the Conflict of Laws* (4th ed., Scoles, E.F. St. Paul, 1964).

Gower, L.C.B., *The Principles of Modern Company Law* (3rd ed.,London,1969).

Graupner, R., *The Rules of Competition of the European Economic Community; A Study of the Substantive Law on a Comparative Law Basis* (The Hague, 1965).

Hermann, A.H. and Jones, C., *Fair Trading in Europe* (London,1977).

Honig, F., Brown, W.J., Gleiss, A. and Hirsch, M., *Cartel Law of the European Economic Community* (London,1963).

Jessup, P.C., *Transnational Law; Storrs Lectures on Jurisprudence* (New Haven, 1956).

Joliet, R. *Monopolization and Abuse of Dominant Position: A Comparative Study of the American and European Approaches to the Control of Economic Power* (The Hague, 1970).

Joliet, R., *The Rule of Reason in Antitrust Law; American, German and Common Market Laws in Comparative Perspective* (Liege, 1967).

Kepteyn, P.J.G. and Van Themaat, P.V., *Introduction to the Law of the European Communities; After the Accession of New Member States* (London,1973).

Kintor, W. and Jooloon, M.R., *An International Antitrust Primer* (New York, 1974).

Korah, V., *Competition Law of Britain and the Common Market* (London,1975).

Korah, V. *An Introduction Guide to EEC Competition Law and Practice* (Oxford,1978).

Kronstein, H., *The Law of International Cartels* (Cornell, 1973).

Kronstein, H., Miller, J.T. and Schwartz, I.E., *Modern American Antitrust Law; A Guide to its Domestic and Foreign Application* (New York,1958).

Leigh, L.H., *The Criminal Liability of Corporation in English Law* (London,1969).

Lipstein, K., The Law of the European Economic Community (London,1974).

McLachlan, D. and Swann, D., Competition Policy in the European Community (Oxford,1967).

McNair of Gleniffer, McNair, A.D., The Legal Effects of War (3rd ed., Cambridge,1948).

Nussbaum, A., Principles of Private International Law (New York,1943).

Oberdorfer, C.W., Gleiss, A. and Hirsch, M., Common Market Cartel Law (CCH 2nd ed., Chicago, 1971).

OECD, Guide to Legislation on Restrictive Business Practices (Paris, loose leaf).

OECD, Restrictive Business Practices; Comparative Summary of Legislation in Europe and North America (Paris,1964).

Oppenheim, L.F.L., International Law, Vol. 1,(8th ed., Lauterpacht, H., London,1963).

Oppenheim, S.C. and Weston, G.E., Federal Antitrust Laws (3rd ed., St. Paul, 1968).

Rahl, J.A., Common Market and American Antitrust; Overlap and Conflict (New York,1970).

Salmond, J.W., On Jurisprudence (11th ed., London,1957).

Smit, H. and Herzog, P. (eds.), Columbia Law School Project on European Legal Institutions; The Law of the European Economic Community, Vol. 2,(New York,1976).

Sørensen, M. (ed.), Manual of Public International Law (London,1968).

Swann, D., Competition and Consumer Protection (London,1979).

Temple-Lang, J., The Common Market and Common Law; Legal Aspects of Foreign Investment and Economic Integration in the European Community, with Ireland as a Prototype (Chicago,1966).

Turner, J.W.C. (ed.), On Crime by W.O. Russell (12th ed.,London,1964).

Van Cise, J.G., The Federal Antitrust Laws (rev. ed., Washington,1955).

Von Mehren, A.T. and Trautman, D.T., The Law of Multistate Problems; Cases and Materials on Conflict of Laws (Boston, 1965).

Wheaton, H., Elements of International Law, Vol. 1,(6th English ed., London,1929).

Whiteman, M.M. (ed.), Digest of International Law, Vol. 1,(Washington, 1963), and Vol. 6 (Washington,1965).

Wilberforce, R.O., Campbell, A. and Elles, N., The Law of Restrictive Trade Practices and Monopolies (2nd ed. London,1966 & Supplements incl. 1969 & 1973).

Williams, G.L., Criminal Law; The General Part (2nd ed., London, 1961).

Wolff, M., Private International Law (2nd ed., Oxford, 1950).

Zwarensteyn, H., Some Aspects of the Extraterritorial Reach of the American Antitrust Laws (The Netherlands, 1970).

ARTICLES

Acevedo, "The EEC Dyestuffs Case: Territorial Jurisdiction" 36 The Modern Law Review 317 (1973).

Akehurst, "Jurisdiction in International Law" 46 British Year Book of International Law 145 (1975).

Allen, "The Development of European Community Antitrust Jurisdiction Over Alien Undertakings" 2 Legal Issues of European Integration 35 (1974).

Baker, D., "Antitrust and World Trade; Tempest in an International Teapot?" 8 Cornell International Law Journal 16 (1974).

Baxter, "Extraterritorial Application of the Domestic Law" 1 University of British Columbia Law Review 333 (1959).

Beckett, "Criminal Jurisdiction Over Foreigners" 8 British Year Book of International Law 108 (1927).

Bentill, "Control of the Abuse of Monopoly Power in EEC Business Law" 12 Common Market Law Review 59 (1975).

Brewster, "Extraterritorial Effects of the United States Antitrust Laws, An Appraisal" 11 American Bar Association, Antitrust Section Rep. 64 (1957).

Buxbaum, "The Applicability of German Cartel Law to Licenses of Foreign Patents" 8 Antitrust Bulletin 925 (1963).

Carlston, "Antitrust Policy Abroad" 49 Northwestern University Law Review 569 (1954).

Caudy, Note, "Sherman Antitrust Law; Applicability to Foreign Commerce" 37 Cornell Law Quarterly 821 (1952).

Cohn and Simitis, "'Lifting the Veil' in the Company Laws of the European Continent" 12 International and Comparative Law Quarterly 189 (1963).

Costouis, "Treaty Making Powers of the EEC; Article 238 and Association Agreements" 15 European Year Book 31 (1967).

Crawford, "The Criteria for Statehood in International Law" 48 British Year Book of International Law 93 (1977).

Dashwood, "The Principle of Direct Effect in European Community Law" 16 Journal of Common Market Studies 229 (1978).

De Aréchaga, "International Law in the Past Third of a Century" 159 Recueil 1 (1978-I).

Del Marmol and Fontaine, "Protection Against the Abuse of Economic Power in Belgium; The Law of May 27, 1960" 109 University of Pennsylvania Law Review 922 (1961).

Dietz, "Enforcement of Antitrust Laws in the EEC" 6 The International Lawyer 742 (1972).

Douglas and Shanks, "Insulation from Liability Through Subsidiary Corporations" 39 Yale Law Journal 193 (1929).

Edwards, C., "The Internationality of Economic Interests" 111 University of Pennsylvania Law Review 183 (1962).

Fawcett, "Trade and Finance in International Law" 123 Recueil 215 (1968-I).

Fitzmaurice, "The General Principles of International Law Considered from the Standpoint of the Rule of Law" 92 Recueil 1 (1957-II).

Forcione, "Intra-Enterprise Conspiracy Under the Antitrust Regulations of the Common Market" 25 The Business Lawyer 1419 (1970).

Fugate, "The Common Market and the United States Antitrust Laws" 38 New York University Law Review 458 (1963).

Furnish, "A Transnational Approach to Restrictive Business Practices" 4 The International Lawyer 317 (1970).

Graupner, "Commission Decision-Making on Competition Questions" 10 Common Market Law Review 291 (1973).

Haight, "International Law and Extraterritorial Application of the Antitrust Laws" 63 Yale Law Journal 639 (1954).

Hanbury, "The Territorial Limits of Criminal Jurisdiction" 37 Problems of Public and Private International Law, The Grotius Society 171 (1952).

Hollmann, "Problems of Obtaining Evidence in Antitrust Litigation; Comparative Approaches to the Multinational Corporation" 11 Texas International Law Journal 461 (1976).

Hug, "The Applicability of the Provisions of the European Community Treaties Against Restraints of Competition to Restraints of Competition Caused in Non-Member States, But Affecting the Common Market" in Cartel and Monopoly in Modern Law, Vol. 2, 639 (1961).

Hunnings, "Enforceability of the EEC-EFTA Free Trade Agreements" 2 European Law Review 163 (1977) and rejoinder in 3 European Law Review 278 (1978).

Jacquemin, "Application to Foreign Firms of European Rules of Competition" 19 Antitrust Bulletin 157 (1974).

Jennings, "Extraterritorial Jurisdiction and the United States Antitrust Law" 33 British Year Book of International Law 146 (1957).

Jennings, "General Course on Principles of International Law" 121 Recueil 327 (1967-II).

Jennings, "The Limits of State Jurisdiction" 32 Nordisk Tidskrift for International Recht 209 (1962).

Katzenbach, "Conflicts on an Unruly Horse: Reciprocal Claims and Tolerances in Interstate and International Law" 65 Yale Law Journal 1087 (1956).

Kincaid, "Sovereign Immunity of Foreign State-Owned Corporation" 10 Journal of World Trade Law 110 (1976).

Koppensteiner, "International Enterprises Under the Antitrust Law of the European Economic Community" 9 Journal of World Trade Law 287 (1975).

Korah, " The Control of Mergers Under Article 86 of the Rome Treaty; Continental Can" 26 Current Legal Problems 82 (1973).

Korah, "Istituto Chemioterapico Italiano Spa and Commercial Solvents Corporation v. Commission of the European Communities" 11 Common Market Law Review 248 (1974).

Krause, "The Multi-Corporate International Business Under Section 1 of the Sherman Act-Intra-Enterprise Conspiracy Revisited" 17 The Business Lawyer 912 (1962).

Krishnamurti, "National and Supra-National Antitrust Legislation; Concerns, Aspirations and Requirements of the Developing Countries" in Cartel and Antitrust Law: Speeches of an International Conference 213 (Gettlieb Duttweilen Institute, October 1973).

Kruithof, "The Application of the Common Market Antitrust Provisions to International Restraints of Trade" 2 Common Market Law Review 69 (1964).

Lawrence, "American Conception of Jurisdiction with Respect to Conflicts of Laws on Crime" 30 Transactions of the Grotius Society 184 (1944).

Lever, "The Extraterritorial Jurisidction of the Restrictive Practices Court" International and Comparative Law Quarterly, Supplement Publication, No.6, 117 (1963).

Lissitzyn, "The Meaning of the Term Denial of Justice in International Law" 30 American Journal of International Law 632 (1936).

McCoy, "The United States Parent Corporation-European Subsidiary Relationship Under the European Antitrust Regulations" 8 Virginia Journal of International Law 46 (1963).

McQuade, "Conspiracy, Multicorporate Enterprises and Section 1 of the Sherman Act" 41 Virginia Law Review 191 (1956).

Malawer, "International Law, European Community Law and the Rule of Reason" 8 Journal of World Trade Law 17 (1974).

Mann, "The Doctrine of Jurisdiction in International Law" 111 Recueil 9 (1964-I).

Mann, "The Dyestuffs Case in the Court of Justice of the European Communities" 22 International and Comparative Law Quarterly 35 (1973).

Mann, "Illegality and the Conflict of Laws" 21 Modern Law Review 130 (1958).

Mann, "Prerogative Rights of Foreign States and the Conflict of Laws" 40 Transactions of the Grotius Society 25 (1955).

Markert, "The Application of German Antitrust Law to International Restraints on Trade" 7 Virginia Journal of International Law 47 (1967).

Markert, "Recent Developments in International Antitrust Cooperation" 13 Antitrust Bulletin 355 (1968).

Metzger, "The Restatement of the Foreign Relations Law of the United States; Bases and Conflicts of Jurisdiction" 41 New York University Law Review 7 (1966).

Miller, "Extraterritorial Effects of Trade Regulation" 111 University of Pennsylvania Law Review 1092 (1963).

Mok, "The Cartel Policy of the EEC Commission 1962-1967" 6 Common Market Law Review 67 (1968).

Murray, "Case Note, Case 48/69, Dyestuffs Cases" 13 Virginia Journal of International Law 375 (1973).

Nebolsine, "Foreign Enterprises Under the Common Market Antitrust Rules" 38 New York University Law Review 479 (1963).

Note, "Extraterritorial Application of the Antitrust Laws; A Conflict of Laws Approach" 70 Yale Law Journal 259 (1961).

Note, 14 Harvard International Law Journal 621 (1973).

Note, "Limitations on the Federal Judicial Power to Compel Acts Violating Foreign Law" 63 Columbia Law Review 1441 (1963).

Note, "The Substantive Rules of Antitrust in the Common Market; Analysis and Approach" 17 Stanford Law Review 263 (1965).

Ongman, "Be No Longer A Chaos: Constructing a Normative Theory of the Sherman Act's Extraterritorial Jurisdiction Scope" 71 Northwestern University Law Review 733 (1977).

Rahl, "American Antitrust and Foreign Operations; What is Covered?" 8 Cornell International Law Journal 1 (1974).

Rahl, "A Rejoinder" 8 Cornell International Law Journal 42 (1974).

Riesenfeld, "The Protection of Competition" in American Enterprise in the European Common Market; A Legal Profile, Vol. 2, (E. Stein and T. Nicholson, eds.) 197 (1960).

Rom, "Restrictive Business Practices in EEC Agreements with Less Developed Countries" 12 Journal of World Trade Law 36 (1978).

Sarkar, "The Proper Law of Crime in International Law" 11 International and Comparative Law Quarterly 446 (1962).

Schapiro, "The German Law Against Restraints of Competition; Comparative and International Aspects" 62 Columbia Law Review I, 236 (1962).

Schwartz, I., "Applicability of National Law on restraint of Competition to International Restraints of Competition" in Cartel and Monopoly in Modern Law, Vol. 2, 701 (1961).

Seidl-Hohenveldern, "Limits Imposed by International Law on the Application of Cartel Law" 5 The International Lawyer 279 (1971).

Sheffer, "The Restrictive Business Practices Law" 14 Economic Quarterly 163 (No. 54-55, October 1967).

Skiöld, Åke, "Antitrust Problems in Connection With Dealings With The Common Market Countries" in the International Bar Association, Ninth Conference Report, 192 (Edinburgh, 1962).

Stanford, "The Application of the Sherman Act to Conduct Outside the United States; A View From Abroad" 11 Cornell International Law Journal 195 (1978).

Steindorff, "Annotations on the Decisions of the European Court in the Dyestuff Cases of July 14, 1972" 9 Common Market Law Review 502 (1972).

Suetens, "Belgium Antitrust Law 'In Action'" 2 Common Market Law Review 325 (1964).

Temple-Lang, "The Procedure of the Commission in Competition Cases" 14 Common Market Law Review 155 (1977).

Timberg, "United States and Foreign Antitrust Laws Governing International Business Transactions" in A Lawyer's Guide to International Business Transactions (Surrey and Shaw, eds.) 619 (1966).

Trautman, "A Study of the International Environment; The International Reach of American Regulatory Legislation Other Than The Sherman Act" in Antitrust and American Business Abroad (K. Brewster) 309 (1958).

Van Oven, "The Intra-Enterprise Conspiracy Paradox" in European Competition Policy 111 (1973).

Verzijl, "The Controversy Regarding the So-Called Extraterritorial Effect of the American Antitrust Laws" 8 Nederlands Tijdschrift voor International Recht 3 (1961).

Waelbroeck, "Enforceability of the EEC-ERTA Free Trade Agreements; A Reply" 3 European Law Review 27 (1978).

Weiner and Parzych, "The Webb-Pomerence Export Trade Act; A United States Antitrust Exemption" 6 Journal of World Trade 119 (1972).

Whitney, "Sources of Conflict Between International Law and the Antitrust Laws" 63 Yale Law Journal 655 (1954).

Willis and Pitofsky, "Antitrust Consequences of Using Corporate Subsidiaries" 43 New York University Law Review 20 (1968).

OTHER SOURCES

American Bar Association, Antitrust Developments 1955 - 1968, A Supplement to the Report of the Atty. Gen. Nat. Comm. to Study the Antitrust Laws (Chicago, 1968).

American Bar Association, Proceedings, Antitrust Section Conference on Antitrust and the European Communities (Brussels and Luxembourg, Sept. 23-26, 1963).

Antitrust Division, U.S. Dept. of Justice, Antitrust Guide for International Operations (1977), reprinted in BNA Antitrust and Trade Reg. Reports, No. 799 (1977), and Trade Reg. Reports (CCH) No. 226, pt. II (1977).

British Aide-Mémoire to the Commission of the European Communities of 20 October 1969. (Text in British Practice in International Law (1969), pp.58-60 (E. Lauterpacht ed.).

Council of Europe, Explanatory Report on the European Convention on the International Validity of Criminal Judgments (1970).

Council of Europe, Report to the Consultative Assembly by the Legal Committee (de Grailly, rapporteur), The Extraterritorial Application of Antitrust Legislation, Doc. 2123 (Jan. 25, 1966).

E.C. Commission, Seventh General Report; April 1963 - March 1964 (June 1964).

E.C. Commission, Eighth General Report; 1 April 1964 - 31 March 1965 (June 1965.

E.C. Commission, First General Report on the Activities of the Communities; 1967 (February 1968).

E.C. Commission, First Report on Competition Policy (April 1972).

E.C. Commission, Second Report on Competition Policy (April 1973).

E.C. Commission, Third Report on Competition Policy (May 1974).

E.C. Commission, Fourth Report on Competition Policy (April 1975).

E.C. Commission, Fifth Report on Competition Policy (April 1976).

E.C. Commission, Sixth Report on Competition Policy (April 1977).

E.C. Commission, Seventh Report on Competition Policy (April 1978).

E.C. Commission, Eighth Report on Competition Policy (April 1979).

Final Report of the European Advisory Committee on Tentative Draft No.2, Restatement of the Foreign Relations Law of the U.S. (Jurisdiction) (A.L.I. 1961).

Harvard Draft Convention on Jurisdiction with Respect to Crime 29 American Journal of International Law Supplement 439 (1935).

Harvard Research in International Law, Jurisdiction With Respect to Crime 29 American Journal of International Law Supplement 435 (1935) Part II.

House Committee on Interstate and Foreign Commerce, 94th Cong., 2nd Session, Hearings on International Uranium Supply and Demand Before the Sub-Committee on Oversight and Investigations (1976).

House Judiciary Committee, 89th Cong., 2nd Session, Hearings on International Aspects of Antitrust Before the Sub-Committee on Antitrust and Monopoly (1966).

House Judiciary Committee, 90th Cong., 2nd Session, Hearings on Economic Concentration; Concentration Outside the United States Before the Subcommittee on Antitrust and Monopoly (1968).

International Law Association, Report of the Fifty First Conference Tokyo (1964).

International Law Association, Report of the Fifty Second Conference, Helsinki (1966).

International Law Association, Report of the Fifty Third Conference, Buenos Aires (1968).

International Law Association, Report of the Fifty Fourth Conference, The Hague (1970).

International Law Association, Report of the Fifty Fifth Conference, New York (1972).

Johnson, Bases of International Jurisdiction, Report of the International Law Conference 1962 (The David Davis Memorial Institute of International Studies).

OECD, Report of the Committee of Experts on Restrictive Business Practices, Export Cartels (Paris, 1974).

OECD, Report of the Committee of Experts on Restrictive Business Practices, Restrictive Business Practices of Multinational Enterprises (Paris,1977).

Report of the Attorney General's National Committee to Study the Antitrust Laws (Washington, 1955).

UNCTAD, Report of the Ad Hoc Group of Experts, Restrictive Business Practices in Relation to the Trade and Development of Developing Countries (1973)(Doc. TD/B/C.2/119).

UNCTAD, Report of the Third Ad Hoc Group of Experts on Restrictive Business Practices, 6th Session (April 17-27, 1979)(TD/250; TD/B/C.2/201; TD/B/C.2/AC.6/20).

UNCTAD, Restrictive Business Practices: Studies on the United Kingdom of Great Britain and Northern Ireland, United States of America and Japan (edited by D. Swann and D. Greer and UNCTAD Secretariat resp., 1973)(TD/B/390).

United Nations Department of Economic and Social Affairs, Report of Group of Eminent Persons, The Impact of Multinational Corporations on Development and on International Relations, UN Doc.E/5500/Rev. 1st/ESA/6 (1974).

LIST OF ABBREVIATIONS

(For full names of periodicals mentioned in the text see Table of Articles)

A.C.	Appeal Cases
All E.R.	All England Law Reports
Art.(s)	Article(s)
BGB	Bürgerliches Gesetzbuch
BGBl.	Bundesgesetzblatt
BGH	Bundesgerichtshof
BKA	Bundeskartellamt
Bull.E C	Bulletin of the European Communities. EC Commission
Ch.	Chancery Division of the High Court
C.M.L.R.	Common Market Law Reports
Cmnd.	Command Paper
EC	European Communities
E.C.R.	European Court Reports
ECSC	European Coal and Steel Community
EEC	European Economic Community
EFTA	European Free Trade Area
Euratom	European Atomic Energy Community
GATT	General Agreement on Tariffs and Trade
GmbH	Gesellschaft mit beschrankter Haftung
I.C.J.	International Court of Justice
I.L.A.	The International Law Association

J.O.	Journal officiel (des Communautés Européennes)
OECD	Organisation for Economic Cooperation and Development
O.J.	Official Journal (of the Communities)
P.C.I.J.Rep.	Permanent Court of International Justice Reports
Rec.	Recueil de la Jurisprudence de la Cour de Justice des Communautés Européennes.
Rec. d. Cours	Recueil des Cours de L'Académie de Droit International.
Reg.	Regulation
SA	Société anonyme
SpA	Società per Azioni
U.N.T.S.	United Nations Treaty Series
W.L.R.	Weekly Law Reports
WuW	Wirtschaft und Wettbewerb

CHAPTER I

The International Dimensions of the European Economic Community Competition Rules

1. IDENTIFICATION OF PROBLEMS CONCERNING THE SCOPE OF ANTITRUST LAWS

A. At the International Level

1-1. A glance at the many antitrust[1] statutes of Western countries might suggest that the antitrust problem is purely domestic in character, since these laws are largely, sometimes exclusively, concerned with restrictions affecting the home market. But there is in truth no reason to expect that the antitrust problem ends at the water's edge. Just as enterprises collude in fixing prices and allocating customers in home markets, so they concert policy in fixing export prices and allocating the world market. The major legal issue in the study is concerned with the fact that enterprises operating under the law of one country can act in a way which has anticompetitive effects in another country. To be able to control such restrictions - which are often referred to in literature as international restrictive business practices[2] - and to do so in an equitable way, it may

1. In North America competition law would be referred to as antitrust law. In this study these two terms are used quite interchangeably. In fact the term "antitrust law" is more convenient in the present context of law against restrictive business practices since the European Economic Community has explored many other avenues concerning competition, such as State aids, taxes and technical barriers to trade which are not topics under the study (see 1-7).

2. The use of the terms "restrictive business practices" and "restraints of trade" is to replace the term "cartel". These terms have a wider sense than the latter, i.e. they include both restrictive agreements (whether cartels among competitors or arrangements between business units from different lines of business who are not necessarily competitors) and monopolies. Such terms as are used in the study refer to all situations in which competition is absent or restricted (see Sheffer, "The Restrictive Business Practices Law" 14 Economic Quarterly 163 (H) (No. 54-55, Oct. 1967).

be necessary for a country to claim, or to appear to claim, "extraterritorial jurisdiction".

It is necessary to state here that the term "extraterritorial" as used in the present context only implies that the antitrust rules reach out to, or bring under the purview of these rules, enterprises situated abroad and/or behaviour that occurred outside the territory. It is no more than a factual observation, and the term "extraterritorial" has to be taken not as a normative but merely a descriptive adjective without legal connotation or value judgment.

1-2. The obvious typesof legal conflicts resulting from the extraterritorial reach of restrictive trade legislation are claims by States of jurisdiction contested by other States. Such conflicts often result in overlapping or concurrent jurisdiction of two or more States and may place transnational enterprises in double jeopardy. In fact the most frequent problem in international trade is the inconsistency of the antitrust laws which raises questions of priority or paramount interest.

Once jurisdiction has been asserted by a State there are issues of extraterritorial enforcement. The enforcement difficulties are on many occasions the structural reasons for a certain degree of inefficiency of antitrust legislation, because of a substantial number of procedural and legal points that create disjunction between jurisdiction and its exercise.[3]

1-3. The extraterritorial reach of restrictive trade legislation is by necessity a conflict-evoking type of legislation and regulation, because

3. See H. Kronstein, The Law of International Cartels 450-456 (1973), where a survey of limited methods to ease the position of plaintiffs in matters of enforcement is given.

of the existing differences with regard to the organization of the national economic systems in the various countries around the world. When commercial practices, resulting from different national regulations of business activity, are extended into the international plane a collision course is often inevitable. The underlying sources of conflicts, which stem largely from these divergencies in policies and economic interests, are listed by Brewster in the following order:

> .....first, we mention differences in legal technique.....; next the basic differences in national attitude and policies toward the cartel question; third, clashes of economic interest which may be fostered by antitrust enforcement; fourth, and perhaps most important, seeds of resentment against our alleged intrusion into the domestic affairs of other countries.[4]

1-4. In view of the increased (and continually increasing) participation by businessmen all over the world in, and the resulting expansion of, transnational business, the dangers of conflicts of all types described before are becoming a greater likelihood. The extraordinary growth of multinational enterprises over the past twenty years, their enormous size and preponderance in the key sectors of industry, indicate that the multinational enterprises may be only too easily tempted to abuse their dominant position anywhere in the world.[5] The striking features of this economic development clearly emphasize the international dimensions required for effective competition policy, and the need for international cooperation in combating restrictive business practices.

1-5. The recent growing interest among governments in the international dimensions of antitrust laws is a result of a host of influences among

---

4. K. Brewster, Antitrust and American Business Abroad 39 (1958).

5. See United Nations Department of Economic and Social Affairs, The Impact of Multinational Corporations on Development and on International Relations, Report of Group of Eminent Persons 83-86 UN Doc. E/5500/Rev. 1 St/ESA/6 (1974). See also European Parliament, Initial Report on the Communication from the Commission of the EEC to the Council (Doc.261/73) on Multinational Undertakings and Community Regulation, Working Documents 1974-1975, No. 292/74, p.15, para. 20.

which we can single out policies of regional economic integration, the general switch in emphasis from tariff to non-tariff barriers to trade, the growing interest in the role and impact of international organizations in controlling international restrictive business practices and the drive to promote the trade and development of the Third World. Various international bodies have often considered the establishment of international mechanisms for the control of international restrictive business practices and for the avoidance and settlement of conflicts which they raise. See 6-41 to 6-44.

B. At the European Economic Community Level

1-6. Articles (hereinafter "Arts.") 85 and 86 of the Treaty Establishing the European Economic Community[6] (hereinafter referred to as the "Treaty") lay down the European Economic Community's antitrust rules;[7] they form the back-bone of rules applying "to undertakings"[8] (the full text of both articles is given in 1-28). In furtherance of the competition policy of the European Economic Community (hereinafter "the Community") Arts. 85 and 86 have been applied to non-Community enterprises[9] (hereinafter "NCES"; in singular "NCE") and to arrangements that have been wholly or partly carried out outside the territorial boundaries of the Common Market. On

6. Treaty Establishing the European Economic Community, Rome, March 1957, UNTS 298, 4 Cmnd. 5179-II.

7. Arts. 87 through 89 prescribe how these rules are to be implemented and administered. Art. 90 applies to public utility undertakings. Art. 91 aims at bringing to an end dumping practices, and Arts. 92 to 94 are concerned with aids granted by States.

8. The meaning of the term "undertaking" is set out in Chapter II of the study. See also 1-29 to 1-30. It is sufficient here to point out that this term is interchangeable with the term "enterprise".

9. Normally references to nationality of enterprises, or other related corporations, are relevant with regard to the place of incorporation, a feature which often composes the traditional definition in private law of a "foreign company" (see Gower, The Principles of Modern Company Law 668 (3rd ed. 1969). However, since the doctrine of nationality may be excluded by the Treaty's competition rules and by the facts of cases, as applicable in antitrust matters, references in the study to NCES relate to international enterprises, comprised of companies or branch-establishments, primarily operating outside the Community. References to Community enterprises relate to enterprises primarily carrying on business within the Common Market.

the basis of these observations one could state that the application of the competition rules has an extraterritorial reach. Further gradual evolution of the international dimensions of the Community competition policy, in view of the preceding survey, is justifiably expected.

1-7. The Community competition legal sphere, like those of many other countries, is but a reflection of the economic and political spheres of the Community policies. For a proper insight into the problems of the extraterritorial reach of the rules it is indispensable first to understand the general role of competition policy.

The Treaty requires in Art. 3(f) "the institution of a system ensuring that competition in the Common Market is not distorted" as one of the activities to achieve the goals of the Community. A detailed description of the importance of competition policy for achieving these objectives (as listed in Art.2) is given by the Commission of the European Communities (hereinafter "the Commission") in the First Report on Competition Policy:

> Competition is the best stimulant of economic activity since it guarantees the widest possible freedom of action to all. An active competition policy pursued in accordance with the provisions of the Treaties establishing the Communities makes it easier for the supply and demand structures continually to adjust to technological development. Through the interplay of decentralized decision-making machinery, competition enables enterprises continuously to improve their efficiency, which is the sine qua non for a steady improvement in living standards and employment prospects within the countries of the Community. From this point of view, competition policy is an essential means for satisfying to a great extent the individual and collective needs of our society.
>
> At both Community and national levels, competition policy endeavours to maintain or to create effective conditions of competition by means of rules applying to enterprises in both the private and public sectors. Such a policy encourages the best possible use of productive resources for the greatest possible benefit of the economy as a whole and for the benefit, in particular, of the consumer. In this respect, the Commission is not only concerned with increasing by means of the rules of competition the quantity of goods available for consumption, but is also taking

> action to promote better information for consumers and to bring about the harmonisation of laws and the removal of technical barriers to trade, in order to provide the best possible opportunities for establishing a genuine common market. 10

1-8. Given the role of the competition policy it seems that a very wide range of situations involving foreign elements may come under the scrutiny of that policy. The variety of those situations could be well illustrated, in terms of persons and conduct, in a description of "international cartels" as given by Friedman and VerLoren Van Themaat:

> .....we ought to consider as international cartels not only those generally recognized as such, namely, cartels whose members are nationals of different states. We should also include those cartels that have international objectives, i.e., cartels composed either entirely of nationals, or foreigners, or both, which affect different national markets.....We should further include cartels whose members are nationals, but whose objectives are entirely foreign. 11

1-9. In this study we are therefore interested in examining in what direction the application of Community competition rules to cases with foreign elements is developing, what shortcomings can be observed and what corrective steps could be suggested.

While there is an abundance of literature dealing with the Community competition rules, one can also observe that the solution of issues connected with the extraterritorial application of these rules is still in an evolutionary stage of development. Allen, in an article on this topic, calls for a profound examination of the aspects which we have selected to research:

> The legal development of antitrust jurisdiction over aliens for the EEC has been marked by considerable theoretical confusion. Academic analysis is necessary in the field to identify the

---

10. First Report on Competition Policy, point 1.

11. W. Friedmann and P. VerLoren Van Themaat, "International Cartels and Combines" in Antitrust Law; A Comparative Symposium 483 (Friedmann ed. 1956).

characteristics of certain principles which have played an active role in the shaping of EEC law in this area, and to deduce any direction, be it apparent or necessary, in which Community law might proceed in this matter. 12

---

12. Allen, "The Development of European Community Antitrust Jurisdiction Over Alien Undertakings" in 2 Legal Issues of European Integration 35 (1974).

2. METHODOLOGY IN THE STUDY OF THE APPLICATION OF THE COMMUNITY COMPETITION RULES TO ENTERPRISES AND ARRANGEMENTS EXTERNAL TO THE COMMON MARKET

1-10. The proposed inquiry into the legal problems of the extraterritorial reach of the competition rules will be undertaken along several approaches: (1) an analysis of the normative aspects of the factually observed behaviour, i.e. the jurisdictional competence of the Community; (2) a detailed description of what factually can be observed, i.e. that the Treaty rules are applied to enterprises and conduct external to the Common Market in a variety of arrangements; (3) examination of the possible difficulties in antitrust enforcement depending on the qualification of the defendant, on the locus of the conduct, or both. Each of these analyses will alternatively be approached along the lines which are set out below.

Chapter I, in the remaining parts, will concentrate on the two main normative legal systems by which limits on the extraterritorial jurisdiction of the Community could be examined, i.e. the general principles of international law and the Community's own domestic rules (the legislative jurisdiction of the Community[13]).

The description of what factually can be observed under the judicial process of the Community with regard to the extraterritorial application of the rules will follow in Chapter II (dealing with jurisdiction over NCES)[14] and in Chapter III (dealing with jurisdiction over the foreign conduct, i.e. the types of prohibited arrangements).

---

13. Clarification of the term "legislative jurisdiction" is given in 1-16.
14. Jurisdiction over NCES is mentioned in the text not in the sense of personal jurisdiction but only as distinct from jurisdiction on the basis of anticompetitive conduct, although this distinction in Community law is often unclear.

The examination of the enforcement difficulties, in Chapter IV, will include matters of substance (the nature of orders and remedies with regard to conduct abroad) and matters of procedure (service of process abroad and the production of documents from outside the Common Market).

Chapter V will concentrate on a comparative study of the extraterritorial reach of antitrust laws other than the Community rules: the legislation of Member States and of the U.S. Such a study is essential for an adequate comprehension of antitrust problems in the international arena. The U.S. antitrust system has a particular importance in the study, since the concepts expressed by the Community in Arts. 85 and 86 were at least partially influenced by the U.S. Sherman Act (Secs. 1 and 2 respectively)[15]. See contents of the pertinent sections in 5-15.

Only after the various aspects of the extraterritorial reach of antitrust rules have been reviewed will a second and more searching look at jurisdictional limitations under international law and in accordance with State practice be taken (Chapter VI).

Eventually we shall attempt to propose a formula for the solution of problems of antitrust jurisdiction and enforcement, aiming at the elimination, reduction and resolution of legal and economic conflicts in ways generally acceptable to the Community.

1-11. Several issues are excluded from the scope of the study:

(1) although Arts. 85 and 86 apply both to the production of goods and the provision of services in all aspects of the Community's economic

---

15. Cf. A. Crotti, Trading Under EEC and United States Antitrust Laws 13-14 (1977).

life, their application in certain fields is subject to a number of exceptions (coal and steel, atomic energy, agriculture, transport by road, rail and inland waterways and transport by inland sea and air)[16]. For the purpose of coherence and convenience we shall not deal with the exceptions nor with special competition rules or regulations which are applicable in those fields;

(2) the present study is concerned only with Arts. 85 and 86 in so far as they are enforced by penal, quasi-penal or administrative sanctions. The problems of jurisdiction and the applicable law in private litigation, concerned with issues such as the validity of agreements and the right to compensation for damages, are not covered as a separate subject. The latter aspects are mentioned only if they have implications relevant to the public policy of the Community. See a brief survey of the private law consequences of the competition rules in 1-22. This is not to say that these problems are unimportant. But they should be studied separately and they are less urgent because they are not likely to give rise to the type of international conflicts which are identified in the study. Cf. 1-21 to 1-24.

---

16. See references in Bellamy, Child and Morris Common Market Law of Competition, secs. 2-71 to 2-75 (2nd ed. 1978).

3. THE SOURCES FOR LIMITATIONS ON THE JURISDICTION OF THE COMMUNITY IN ANTITRUST MATTERS

1-12. In assessing the reach of the Community competition law it is necessary, on the one hand, to determine what are the inherent limits of that law within the Common Market and, on the other hand, to determine what limits, if any, international law[17] imposes on the extraterritorial application of Community law. The remainder of the present chapter will attempt to set out first the general terms of international law and then those of the relevant Community law, in order to provide the framework within which the present study will seek to evaluate the extraterritorial reach of the competition law.

A. The International Law Governing Jurisdiction in Antitrust Matters With References to Community Competition Law

> Jurisdiction is a manifestation of State sovereignty and the classical function and purpose of traditional international law has been, after all, to set limits to the lawful exercise of State power to the end that sovereign States might live without strife. 18

(1) The Relevance of International Law in Determining the Scope of Community Competition Rules

1-13. International law comprises those rules of law and principles that govern the relations between States including matters of treating

---

17. The term "international law" in the study always refers to public international law as distinct from private international law, unless it is otherwise expressly stated.

18. Jennings, "The Limits of State Jurisdiction" 32 Nordisk Tidskrift for International Ret. 209 (1962).

nationals of other States.[19]

Within its own territory a State is virtually supreme. However, under international law, a State is required to conform to certain minimum standards of conduct towards aliens (regardless of how it treats its own nationals).[20] In the absence of treaties, and until States can reach agreement to establish conventional international law, customary international law provides the only restraint upon the conduct of nations in the area of extraterritorial application of antitrust law.

1-14. In approaching the subject of the application of the Community competition rules to enterprises and conduct external to the Common Market, as governed by international law, one would, then, first have to establish how far a sovereign State is entitled under international law to give extraterritorial application to its antitrust laws and after that one would have to look at the special position in this respect of the Community, which is not a sovereign State but a community of sovereign States to which those individual States have delegated certain aspects of their sovereignty. The delegation of sovereignty is to be found in the Treaty and related documents, and in the implementing rules and regulations.

These two questions will be examined in Chapter VI of the study. Nevertheless, a short survey of the theory and the principles of jurisdiction in international law seems necessary here. This will enable the Community antitrust policy to be examined throughout the study in

---

19. See Whiteman, Digest of International Law, vol. 1, p.1 (1963).
20. For example, see Restatement (Second) of Foreign Relations Law of the United States, Sec. 165 (1965) (hereinafter cited "Restatement of Foreign Relations Law").

view of the principles of international law, and finally it will be convenient to state any conclusions that may be drawn.

(2) The Theory of Jurisdiction in International Law

1-15. "Jurisdiction" is a measure of the limits within which one State may prescribe and enforce rules of law without violating or infringing the sovereignty of another State. In a more positive sense "jurisdiction" could be described as an expression of the inherent power of a State to govern.[21] The problem of State jurisdiction only arises in matters not exclusively of domestic concern; if a State acts with respect to persons, things or events beyond the scope of its jurisdiction, the act, as a matter of international law, is not only a nullity and may be ignored, but any State injured thereby (or having nationals so injured) has a claim for redress.[22]

1-16. Because the word "jurisdiction" is used by different writers to denote a wide variety of different things, it seems advisable to start by defining the senses in which this term will be used in the study. As a particular aspect of the general legal competence of a State, "jurisdiction" refers to legislative, judicial and enforcement competence.[23] "Legislative

---

21. For an extensive treatment of the subject of jurisdiction see Whiteman _supra_, note 19, at 216-219, and vol. 6, pp.88-183 (1965); Akehurst, "Jurisdiction in International Law" 46 _Brit. Y.B. Int. L._ (1975) pp.145-212; Jennings, "General Course on Principles of International Law" 121 _Recueil_ (1967-II) pp. 515-526; Mann "The Doctrine of Jurisdiction in International Law" 111 _Recueil_ (1964-I) pp.9-158; Jennings, _supra_, note 18, at 209-229; Jennings "Extraterritorial Jurisdiction and the United States Antitrust Law" 33 _Brit. Y.B. Int. L._ (1957) 146-175.

22. Mann, _supra_ note 21, at 14.

23. See Oppenheim, _International Law_, vol. 1, 19 (8th ed., Lauterpacht 1963); Salmond, _Jurisprudence_ 75 (11th ed., Glanville Williams 1957); Fitzmaurice "The General Principles of International Law" 92 _Recueil_ (1957-II) 216-217; Johnson, _Bases of International Jurisdiction, Report of the International Law Conference 1962_ (The David Davis Memorial Institute of International Studies) 33-35; Jennings, _supra_ note 18, at 212-213; Brownlie _Principles of Public International Law_ (2nd ed. 1973).

jurisdiction" (or "prescriptive jurisdiction") is the power of a State to make rules. "Judicial jurisdiction" refers to circumstances where the initiative for the decisions lies with the judiciary or with the quasi-judiciary, i.e. the power of the State's courts to try cases. The notion of "enforcement jurisdicion" (known also as "prerogative jurisdiction" or "administrative jurisdiction") deals with the power of the State, or the administrative authority, to take executive action in pursuance of or consequent on the making of decisons or rules.

1-17. The limits of State jurisdiciton under international law are established by several distinct principles which have received varying degrees of support from practice and opinion. In his foreword to the Harvard Research in International Law, Jurisdiction With Respect to Crime,[24] Dickinson, the Reporter, summarized the practice of States with respect to extraterritorial penal jurisdiction as follows:

> Analysis of modern national codes of penal law and penal procedure, checked against the conclusions of reliable writers and the resolutions of international conferences or learned societies, and supplemented by some exploration of the jurisprudence of national courts, discloses five general principles on which a more or less extensive penal jurisdiction is claimed by States at the present time. These five general parinciples are: first, the territorial principle, determining jurisdiction by reference to the place where the offence is committed; second, the nationality principle, determining jurisdiction by reference to the nationality or national character of the person committing the offence; third, the protective principle, determining jurisdiction by reference to the national interest injured by the offence; fourth, the universality principle, determining jurisdiction by reference to the custody of the person committing offence; and fifth, the passive personality principle determining jurisdiciton by reference to the nationality or the national character of the person injured by the offence. 25

---

24. Research in International Law Under the Auspices of the Harvard Law School, Jurisdiction With Respect to Crime 29 Am. J. Int. L. Supp. 435 et seq. (1935)(Including an extensive bibliography of the literature)(hereinafter cited the "Harvard Research").

25. Ibid. at 444-445.

If one examines the various drafts drawn up for an international convention similar principles of jurisdiction are constantly reflected in them.[26]

(3) Difficulties in the Application of the Principles of Jurisdiction of International Law to the Community Jurisdiction in Antitrust Matters

(a) How Adequate are the Principles of Jurisdiction to Determine the Scope of Antitrust Jurisdiction in General?

(i) The Principle of Territoriality.

1-18. The principle of territoriality has been described as a fundamental and unchallenged proposition of international law.[27] The draftsmen of the Harvard Draft Convention on Jurisdiction with Respect to Crime regarded this statement on the principle as so well established that they refrained from an extensive citation of authorities to support it.[28]

26. For example, see the Montevideo Convention, 1940 (Secundo Congresso Sudamericano, Buenos Aires, 1940) p.376 et seq.; the Draft Convention on Jurisdiction with Respect to Crime, of the Harvard Group 29 Am. J. Int. L. Supp. 439 (1935); the Report by Brierly - C. De Visscher to the League of Nations in 19 Am. J. Int. L. Supp. 253 (1926); the Resolution on International Penal Law, adopted at the International Congress for Comparative Law, held at The Hague, printed at the end of the above mentioned draft, p.644; the Resolution of the Institute de Droit International, Cambridge 1931 (Ann. II, 1931, p.235); the Conference for Unification of International Penal Law, Warsaw, 5th November, 1927 (Actes de la Conference I, p.131).

27. See Lord Finlay, in The Case of the S.S. "Lotus",P.C.I.J. Ser. A. No. 9 p.56 (1927). See also the opinion in this case of Judges Loder (pp.34, 35), Weiss (p.44), Nyholm (p.63), Moore (pp.92-94) and Altamira (p.95); Wheaton, Elements of International Law 270-274 (6th Eng. ed., Keith, 1929); Hanbury, "The Territorial Limits of Criminal Jurisdiction" 37 Prob. of Pub. and Private Int'l Law, The Grotius Society 171 (1952); Beckett,"The Exercise of Criminal Jurisdiction Over Foreigners" 6 Brit. Y.B. Int. L. (1925) p.44; "Criminal Jurisdiction Over Foreigners" 8 Brit. Y.B. Int. L. (1927) 108. For the viewpoint of conflict of laws see Goodrich and Scoles, Conflict of Laws (1964); Cheatham, Griswald and Reese, Cases and Materials on Conflict of Laws 93 (5th ed. 1964).

28. Supra note 26, at 480.

Jennings states that this principle is everywhere approved as of primary importance and that it commends universal assent.[29]

The principle of territoriality implies that a State is entitled to prescribe rules governing the acts of all persons which take place within the territory of that State. However, in modern times States have gone to great lengths to relax and avoid the restrictiveness of this principle. They have extended it by the adoption of: (1) the "subjective territorial principle" which establishes the jurisdiction of the State to prosecute and punish for crimes commenced within the State, but completed or consummated abroad;[30] (2) the "objective territorial principle" which establishes the jurisdiction of the State to prosecute and punish for crimes commenced without the territory of the State, but consummated within the territory.[31] Thus, a State may claim jurisdiction for an offence which has been committed, in part or in whole, in its territory in cases where a constituent element of the offence occurred in its territory. This concept is formulated in the Lotus Case,[32] by the Harvard Draft Convention on Jurisdiction with Respect to Crime,[33] by the criminal codes of many countries[34] and by judicial decisions in many countries.[35] Less certain is the opinion, examined in detail below, that States are also entitled to claim jurisdiction over offences committed abroad which merely produce effects in their territory even though those effects were a constituent element of the offence.

---

29. Jennings, "Extraterritorial Jurisdiction and the United States Antitrust Law" 33 Brit. Y.B. Int. L. (1957) p.148.
30. Harvard Research, supra note 24, at 486.
31. Harvard Research, supra note 24, at 487.
32. Supra note 27, at 23, 30.
33. Supra note 26, at 480 (Art. 3).
34. For example, the French Code of Criminal Procedure, Art. 693.
35. As to Common Law countries, cf. Halsbury's Laws of England, vol.10, 318 (3rd ed.). For an example in German Law see Mann, supra note 21, at 85.

1-19. The debate on the adequacy of the principle of territoriality as a basis for jurisdiction in antitrust matters, where only effects of offences committed abroad are found within the territory, has tended to concentrate on the meaning of the objective territorial principle. The problems in that connection are stated by Jennings in the following paragraph:

> The objective territoriality test began of course with cases of direct physical harm, e.g. shots across a border. Difficulties began to arise when it was extended to more complicated situations on the basis of more or less remote effects, as in cases of defamation.....and in antitrust cases, 'effects' upon trade. The problem is how to limit the field of application of the objective territoriality test once it is liberated from the simple case of direct physical harm. For, unless the objective territoriality test is limited at some point, it is destructive of the territoriality principle itself on which it purports to be based, and what purports to be a mere extension or interpretation of the territoriality principle is found to have become a 'ubiquity' principle of jurisdiction. 36

The Harvard Research states that in the application of the objective territorial test the effect is indistinguishable from the act; each has been said to constitute an "essential constituent element" or "part" of the crime, thus justifying the exercise of territorial jurisdiction.[37] In the Lotus Case the Permanent Court of International Justice pointed out that the elements of the offence were "legally, entirely inseparable, so much so that their separation renders the offence non-existent".[38] The assumption that "the place where the effect is produced is the place where the act was committed is in every case a legal fiction" and is only justified "where the act and its effect are indistinguishable".[39] The difficult problem in the application of the objective test of territoriality to antitrust cases which do not concern "direct physical harm" is therefore the extent to which the

---

36. Jennings in I.L.A., Tokyo Conference 355.
37. Harvard Research, supra note 24 at 494-495.
38. The Lotus Case, supra note 27, at 30.
39. Ibid. at 37 (M. Loder).

requirement of a "constituent element" of the offence, occurring within the territory can be applied where only economic effects of the antitrust offence have taken place within the territory. This problem is best understood when set against the background of the meaning of effects of antitrust offences as explained in the following paragraph:

> .....we may with certainty deduce only that the restraint of competition does not have to be realized by any acts within the national territory. On the contrary, it is sufficient if a restrictive act caused abroad simply has result or consequence in the national territory.
>
> The point of contact presupposes that the place where a restraint of competiton is legally completed (for instance by the conclusion of a cartel agreement) and the place where the effects of the restraint of competition take place, frequently diverge (for instance, if a restrictive agreement relating to the national territory is concluded abroad). In one word, 'effect' is something quite different from execution, putting into practice, or any other term denoting an activity. The effect on the national territory is the consequence of an act done in a foreign country. 40

The theory which supports the exercise of jurisdiction upon effects of antitrust offences is often named in literature as an "effects doctrine". However as is evident from the difficulties mentioned above, the scope, as well as the very validity of such a doctrine, is subject to a lively debate. We shall attempt, at the end of the study, to identify the position and the possible limits of an "effects doctrine" from the point of international law. This will be done after the obtainment of more information on the possible operation of such a doctrine in various legal systems including of course that of the Community.[41] The substance of the proposed inquiry in cases where

40. Schwartz,"Applicability of National Law on Restraints of Competition to International Restraints of Competition" in Cartel and Monopoly in Modern Law, vol. 2, p.715 (1961).
41. According to the OECD Committee of Experts on Restrictive Business Practices the criterion of "effects" is embodied in the legislation of Germany, Austria, Denmark, Spain, France, Sweden and Finalnd; it has moreover been recognized in the case law of Canada, Japan, Switzerland,the United States and the European Communities and attested by doctrine in Belgium (see OECD, Committee of Experts on Restrictive Business Practices, Restrictive Business Practices of Multinational Enterprises" sec. 120 (1977)). See also a detailed survey of legislation of the Member States of the EEC and U.S., in that respect, in Chap. V.

the legislation mentions the term "effects" will be in line with the following formulation by Jennings:

> Is "effect" used in the somewhat strict sense.....to mean a "constituent element" of the crime itself; or is it merely a question of causation? If it is a mere question of causation, what tests may be employed to find out which "effects" are too remote from the originating act to cause the matter to become constructively territorial? 42

(ii) Principles of Jurisdiction Other Than Territoriality.

1-20. The application of the principle of nationality - upon which a State is entitled to claim jurisdiction on its nationals wherever they are - in antitrust matters is not internationally recognized and may have some shortcomings (see 6-7). However, some writers admit that the principle is applicable in antitrust cases[43] and some legislations also do so.[44] The borrowing of the concept of nationality, as a mark of allegiance and an aspect of sovereignty which developed in relation to individuals, for the domain of legal persons is awkward in some respects but is now well established.[45]

It is, however, unlikely that the protective principle will be applicable in antitrust matters. Although, under the protective

---

42. Jennings in I.L.A., Tokyo Conference, 356.

43. See Jennings, supra note 29, at 153-154.

44. For example see Restatement of Foreign Relations Law, Sec. 30 (in the language of Sec. 30 "A State has jurisdiction to prescribe a rule of law (a) attaching legal consequences to conduct of a national of the State wherever the conduct occurs....."); Jugoslovenka Reviga za Medunarodno Pravo, II (1964) pp.113-114 (Yugoslav antimonopoly legislation which applies to all acts of Yugoslav corporations regardless of where they occur). See also the Official Statement of the British Government on the principles according to which jurisdiction may be exercised over foreign corporations in antitrust matters (published in Brownlie, supra note 23, at 305-306). The application of the concept of nationality is restricted by interference with the legitimate affairs of other States.

45. See Brownlie, supra note 23, at 409. See also note 9 below.

principle an alien may be prosecuted by an offended State for conduct wholly outside its borders whether or not the conduct was lawful at the place where it occurred (there need be no effects within the territory of the offended State, nor any connection between the conduct and activity within the State), this principle takes in only a specific variety of political, currency, immigration and some economic offences.[46] According to a generally accepted opinion this principle has no application as a basis of jurisdiction in antitrust cases apart from circumstances of the most exceptional kind. See 6-6.

There is no disagreement among writers that the principles of universality and the passive personality are not an adequate basis for antitrust jurisdiction.[47]

(b) The Dependence of the Limits Upon the Community Jurisdiction Under International Law on the Nature of the Applicable Community Law

1-21. As a general rule the jurisdictional limitations reflected in the principles of international law depend on the nature of the law applicable, whether it is criminal law and public law concerned with the functioning of public bodies or with the sovereign rights of States or whether these are laws of other areas of municipal law.[48] International law sets limits to that part of the law which embodies its peculiar notions by public order and is attended by penal sanctions. The converse of these rules of international law are those rules of private international law whereby municipal courts commonly refuse to apply

---

46. See Sarkar, "The Proper Law of Crime in International Law" 11 I.C.L.Q. 462-466 (1962).

47. The use of these principles as a basis for jurisdiction is confined to certain qualified circumstances only; see Brownlie, supra note 23, at 297-298.

48. Cf. Akehurst, supra note 21, at 170; Jennings, supra note 18, at 210.

certain aspects of a foreign law, e.g. penal and revenue laws, or laws contrary to the local ordre public.[49]

Community antitrust law seems difficult to fit into this system because breaches of the rules could be sanctioned by administrative (regulatory) or criminal proceedings and by civil (private) proceedings.

1-22. Arts. 85 and 86 of the Treaty were introduced in the public interest of the Community, and hence, are primarily rules of public law. The rules are backed by the power of the Community in the form of various sanctions. Some sanctions could be described as administrative,[50] but where the sanctions take the form of "fines" or "penalty payments" imposed by the public authority - as under Arts. 15 to 17 of Regulation (hereinafter "Reg.") 17[51] - the remedies, and also the proceedings, seem to be criminal or quasi-criminal.[52]

Arts. 85 and 86 also have implications within the Member States and could be exercised by authorities other than the Community. These articles are Treaty provisions with direct effect, in the sense that once the Treaty has been incorporated as part of the law of each Member State

---

49. See Jennings in I.L.A., Tokyo Conference 354. Even in private law cases limitations on the extraterritorial application of the law exist where its application to events occurring in another State would thwart the economic policy of the other State.

50. In the Dyestuffs Cases (Cases 48, 49, 51-57/69)[1972] E.C.R. 619) the Advocate-General stated that sanctions under Arts. 85 and 86 are of administrative nature (p.697).

51. Regulation 17 of the Council of 6 February 1962, First Regulation Implementing Articles 85 and 86 of the Treaty, J.O. 1962, 204; O.J. (Special Edition 1959-1962) p.87.

52. See Akehurst, supra note 21 at 190; Oberdorfer, Gleiss and Hirsh, Common Market Cartel Law, sec. 22 at pp.33-34 (2nd. ed. 1971); Steindorff "Annotations on the Decision of the European Court in the Dyestuffs Cases of July 14 1972" 9 C.M.L. Rev. 510 (1972); Hug "The Applicability of the Provisions of the European Community Treaties Against Restraints of Competition to Restraints of Competition Caused in Non Member States, but Affecting the Common Market" in Cartel and Monopoly in Modern Law, vol. 2, 656 (1961).

such articles are to be given legal effect in the Member States without further enactment being necessary and can create both rights and obligations enforceable by individuals.[53] Reg. 17 provides that authorities in the Member States responsible for administering domestic legislation on competition[54] are competent to determine whether or not the prohibitions of Arts. 85 and 86 apply, but only until such times as the Commission initiates a procedure with regard to request of negative clearance or exemption under Art. 85(3) or requiring termination of an infringement (Art. 9(3) of Reg. 17). In exercising their competence the national authorities have no means of granting exemption under Art. 85(3) or of issuing a negative clearance.[55] For the purpose of classifying these proceedings as of private or of public law nature it is however essential to observe that the jurisdiction of the national authorities is concurrent to that of the Community authorities, and that a distinction is drawn between the "national authorities" as mentioned here, on the one hand, and those authorities responsible for determining the legal consequences of such agreements and practices in civil proceedings in accordance with the national law, on the other hand.[56]

Clear private law consequences of the competition law follow from the provision in Art 85(2) that agreements and decisions forbidden by Art. 85(1) are null and void. It thus ensures that, irrespective of the fate of the agreements and decisions that violate prohibitory

53. See Columbia Law School Project on European Legal Institutions; The Law of the European Economic Community, vol. 2, sec. 85-04 (Smit and Herzog eds. 1976) (hereinafter cited as "Smit and Herzog"); K. Lipstein, The Law of the European Economic Community 21-45 (1974). See generally for the principle of "direct applicability" Dashwood "The Principle of Direct Effect in European Community Law" 16 J. of C.M. Studies 229 (1978).

54. For the meaning of "national authorities" see Barounos, Hall and James, EEC Antitrust Law; Principles and Practice 292-293 (1975).

55. The question when the Commission initiates a procedure was decided by the Court in the Haecht (No.2) Case (Case 48/72 [1972] E.C.R. 77).

56. See Barounos, Hall and James, supra note 54, at 292-293.

provisions under the law of Member States, agreements and decisions forbidden by Art. 85(1) shall, by virtue of Community law, lack legal validity. But, Subsection 2 does not deal explicitly with possible civil law consequences of violation of Art 85, such as a declaration that an agreement is prohibited, or an action in tort. According to a report published by the Commission in 1966, private suits of this type would be possible in Belgium, Luxemburg, France and Italy and private individuals might be able to recover damages in Germany and the Netherlands, though a final answer could be given only after this issue has been settled by the courts.[57] In a recent private communication with J. Temple-Lang, a Legal Adviser to the Commission, the following statement was given as descriptive of the present situation:

> There is as yet no provision for multiple damages, and private actions for single damages have so far always been settled out of court and so have gone unreported. However, they are available under the laws of all the Member States of the EEC. Such actions would greatly improve antitrust compliance.
>
> Findings by the Community institutions that a firm has violated Community antitrust law would greatly facilitate private actions for damages in national courts. Such actions would not necessarily have to be in the courts of EEC Member States; a ruling of the Commission or the Court could help a plaintiff in a damage action even if he was suing in a U.S. court under U.S. law.[58]

1-23. We may now reach the conclusion that any a priori attempt to classify the Community competition rules within one of the existing categories (such as private law, public law, criminal law, administrative

---

57. La Répration des Conséquences Dommageables d'une Violation des Articles 85 et 86 du Traité Instituant la CEE, Série Concurrence 1 (Brussels 1966). Opinions differ as to whether such private suits are possible in the U.K. According to J. Cunningham a private suit is not possible in the U.K. (Competition Law of the EEC; A Practical Guide 62 (1973)). However, for Bellamy, Child and Morris it is still an open question (see supra note 16, at 4 - 10).

58. An interview in Brussels, 2nd October, 1979. Temple-Lang indicates that a tort action could be for triple damage as is the practice in the U.S.

law) is doomed to fail, because the law contains elements of all of these.

It is therefore noteworthy that the description of a remedy or of the proceeding in the law is not always material where the remedy or the proceeding are considered under international law. As a general rule we propose that the nature rather than the name of the sanction or the proceeding is decisive for limiting the exercise of the jurisdiction of States over aliens.[59] Thus, for example, it is immaterial that Art. 15(4) of Reg. 17 specifically provides that the fines resulting from the proceedings under the regulation are not criminal in character.[60] A provision similar to Art. 15(4) of Reg. 17 can be found in Sec. 38 of the German Federal Cartel Law.[61] Nevertheless, most German writers regard Sec. 38 as having a penal character and this practice has even been criticised because it subjects citizens to such sanctions without giving them the guarantees of criminal law.[62] The problem of classification in the U.S. is more difficult given the welter of proceedings and remedies which may be available to ensure compliance with the substantive antitrust rules or to reinstate the _status quo ante_[63] (see 5-23).

---

59. Cf. Akehurst, _supra_ note 21, at 190 (see particularly n.30) and 191. See also European Parliament, Working Documents 531/76, p.10, at para. 8.

60. Art. 15, para. 4, provides: "Decisions taken pursuant to paras. 1 and 2 shall not be of a criminal nature".

61. Act Against Restraints of Competition of 27 July 1957, as amended (the Act was consolidated in 1973). For the full text in English see OECD, _Guide to Legislation on Restrictive Business Practices_ vol. 2, Germany 1.

62. Cf. Kruithof, "The Application of the Common Market Antitrust Provisions to International Restraints of Trade" 2 _C.M.L. Rev._ 71 (1964).

63. Referring to the U.S. antitrust laws Jennings states that antitrust offences manifestly come within the definition of "crime" whatever the procedure which is used. Nevertheless, "crime", according to this opinion, never includes mere civil wrongs which may be expiated by restitution or reparation to the injured individual. See Jennings _supra_ note 29, at 147 (the definition of "crime" in the article is based _inter alia_ on the Harvard Research).

Because of the peculiar character of the competition rules of the Community the limitation on the scope of the study, i.e. its concern with Arts. 85 and 86 only in so far as they are enforced by remedies and proceedings which are criminal, quasi-criminal or administrative (see 1-11), seems proper. We shall consider all such proceedings and remedies as demonstrating the application of public law although we shall refer at a later stage to differences between the possible reach of criminal and administrative remedies (see 6-31 and 6-32).

1-24. The detailed illustration of the special character of the Community competition rules as set out above does not only emphasize the point that the principles of international law pertaining to the extra-territorial reach of criminal or administrative antitrust law are different from those which deal with private antitrust law. It also indicates that any comparative study of antitrust laws of different nations must take the similar peculiarity of the laws into account. Moreover, any attempt to arrive at an harmonization of antitrust legislation in the international Community of nations must reflect an awareness of the special character of the laws.

B. The Limitations on Community Jurisdiction in Antitrust Matters With Foreign Elements According to the Community Legislation

1-25. From the formal viewpoint Community law belongs to international law. In fact, it is partly embodied in, partly based on a Treaty concluded between sovereign States. From the viewpoint of its content Community law is a common internal law in the Member States rather than a law between these States.[64] Before we examine the scope of the

64. See Kapteyn and VerLoren van Themaat, Introduction to the Law of the European Communities: After the Accession of New Member States, 25 (1973).

particular antitrust provisions of this law it is necessary to inquire whether this type of law has rules of conflict which may grant or prevent jurisdiction in cases involving foreign elements.

(1) Community Competition - Conflict of Laws Rules

1-26. The Treaty, apart from general provisions, containsno actual rules of conflict of laws. Therefore, the traditional principles of the latter doctrine must serve here as obvious guidelines.[65] In so far as the antitrust provisions are penal in character the general rules of the private international criminal antitrust law or private international administrative antitrust law of the forum apply. According to these rules the power of the parties to choose the applicable law may be limited by consideration of "public policy". The concept of "public policy" dictates the application of the mandatory public and private laws of the forum and is resorted to whenever forum law is to be applied instead of the foreign law which could have been indicated to be applicable by the conflict rules.[66] The judge in such cases must determine that the issue is of such essential importance that foreign law does not apply.[67] The principle of "public policy" implies that the conflict rules of public law generally restrict themselves to defining their own law and are unilateral, i.e. conflict rules determining the subject matter to which their own public law shall apply. In distinction conflicts rules of private international law, which otherwise apply,

---

65. See Hug, supra note 52, at 650.

66. The subject of "public policy" in conflict of laws and its implications is discussed in every text book on the conflict of laws. See, for example, Cheshire and North, Private International Law 148 et seq (9th ed. 1974); Wolff, Private International Law 165 et seq. (2nd Ed. 1950); Ehrenzweig, A Treatise on the Conflict of Laws 342 et seq (1962).

67. For example, see Restatement (Second) of Conflicts of Laws, Sec. 187 (1971).

determine the applicability of one or the other of several legal systems and are, therefore, bilateral.[68]

Public law rules, like Arts. 85 and 86, have therefore been described by Schwartz as "hidden rules of conflict of laws":

> The antitrust laws protect the domestic economy and the economic freedom of the individual. In other words, the antitrust laws protect competition, as well as freedom of competition and activity on the domestic market which in a territorial as well as in a material sense includes imports. Therefore, the place of conclusion or performance of an agreement, or the law or venue agreed upon by the parties, are of no importance as points of contact. Also, the nationality of the party concerned, the domicile of natural and the seat of legal personalities are of no or of minor importance in determining the applicable law. 69

(2) Terms in Articles 85 and 86 Implying Jurisdictional Limitations

1-27. If the extraterritorial application of the Community competition rules raises jurisdictional problems, those problems are raised by the terms of Arts. 85 and 86. Therefore, before the Community case law is discussed in subsequent chapters, a preliminary analysis of the relevant terms of Arts. 85 and 86, from a jurisdictional point of view, is required.

We have to emphasize here that throughout the study we shall assume a general knowledge of the substantial and procedural competition rules of the Community, and will elaborate on them only in so far as they are concerned with enterprises or conduct external to the Common

68. See Mann, *supra* note 21, at 69-70; Ehrenzweig, *supra* note 66, at 312. A comparative study of the operation of antitrust laws which contain no specific conflict rules is found in C. Edwards, *Control of Cartels and Monopolies; An International Comparison* 30 (1967).

69. Schwartz, *supra* note 40, at 707 *et seq*. Compare the implementation of the principle of "hidden rules of conflict of laws" in U.S. antitrust jurisdiction in Kronstein, Miller and Schwartz, *Modern American Antitrust Law* 284-289 (1958). However, much has also been written in the U.S. in objection to this principle on the basis that normal contract law has been abandoned for the aims of antitrust policy (e.g. Haight, "International Law and Extraterritorial Application of the Antitrust Laws" and Whitney "Sources of Conflict Between International Law and Antitrust Laws" 63 *Yale L.J.* 639 and 655 resp. (1954).

Market.

1-28. Art. 85 and 86 provide:

Article 85

1. The following shall be prohibited as incompatible with the common market: all agreements between undertakings, decisions by associations of undertakings and concerted practices which may affect trade between Member States and which have as their object or effect the prevention, restriction or distortion of competition within the common market, and in particular those which:

(a) directly or indirectly fix purchase or selling prices or any other trading conditions;
(b) limit or control production, markets, technical development, or investment;
(c) share markets or sources of supply;
(d) apply dissimilar conditions to equivalent transactions with other trading parties, thereby placing them at a competitive disadvantage;
(e) make the conclusion of contracts subject to acceptance by the other parties of supplementary obligations which, by their nature or according to commercial usage, have no connection with the subject of such contracts.

2. Any agreements or decisions prohibited pursuant to this Article shall be automatically void.

3. The provisions of paragraph 1 may, however, be declared inapplicable in the case of:

- any agreement or category of agreements between undertakings;
- any decision or category of decisions by associations of undertakings;
- any concerted practice or category of concerted practices;

which contributed to improving the production or distribution of goods or to promoting technical or economic progress, while allowing consumers a fair share of the resulting benefit, and which does not:

(a) impose on the undertakings concerned restrictions which are not indispensable to the attainment of these objectives;
(b) afford such undertakings the possibility of eliminating competition in respect of a substantial part of the products in question.

Article 86.

Any abuse by one or more undertakings of a dominant position within the common market or in a substantial part of it shall be prohibited as incompatible with the common market in so far as it may affect trade between Member States. Such abuse may, in particular, consist in:

(a) directly or indirectly imposing unfair purchase or selling prices or other unfair trading conditions;
(b) limiting production, markets or technical development to the prejudice of consumers;
(c) applying dissimilar conditions to equivalent transactions with other trading parties, thereby placing them at a competitive disadvantage;
(d) making the conclusion of contracts subject to acceptance by the other parties of supplementary obligations which, by their nature or according to commercial usage, have no connection with the subject of such contracts.

Since Art. 86 reintroduces many of the terms included in Art. 85[70] those terms do not require repeated examination in the present context. We therefore propose to explore the meaning of the following terms as determining the legislative jurisdiction of the Community:

(1) undertakings

(2) agreements between undertakings

(3) affect trade between Member States

(4) within the Common Market (or a substantial part of it)

(5) may affect

(6) object or effect

(a) "Undertakings"

(i) Definition.

1-29. The term "undertaking" has not been defined for the purpose of the Treaty but assumed that its meaning is understood.[71] The term "undertaking" is that of the authentic English version of the Treaty, corresponding to the French "enterprise", for which "enterprise" will be found in many translations made before the accession of the U.K. to

---

70. See Smit and Herzog, *supra* note 33, sec. 86.04(a).

71. References to "undertakings" are also to be found in Arts. 52 and 80 of the *EEC Treaty*. Both the *ECSC Treaty* (Art. 80) and the *EURATOM Treaty* (Art. 196) contain definitions of an "undertaking" for the purposes of those treaties.

the European Communities. The latter term started its life as a designation of an object of rights, a going business which in various ways was protected by the law, in part by the law relating to delicts and in part by the law relating to unfair competition.[72] But, in the course of time it has become possible to refer to "enterprise" as the holder of rights. Enterprise, in fact, may enter into transactions in a way which heretofore would appear to have been reserved to persons, both natural and legal.[73] In this sense the term seems to have evaded Arts. 85 and 86 of the Treaty while it may be used differently in the context of other legal provisions.[74]

The use of the term "enterprise" in the study is to include "association of undertakings" where appropriate in the context.

1-30. More specifically the quest for a proper interpretation of the term "undertaking" in Arts. 85 and 86 consists of efforts to determine whether the term is used in a technical, legal or economic sense. With regard to the "reaching out" of the competition rules, the determination of the degree of economic autonomy of a subsidiary may either broaden or restrict the jurisdiction of the Community over a NCE. For example, the presence and activities in the Common Market of a locally organized subsidiary may give the Community direct jurisdiction over the non-

---

72. See Cohn and Simitis, "Lifting the Veil in the Company Laws of the European Continent" 12 Int. and Comp. L.Q. 218-219 (1963).

73. Cf. A. Deringer, The Competition Law of the European Economic Community, sec. 105 (CCH ed. 1968).

74. Ibid. See also Bebr, Judicial Control of the European Communities 65 (1962). However, it is noteworthy that the term "unternehmen" in the German Act Against Restraints of Competition (supra note 61), sec.1, bears the same sense as the term "undertaking" in the Treaty. The German term was translated to "enterprise" in the OECD, Guide to Legislation (see supra note 61).

Community parent company, in certain circumstances, if an interpretation of the term "undertaking" in an economic sense is adopted. The reasoning which may support a possibility of direct jurisdiction over a NCE, in such circumstances, concerns the contention that the conduct of the subsidiary is imputed to its parent, since the subsidiary is the "alter-ego" of the parent company in an economic sense. The ascription of restrictive behaviour may, of course, take place in domestic situations as well as in cases involving NCES. However, it takes on special significance in the latter incidents, which are our immediate interest.

If the Community is to base its jurisdiction over NCES on the basis of the so-called economic unit theory it is important that a workable guide (e.g. measures of independent management, types of ownership, etc.), as a reliable criterion for the interpretation of "undertaking", be found to determine in what circumstances attribution of conduct is justified.

Art. 86, in contrast to Art 85, prohibits abuse of a dominant position by "one or more undertakings" and so implies that where several enterprises are consolidated in a combine, it is irrelevant, notwithstanding their legal independence, that they may be considered to be one or several enterprises from an economic point of view. In other words, Art. 86 could reach dominant position based on overt collusive agreements within the meaning of Art. 85, as well as groups of enterprises which constitute legally distinct entities, but which are subject to a unified control, and also certain oligopoly situations.[75]

75. Cf. R. Joliet, Monopolization and Abuse of Dominant Position: A Comparative Study of the American and European Approaches to the Control of Economic Power, 237 (1970).

(ii) Points of Contact Between "Undertakings" and the Community.

(1) Nationality.

1-31. No attempt has been made by the draftsmen of the Treaty to restrict the application of the competition rules to enterprises which are nationals of one of the Member States. The implications of the absence of a legislative provision which creates a national status for an "undertaking" are very likely to be that the relevance, if any of a requirement for a Community nationality does not seem of much importance in this context. This conclusion may follow from the observation that the requirement of nationality tends to depend on the context of the particular rule of law involved, e.g. rules of public policy purpose do not tend to be based on nationality.[76]

1-32. Before noting the proper judicial approach of the Community towards basing its jurisdiction on the principle of nationality, it would be of no use to attempt to define "nationality" for Community enterprises. Any such definition may later be found irrelevant in view of a possible rejection of this principle as a basis of jurisdiction. Nevertheless, if the concept of "nationality" of enterprises is adopted by the case law, a few preliminary illustrations may broadly indicate the possible scope of the competition rules.

One can certainly say that the jurisdiction of the Community over a Community subsidiary of a NCE, i.e. a subsidiary incorporated in the Common Market and operating therein, would not seem to be open to question. Since there is now general consensus that foreigners who

---

76. Brownlie, supra note 23, at 409.

do business in a country are subject to its laws, the fact that foreigners are participants in a domestic restrictive arrangement does not, in itself, create problems in coping with the arrangement by a domestic law. Foreign ownership of a subsidiary within the Common Market, for instance, would not free it from the liability which is imposed on a company organized in the Common Market and owned by nationals of Member States, because considerations of antitrust laws, as public laws, will apply.[77]

In accordance with the principle that, as regards its own nationals, a State has authority, consistent with its own fundamental laws, to regulate their conduct both within and outside its own territory, it seems that jurisdiction over an offence committed abroad by a Community enterprise, which falls within the framework of Arts. 85 and 86, is in line with the rules of international law. There would, however, be limitations in this case on the enforcement jurisdiction of the Community.[78]

Where a non-Community subsidiary of a Community enterprise is a national of the country of its organization and operation it is subject to that foreign country's regulation, as is normally the case. Nevertheless, such a subsidiary, through control by its Community parent, will be subject to the Community regulation, even though the Community may not have jurisdiction to prescribe rules directly applicable to it.[79]

---

77. See Nebolsine, "Foreign Enterprises Under the Common Market Antitrust Rules" 38 N.Y.U.L. Rev. 481 (1963).

78. Cf. Jennings, *supra* note 29, at 153-154.

79. The Restatement of Foreign Relations Law uses the term national to include a corporation organized under the law of the claiming State (secs. 27 and 30), but the commentary to Sec. 27 states that where a foreign corporation is owned or controlled by nationals of the claiming State it is not a "national" of that State but may be effectively regulated by it through its jurisdiction over the controlling interests (Comment d).

(2) Place of Business

1-33. Clearly, the Commission can exert jurisdiction over a Community partner of a NCE and may declare illegal an agreement it has with the foreign enterprise. But, would the term "undertakings" include only NCES which have a place of business within the Common Market upon which the Community can exercise direct jurisdiction in antitrust matters?

Arts. 85 and 86 do not restrict their application to "undertakings" whose place of business is within the Common Market. Words denoting "undertakings" "belonging" to one of the Members States, or described as having their offices within the Common Market, appear in Reg. 17 (Art. 11(2)) and are mentioned particularly in connection with investigations and verifications. Form A for negative clearance (now attached to Form B) indicates that the Commission may wish to limit its judicial competence to cases in which the enterprises involved have at least an establishment or representative within the Common Market.[80]

The only conclusion now which could be based on the language of the implementing regulations, before judicial analysis, is that all NCES having their offices within the Common Market may be said to be directly subject to the competition rules, as those organized in the Member States. Such a conclusion may, in view of the definition of "undertaking", still be subject to qualifications as to the nature of the independence of the branches or divisions within the Common Market. If the latter are qualified as distinct economic entities they would be put

80. See point 6 in Form A/B, attached to Regulation 27/62 of the Commission of 3 May 1962, First Regulation Implementing Council Regulation 17/62, J.O. 1962, 35/1118; O.J. (Special Edition 1959-1962) p.132.

under the direct jurisdiction of the Community rather than the foreign parent abroad.

(3) Absence of either Community Nationality or Place of Business Within the Common Market

1-34. It will not be possible in all situations to show the economic identity between a foreign parent company and its subsidiary. The NCE might not also be operating in the Common Market through a subsidiary but through an exclusively independent distributor, or even that link with the Common Market might be lacking. For example, the concerted practices between the undertakings could be simply to respect each other's national territories or to observe certain production quotas. Therefore, the remaining question in reference to the term "undertaking" is whether this term may include an enterprise situated outside the Common Market and not having any establishment of whatever kind within the Common Market. A positive answer to this question will probably attach jurisdictional significance to the conduct of that enterprise rather than to its location.

(b) "Agreements Between Undertakings"

1-35. The question of the relationship between parent and subsidiary comes again under consideration in view of the examination whether parent and subsidiary are two distinct enterprises as regards the agreements between them. In other words, when, if ever, are related corporations (if one or both are situated outside the Common Market) to be considered as enterprises capable of the kind of anticompetitive cooperation which is forbidden by the provisions of the Treaty?[81] Or would an agreement, which comes under the scope of this study, between a subordinate undertaking and its parent company, be attacked only as abuse of a dominant position under Art. 86?

(c) "Affect Trade Between Member States"

1-36. It is often difficult to localize restrictive business practices in a certain territory; they frequently take the form of a complicated pattern of conduct, extending over a long period of time and over a wide geographical area. But the literal text of Arts. 85 and 86 seems to suggest that it may reach arrangements external to the Common Market which, by imposing restraints upon market behaviour outside the Common Market, may affect interstate trade within the territory of the Common Market. However, it is not clear, from the Treaty, how far the Community will go in that direction.

1-37. Broadly speaking the words "affect trade between Member States" seem to serve to distinguish consequences which are prohibited altogether from those which are prohibited, if at all, only under national restrictive practices legislation. This requirement implies a certain territorial scope by intending to confine the legislative jurisdictional sphere of application of the rules. Whether there is also a substantive significance to this requirement is a question connected with the terms determining the nature and impact of the restraint on trade and on competition within the Common Market, and will be discussed in due course

81. Related corporations include parents and their subsidiaries, two or more subsidiaries of a common parent (affiliates), or two or more corporations, the stock in each of which is owned by the same natural person or persons; cf. Report of the Attorney General's National Committee on the Antitrust Laws 30 (1955).

in that particular context. See 3-3 to 3-5 and 3-9.

1-38. It seems that the provisions of the Treaty do not have a "foreign trade" clause, which would prohibit restrictions on trade between the Common Market area, as an economic bloc, and outside countries.[82] The term "trade between Member States" implies, for instance, that agreements restraining competition in countries outside the Common Market (in particular export cartels) are permitted, provided that competition within the Common Market remains unrestricted. The ommission of the term "foreign trade" in the articles has been argued to have significant consequences, and to leave beyond the reach of the rules many restraints of trade that in the first instance restrict trade between Member States and third countries. See 2-124. The question whether limits on the extraterritorial reach of the rules result from the absence of such a clause, or from the philosophy behind the law as well as from self-imposed restraints will be examined in a case to case judicial review. All types of combinations relating to exports and imports (e.g. prohibitions against foreign enterprises importing from the Common Market or export prohibitions on customers in a third country) must therefore be subject to individual scrutiny, whether or not they have effects on trade between Member States.

(d) "Within the Common Market" ("or a Substantial Part of It")

1-39. This requirement seems to have geographical significance only and is satisfied as soon as the competition is affected within the

82. The term "foreign trade" as it has developed in the U.S. antitrust jurisprudence is mainly concerned with restraints upon exports from or imports into a State (see Chapter V 5-31 to 5-34).

territory defined in Art. 227 of the Treaty. It also supports the interpretation that the localization of the effects of prohibited practices within the Common Market as previously explained, may give the Community jurisdiction in that case. Thus if competition inside the Common Market is not restrained, activities of Community enterprises which are directed outwards will be beyond the reach of the rules.

(e) "May Affect" (trade)

(f) "Object or Effect" (restriction of competition)

1-40. These two requirements further qualify the nature of the "effect" which is required within the territory of the Common Market according to the preceding terms. However, while the terms which were discussed before have a special function of serving as a criterion of territorial effect, the terms under consideration here indicate what should be the significance of the market effect (i.e. negligible or substantial) and how remote and slight the "effect" could possibly be.

1-41. In particular the questions under these two terms are: "May affect" - what actual degree of the effect on trade warrants the exercise of jurisdiction? Would it suffice that the effect be potential or possible, and not actual? Should the effect be direct or indirect? "Object of effect" - this requirement (in Art. 85 only) has an alternative nature. However the text does not justify a preference. Does the article imply that the effect must have been intended foreseeable, or how much careless disregard is sufficient? Will an intent that can reasonably result in a restrictive practice come within Art. 85? How relevant is the fact that the practice also seeks to achieve other ends and the restraint is only ancillary to the main purpose?

The interpretation of these two terms poses the whole issue of the causal relationship between the practice and the effect and it will be important to clarify what is the properly applicable doctrine of causation.

The use of the term "effect" above is both with regard to the effects on trade between Member States and the effects on competition within the Common Market. It thus becomes important also to establish what is the link between the requirements that trade is affected and that restrictive effects are touching upon competition (or the existence of a dominant position).

CHAPTER II

Theories and Principles in the Application of Community Competition Rules to Non-Community Enterprises

1. "UNDERTAKINGS" AND THE ECONOMIC UNIT THEORY

INTRODUCTION

2-1. It is clear that in order to obtain comprehensive antitrust protection the term "undertaking" should be interpreted most liberally. In the legislative analysis of this term it has been questioned whether its interpretation should be determined on the basis of economic considerations. See 1-31. Most writers have supported such an interpretation as being in keeping with the purpose of Arts. 85 and 86, rather than merely stressing technical or legal concepts which relate to the separate legal personalities of the bodies involved.[1] From the language of the articles there seems to be no reason why the term "undertaking" should not include almost any legal or natural person carrying on activities of an economic nature, or have a reasonable degree of economic autonomy.[2] It also follows from the articles that the legal form of an "undertaking" is not decisive; it

1. See, for example, Columbia Law School Project on European Legal Institutions; The Law of the European Economic Community, vol. 2, sec. 85.11, at p.3-91 (Smit and Herzog eds. 1976)(hereinafter cited as "Smit and Herzog"); R. Graupner, The Rules of Competition of the European Economic Community 11 (1965); D. McLachlan and D. Swann, Competition Policy in the European Community 130 (1967); Note, "The Substantive Rules of Antitrust in the Common Market; Analysis and Approach" 17 Stanford L. Rev. 263 (1965).

   The meaning of the term "undertaking" for Art. 86 need be, of course, the same as for Art. 85 (see 1-30).

2. Cf. Bellamy, Child and Morris, Common Market Law of Competition, sec. 2-03 (2nd ed. 1978).

could include corporate bodies, unincorporated associations, partnerships and individual traders.[3] The definition of "undertaking", as it may be based upon economic concepts, embodies the principle of "lifting the veil" which, as a judicial inroad into the corporate entity, is used by courts following the lead of the legislature.[4] An economic unit theory, as may be applicable in competition cases, is a step in that direction and rests on the basis of corresponding justifications.

To understand the type of incidents which lend themselves to the application of a possible economic unit theory it is advisable to refer first to a functional definition of that theory, like the one proposed by the OECD Committee of Experts on Restrictive Business Practices:

> The theory of enterprise unity involves considering as a single economic entity, and even though they have separate legal personalities, enterprises belonging to the same group and subject to the same control.....The theory of enterprise unity is thus to be understood as an example of the application of the behaviour principle, but should not lead to automatically imputing the subsidiary's behaviour to the parent nor to denial of any independence of action on the part of the subsidiaries, which have been established in countries in which they operate. 5

The economic unit theory defines a corporation as a method and not as a thing; its definition varies and for one purpose it may be totally different from the definition for another.[6] In the present

---

3. Cf. ibid.; Honig , Brown, Gleiss and Hirsh, Cartel Law of the European Economic Community 9 (1963).

4. See Gower, The Principles of Modern Company Law 213-217 (3rd ed. 1969).

5. OECD, Committee of Experts on Restrictive Business Practices, Restrictive Business Practices of Multinational Enterprises, secs. 130-131 (1977)(hereinafter referred to as "OECD, Restrictive Business Practices of Multinational Enterprises").

6. See Douglas and Shanks, "Insulation From Liability Through Subsidiary Corporations" 39 Yale L.J. 194-195 (1929). This article is mostly concerned with the liability of parent companies in contracts and torts.

connection an implementation of the economic unit theory may purport to fulfil a purpose of competition law, so that the parent company will not be protected against antitrust proceedings by the affiliate's position as an independent legal personality, because in antitrust proceedings criteria of antitrust law, and not of corporation law, are regarded as authoritative.[7] In competition law particular account is expected to be taken of the public interest in prosecuting violations of the antitrust laws where initiated by foreign enterprises having subsidiaries within the territory.

The ascription of restrictive behaviour of a subsidiary to its parent may, of course, take place in domestic situations as well as in cases involving NCES. However, it may take on special extraterritorial jurisdictional significance in the latter incidents, which are our immediate interest in the present study. Would, therefore, the term "undertaking" in the Treaty be in practice interpreted by the Commission and the Court, so that the presence and the activities in the Common Market of a locally organized subsidiary of a NCE gives the Community direct jurisdiction over the foreign parent company?

Where foreign elements are involved the economic unit theory may have implications other than the one questioned above: a Community enterprise may be held liable by a foreign government for acts done abroad by its subsidiary there, and it could also be responsible before the Community for infringements of the Community competition rules by its foreign subsidiary. If the foreign subsidiary is actually part of the corporate family then it means that the parent would not be able to evade responsibility for the subsidiary's acts in either of

7. Cf. Schwartz, "Applicability of National Law on Restraints of Competition to International Restraints of Competition" in Cartel and Monopoly in Modern Law, vol. 2, 702-703 (1961).

these situations.

The question whether the economic unit theory will exempt restrictive agreements or conspiracy between related legal bodies of the same group points to a different issue which has relevance to the extra-territorial application of the competition rules (the "intra-enterprise conspiracy"). This issue is discussed in Section 2 of the present chapter.

The economic unit theory, as evolved in various legal systems, allows not only the question of the responsibility of foreign enterprises to be settled, but also a solution to be found to problems of investigation, service of process and enforcement, with regard to such enterprises. The latter incidents employ many of the operational features of the economic unit theory, but the incidents themselves are analytically different. The question in the latter case hinges on the application of the "presence" test,[8] for specific purposes, but without regard to the questions of substantive jurisdiction, i.e. those are mostly matters of personal jurisdiction and divorced from the varied issues of liability under the legislative jurisdiction.

A. The Economic Unit Theory in the Community Case Law

2-2. The economic unit theory was used by the Court for the first time as a jurisdictional basis in the Dyestuffs Cases,[9] although it had been

8. See Douglas and Shanks, supra note 6, at 204-205.

9. The relevant judgments for our survey from the complex of the Dyestuffs Cases are the following: Case 48/49 Imperial Chemical Industries Ltd. v. Commission [1972] E.C.R. 619 (hereinafter cited as the "I.C.I. Case"); Case 52/69 Geigy AG v. Commission [1972] E.C.R. 787 (hereinafter cited as the "Geigy Case"); Case 53/69 Sandoz AG v. Commission [1972] E.C.R. 845 (issues of fact and law and the grounds of judgment in the latter case are identical to those of the Geigy Case).

mentioned by it before.[10] The Dyestuffs Cases involved several defendants but concerned the same set of facts, as described below, with regard to each of the parties.[11]

The Commission carried out an investigation following information supplied by the representative trade bodies in the leather, textile, dyeing, and printing industries in several Member States. Price increases in those Member States were introduced in 1964, 1965 and 1967 by ten dyestuffs manufacturers, four German, one French, one Italian, three Swiss (Ciba, Geigy and Sandoz), and one English (I.C.I.).[12] Between the 7th and 20th of January, 1964, a uniform increase of 15% was made in the prices of certain dyestuffs in Italy, Holland, Belgium and Luxembourg. On 1st January, 1965, the same 15% increase was extended to Germany, and nearly all the manufacturers made a uniform 10% increase in the prices of the remaining dyestuffs and pigments in all five countries. On the 16th of October, 1967, an increase of 8% was made by nearly all the producers in Germany, Holland, Belgium and Luxembourg; the increase in France was 12%; there was no increase in Italy.

With respect to the uniform and simultaneous price increases the Commission noted that messages by telex or telegram were sent to subsidiaries or representatives, with similar contents. It accused the

---

10. Some of the economic considerations upon which the theory is based were previously mentioned in a different connection (see the intra-enterprise conspiracy doctrine in Section 3 of this chapter) and have already been entertained by the Court in the Béguelin Case (Case 22/71 [1971] E.C.R. 949; for a factual description of this case see 2061).

11. For the method of summarizing important facts of cases it will suffice if only the most significant aspects of the most important cases are given. When a case serves to illustrate concepts in different connections, the whole extract from the case will appear in only one of those contexts and a reference to it will be contained in the other contexts.

12. The U.K. was not then a Member State of the Community.

manufacturers of aniline dyestuffs of participating in concerted practices constituting infringements of the provisions of Art. 85(1). It, therefore, imposed fines on those undertakings which in the case of the four NCES amounted to 50,000 units of account.[13]

2-3. The arguments of the applicants, whose registered offices were outside the Community, were almost identical. They contended before the Court that the Commission had had no jurisdiction to impose fines upon them for acts they may have committed outside the territory of the Common Market. I.C.I., in particular, adduced the argument that since the contracts for supply of dyestuffs were both made in and governed by English Law, the corporation had not, for its part, carried on any activity inside the Common Market of which the law could take cognizance.

Nevertheless, the Court was satisfied that the price increases, put into effect within the Common Market by the respective subsidiaries of the applicants, were in fact the prohibited conduct of the NCES for which they themselves were responsible. The Court rejected the applicants objections to the Commission's jurisdiction as unfounded and delivered the following explanations:

> The fact that a subsidiary has separate legal personality is not sufficient to exclude the possibility of imputing its conduct to the parent company. Such may be the case in particular where the subsidiary, although having separate legal personality, does not decide independently upon its own conduct on the market, but carries out, in all material respects the instructions given to it by the parent company. 14
>
> In these circumstances the formal separation between these companies, resulting from their separate legal personality, cannot out-weigh the unity of their conduct on the market for the purposes of applying the rules on competition. It was in fact the applicant undertaking which brought the concerted practice into being within the Common Market. 15

---

13. See the Aniline Dyes Cartel [1969] C.M.L.R. D23 (hereinafter cited as the "Dyestuffs Decision").

14. I.C.I. Case 662, at paras, 132-133.

15. Geigy Case 836, at para. 45.

2-4. It is noteworthy that the Commission's contested Dyestuffs Decision did not consider the economic unit theory at all. However, the Commission asserted this theory in its statements of defence before the Court, saying that the applicants' conduct, against which objection was made, had taken place inside the Common Market. The reasons which originally had sustained the decision (see 2-51) appeared only as an alternative ground in the Commission's submissions to the Court.

The objectionable practices of the applicants consisted, according to the Commission's defence, in the fact that they gave orders to their Community subsidiaries to increase prices. The fact of influencing the behaviour of the subsidiaries constituted, in the Commission's view, conduct on the part of the applicants within the Common Market. The subsidiaries simply carried out the orders, so that when one considered their competitive situation in respect of third parties, they appear as mere extensions of the applicants within the Common Market.[16] The Commission indicated that the concept of legal personality, in the case of an industrial concern, is far from being an absolute concept and stressed that it should only be applied in so far as it does not result in unjust and unacceptable consequences within the legal order.[17]

2-5. A further application by the Court of the economic unit theory approved in principle the Commission decision which for the first time applied this theory.[18] The facts of the Continental Can Case[19]

---

16. See Ibid, 795.
17. See I.C.I. Case, 632.
18. Continental Can Co. Inc. [1972] C.M.L.R. D11 (hereinafter cited as the "Continental Can Decision").
19. Case 6/72 Europemballage Corporation and Continental Can Company Inc. v. Commission [1973] E.C.R. 215 (hereinafter cited as the "Continental Can Case"). The Court rejected some of the factual appraisals made by the Commission and thus reversed the decision.

provided an occasion which was particularly suitable for the application of the economic unit theory in the context of Art. 86.

Continental Can Company Inc. (Continental) of New York (USA), a company manufacturing metal packages, packaging materials of paper and plastic and machines for manufacturing and using these packages, by successive purchases during the year 1969, brought its share in Schmalbach-Lubeca-Werke AG (SLW) of Brunswick (Germany) to 85.8% of the nominal capital. During the same year, Continental contemplated the formation, with The Metal Box Company Ltd. (MB) of London, of a European holding company for packaging, in which the licensees of Continental in the Netherlands and in France, Thomassen & Drijver-Verblifa N.V. (TDV) of Deventer and J.J. Carnaud and Forges de Basse-Indre (Carnaud) of Paris, would be invited to participate. However, Carnaud indicated at the end of August 1969 that it could not participate in the contemplated holding company. On 16 February 1970 an agreement was signed between Continental and TDV whereby it was agreed:

(a) that Continental would set up in Delaware (USA) a company (subsequently called Europemballage Corporation) to which it would transfer its interests in SLW;

(b) that Continental would induce Europemballage to offer to the shareholders of TDV other than MB and Carnaud, a sum of 140 florins cash for each TDV share of 20 florins nominal value. Each TDV shareholder offering his shares would also receive a certificate granting him a preferential right to purchase ordinary shares in Europemballage when these should be offered to the public. Continental would provide Europemballage with the necessary funds for such a purchase by acquiring additional shares in Europemballage.

In the implementation of this agreement: on 20th February, 1970, a company called Europemballage Corporation (Europemballage) was set up in Wilmington, under the legislation of the State of Delaware, and opened an office in New York and another in Brussels; on 16th March, 1970, TDV published the take-over bid made by Europemballage.

After the Commission drew the attention of the corporations concerned to the possible incompatibility of the transaction contemplated with the provisions of Art. 86 of the Treaty, MB indicated that it was postponing its contemplated transaction with Europemballage. In April 1970, Europemballage carried out the purchase of the shares and debentures of TDV offered up to the date, thus bringing the initial share of Continental in TDV to 91.07%

The Commission, in decision, found that the above take-over constituted such an increase of Continental's dominant position, that no room for effective competition on the market was left and that, therefore, the merger would be considered an abuse of that dominant position. This would be true, the Commission held, although the dominant position itself was not used in the realization of the acquisition. Continental Can was required to put an end to the infringement of Art. 86 and to submit proposals for this purpose to the Commission.

2-6. On appeal Continental argued before the Court that it did not have a registered office, and did not exercise any activity, in the territory of a Member State and that, therefore, the Commission had exceeded its jurisdictional powers. However, the grounds for the Commission's jurisdiction over Continental were approved by the Court, on the basis of acts performed by a subsidiary within the territory of the Common Market. In explaining its judgment the Court used the following language:

> .....the circumstance that this subsidiary company has its own legal personality does not suffice to exclude the possibility that its conduct might be attributed to the parent company. This is true in those cases particularly where the subsidiary company does not determine its market behaviour, but in essentials follows directives of the parent company.....The circumstance that Continental does not have its registered office within the territory of one of the Member States is not sufficient to exclude it from the application of Community Law.20

2-7. A far more comprehensive elaboration of the economic unit theory (although not without modifications as to the prerequisites and the standard of proof required for the theory; see 2-18, 2-26) was manifested both by the Commission and the Court in the Commercial Solvents Case.[21] The factual background of the case was the following.

Commercial Solvents Corporation (CSC) of New York, is the world's only industrial producer of nitropropane and aminobutanol. Both are intermediary products for the manufacture of ethambutol, an anti-tuberculosis drug. In 1962 CSC acquired a majority of the voting stock in Istituto Chemioterapico Italiano SpA (Istituto) in Milan and representation in the "Consiglio di amministrazione" and in the "Comitato Esecutivo". Until 1970 Istituto acted as a reseller of aminobutanol produced by CSC. A customer of Istituto for this product was Laboratorio Chemico Farmaceutico Giorgio Zoja SpA (Zoja), to which Istituto began selling it in 1966. Zoja used the product in the manufacture of ethambutol-based specialities. In 1968 Istituto

---

20. Continental Can Case 242, at paras. 15-16.

21. Joined Cases 6 and 7/73, Istituto Chemioterapico Italiano SpA and Commercial Solvents Corporation v. Commission [1974] E.C.R. 223 (hereinafter cited as the "Commercial Solvents Case"). Reference to the decision of the Commission is given in note 22).

initiated efforts to bring about a merger with Zoja, but such efforts broke down in 1969. Istituto started the production of its own ethambutol-based specialities in 1970. Early in 1970 CSC decided that it would no longer supply nitropropane and aminobutanol to the Common Market, only dextro-aminbutanol, an up-graded intermediate product which Istituto would convert to bulk ethambutol for sale in the Common Market and elsewhere, and for the manufacture of its own specialities. In the spring of 1970 Zoja cancelled its order for 20,000 kg of aminobutanol because a number of independent distributors were supplying large amounts of aminobutanol at lower prices, but at the end of 1970 Istituto informed CSC that Zoja had placed a new order for aminobutanol. CSC replied that none was available. After further attempts to obtain supplies of aminobutanol on the world market had failed, Zoja, by letter dated 8th April, 1972, applied to the Commission for the institution of proceedings against CSC and Istituto, under Art. 3 of Reg. 17, for infringement of Art. 86 of the Treaty.

By its decision of 14th December, 1972, the Commission found that CSC's denial of aminobutanol through Istituto to Zoja constituted an abuse of a dominant position within the Common Market and thus a violation of Art. 86.[22] Therefore, it required CSC to supply Zoja with sufficient raw materials for its production destined for Zoja's entire market (within and without the Common Market). It further imposed on CSC and Istituto jointly and severally a punitive fine and a periodic penality payment for any delay in the event of a failure promptly to resume supplies to Zoja.

---

22. Zoja SpA v. Commercial Solvents Corporation and Istituto Chemioterapico Italiano [1973] C.M.L.R. D50 (hereinafter cited as the "Zoja Decision").

2-8. Many of the jurisdictional implications of this case are discussed throughout the study, but it is noteworthy, at this stage, that the Commission based its claim for jurisdiction over CSC solely on the basis of the economic unit theory, as it did in the Continental Can Decision. (However, in distinction from the latter case, the Commission proposed on appeal an alternative basis for its jurisdiction; see 2-53). The Zoja Decision concluded, in principle, that the subsidiary's conduct in the territory of the Common Market was influenced by the parent company so that there was no ground for distinguishing between the will and acts of CSC and Istituto.[23]

The Court's pronouncement on the application of the economic unit theory was as follows:

> .....the conduct of CSC and Istituto has thus been characterized by an obviously united action, which, taking account of the power of control of CSC over Istituto, confirms the conclusions in the decision that as regards their relations with Zoja the two companies must be deemed an economic unit. 24

2-9. The Commercial Solvents Case remains the latest detailed pronouncement on the manifestation of the Court's approach towards the use of economic concepts as a tool in establishing the jurisdiction of the Community over NCES. Since that judgment the Commission and the Court have applied the economic unit theory in a number of cases as a matter of practice. They gave very little explanation of the basis of the theory and no objections were raised by parties to the justification of the theory.

---

23. Zoja Decision D6, at para A4.

24. Commercial Solvents Case 254-255, at para 41.

Among the clear examples of the application of the theory is the United Brands Case,[25] in which the Commission, and later the Court, found that a New York enterprise, together with United Brands Continental BV of Rotterdam, and its other subsidiary companies, formed a single economic unit. The only relevant reference to the economic unit theory in the case was the Commission's statement that the subsidiaries were under the control of the parent company and "do not possess any real autonomy".[26] The Commission had found that United Brands Company had abused its position in four respects, namely forbidding ripeners/distributors to resell green bananas, refusing to continue to supply a ripener/distributor who had taken part in an advertising campaign for a rival brand of bananas, discriminating between trading partners by charging prices which differed considerably according to the purchaser's country, and charging some of its customers unfair prices. The Court upheld the Commission's findings on the first three counts and rejected the fourth for lack of proof. It accordingly reduced the fine.

Another decision in which the economic unit theory has been applied was issued by the Commission under Art. 86 against Hoffmann-La Roche (Roche), a multinational group with its headquarters in Switzerland and the world leading vitamin manufacturer.[27] The Commissior considered that Roche, which operated in the Common Market through its

---

25. United Brands Company (Chiquita) [1976] C.M.L.R. D46, at para. 75 (hereinafter cited as the "United Brands Decision"). On appeal Case 27/76, United Brands Company and United Brands Continental V.B. v. Commission [1978] E.C.R. 131 (hereinafter cited as the "United Brands Case").

26. See United Brands Decision D46, at para. 75.

27. See Hoffman-La Roche & Co. AG [1976] C.M.L.R. D42, at para 74.

eight subsidiaries, located in several Member States, was abusing its dominant position by concluding exclusive or preferential contracts, since the effect of the contracts was to tie the most important buyers of bulk vitamins to it and to prevent its chief competitors from supplying them. The decision, which imposed on the Swiss enterprise a fine of 300,000 u.a. or DM 1,098,000 (as Roche has an important subsidiary in the Federal Republic of Germany), did not even mention that it applied the economic unit theory. This decision was fully approved by the Court.[28]

A later decision of the Commission in this series concerned a Swedish manufacturer of cash registers, Liptons Cash Registers, who refused to supply spare parts to an independent English firm by prohibiting its wholly-owned subsidiaries and distributors within the Common Market from selling such spare parts outside a fixed distribution network (contrary to Art. 86).[29] The decision was, however, reversed by the Court on another ground.[30]

B. Technicalities and Operation of the Economic Unit Theory

(1) The Guiding Principles

2-10. The issues which were left without an analysis in the preceding survey of the application of the economic unit theory could be simply

28. In Case 85/76, Hoffmann La-Roche and Co. AG v. Commission [1979] E.C.R. 461.

29. See Lipton Cash Registers and Business Equipment Limited v. Hugin Kassaregister AB and Hugin Cash Registers Limited [1978] 1 C.M.L.R. D42, at para 74.

30. Case 22/78, Hugin Kassaregister & Hugin Cash Register Ltd. v. Commission [1979] E.C.R. 1869.

reduced to the question: under what conditions would a parent company and its subsidiary, with a separate legal identity, be treated as a single economic unit for the purposes of the Community competition law?

The assertion that the isolation will be broken down where the subsidiary is an "extension" or "the will and the acts" of the parent company is not helpful for the application of the theory. These concepts themselves need defining; at best they merely point out the results, and the results are significant only in the light of the facts. The conclusion that the parent company will be held liable when the use of the subsidiary is "unjust",[31] also falls short of describing the standard of conduct and the prerequisites for the application of the theory, which the facts of the cases permit.

2-11. The explanations in the Community case law of what constitutes an economic unit concentrate on the notion of "control".[32] But, since "control" may assume different guises, we have to examine the facts concerning the manner and method of organization and operation of enterprises.[33] The examination of the relevant facts will be in line with a summary of guiding principles which, we submit, follow the tests in the Commission decisions and the Court judgments. Other useful

31. Cf. I.C.I. Case, submission and arguments of parties (the Commission) 632.

32. Cf. notes 14, 20 and 24 above.

33. Although no specific Community enactment on the operation of the economic unit theory exists, the Commission laid down , in a Notice, some guidelines in this direction, for the specific purpose of calculating aggregate turnover of enterprises which are parties to agreements under the scope of that Notice; see Notice, Concerning Agreements, Decisions and Concerted Practices of Minor Importance Which Do Not Fall Under Article 85(1) of the Treaty Establishing The European Economic Community, J.O. 1970, C64, p.1.

factors may also suggest themselves, but the following guidelines may, where taken with regard to their aggregated impact, prove sufficient to establish "control":

(a) The structural and managerial test:

(i) Majority of stock ownership - the holding by the parent company of the majority (usuàlly more than half) of capital of issue shares of the subsidiary. An ownership by the same company of the majority stock of both the parent and the subsidiary may also come under this guideline.

(ii) Managerial and administrative involvement - the parent company, in addition to having a majority of the voting stock of the subsidiary, is represented by its officials and directors on various boards of the subsidiary.

(b) The functional and operational test:

(i) Evidence of actual influence (control), in all material and essential respects, in a manner binding on the subsidiary, or at least the

(ii) ability and possibility to influence (to control) in a decisive manner the behaviour of the subsidiary.

(c) The extent to which the parent company was causally influencing the specific prohibited conduct of the subsidiary.

2-12. It is apparent that the majority of stock ownership mentioned in the first guiding principle above, which appears as constant, usually implies a controlling interest; otherwise the question would normally not arise. Stock ownership gives the stock-holders, either by statute, judicial decision, or by normal corporation procedure, the exercise of control. This control is realized in the election of directors, the making of by-laws, the increase or decrease of the authorized capital stock, and the performance of other acts incident to the legal status of stock-holders.[34] The extent of the parent's involvement in the management and administration of the subsidiary becomes material where no formal barriers between the two management structures are maintained; separate meetings are not observed, and activities of the same individuals serving on the two boards cannot be described, so as to distinguish always between their acts as directors of the subsidiary or directors of the parent.

One qualification of the assertion of connection between the majority of stock ownership and the managerial and administrative involvement, as implied above, seems appropriate. If, despite complete ownership of the subsidiary by the parent, control is effectively in independent hands, the subsidiary may still be a distinct economic unit within the meaning of Arts. 85 and 86. This situation may occur where by an effective legal measure, such as a management contract, the management of the subsidiary is entrusted to persons over whom the parent has no control. In cases where subsidiaries are not wholly owned a holder of the minority interests may sometimes have more administrative influence than those who own the remainder of the stock and a greater interest in the administration of the subsidiary. If the remainder stock is owned by persons who are not themselves actual or potential actors in the relevant market the holder of the minority share-capital will have the administrative power. This situation will ordinarily occur when small private investors or banks hold the remaining interest, which may be less than half of the stock.

The question of a judgment on the subsidiary's autonomy seems to require <u>inter alia</u> a careful consideration of the company law applicable

---

34. See, for example, Gower, <u>supra</u> note 4, at 343-347.

to the subsidiary and seems dependent on various concepts of that law. For example, one is supposed to take account of the fact that under most company laws the directors of a company are under a legal obligation to conduct the company's business in conformity with its own interest. This principle is incompatible with an obligation to execute orders emanating from persons outside the company. Even if the majority shareholder is directly or indirectly able to determine the executives of the company the latter must abide by the above rules of company law. Therefore, a point to consider is whether company law permits the required intensity of integration between parent and subsidiary; otherwise an illegal situation would be accepted as the basis of antitrust jurisdiction.[35] But, the reliance upon the national law of the subsidiary raises the problem whether the result of the case might vary under the law of another Member State not having such a provision. We submit that if the actual exercise of directive power can be established, company law standards to the contrary should not be accepted as a valid defence, for this would imply that potential addresses of antitrust provisions could rely on legal principles even if it could be shown that they did not feel obliged to observe them.

2-13. The second guiding principle speaks clearly about "control"; it describes situations where the day-to-day business of the units is not kept separate and where some process cannot be described so as to identify it with the activity of one unit or the other. Attention must be paid to the fact that in a case where the two businesses are merely units in a line of production their description as separate

---

35. See Koppensteiner, "International Enterprises Under the Antitrust Law of the European Economic Community" 9 J.W.T.L. 296 (1975).

businesses will occasionally be difficult, except in so far as economy and efficiency in operation have necessitated duplication at strategic points. The non-observance of separate financial units between the parent and the subsidiary may serve in particular as an important indication that the business units should be treated as assimilated.

A distinct requirement within the framework of this guiding principle is that it will suffice for that principle to apply that only mere ability and possibility to control by the parent company exist. A better understanding of that situation will be gained later when this principle is examined in factual circumstances.

2-14. The third guiding principle relates to a constituent element in the definition of an economic unit in a particular case, and this establishes the responsibility of the parent company in the relevant circumstances. Of course it is possible for two companies which usually do not form an economic unit to act in unison with regard to a specific activity; in that case the rules are laid down in Art. 85, dealing with restrictive agreements and with concerted practices. Therefore this guiding principle does not imply that two companies which, as entities, do not form an economic unit, are to be considered as an economic unit in one particular aspect or with regard to one particular activity. It has been emphasized before that all three guiding principles have to be taken as one complex of accumulating requirements.

(2) Implementation of the Guiding Principles in the Case Law

2-15. In illustrating the implementation of the guiding principles and the quality of proof required for an economic unit we shall refer to the facts of the decisions and judgments which were described at the outset of this chapter to indicate the general recognition and use of an economic unit theory in Community law. As already mentioned the ruling in the Commercial Solvents Case lends itself in particular to significant conclusions regarding the main aspects of the economic unit theory and, therefore, is the first to be examined under each of the guiding principles, with exceptions where it clearly deviates from other rulings.

(a) The Structural and Managerial Test

(i) Majority of Stock Ownership

2-16. Commercial Solvents Corporation held 51 per cent of the share capital of its Italian subsidiary, Istituto. In order to establish the importance of this fact the Commission referred, in the decision, to provisions of the national law of the subsidiary. Holding a majority of the (voting) stock implies, according to Italian Company Law (Article 2359 of the Civil Code[36]), that the parent company has the control of the subsidiary. However, it is not clear whether that "control", as mentioned in the company law, relates directly to the control sought by the competition rules of the Treaty, based on the control of the subsidiary market behaviour. The applicants indeed contended that the Italian law applied only to the prohibition of crossed-share holdings between the parent and a "controlled" subsidiary for the protection of the creditors of the parent.[37] In its defence the Commission further attempted to strengthen the inference of "control" by referring to company laws of other Member States, to a

36. For the text of the Italian article see the Zoja Decision D56.
37. See Commercial Solvents Case 229.

proposal for enacting Community company law, and to the German Competition Law.[38] The Court, for its part, did not comment on those inferences of "control", so that their real evidential value is not yet definite.

In all of the remaining cases, which implemented the economic unit theory before the Commercial Solvents Case, the parent companies held, at the time of the offence, all or at any rate the majority of the shares in their subsidiaries and this point was presumed to imply control.[39]

(ii) Managerial and Administrative Involvement

2-17. The relations and dependence between this requirement and the requirement of majority of stock ownership was described by the Commission, in general terms, in the Zoja Decision:

> (CSC's majority of the stock ownership -B.B.).....permits it to exercise permanently a determining action over the formation of the corporate will and thus over the management of Istituto Chemioterapico, given that the general meeting, by the favourable vote of a number of shareholders representing more than the majority of the same capital, has, *inter alia*, the power to appoint the directors to discuss their responsibilities, to approve the balance sheet. 40

The involvement of CSC in the management and administration of its subsidiary was evidenced by the composition of the management board and the executive committee of Istituto. In fact 5 of the 10 members of the management board of Istituto were representatives of CSC and held important executive posts. In practice the president of CSC

38. See *ibid*.

39. See, for example, I.C.I. Case 662, at paras. 136 *et seq.*

40. Zoja Decision D56, at para. A2.

was also the chairman of this management board and had the casting vote. The applicants claimed that the president's casting vote had never been used, but the Commission seemed to be satisfied with the mere possibility of the president's determining the power relations within the group, if necessary.[41] The Commission also rejected the argument that under Istituto's articles of association the two "consiglieri-delegat" (delegates of CSC) still had full power to direct the company, except in relation to investments, as being too remote from such actual possibility.[42] The articles of association did not seem, therefore, to have any relevance in connection with the economic unit theory. With regard to the executive committees of Istituto, among six members, three were representatives of CSC, which revealed "the intention of CSC to follow closely, day by day, the business, even the routine business, of Istituto".[43]

In all of the remaining cases which applied the economic unit theory the Commission and the Court paid less attention to the second guiding principle, probably because of the absence of arguments from the parties denying the existence of such an actual state of affairs as the principle requires.

(b) The Functional and Operational Test

2-18. The "control" which is a feature of all the guiding principles is classified under this principle in two degrees of intensity, one of a mere possibility and ability to control, and the other of a continuous factual control.

---

41. Cf. Commercial Solvents Case 232.

42. Ibid. at 228-229.

43. Zoja Decision D56, at para A4.

The case law of the Community indicates that the Commission and the Court resorted to findings of control on the basis of circumstantial evidence. In the Dyestuffs Cases the Court found that the subsidiaries had carried out "in all material respects" the instructions given to them by the parent companies.[44] A similar observation was repeated by the Court in the Continental Can Case where it emphasized that the subsidiary "in essentials followed directives" from the parent company.[45]

A departure from the test of actual influence in all material and essential respects could be observed in the Commission's position in the Commercial Solvents Case where it argued that an "entity" relationship between CSC and Istituto would need only to be proved in respect to the specific conduct in question:

> .....CSC controls Istituto and exercises its control in fact at least with respect to Istituto's relations with Zoja. Therefore, there is no ground for distinguishing between the will and the acts of CSC and those of Istituto. Regarding their relations with Zoja the Commission considers them as constituting one economic entity.[46]

This argument may impair the requirement that, in order to establish the economic reality of a complex of legal and factual data, it is important that the subsidiary is under actual and continuous influence of its parent company in all material respects. Although the change might appear to be a tactical retreat from a larger assertion, it held, in fact, implications for the broadening of the economic unit test. This approach was criticized by the applicants as an unwarranted change in ground.[47] The Court in its ambiguous language did not remedy the impairment of the initial requirement as

---

44. Cf. I.C.I. Case 662, at paras. 132-135; Geigy Case 835,at para 44.
45. Continental Can Case 242, at para. 15.
46. Commercial Solvents Case, pleas and arguments of the parties, 228, at para. 9.
47. Cf. ibid. judgment 254, at paras. 37-38.

appeared in its previous judgments:

> .....the conclusion is reached that CSC holds the power of control of Istituto and exercises its control in fact at least with respect to Istituto's relations with Zoja.....there is no foundation in the complaint, which must therefore be rejected, that the Commission altered its position during the course of the present proceedings in that after having agreed in its Decision that the two companies constituted an economic unit in every respect, it restricted its position to the argument that in any case they acted as such a unit in their relations with Zoja. 48

If the implicit change from former rulings is to be taken as to require only enough proof of factual influence to show economic unit in the narrow scope, concerning the specific prohibited conduct, it is still necessary to satisfy the requirement of ability and possibility (as distinguished from actual control) the parent company to influence, in a decisive manner, the general behaviour of the subsidiary. This is evident from pronouncements of both the Commission and the Court, referring in general terms to the existence of control in the latter case.[49]

(c) <u>The Extent to Which the Parent Company Was Causally Influencing the Specific Prohibited Conduct of its Subsidiary</u>

2-19. The attribution of Istituto's activities, *vis à vis* Zoja, to CSC was justified by the Commission and the Court on the basis of the following points:

(1) The highly significant coincidence of the periods when CSC decided to prolong its production to a stage beyond finishing and when Istituto, a former distributor of nitropropane aminobutanol, began its activities as a producer. The latter development was clearly influenced

48. *Ibid*. at 254, para. 38.

49. Accord, Koppensteiner, *supra* note 35, at 311.

by CSC since the activities of Istituto as a producer required investments for which CSC had a blocking vote.

(2) The association of the decision by CSC no longer to sell nitropropane and aminobutanol with the fact that it made an exception in favour of Istituto, which was supplied with dextroaminobutanol for the purposes of its own production of ethambutol and specialities based on this product. The latter action indicated the intention of CSC to prevent Zoja being able to obtain supplies of raw material, and showed to what extent CSC exercised close surveillance over the activities of Zoja.[50]

(3) The significance of the fact that Istituto bought quantities of nitropropane, which was still available on the market for resale to paint manufacturers, who were forbidden to resell for pharmaceutical purposes outside the Common Market.

These points were also connected, in the decision, with the failure of merger discussions between Zoja and Istituto, which contributed, according to the Commission, to the unlikelihood that CSC had refrained from exercising, in fact, its power of control over Istituto in that respect.[51]

2-20. In the Continental Can Case, although no direct evidence of an "order" to Europemballage, concerning the acquisition of the TDV shares was found, the Court confirmed the finding that Continental Can had "caused" Europemballage to perform that act. This finding was probably inferred from the undisputed fact that Europemballage was set up for the purpose of buying the TDV shares, that at the time of the take-over bid it was not fully organised, and that funds necessary for the transaction were provided by Continental Can.[52]

---

50. See Zoja Decision D57, at para. A6.
51. See ibid.
52. Continental Can Case 242, at para 16.

It is noteworthy that "control" as required for the application of the economic unit theory may even be indirect if sufficiently influential. The applicants in the Continental Can Case contended that the legal person which committed the alleged abuse (Europemballage) was not the same as that which held the dominant position in the Common Market (Continental Can). However, the Commission and the Court denied any relevance to the undisputed fact that SLW was placed only under the indirect control of Continental Can.[53]

2-21. In the Dystuffs Cases the requisite of factual influence upon the occasion of price increases in the Common Market was evidenced by telex messages, relating to the 1964 increase, sent by the applicants to the subsidiaries, with specific orders as to the prices and conditions of sale. In the absence of evidence to the contrary, it was assumed that on the occasion of the increases of 1965 and 1967 the applicants acted in a similar fashion.[54]

2-22. A firm conclusion as to the importance of the third guiding principle for the operation of the economic unit theory results from all the cases mentioned above. In each case the Commission and the Court insisted that evidence of influence in relation to the specific prohibited conduct is an indispensable prerequisite for the operation of the theory. We submit that any different view, which may propose that once it was explained that a subsidiary had acted on the actual or presumed instructions of its parent company the latter would also be held liable for any alleged breach of the relevant competition rules,

---

53. See further arguments of the applicants in the Continental Can Case 223.

54. See I.C.I. Case, judgment 663, at paras. 144-145.

even if the circumstances of the specific concerned conduct are different,[55] is too wide a view and is unacceptable in its scope of attribution of liability.[56]

(3) The Standards of Proof Required by the Economic Unit Theory

2-23. The first guiding principle is established upon constant facts. However, the second and the third seem to require a certain degree of inferential evidence on the relationship between parent and subsidiary. The quality of proof or the type of evidence of the intensity of control, with regard to those principles, is to be determined by the Community in each case under consideration so that generally accepted notions of justice would be regarded.[57]

2-24. The Dyestuffs Cases' judgments seem to represent a departure from a rigid formula of proof, since it was presumed on the basis of one telex message that the applicants acted similarly on other occasions. If the judgments really implied that parent and subsidiary are an entity for all purposes, whenever it can be shown that they acted as one in similar circumstances or in a related offence, these judgments might establish that the burden of proof shifts to the parent to prove that the case in a later offence is different. Such a possible shift in the

---

55. In the Dyestuffs Cases the Commission inferred actual offences upon evidence of action in one similar event only (see 2-21), but this is not the case where such inferences are made with regard to a specific offence which occurs in completely different circumstances, as mentioned in the text. The Dyestuffs Cases were, nevertheless, criticized for a certain departure from the strict formula of proof as suggested here. See 2-24.

56. But see Bentill "Control Over the Abuse of Monopoly Power in EEC Business Law" 12 C.M.L.Rev. 65 (1975).

57. In the last chapter of the study we indicate that the standards of proof to establish an economic unit for a jurisdictional purpose in a specific field may come under the scrutiny of the principles of jurisdiction of international law. See 6-9.

the burden of proof, in a case that may result in the imposition of substantial fines, attracted strong criticism from writers.[58] Mann, in particular, expresses doubt whether the judgments contained the sufficient elaborate, detailed and painstaking investigation necessary to disregard distinct legal personalities.[59] Referring to that particular fact, i.e. the telex messages, Mann says:

> .....the text of these messages can nowhere be found - not in the decision of the Commission, nor in the speech of the Advocate-General, nor in the judgment of the Court. No such messages were proved to have been sent in 1965. Yet the Court felt entitled to say that 'in absence of contrary indications it must be assumed' that I.C.I.'s attitude was similar. Thus the whole case covering acts in three different years rests on a single telex message of unknown and therefore unreviewable content. 60

Nevertheless, it is important to stress that the evidence before the Court with regard to the first price increases (the 1964 telex messages) was convincing, and that the Commission could produce some concrete evidence of influence exerted by the parent corporations over the subsidiaries. In any event, it is evident from the proof actually required by the Court in these Cases, that the requirement that a subsidiary be unable to determine its behaviour in an autonomous manner is not as strict a test in practice as it would appear.[61]

2-25. Before venturing any further into the case law to ascertain the standards of proof required, it may be important to examine a proposal of the Advocate-General Warner that a subsidiary, by its definition, will presumably act in accordance with the wishes of its parent company.

---

58. See Mann "The Dyestuffs Case in the Court of Justice of the European Communities" 22 Int. & Comp. L.Q. 48-49 (1973); Allen, "The Development of European Community Antitrust Jurisdiction Over Alien Undertakings" 2 Legal Issues of European Integration 58-59 (1974); Steindorff "Annotation on the Decision of the European Court in the Dyestuffs Cases of July 14, 1972" 9 C.M.L. Rev. 506 (1972); Murray, "Case Note, Case 48/69, Dyestuffs Cases" 13 Va. J. Int. L. 381 (1973).

59. See Mann, ibid. at 49.

60. Ibid. at 48-49.

61. See Allen, supra note 58, at 59.

The Advocate-General argued this presumption before the Court in the <u>Commercial Solvents Case</u>:

> .....unless the presumption is rebutted, it is proper for the parent and the subsidiary to be treated as a single undertaking for the purposes of Articles 85 and 86 of the EEC Treaty, and .....the presumption can only be rebutted if it is shown affirmatively, by those concerned to rebut it, that the subsidiary in fact conducted its business autonomously. 62

Advocate-General Warner stressed that the necesity for that presumption is derived from the characteristics of the sphere of competition law. He indicated that neither Art. 85 nor Art. 86, anywhere refer to "persons", but are directed to "undertakings", a much wider and looser concept. The export of the doctrine of separate legal personality into branches of the law where it has little relevance could, as the opinion stated, serve only to divorce the law from reality.[63]

However, Advocate-General Warner gave no indication what would be a definition of a "subsidiary" for this presumption. Since this term is being used to imply "control", one might think it should be based either on the majority of stock ownership, or on the involvement in the management or administration of another corporation.[64] In any event, the presumption proposed is very far reaching in view of the Advocate-General's observation that rebutting the presumption is a very difficult onus to discharge and that it is almost impossible to discharge it in the ordinary case of a parent and subsidiary on related business.[65] The

---

62. <u>Commercial Solvents Case</u> 264.

63. <u>Ibid.</u> at 263-264.

64. See V. Korah "Istituto Chemioterapico Italiano SpA and Commercial Solvents Corporation v. Commission of the European Communities" 11 <u>C.M.L. Rev.</u> 252 (1974). The writer observes that such a definition for a "subsidiary" would not be very different from the definition of "inter-connected bodies corporate" in section 159 of the <u>English Companies Act</u> 1948.

65. See <u>Commercial Solvents Case</u> 264.

Commission and the Court did not resort to the proposed presumption and instead searched for findings of actual control based on circumstantial evidence. (With regard to the Commercial Solvents Case see 2-18 and 2-19). We submit that the burden of proof has to lie with the prosecuting authority; the actual exercise of the parent's power of control must be shown by those who request the veil to be lifted. For even in the cases of complete ownership it is perfectly conceivable that the parent may choose not to use its ultimate authority.

2-26. In the Commercial Solvents Case emphasis was placed, as indicated before, on inferences from circumstances surrounding the relations between the parent company and its subsidiary in relation to the third party concerned. See 2-18. Such an approach may imply a change with respect to the legal concept of the economic unit theory, since that approach requires that the decisive elements for establishing actual control, in the act to be imputed to the parent company, should be unilateral acts by the parent company. The economic unit theory, as reflected in the Commercial Solvents Case seems to become a "united action" theory.[66] In the Commission's Fifth Report on Competition Policy the latter theory is referred to as the "unity of conduct on the part of parent company and subsidiary".[67] Thus the economic unit theory may become in the case law a guise for an antitrust version of an implied agency theory.[68] The agency theory in fact gives a reasonable explanation why in the Zoja Decision fines were imposed jointly and severally on the parent company and its subsidiary.

---

66. Cf. Allen, supra note 58 at 73.
67. Fifth Report on Competition Policy, point 38.
68. See Allen, supra note 58, at 73.

2-27. Corporations in various legal systems have long been liable for offences of both strict and vicarious liability. The latter concept is explained by Leigh in the following paragraph:

> Vicarious liability is directed toward imposing a police function upon the master in respect of the actions of his servants or agents. Corporations are in the same position as any other master. Vicarious liability can mean either of two things. If liability is imposed respondeat superior, in the absence of a requirement of intent, it may mean no more than that a servant, in performing a routine task has supplied an actus reus which will be imputed to the master as his personal actus reus. Alternatively, if liability is imposed where the servant enjoys a delegated power, the offence is essentially that of the servant, liability for it being ascribed to the master. In both cases, the rationale of liability relates to the failure of an employer adequately to perform a supervisory function. In either case, because liability is vicarious, it usually matters little whether the offence is that of the master or of the servant. 69

The invocation of the concept of an agency for the purpose of vicarious liability in many aspects of national legislations is not unknown; courts have made use of the agency concept to pierce the corporate veil, where the corporate personality was used for the evasion of statutory regulation, e.g. tax laws.[70] It is of course necessary to ascertain the authority of the agent in each case, as a question of fact, and courts have developed yardsticks for that purpose, often based on the quest for a controlling interest.[71] Any use of the concept of vicarious liability by the Community for the assertion of jurisdiction over foreign parent companies will, therefore, be based on principles not of antitrust law but of criminal law and tort.[72]

---

69. L. Leigh, The Criminal Liability of Corporation in English Law 75 (1969); see also R. Cross and P. Jones, An Introduction to Criminal Law 106-107 (7th ed. 1972).

70. See Gower, supra note 4, at 203-204.

71. For example in Smith, Stone & Knight v. Birmingham Corporation [1939] 4 All E.R. 116 (per Atkinson J.), six points were considered relevant for determining the question of implied agency; some of them are similar to the guiding principles of the economic unit theory. See also Badische Anilin und Soda Fabrik v. Basle Chemical Works, Bindschedler [1898] A.C. 200 H.L.

72. Cf. Steindorff, supra note 58, at 506-507.

The important elements involved in a possible agency theory, in competition cases, would be of complicity and of procurement. These elements raise questions as to the degree in which the two distinct legal personalities have participated, i.e. whether they are principal offenders, accessories, or abettors, or whether their participation is innocent so that the acts done by them do not make them participes criminis.[73] In the case of antitrust law it is rather likely that the subsidiary would be found an "intelligent agent" interposed in the violation of criminal law. In such a case it may seem to be improper to hold simply that the agent's behaviour should only be imputed to the parent company, because the agent does not enjoy real autonomy and acts under the order of the parent. Should we not rather demand from the subsidiary that it resist an order, if its execution would violate the law?[74] Steindorff suggests that the subsidiary's action may be imputed to the non-Community parent company only if the subsidiary is an innocent agent.[75]

2-28. Apart from the Commercial Solvents Case, where it is possible to observe that the Community has pursued a line of reasoning justified by an agency theory, there are very few indications of the adoption of that approach in the case law.

The idea that a subsidiary could act as an "intelligent agent" and be responsible for its action, in addition to the liability of the

73. See Russell on Crime, vol. 1, 128 (12 edition, Turner ed.,1964).

74. See Steindorff, supra note 58, at 507.

75. Ibid. On the concept of an "innocent agent" see also Cross and Jones, supra note 69, at 103. In their eighth edition, sec. 19.2, the authors describe an "innocent agent" as one who commits the actus reus of an offence, but is himself devoid of responsibility. See also Russell on Crime, supra note 73, at 129; an "innocent agent" is defined as a mere machine whose movements are regulated by the offender by Glanville Williams, Criminal Law, sec. 120 at 350 (2nd. ed. 1961).

parent company, was reflected in the Pittsburgh Corning Decision.[75a] In this decision the Commission stated that, for a concessionary (*in casu*, a subsidiary) to apply a discriminatory price policy at the request of the grantor of the concession constitutes a concerted practice within the meaning of Art. 85(1). In the Comission's view the fact that the concessionary agreed only for fear of having its concession contract terminated makes no difference. However, in spite of holding the subsidiary liable for its part in the prohibited conduct, the Commission fined only the parent company, which was a NCES having an office within the Common Market.

In a recent judgment the Court approved a decision implying that a subsidiary company and dealers which worked for it each could pursue a separate course of action in spite of instructions or directions given to them.[76] The actions were brought to the Court in March 1978 by BMW Belgium and 47 BMW dealers in Belgium against the Commission's decision of 23rd December 1977.[77] Under that decision the applicants were held to have infringed Art. 85(1) by agreeing on the basis of two circulars dated 29th September 1975 to a general prohibition on exports, and maintaining the prohibition in force until 29th February 1976, and were fined 150,000 u.a. in the case of BMW Belgium, and either 2,000 or 1,500 u.a. each in the case of the dealers. BMW argued that since it was a wholly-owned subsidiary of BMW Munich, it was unable to pursue different objectives than those imposed by the parent company: the Court dismissed this argument as irrelevant, observing that the relationship of such a dependence between

---

75a. See Re Pittsburgh Corning Europe [1973] C.M.L.R. D6 at para 5.

76. See Cases 32 and 36-82/78, BMW Belgium SA and others v. Commission (1979) E.C.R. 2435.

77. BMW Belgium NV and Belgian Dealers [1978] C.M.L.R. 126.

parent and a subsidiary company does not exclude either a divergence of conduct, or a divergence of interests as between the two companies. The BMW dealers argued along similar lines (this argument being relevant also to the question of the amount of fines), that their economic dependence vis-à-vis BMW Belgium was of such a nature as substantially to invalidate the fact of their agreement to the circular. The Court held that although the relationship of economic dependence between the BMW dealers and BMW Belgium was capable of conditioning the former's freedom of initiative and decision, it was not such as to have made it actually impossible for the dealers to refuse to give their agreement to the circulars, as was borne out by evidence to the effect that a significant number of the dealers (43 out of a total of 90) had abstained from signing the circulars; in any case, this line of argument had already been fully taken into account by the Commission in arriving at the amount of the fines.

It is yet too early to deduce any conclusions about the full adoption of an agency theory in Community case law. It is to be observed that the theoretical basis of vicarious liability is different from the theory of identification of separate legal bodies as one in all relevant aspects; the economic unit theory identifies the related corporations as having the same directing mind and will, centre, ego and brains.[78] For the Community case law an agency theory would therefore mean an adoption of a less strict standard to apply to NCES with subsidiaries within the Common Market.

---

78. Cf. Cross and Jones, supra note 69, at 108.

2. " AGREEMENTS BETWEEN UNDERTAKINGS" AND THE CONCEPT OF AN INTRA-ENTERPRISE CONSPIRACY

INTRODUCTION

2-29. An interpretation of the term "undertaking" with regard to economic considerations, seems, prima facie, to prevent the application of Art. 85(1) to prohibited arrangements between related corporations. Nevertheless, there are some cases relating to the application of Art. 85(1) in that respect. The concept connected with these cases is that of the intra-enterprise conspiracy which implies, in fact, a contrary meaning and a different purpose from those connected with the economic unit theory (see Section 2 of this Chapter). The intra-enterprise conspiracy is a concept mostly used in American antitrust jurisprudence to indicate that agreements or concerted practices between one or more of the subsidiaries and the parent company, or between the subsidiaries themselves, should be regarded as conspiracy within the meaning of the law.

Most of the conclusions reached in the following survey are applicable in domestic settings as well as in circumstances involving arrangements and enterprises external to the Common Market. However, in the international context the application of the intra-enterprise conspiracy concept presents high risks to some of the typical organizations of multinational enterprises, where the "subsidiary" is used, more often than not, as a substitute for the domestic division or branch.[79] Therefore, the following examination of the concept will,

---

79. See Krause "The Multi-Corporate International Business Under Section 1 of the Sherman Act - Intra-Enterprise Conspiracy Revisited" 17 The Business Lawyer 912 (1962).

in particular, focus on incidents that enabled the Community to bring NCES and their activities under the jurisdictional scope of the competition rules of the Treaty.

The question of the autonomy of a subsidiary (which comes under discussion in connection with the intra-enterprise conspiracy concept) should of course be determined by the same guiding principles as used for the economic unit theory. See 2-11. In order to avoid a repeated search for these guiding principles in each case we shall confine ourselves here to a discussion of already evident cases where the control of the parent company over the subsidiary, or between other related corporations, is satisfied by the tests which those guiding principles provide.

The Commission has developed a substantial jurisprudence regarding the intra-enterprise conspiracy concept while the Court's approach is not as yet so developed. Therefore, the decisions of the Commission will be examined first and only then we shall elaborate the judgments of the Court.

A. The Intra-Enterprise Conspiracy Concept in Decisions by the Commission

2-30. The first Commission decision dealing with problems of the intra-enterprise conspiracy was the Christiani & Nielsen Decision.[80] The following were the factual circumstances.

---

80. Christiani & Nielsen N.V. [1969] C.M.L.R. D36 (herinafter cited as the "Christiani & Nielsen Decision").

On 23rd February, 1963, the wholly-owned Dutch subsidiary of the Danish corporation, Christiani & Nielsen A/S, submitted to the Commission a request for a negative clearance (before the accession of Denmark to the EEC) in respect of an agreement between it and its parent. Under the agreement, the parent, a construction company, undertook to place at the disposal of the subsidiary, also a construction company, its patents, inventions and know-how and to provide the subsidiary with technical assistance. In return, the subsidiary agreed to pay its parent a fee, to restrict its operations to the Netherlands and to carry out the parent's instructions. The parent also reserved the right to appoint the officers of the subsidiary and agreed not to operate in the Netherlands. The agreement was terminable only upon the consent of both parties. Subsidiaries had also been set up in other Member States and it appeared that all of them had to abstain from activities in countries where other subsidiaries were situated.

In view of the state of affairs described above, the Commission reached the following decision:

> For Article 85(1) of the Treaty to apply, there should, between the undertakings in question, be competition which is capable of being restricted. This requirement is not necessarily fulfilled, in relations between two undertakings which carry on their activities in the same sector, by the mere fact of the existence of a separate legal personality for each of the undertakings.....the division of markets laid down in the agreement is, in the end, only a distribution of tasks within a single economic entity. 81

2-31. At first glance it seems that the Commission, in the decision above, repudiated the concept of intra-enterprise conspiracy, since no internal restriction of trade was concerned. But the Commission did not consider whether a restriction of trade can be said to exist if restrictions are put upon the freedom of action of third parties, such

---

81. <u>Ibid.</u> at D38-D39.

as competitors, customers or suppliers. As the prohibition of Art.85(1) equally applies to agreements which distort competition with and/or, between third parties - for instance vertical agreements[82] - the decision was described by Van Oven as obviously based upon unsound ground.[83] It therefore may be deduced from the decision that intra-mural competition may be protected by the rules in circumstances where the related corporations aim to restrict competition between themselves.[84]

2-32. One week prior to its decision in Christiani & Nielsen, the Commission issued a press release describing its intervention in a matter involving the American Sperry Rand Corporation, its Italian subsidiary, Remington Rand Italia SpA, and a non-related third party who had imported some Remington Rand electric shavers into Italy for resale on the Italian market.[85] An agreement between the parent company and its exclusive Italian subsidairy concerned a transfer of a trade-mark and guaranteed for the latter complete territorial protection. The Commission advised the corporations that it might regard the agreement as infringing Art. 85(1). The Commission was, in the circumstances concerned, faced with a situation where the alleged impact of an arrangement between a parent corporation and its operating subsidiary was external to the corporate group; its alleged anti-competitive purpose or effect being directed at a non-related third party. The case was settled amicably after the corporations concerned promised not to make any use of the trade-mark for preventing parallel imports from other Member States. The Commission did not comment, in

82. See Smit and Herzog, supra note 1, at secs. 85.62 et seq.

83. Van Oven "The Intra-Enterprise Conspiracy Paradox" in European Competition Policy 111-112 (1973).

84. Ibid. at 112.

85. Sperry-Rand Press Release, Bulletine of the E C , No.8, 1969, secs. 40-41.

its communication, on any consideration of the intra-enterprise conspiracy concept in those circumstances. Thus, only with some possible qualifications on the application of the concept in this incident, e.g. the absence of a formal decision following a profound scrutiny of the case; a possible finding that the subsidiary was sufficiently independent, etc., may the press release be taken to mean that the Commission took into account harm, or intended harm, to non-related third party competitors.[86]

2-33. In a subsequent case the decision of the Commission seems to be inconsistent with what appeared to be the Commission's attitude with regard to the reasons for repudiating the intra-enterprise conspiracy concept in the Christiani & Nielsen Decision. The Kodak Decision[87] concerned the following facts:

Five Community subsidiaries of the American Eastman Kodak Corporation sold their products in the Common Market subject to uniform conditions which imposed certain restrictions on their customers, *inter alia*, as regards resale and export. The Kodak group in the Common Market did so on the instructions of their parent company, with which they were bound to comply. The Commission considered the subsidiaries entirely dependent on the parent company and, therefore, incapable of indendent action in their mutual relations. It then reached the following conclusion in response to an application for a negative clearance:

> The uniformity of the sales conditions of the Kodak corporations of the Common Market does not result from an agreement of concerted practices between the parent company and its subsidiaries or between the subsidiaries themselves. [88]

---

86. Cf. Koppensteiner, *supra* note 35, at 290.

87. Re Kodak [1970] C.M.L.R. D19 (hereinafter cited as the "Kodak Decision").

88. *Ibid.* at D21-D22.

Before granting a negative clearance the Commission also examined the contents of the sales conditions between the Kodak corporations and their customers. The conditions of sale, apart from the fact that they were identical, seemed to constitute agreements between undertakings, because they were necessarily the subject of a contract between the Kodak companies and each of their purchasers. They were subsequently amended and provided no grounds for the Commission to act against the sales conditions.

2-34. The startling discrepancy in the reasoning between the Kodak Decision and the Christiani & Nielsen Decision is described by Van Oven as being that while "in the latter case the lack of independence of the subsidiaries led to the conclusion that no restriction of competition existed, in this Case (the Kodak Decision - B.B.) no conspiracy existed. Thus the impression is that the Commission in its last decision deliberately and entirely repudiated the intra-enterprise conspiracy doctrine, at least as regards cases when the subsidiaries are completely dependent."[89]

Also in distinction from the Christiani & Nielsen Decision the Commission seemed, in the Kodak Decision, to take account of external effects of agreements between related corporations. This conclusion becomes apparent in the interpretation given to the decision in the First Report on Competition Policy:".....It was considered that restrictions imposed on third parties fall under the prohibition laid down in Article 85(1)."[90] Again in the Fourth Report on Competition Policy the Commission stated that in its view Art. 85(1) does not

---

89. Van Oven, supra note 83, at 113.
90. First Report on Competition Policy, point 5.

exempt agreements concluded within a corporate group "if they have wider implications, for instance agreements which restrict the scope for non-member undertakings to penetrate a given market."[91]

2-35. The assertion that a practice engaged in by separate legal bodies of the same group is prohibited if it affects third parties has probably been a main reason for the conclusion in a recent decision of the Commission concerning subsidiaries of the Japanese firm Kawasaki Heavy Industries Ltd.[92] Kawasaki Motors (UK) Ltd., which undertook, through a network of appointed dealers in the U.K., the distribution of motor-cycles and related parts made in Japan and supplied by its parent company (Kawasaki Heavy Industries Ltd.) and its subsidiary companies, imposed on its dealers an export prohibition. The German subsidiaries, Kawasaki Motoren GmbH - a wholly-owned company of the Japanese corporation - undertook the same function in the Federal Republic of Germany. Although it had neither entered into a relevant agreement with the English subsidiary, nor was a party to the agreement between the English company and the English dealers, the German subsidiary benefitted from the export ban and assisted in its enforcement (by disclosing the frame-numbers of machines exported to Germany and thus making it possible to identify U.K. dealers effecting such exports). The export ban was not restricted to sales to unauthorized dealers and was found by the Commission to restrict competition within the Common Market. The Commission held that the German subsidiary itself was infringing Art. 85, but fined only the English company because "it was a member of the Kawasaki group of companies which made the agreement in question". The decision did not state the basis for the liability

---

91. Fourth Report on Competition Policy, point 52.

92. See M. Putz v. Kawasaki Motors (U.K.) Ltd.; The Community v. Kawasaki Motoren GmbH. [1979] 1 C.M.L.R. 448.

of the German subsidiary, whether as an intra-enterprise conspiracy (a concerted practice in the group or informal agreement) or a form of once-removed vicarious liability via the foreign parent company and group membership.

B. The Court of Justice and the Intra-Enterprise Conspiracy Concept

2-36. Some of the host of questions concerned with the application of the intra-enterprise conspiracy concept were considered by the Court, presumably for the first time, in a preliminary ruling in the Béguelin Case.[93] The Court's ruling pointed out that a transfer, by a parent company to a subsidiary, wholly-owned and controlled by it, or the authorization of transfer to that subsidiary, of rights held by the parent company, does not constitute an agreement "between undertakings" within the meaning of Art. 85(1).[94] The Court confirmed that the subsidiary in this case constituted an internal reorganization of the parent corporation for the purpose of taking advantage of the grant of an exclusive dealership which the parent company originally owned.

2-37. It is argued whether it would be wrong to infer from this ruling, on the face of it, any repudiation of the intra-enterprise

---

93. Case 22/71, Béguelin Import Co. v. GL Import-Export SA [1971] E.C.R. 949 (hereinafter cited as the "Béguelin Case").For the details of the case see 2-61. This case is a good example for a consideration of the intra-enterprise conspiracy in a domestic setting since both the parent company and the subsidiary were situated within the Common Market.

   Although the Court failed to deal with the concept in a previous case (Case 78/70, Deutsche Grammophon Gesellschaft MbH v. Metro-SB Grossmärkte CmbH & Co. KG [1971] E.C.R. 487 (hereinafter cited as the "Deutsche Grammophon Case")), Advocate-General Romer, relying on the Commission's position in the Christiani & Nielsen Decision and the Kodak Decision, argued that Art. 85(1) was inapplicable to a mere division of functions within a single economic unit. The Court seemed only to imply that as far as parent-subsidiary arrangements are concerned, Art. 85(1) does not operate.

94. See the Béguelin Case 959, at paras 8-9.

conspiracy concept.[95] Van Oven's opinion is that the Court only stated a simple truth, i.e. "that practices which do not result in a restriction of trade cannot come under the prohibition laid down in Art. 85(1) merely on the ground that they emanate from economically affiliated companies"; therefore, in his opinion, it may rather be inferred that the Court deliberately wanted to leave the question of the "intra-enterprise conspiracy" concept open.[96]

2-38. The next pronouncement of the Court on this concept took place in the context of an application of the economic unit theory. In the Dyestuffs Cases[97] the Court applied the latter theory and declared inadmissable the application of the intra-enterprise conspiracy concept, since an application of the two methods would have led to contrasting results:

> Where a subsidiary does not enjoy real autonomy in determining its course of action in the market, the prohibitions set out in Article 85(1) may be considered inapplicable in the relationship between it and the parent company with which it forms one economic unit. 98

Contrary to the judgment in the Béguelin Case, the Court did not state this time which of the prerequisites of Art. 85 it thought were not fulfilled, i.e. plurality of actors, a need that the actors would cooperate like independent corporations or the existence or the

---

95. See Van Oven, supra note 83, at 114. The writer claims that the ruling does not imply repudiation of the intra-enterprise conspiracy concept, but see Fourth Report on Competition Policy (at point 52) where the assertion is made that the case is in line with the Commission's previous decisions which had repudiated the concept. See also Koppensteiner, supra note 35, at 212, where the writer argues that in the Béguelin Case the Court found the decisive criterion in the impossibility of competition between parent and subsidiary (but he regards the ruling on this point as an obiter dicta).

96. Van Oven, ibid.

97. For details of the Dyestuffs Cases see 2-2.

98. I.C.I. Case 662, at para. 134.

possibility of anticompetitive effects.

2-39. In a further preliminary ruling the question of intra-enterprise conspiracy attracted the Court's attention only indirectly. The primary approach with regard to an agreement between parent and subsidiary was taken by the Court in the Centrafarm Case,[99] upon the provisions which concerned the free movement of goods under Art. 36. The issue in question was the use of industrial property rights, and the Court concluded that the exercise by the patentee (in casu, a company incorporated in the State of New York, USA) of the right, which it enjoys under the legislation of a Member State, to prohibit the sale in that State of a product, protected by the patent, which has been marketed in another Member State by the patentee or with his consent, is incompatible with the rules of the Treaty (Art. 36). The licensee in this case was a subsidiary controlled by its parent company, the patentee. Nevertheless, the Court ruled that in this connection "it is of no significance to know whether the patentee and the licensee do or do not belong to the same concern."[100]

Would the parent-subsidiary relations matter if the judgment had been considered under the rules of competition? The Court admitted that the competition rules can be applicable in circumstances where manipulation of industrial property rights may cause prohibited effects within the Common Market,[101] but then referred, in general terms only, to the already existing practice towards the concept of intra-enterprise conspiracy:

> Aritcle 85.....is not concerned with agreements or concerted practices between undertakings belonging to the same concern and having the status of parent company and subsidiary, if the

---

99. Case 15/74, Centrafarm BV and de Peijper v. Sterling Drug Inc. [1974] E.C.R. 1147 (hereinafter cited as the "Centrafarm Case").

100. Ibid. at 1164, para. 21.

101. Ibid. at 1167, paras. 38-40.

> undertakings form an economic unit within which the subsidiary has no real freedom to determine its course of action on the market, and if the agreements or practices are concerned merely with the internal allocation of tasks as between undertakings. 102

The above view of the Court seems to imply that the legally decisive reason for the elimination of Art. 85(1) is the absence of competition, and not conspiracy, within the group. The Commission in the Fourth Report on Competition Policy regarded the Centrafarm Case as confirming the line which it had already taken, both in the Christiani & Nielsen Decision and the Kodak Decision, and by the Court itself in the Béguelin Case.[103] Previously we have indicated that the Kodak Decision may, however, imply a different approach from that implied by the Court in the Centrafarm Case (the decision was interpreted to mean that no conspiracy exists between parent and subsidiary; see 2-34). Koppensteiner considers that other decisions and pronouncements - which we have not mentioned here - indicate a change in the position of the Commission from the one it expressed in the Kodak Decision.[104] We regard those decisions and pronouncements as still insufficient to define the exact approach of the Commission in the case law,[105] and submit that only on the basis of more cases to come will it be possible to ascertain whether the Commission and the Court are now consistent in repudiating the concept of the intra-enterprise conspiracy in the absence of competition but not conspiracy.

2-40. In the Centrafarm Case the Court totally ignored the possibility of the licensing agreement having effects on third parties within the

---

102. Ibid. at 1167, at para. 41.

103. See Fourth Report on Competition Policy, point 52. It is interesting to note that in this comment the Commission does not distinguish between the Christiani & Nielsen Decision and the Kodak Decision in points of lack of competition or lack of conspiracy.

104. See Koppensteiner, supra note 35, at 293.

105. For example the Commission repeated its position in the Kodak Decision in observations submitted to the Court in the Deutsche Grammophon Case (see supra note 93) which indicates adherence to the opinion mentioned in that decision.

Common Market. Although it ruled that in principle the prohibited practice cannot prejudice the application of the competition rules, it stated that the practice in question was exempted from the application of those rules (as explained in 2-39), in spite of it being, in our opinion, contrary to the competition policy because of effects on third parties.

In the Fourth Report on Competition Policy the Commission found it necessary to stress that in its view the judgment in the Centrafarm Case does not exempt from the prohibition in Art. 85(1) agreements concluded within a corporate group, if they have wider implications, i.e. effects on third parties.[106] In distinction from the Court's ruling, the Commission in its written observations to the Court put forward a proposal for the possibility of giving wider implications to Art. 85(1) in the circumstances of the case:

> .....if agreements concluded within the concern are of wider scope, if for example they restrict possibilities open to undertakings outside the concern of penetrating a given market such agreements must be held to be covered by the provisions of Article 85(1). 107

Advocate-General Trabucchi, in his opinion to the Court, justified an application of Art. 85(1) on the factual background of the case:

> .....consideration can reasonably be given to the applicability of the prohibition laid down under Article 85(1) when, instead of being confined to regulating internal relationship, the agreements between the undertakings in a group are designed to raise barriers against third parties, and to block the avenues open to them for trade and competition. 108

The practice agreed between the parent company and its subsidiary had, in our opinion, as its object, the means and consequence, to regulate differently, for various Member States, the conditions on the

106. See point 52.
107. Centrafarm Case, observations submitted by the Commission, 1159.
108. Centrafarm Case 1180.

market in respect of the goods protected by the patents, and indeed it could affect third parties.[109] We therefore believe that the ruling in the Centrafarm Case should have dealt directly with the question whether concerted practice or agreements, which do result in restriction of trade and competition, are illegal in spite of the fact that they emanate from economically affiliated companies (in contradistinction to the interpretation of the Béguelin Case as proposed in 2-37). However, the opportunity to rule on the illegality of external effects of an agreement between related corporations, which had come the Court's way, had not been properly taken to express the Court's still unknown opinion on this point. The Court's failure to examine the situation from the point of view of third parties and its having based the ruling on the Treaty's provisions on the free movement of goods, could mean that some prohibited practices would be beyond the reach of Arts. 85 and 86. We submit, however, that the application of the competition rules in such incidents would appear to be more effective than those deduced from provisions on the free movement of goods.[110]

One justification for a total repudiation of the intra-enterprise conspiracy - with regard to both the relations between parent and subsidiaries and the effects on third parties - in situations similar to the Centrafarm Case cannot, however, be ignored. In view of the of the territorial character of national industrial property laws, disproportionate advantages, in relation to Art. 85(1), could occur from a different view, due to the fact that an enterprise effects its trade in the Common Market by means of subsidiaries instead of unincorporated divisions.[111] But, there is of course no exemption for

---

109. In this context see opinion of the Advocate-General in Deutsch Grammophon Case (supra note 93) 509-510 and his summary at 512 (point 2).

110. Cf. Smit and Herzog, supra note 1, at sec. 86.25 (p.3-281).

111. See Van Oven, supra note 83, at 115-116. But see a different view in 2-45.

prohibited manipulation of industrial property rights by virtue of other rules of the Treaty.

It is correct to conclude here that many questions are still unresolved and many areas of uncertainty exist with regard to the intra-enterprise conspiracy concept, but they seem to relate more to the scope of the exemption given than to its availability.

C. The Confusion Concerning the Rationale and Operation of the Intra-Enterprise Conspiracy Concept in Community Law

2-41 We are here faced with an objection which is indeed necessarily inherent to the application of rules of law which refer to concepts of an economic nature and, therefore, vaguely defined in law. 112

This observation by Van Oven identifies the difficulty in question, that in the interpretation of rules which govern business relations, the economic meaning of concepts, rather than the legal form in which the phenomena present themselves, is of paramount importance. The intra-enterprise conspiracy seems, therefore, to have been born out of confusion of thought, since in the case of a subsidiary cooperating with its parent company, the parent company, which decides whether the actions are to take place, is responsible for them, whereas this concept indicates otherwise, i.e. that the two corporations are considered as separate actors each responsible for the offence.

2-42. There have been some efforts in Community case law to explain this striking confusion. In the Dyestuffs Cases the Commission remarked in its defence, that the purpose of both methods - the economic unit

112. Van Oven, supra note 83, at 118.

theory and the intra-enterprise conspiracy - is that enterprises should not make wrongful use of the possibility of establishing subsidiaries in either way:

> The Commission has already taken favourable note of the particular situation of members of a combine in giving negative clearance on 18 June 1969 (Christiani & Nielsen Decision -B.B.) .....Thus while the existence of a group-relationship can have favourable consequences for undertakings as regards the application of Community competition law, it must be admitted on the other hand that unfavourable consequences can also follow. 113

In the Centrafarm Case Advocate-General Trabucchi stated that precedents of the Court (the Béguelin Case, I.C.I. Case, Geigy Case, Sandoz Case and Commercial Solvents Case) in which the unity of a group forming an economic whole was stressed, do not in principle preclude the applicability of Art. 85(1) to agreements or practices in which the component companies of a group alone participate. These cases, the Advocate-General argued, were concerned with establishing whether anticompetitive conduct, on the part of a company established in the Common Market, could be laid at the door of the parent company which controlled it and which was established in a third country:

> .....this enables us to rule out the possibility that these precedents, which were designed to meet clearly defined situations, can militate against application of Article 85(1) in the case of agreements and practices operating between the members of the same group where such instruments and practices have the object or effect of restraining competition from third parties. 114

2-43. In the present connection it is also important to refer to a general observation on the limits inherent in the application of the principle of lifting the veil in company law, as stated by Gower:

---

113. I.C.I. Case 632.

114. Centrafarm Case 1180. See also Commercial Solvents Case, opinion of the Advocate-General, 262.

> .....in some cases where they (the courts - B.B.) have ignored corporate entity in the interests of third parties, they have refused to allow members to take advantages of this relaxation in similar circumstances. Though unexpresed there is, perhaps, a very reasonable feeling that those who seek the advantages of corporate personality must accept the corresponding burdens. 115

2-44. For a more detailed explanation of the application of a possibly limited intra-enterprise conspiracy concept, in accordance with Art.85(1) it is necessary to return to the three substantive prerequisites for this article's violation: 1. there must be two or more undertakings; 2. they must cooperate; 3. their cooperation must have anticompetitive purpose or effect.

(1) Plurality of Actors

2-45. If the application of the intra-enterprise conspiracy is repudiated, at least with regard to intra-mural conspiracy, it seems necessary first to formulate tests for the identification of parent and subsidiary as one unit in the relevant sense. Community case law has applied for that purpose the same guiding principles which it uses with regard to the economic unit theory.[116] These principles are listed in 2-11. For an exemption of conspiracy between related enterprises it is important to regard each of the guiding principles as necessary, but not as sufficient to discard the intra-enterprise conspiracy; the absence of sufficient degree of proof for establishing an economic unit may be thought to change this picture and make even an effective intra-"family" restraint possible.[117] It has to be stated that in certain

115. Gower, supra note 4, at 216 and notes 78 and 79 in the same page.
116. The best illustration for the use of all those guiding principles in the context of the intra-enterprise conspiracy concept is the Christiani & Nielsen Decision.
117. See Dietz "Enforcement of Antitrust Laws in the EEC"6 The International Lawyer 746 (1972).

circumstances even a partly-owned subsidiary would be regarded as a member of the "family" (as indicated previously in 2-12), so that the possibility of conspiracy within the group will be rejected. It is here that the clear distinction between the partly-owned subsidiary and what may be called a "joint venture" situation must be emphasised. It may be appropriate to characterize the "joint venture" situation as one that involves a "distinguishable third person" in addition to the parent and subsidiary. Simply stated this would be a situation in which a conspiracy, if one were found to exist, would be considered to involve primarily two or more preexisting interests who had combined in the joint venture.[118]

Although the guiding principles mentioned above do not give too great weight to the existence of separate legal bodies, the concept of intra-enterprise conspiracy seems to regard incorporated bodies as the main subjects for its application. Thus, for example, cooperation and planning between unincorporated divisions, or separate plants or outlets within a corporate enterprise, or distinct stages in vertically integrated enterprises, ordinarily may not seem to be treated as subjects of the "conspiracy". Nevertheless, we submit that the antitrust laws ought to concentrate, eventually, on differences in substance rather than form and that a distinction between multi-corporate and multi-branch enterprises seems inappropriate. Such an interpretation would be in keeping with the proper meaning of the requirement in Art. 85(1) of plurality of actors. Thus the application of the intra-enterprise conspiracy concept can at least guarantee that wholly-owned and completely dominated subsidiaries, which are exactly the same as unincorporated branch offices or divisions, would be immune from the application of Art. 85(1), when "intra-enterprise conspiracy" is concerned. At the same time prohibited arrangements can exist where

118. See opinion of Advocate-General Dutheillet De Lamithe in the Béguelin Case 966.

management makes provision for independent decisions by branches or divisions which enjoy a measure of autonomy.[119]

Nevertheless, the application of the intra-enterprise conspiracy concept only where a certain practice between the same related companies restricts competition with regard to third parties embodies a paradox. For if the conspirators are one and the same economic unit how could they still satisfy the requirement for plurality of actors of Art. 85(1)? From an economic point of view there is therefore still an indefensible discrimination in the application of the intra-enterprise conspiracy concept.

(2) The Need to Cooperate

2-46. Obviously, inter-dependent related corporations cooperate and their cooperation is not the kind of cooperation Art. 85(1) is concerned with; the latter type of cooperation whether evidenced by a formal agreement or otherwise, is not that of parties which are not in fact independent. Therefore, with respect to this requirement the relationship between the corporations should be characterized with reference to considerations which are realistic from the standpoint of economic substance and not with reference to matters of form. The issue raised by the requirement in Art. 85(1) as to the capacity of the corporations to cooperate can be satisfactorily resolved only by determining the actual independence or interdependence of the corporations.[120]

119. See A. Deringer, The Competition Law of the European Economic Community 10, at secs. 113-114 (CCH Edition, 1968).

120. See Forcione "Intra-Enterprise Conspiracy Under the Antitrust Regulations of the Common Market" 25 The Business Lawyer 1434(1970)

The application of the intra-enterprise conspiracy concept, as developed in Community law, indicates that if related corporations are held to be sufficiently inter-dependent, so as to be incapable of competing with each other, they may still be held to be sufficiently independent so as to constitute a plurality of separate enterprises with regard to outsiders. The limited liability of the intra-enterprise conspiracy should, therefore, focus on those incorporated subsidiaries, or in some instances even divisions or branches, which present themselves as competitors, and on those undertakings that specifically intend to use subsidiaries to achieve anticompetitive results.[121] The cases which are subject to the qualified application of the intra-enterprise conspiracy concept are situations where the multi-corporate enterprise has not developed "out of itself", but represents a combination of former competitors, or the result of a calculated programme of integration to achieve market power. In terms which imply economic sense we can conclude that the distinct legal personality of a company, in a group of related companies, should, for the purpose of the "conspiracy", be respected by third parties, among whom will be cartel authorities and the courts, as much as, but no more than, it is respected by the parent company and the other related companies themselves for the explicit purpose of restriciting trade and competition. The leading motive in this test, as has already been stated before, is that corporations cannot enjoy the benefits of separate corporate identities and escape consequences of an illegal combination in restraint of trade by insisting that they are in effect a single economic unit.

The common plan or scheme between the actors must be distinguished from the command by a parent to its subsidiary to do something. In such

121. See Willis and Pitofsky "Antitrust Consequences of Using Corporate Subsidiaries" 43 N.Y. Un. L. Rev. 20 (1968).

instances of straight-forward control and instruction by the parent, the question would be a matter of parent liability, along with the subsidiary, for the subsidiary's illegal action in the master-servant theory of liability (see 2-27). In a conspiracy it is not necessary that the plan or decision be acted upon or, even if carried out, that it be successful. Once the conspiracy has been established, every conspirator becomes liable for the acts of his conspirators in the carrying out of the conspiracy.

(3) Anticompetitive Object or Effect

2-47. Difficult problems exist in establishing the borderline between restrictions of trade vis-à-vis third parties and restrictions affecting internal competition. The difficulties involved should imply in our view that only in rare cases can it be shown that the anti-competitive conduct with regard to third parties is clearly abusive and comes under Art. 85(1). This approach corresponds to the reasoning for the application of the intra-enterprise conspiracy concept, that litigation in this area should involve only defendants who, in one way or another, have engaged in conduct that was not entirely "innocent" in relation to the "spirit", if not the letter, of the law.[122] As a practical matter, few intra-enterprise "restraints" would be prohibited under the limited-exemption theory, unless they were specifically designed to restrain the trade of a third party. Where they are so designed, however, the application of Art. 85(1) would not inhibit normal business activity, and therefore would not be objectionable. An example of such prohibited effects could be seen in the Centrafarm Case

---

122. This point has been given particular significance in American jurisprudence: see Krause, supra note 79, at 927-928.

and in some situations of licensing patent agreements, or in the assigning of trade marks to subsidiaries, which in particular illustrates the possible danger of application of Art. 85(1).[123]

D. Conclusions on the Scope of Application of the Intra-Enterprise Conspiracy Concept in Community Law

2-48. The exemption as given by the Commission may be a limited one, available only in so far as the cooperation of the corporations results in no more than competitive injury to non-related third parties. In other words, where related corporations constitute a plurality of cooperating actors, with the result that it is necessary to consider the consequence of their conduct, their cooperation can have the kind of anticompetitive consequences forbidden by Art. 85(1), except in cases where it merely results in the absence of competition between them. It is still unclear whether the Commission considers that it is impossible for a conspiracy to exist in such circumstances or whether it is merely satisfied with the fact that no competition in fact exists. The Court, as stated above, has not yet clearly fixed the boundaries of the exemption as to whether interdependent related corporations should be exempted from the requirement of Art. 85(1) where arrangements between them produce anticompetitive effects upon third parties. Otherwise, the Court's approach seems to be in line with that of the Commission.

The limited-exemption theory cannot, however, be exempt from criticism. This criticism has been, somewhat uncharitably, translated by an American writer as follows: "Form matters. Form does not really

---

123. See Van Oven, *supra* note 83, at 115-116.

matter. Even if form did really matter, you are stuck anyhow."[124] The theoretical "vice" of the limited-exemption line of reasoning, in the opinion of Forcione, is mainly the following:

> It does not deal correctly with the requirement that the corporations be sufficiently independent, as a matter of fact, so as to be capable of the kind of cooperation contemplated by Art. 85(1). Instead, it assumes such capability, on the basis of the determination that the corporations constitute separate entities for purposes of the requirement of a plurality of actors. In so doing it applies the same formal criteria to both requirements. 125

The limited-exemption theory is nevertheless appealing, as stated by Forcione, because it preserves respect for the corporate form (e.g. by rejecting to a certain degree - in cases affecting third parties - the economic unit approach in connection with the requirement of a plurality of actors) and because, at the same time, it seems to ensure a result that is economically realistic (e.g. by bringing economically realistic considerations to bear on the requirement of an anticompetitive purpose of the effect where dealing with internal matters of the enterprise).[126]

In the present context we have to observe that Art. 86 may also be used as a device which offers a basis in antitrust law for coping with unreasonable single-firm business conduct.[127] The article which deals with monopolistic practices does not directly bear on the intra-enterprise conspiracy question, but the limited scope of its potential impact in that direction provides one possible explanation for the

---

124. See McQuade "Conspiracy, Multicorporate Enterprises and Section 1 of the Sherman Act" 41 Va. L. Rev. 191 (1956).

125. Forcione, supra note 120, at 1433.

126. Forcione, supra note 120, at 1431-1432.

127. Cf. Deringer, supra note 119, at secs. 112 and 547. See also Forcione, supra note 120, at 1431-1432.

development of what may seem to be a limited-exemption theory with regard to the intra-enterprise conspiracy. A solution based on Art. 86 necessitates of course that all requirements of the article be present and this cannot always be realized.

3. THE APPLICATION OF THE COMMUNITY COMPETITION RULES TO NON-COMMUNITY ENTERPRISES MERELY ON THE BASIS OF "EFFECTS" ON TRADE AND ON COMPETITION WITHIN THE COMMON MARKET

INTRODUCTION

2-49. In the legislative analysis of the provisions of the Treaty, in Chapter I, we have observed that the combined effects on trade and on competition within the Common Market could be sufficient for the application of the competition rules to NCES which are responsible for such effects. See 1-37. In this section we shall attempt to indicate whether and to what extent this approach has actually been exercised in Community law. For the purpose of the proposed inquiry we shall describe such a jurisdictional approach as an effects doctrine. In order to establish the qualitative difference bwtween an effects doctrine and other jurisdictional approaches relied upon by the Community we shall occasionally have to refer to the corresponding concepts in international law. These references are essential since the term effects doctrine derives its basic meaning from the context of jurisdiction in international law; in fact it is only by reliance on the concepts of international law that the following survey becomes meaningful.

A. An "Effects Doctrine" in the Community Case Law

In the following we shall first consider the decisions of the Commission and only then refer to judgments of the Court, since the Court seemed to avoid judging directly on an effects doctrine and found alternative ground for its jurisdiction.

(1) The Commission and an "Effects Doctrine"

2-50. The Commission's very first decision under the competition rules indicates, in fact, the entertaining of considerations characteristic of an effects doctrine.

In the Grosfillex Decision,[128] a French manufacturer of plastic goods appointed the Swiss firm Fillistdorf as its exclusive dealer for the territory of Switzerland. Certain provisions of the agreement prohibited Fillistdorf from selling in the Common Market countries the goods covered by the agreement and any others likely to compete with these, whether manufactured within or outside the Common Market. The Commission, while inquiring whether the consequences of the provisions in the contract between the two companies had the effects prohibited within the Common Market, gave particular significance to some circumstances which are discussed in this study in a different context (see 3-48). Those circumstances indicated that competition within the Common Market was not prevented, restrained or distorted to any appreciable extent as a result of the contract in question and consequently the negative clearance sought was granted.

The fact that, given the factual situation above, the Commission had to trace possible consequences within the Common Market of activities carried out abroad by a NCE exemplifies the operation of an effects doctrine. Consequently, the Commission was of the opinion that the territorial scope of application of Art 85 is determined neither by the domicile of the enterprises concerned nor by the place where the

128. Grosfillex [1964] C.M.L.R. 237 (hereinafter cited as the "Grosfillex Decision").

agreement is concluded or carried out. On the contrary, the sole and decisive criterion is whether an agreement of an enterprise affects competition within the Common Market or is designed to have this effect.

Since no prohibited effects were found within the Common Market the decision cannot indicate precisely which effects would have been sufficient for the Community to assume jurisdiction over a NCE. The decision, nevertheless, illustrates the difficulties of localizing effects within the Common Market and implies that even activities of a Community enterprise which are directed abroad may come under the scrutiny of the competition rules.

At such an early stage in the development of Community law the Grosfillex Decision seemed particularly significant, as is evident from the following paragraph in the Seventh General Report on the Activities of the Community:

> .....this decision is important in that there are numerous similar cases of excluding dealing agreements with enterprises in non-member States.....As a result of this case the Commission's views on the matter are made available to any one signing such contracts. 129

The Grosfillex Decision was later referred to by the Commission on various occasions, as an important corner-stone in the evolution of an effects doctrine. In the Dyestuffs Cases, after the Commission had based its decision on an effects doctrine, it relied on such a doctrine in its defence before the Court and referred to its own previous decisions in the following language:

---

129. Seventh General Report on the Activities of the Community: April 1963-March 1964 (June 1964), point 67. See also Guide Practique, where the Commission firstmade its approach about arrangements and enterprises external to the Common Market known (Practical Guide to Articles 85 and 86 of the Treaty of Rome, unofficially translated in the Board of Trade Journal, 9th October, 1962, and reprinted in Campbell, Common Market Law, vol.2, sec.2605 (1969))

.....the defendant argues that, should it be the case (which it has already denied under the first head of its arguments) that the conduct of the applicant company took place wholly outside the Community, the jurisdiction of the Community is justified by reason of the economic effects that his conduct has produced in the Common Market and of the resultant disruption of the public policy of the Community as regards a prudent application of the doctrine of economic effects, taking into account the extent of the direct economic effects resulting from the conduct of the applicant.....This conclusion also accords with the previous practice of the Commission, as appears from its decisions in the cases of Grosfillex (J.O. 1964, p.915), Bendix (J.O. 1964, p.1426), Vitapro (J.O. 1964, P.2287), Transocean (J.O. 1967, No.163, p.10) and the European Machine Tool Exhibition (J.O. 1969, No. L69, p.13). 130

The Grosfillex Decision was also listed in the Commission's Sixth Report on Competition Policy, among other decisions, as indicating that the Commission has power to act against a NCE whenever the effects of the restrictive practices are felt within the Common Market.[131]

2-51. In the Dyestuffs Decision (for details of the case see 2-2), the Commission expressed an explicit and clear statement adopting an effects doctrine for the purpose of imposing fines on NCES:

It is clearly apparent in these various circumstances that the increases in price found by the Commission are at very least the effect of concerted practices within the meaning of Article 85(1); there is, therefore, no need to examine whether the increases are the result of agreement. 132

This decision is applicable to all the undertakings which took part in the concerted practices, whether they are established within or outside the Common Market.....the competition rules of the Treaty are, consequently, applicable to all restrictions of competition which produce within the Common Market effects set out in Article 85(1). There is therefore no need to examine whether the undertakings which are the cause of these restrictions of competition have their seat within or outside the Community. 133

---

130. I.C.I. Case, submission and arguments of the parties, 629.

131. Sixth Report on Competition Policy, point 36.

132. Dyestuffs Decision, D28.

133. Ibid. D33.

Much criticism has been levelled against the summary nature of the Dyestuffs Decision and in particular on the gaps in the treatment of certain areas of pertinence, e.g. it might have ignored the implications of international law while taking a strictly "provincial" attitude.[134] As to the application of an effects doctrine, the Commission did not indicate where the concerted practices should be located, but held the seat of the enterprises to be irrelevant and regarded the effects alone to be determinative. Allen argues that this ground for the decision, taken literally at least, represented only "a temporary beach-head" for an effects doctrine according to its meaning in international law.[135] See discussion of an effects doctrine in the context of international law in 1-19.

2-52. On appeal the Commission extensively commented on the necessity to use an effects doctrine in Community law based on equivalent terms in national laws of the Member States and in International law. However, the complexion of the theoretical arguments of the Commission as stated in the Decision seemed to change slightly when the Commission attempted to present before the Court an effects doctrine together with the economic unit theory as two alternative grounds for jurisdiction.[136] In fact, the Commission pleaded that in the first place it had jurisdiction in this case because the NCES had acted within the Common Market.[137] A possible explanation for that change of approach is that perhaps the Commission regretted its boldness and thus sought to present to the Court an alternative which would leave it with another option

134. Steindorff, supra note 58, at 504.

135. Allen, supra note 58, at 52.

136. As to the explanation on the alternative ground for jurisdiction, on the basis of the economic unit theory, see 2-4.

137. I.C.I. Case 627.

to either adopt a debatable effects doctrine or remove much of the effectiveness of the competition laws.[138] Another explanation could be that the Commission, by a change of position, wanted to avoid political sensitivities with regard to a disputed principle of international law.[139]

The Commission's submissions to the Court are also instructive by virtue of a considerable conceptual contrast to the decision. The Commission's plea for jurisdiciton before the Court could be contrasted with the distinction the Commission had seemingly made in its decision, that the concerted practices (the prohibited conduct) were separate from their implementation (the consequences). Before the Court the Commission argued that it had found it sufficient to warrant jurisdiction, on the basis of the economic unit theory, that the implementation of price increases within the Common Market were considered as activity in reality by the parents. Allen considers that this change in the attitude of the Commission may give new significance to the wording of the decision:

> .....if the parent and subsidiary can be regarded as a single entity, then the implementation (though it is not specifically the prescribed conduct) might nevertheless be deemed conduct in the furtherance of the concerted practice.....the words used by the Commission then suggested that it had revised its own view of the effects doctrine as a constituent element of the offence.....140 [by demanding implementation by the parent in the Common Market].

Was not the assertion of jurisdiction in the Commission's arguments before the Court very much like the objective territorial principle?[141] Allen raises the question whether the change in the Commission's position in this case exemplifies conceptual confusion,

---

138. Allen, supra note 58, at 52-53.

139. See for example, Note in 14 Harv. Int'l L.J. 627 (1973).

140. See Allen supra note 58 at 53. The Commission also indicated that it regarded the effects doctrine as limited by the protective principle of jurisdiction. See comment on the latter point in 6-6.

141. Cf. Acevedo "The EEC Dyestuffs Case: Territorial Jurisdiction" 36 Mod. L. Rev. 320 (1973).

semantic acrobatics or serious reconsideration of the applicable principle.[142] Such vagueness of opinion does not, of course, help clarify what the actual conceptual approach of the Commission is.

2-53. A further mention of effects as a subsidiary ground for jurisdiction followed in the submissions of the Commission to the Court in the Commercial Solvents Case (but not in the Commission's decision). In its defence the Commission noted that ".....the conduct of Commercial Solvents Corporation in question produces effects in the territory of the Common Market which are direct and immediate, reasonably forseeable and substantial."[143]

2-52. In October 1972 the Commission published an opinion about the importation of Japanese products into the Common Market. The opinion contained an express statement about the possible application of an effects doctrine:

> In recent years and with increasing frequency, cases have occurred in which Japanese industries prepare measures, partly autonomously and partly in concentration with corresponding European industries, that are designed to limit imports of Japanese products into the Community or to control them in another manner, from the point of view of quantities, prices, quality or in any other respect.
>
> The Commission considers it necessary to draw the attention of those concerned to the fact that, by virtue of Article 85..... the fact that several or all of the participating enterprises have their head-offices outside the Community does not prevent the application of this provision, in so far as the effects of these agreements, decisions or concerted practices extend to the territory of the Common Market. 144

This opinion formulated a wide effects doctrine according to which even unilateral activities of NCES, which do not have any link

142. Allen, supra note 58, at 52-53.

143. Commercial Solvents Case 230.

144. Commission of the EEC, Opinion Governing the Applicability of the Treaty of Rome to the Importation of Japanese Products into the Community, J.O. 1972, C111/13. See also Second Report on Competition Policy, points 17 and 24.

with the territory of the Common Market, but which produce effects therein, may come under the jurisdiction of the Community.

2-55. Almost two years after its publication the opinion on the importation of Japanese products into the Common Market was implemented in the Franco-Japanese Ballbearings Decision.[145] The agreement under consideration here, which was not notified to the Commission, consisted largely of an exchange of letters between trade associations from both countries and revealed a consensus on the part of the parties that the price of Japanese ballbearings imported into France should be increased so as to align such prices with bearings of French production. The Commission condemned the bilateral measures of the associations and declared the agreement contrary to Art. 85.[146]

In explaining the basis for its jurisdiction over the foreign trade association and its respective members the Commission referred to the opinion mentioned above.[147] It noted that the effects of the restrictions could be felt throughout the French market, with the additional possibility that there could also be an effect on trade with other Member States, which could not have arisen in the absence of such an agreement.[148] The intended effects on competition were to neutralize the function of price competition, which is to keep prices as low as possible. However, no actions were taken against the parties involved, though the Commission declared the arrangement invalid.

145. Re Franco-Japanese Ballbearings Agreement [1975] 1 C.M.L.R. D8 (hereinafter cited as the "Franco-Japanese Ballbearings Decision").

146. Ibid. at D18-D19.

147. Ibid. at D19, para. 32.

148. Ibid. at D14-D15, para. 16-18.

2-56. The opinion on the importation of Japanese products into the Common Market was again mentioned in the Franco-Taiwanese Mushroom Packers Decision.[149] The agreement in question here was made between the Taiwan Mushroom Packers United Export Corporation, the national trade association representing all Taiwan exporters, and five of the principal French producers of preserved mushrooms. The object of the agreement was to fix prices and to divide the German market between the parties.

The Commission found the agreement, which was not notified to it, prohibited under Art. 85. It repeated its opinion of the incompatability of such agreements with the rules of the Treaty, and stressed that this opinion made it clear that an agreement entered into by enterprises having their seat outside the Community falls within the field of application of Art. 85(1) to the extent that the effects of the agreement extend to the territory of the Common Market.[150] However, the Commission chose not to punish the Taiwanese partner to the agreement and imposed fines only on the French partners.

2-57. A further affirmation of the application of an effects doctrine was illustrated by a Commission decision which concerned a manufacturer in a non-Member State, in casu, the U.K. before it became a Member State of the EEC.[151] The decision stated that a manufacturer who does not have a presence within the Common Market may, nevertheless, be guilty of offence under Art. 85, by prohibiting his local

149. Re the French and Taiwanese Mushroom Packers [1975] C.M.L.R. D83 (hereinafter cited as the "French and Taiwanese Mushroom Packers Decision.")

150. Ibid. at D90, para. 21.

151. Theal/Watts [1977] 1 C.M.L.R. D57, at para. 69.

dealers abroad from exporting his goods into the Common Market. A fine which was imposed on the NCE related, inter alia, to activities of that manufacturer which continued after the U.K. joined the EEC.

2-58. In a decision concerning members of the Genuine Vegetable Parchment Association[152] the Comission imposed fines, inter alia, on a NCE (Finnish) for violations of Art. 85 through concerted practices with other Community enterprises. There was no evidence in the decision that the Finnish company had a presence within the Common Market. The offence consisted of that company discussing with its fellow members of the trade association the prices to be charged for the relevant product in certain Member States and thereupon charging such prices in one such country to which it sold the product. The restrictive practices in question were wholly arranged within the framework of the relevant international trade association which has its headquarters in Sweden. Another NCE (Australian) member of the trade association did not export to the Common Market and was not considered in the decision.

It is obvious that the basis for the Commission's jurisdiction over the NCE in this case is merely the effects which occurred within the Common Market.

2-59. A recent decision of the Commission related, inter alia, to restrictive practices of the British corporation Associated Lead Manufacturers Ltd.[153] in a period before the accession of the U.K. to the EEC. The corporation did not have a commercial presence within the

---

152. The Community v. Members of the Genuine Vegetable Parchment Association [1978] 1 C.M.L.R. 534.

153. The Community v. Associated Lead Manufacturers Ltd. and Others [1979] 1 C.M.L.R. 463.

Common Market, but was held to be subject to Art. 85 for collaborating with Community enterprises in setting up and operating a notification and quota system extending to the whole territory of the Common Market. In its reasoning the Commission explicitly rejected arguments of the defendant that the competition rules are not applicable to it on the basis of effects alone.[154]

2-60. In the Sixth Report on Competition Policy the Commission very clearly states that it has adopted an effects doctrine which operates as follows:

> In terms of legislation, administrative practice and court rulings, the legal theory here - the 'effects' theory - is based on a broad interpretation of the principle that the authorities can act against restrictions of competition whose effects are felt within the territory under their jurisdiction, even if the companies involved are located and doing business outside that territory, are of foreign nationality, have no link with that territory and are acting under an agreement governed by a foreign law. 155

(2) The Court and an "Effects Doctrine"

2-61. In the Béguelin Case,[156] which came before it for a preliminary ruling, the Court did not preclude a holding that Art. 85 is applicable in circumstances that fit an application of an effects doctrine. The facts of the case are as follows:

The Belgian company Béguelin Import Co. concluded an agreement on 1st March, 1976, with the Japanese firm Oshawa under which the latter made it exclusive distributor for Belgium and France in WIN gas pocket lighters manufactured by that firm. From 18th March, 1976, the company

154. Ibid. at para. 32.

155. Sixth Report on Competition Policy, point 37.

156. See reference for the Béguelin Case in note 93, supra.

Béguelin Import Co. France, a subsidiary of the Belgian Béguelin Company, and wholly dependent upon it economically, took over the exclusive concession for France. On 25th March, 1967, it concluded an agreement to that effect with Oshawa.

In Germany the company Gebrüder Marbach enjoys a similar exclusive concession.

In 1969 the company G.L. Import Export of Nice, imported into France approximately 18,000 WIN lighters. These had first been sent to Hamburg, to Gebrüder Marbach, and there remained under customs seal; they were then despatched and cleared through customs in France. The Béguelin companies brought actions before the Tribunal de Commerce De Nice for an injunction to forbid G.L. Import Export and Gebrüder Marbach marketing the articles in France, and for damages for unlawful and unfair competition. The defendants submitted that the exclusive concession contract concerting France was void as contrary to Art. 85 of the Treaty and as constituting an obstacle to the freedom of trade within the Common Market, since the French Béguelin company was only a subsidiary of the Belgian Béguelin company and had common economic interests with it. The Tribunal de Commerce De Nice decided to ask the Court for a preliminary ruling.

The first question referred to the Court concerned, <u>inter alia</u>, the validity of an agreement, which had not been notified to the Commission, under which a producer established in a third country granted to an undertaking, subject to the law of a Member State, the exclusive right to distribute his products on the territory of the State. The Court ruled on this point:

> To be incompatible with the Common Market and prohibited under Article 85, an agreement must be one which 'may affect trade between Member States' and have 'as [its] object or effect' an impediment to 'competition within the Common Market'. The fact that one of the undertakings which are parties to the agreement is situate in a third country does not prevent application of that provision since the agreement is operative on the territory of the Common Market. 157

One qualification on this ruling, which implies or indicates consideration of an effects doctrine, must be spelt out immediately. The Court's pronouncement is only an obiter dictum since the question of actual jurisdiction of the Community over a NCE, for acts performed abroad, was never raised and at no time was the issue of punishing the foreign manufacturer, or any other alien, before the Court.[158] Mann considers this ruling so lacking in clarity, in many aspects, that it can hardly be treated as "the source of a legal rule of great width and impact".[159] According to another view the Béguelin Case is not a clear example of an effects doctrine, in any event, because "effects" seem to be used as a synonym for "result" of the conduct.[160] See preliminary observations in 1-19 which attempt to explain that distinction.

Nevertheless, the Béguelin Case was referred to by the Commission and the Advocates-General in subsequent proceedings before the Court as the latter's first recognition of an effects doctrine. The Commission mentioned the Béguelin Case, in that connection, in its defence in the

---

157. The Béguelin Case 959, at paras. 10-11.

158. Cf. Acevedo, supra note 141, at 320; Allen, supra note 58, at 71. But see a letter by Dr. Schlieder, Director-General of Competition, in answer to a letter by Mr. J.P. Cunningham, in Financial Times, Newsletter, October 1972, p.13 (the view expressed in the letter is that the ruling implies an effects doctrine).

159. Mann, supra note 58, at 49.

160. Acevedo, supra note 141, at 320, n.10.

Commercial Solvents Case.[161] and so did Advocate-General Warner who rejected a distinction, argued by the applicants, that the Béguelin Case is not a proper precedent as it was concerned only with private international law, namely the validity of a contract.[162] An earlier mentioning of the Béguelin Case, in the same connection, is found in the opinion of Advocate-General Mayras in the Dyestuffs Cases.[163]

The Béguelin Case was also cited by the Commission with regard to an effects doctrine in several of the annual reports on competition policy.[164] This case was recognized by the OECD Committee of Experts on Restrictive Business Practices as the only express ruling (at the time[1977]) of the Court on the application of an effects doctrine in Community law.[165]

It may be interesting to note that in the Béguelin Case Advocate-General Dutheillet De Lamothe argued that in an earlier ruling the Court had already implied an application of an effects doctrine:

> .....so long as the agreement in question is operative within the Common Market this has no effect on the application of Article 85(1) of the Treaty. In my opinion, this emerges very clearly from your judgment in Sirena in which you recognized that the national court needed to consider the question whether Article 85(1) applies to contracts binding an American firm to undertakings in the Common Market. 166

---

161. See Commercial Solvents Case 230. Recently the Béguelin Case was mentioned in that context in the Associated Lead Manufacturers Decision (at para. 32).

162. See Commercial Solvents Case 265.

163. See I.C.I. Case 692.

164. Cf. Eighth Report on the Activities of the EEC (1965) para. 67: Second Report on Competition Policy, point 24: Sixth Report on Competition Policy, point 38.

165. OECD, Restrictive Business Practices of Multinational Enterprises, supra note 5, at sec. 128.

166. The Béguelin Case 967-968. Reference for the Sirena Case which is mentioned in the opinion of the Advocate-General is: Case 40/70 Sirena v. Eda and Others [1971] E.C.R. 69. The relevant pronouncement of the Court in the latter case is the following: ".....
if the above mentioned agreements were concluded before the Treaty entered into force, it is both necessary and sufficient that they continue to produce their effects after that date" (p.84).

2-62. The Court's judgments in the Dyestuffs Cases is surprising in that they entirely ignored the possible application of an effects doctrine after the Commission, in its decision, had relied solely upon an effects doctrine as a basis for its jurisdiction, and repeated that doctrine before the Court in its defence. Instead the judgment found that the applicants had acted within the Common Market by attributing to them the behaviour of their subsidiaries within the Common Market.

The pleas and arguments of all parties before the Court in the Dyestuffs Cases were in fact primarily concerned with an effects doctrine.[167] Objecting to the view of the Commission were not only the defendants but also the Government of the United Kingdom (at the time not a Member State), since one of the companies involved was a company incorporated in a Member State and carrying on business in the U.K. It, therefore, submitted to the Commission an Aide Mémoire[168] in which it stated that it objects to the assumption of extraterritorial jurisdiction in antitrust matters by the courts, or authorities of a foreign State, when that jurisdiction is based upon what is termed an effects doctrine. Advocate-General Mayras dealt with an effects doctrine in his opinion by indicating, however, that the adoption of an effects doctrine is supportable by the language of the Treaty, the statutory and case law of the Member States, the laws of non-Member States, Community law and the "law of nations". The Advocate-General concluded concerning the legal situation as follows:

---

167. For example, see I.C.I. Case, submissions and arguments of the parties, 630.

168. The Aide Mémoire was published in (E. Lauterpacht Ed.) British Practice in International Law (1969) pp.58-60 and in the International Law Association, The Hague Conference 185-188.

> You will have to decide, for the first time, so far as I know, the important question whether undertakings whose registered offices are outside the Community.....can be fined in application of Regulation no. 17/62 for their participation in concerted practices detrimental to competition put into effect inside the Common Market. 169

Advocate-General Mayras's lengthy observations in favour of an effects doctrine extended to exclude other jurisdictional theories that indicated, according to his opinion, hesitation, if not certain unwillingness, to entertain an effects doctrine in the case under consideration. In the Advocate-General's words, "surely, the Commission would be disarmed if it was deprived of the power to take any decision against undertakings situated outside the Common Market".[170]

In view of these opinions the Court's failure of either referring to or rejecting an effects doctrine was "anticlimatic and might be regarded as the easy way out".[171] Mann expresses his wonder about this fact as follows:

> .....an unusually fascinating fact that in its judgment the Court succeeded in avoiding the decision of a great problem of international law argued before it, refrained from any pronouncement upon them or upon any question of international law, and travelled its own independent and unexpected road. 172

One observation which throws light on the approach of the Court in the Dyestuffs Cases should not, however, be ignored. In contrast to formal restrictive agreements, which fall under Art. 85, irrespective of their implementation, concerted action, as the term indicates, presupposes action. A mere understanding to act pursuant to a common

---

169. I.C.I. Case 668.

170. I.C.I. Case 679.

171. See Allen, supra note 58, at 58.

172. Mann, supra note 58, at 46. But see in the same page, note 41, where Mann observes that a certain pronouncement of the Court cannot be taken to assume that the Court intended that there was no room for the problem of international law.

plan is not sufficient. See 3-14. Taking this into account, the price increases by the subsidiaries involved in the Dyestuffs Cases provide at least an indispensable element for finding concerted action. Viewed in this perspective the Court's disposal of the cases seems correct.[173]

2-63. In the Continental Can Case, which was a further manifestation of the Community extraterritorial jurisdiction in antitrust cases, neither the Court's judgment nor the Commission decision produced any opinion on an effects doctrine. Such a doctrine was, however, mentioned in this case by Advocate-General Roemer who remarked that the doctrine has been recognized in the Court's case law:

> .....according to this case-law it is sufficient, to enable the Community authorities to take an action on the basis of the Community law of competition, that a certain type of behaviour becomes apparent within the Common Market (Case 52/69.....) that the effects of actions by undertakings in third countries had become apparent within the Common Market (Case 22/71.....)174

It is apparent that while Advocate-General Roemer interpreted the Béguelin Case as an example of the application of an effects doctrine he felt that such an exercise of jurisdiction was unnecessary in the present case.

It is likely that the facts of the Continental Can Case fitted more comfortably into the criteria for the economic unit theory than did the facts in the Dyestuffs Cases. But in the opinion of the commentators it is debatable whether the judgment in the Continental Can Case implies an entertainment of an effects doctrine. While Hermann holds the view that the judgment is an example of an effects doctrine,[175]

173. See Koppensteiner, supra note 35, at 310.

174. Continental Can Case 263.

175. See A. Hermann, Financial Times, Antitrust Policy in Europe 100 (1973).

Malawer contends that the extraterritorial jurisdiction was at issue, but that the Court did not apply an effects doctrine.[176] Ellis considers that the judgment does not involve an effects doctrine because the act of acquiring the Netherlands' competitor was performed within the Common Market, via a public order in the Amsterdam Stock Exchange, for the purchase of all issued shares and convertible bonds of the Netherlands' company.[177] Smit and Herzog note that the Continental Can judgment uses general language that would fit the extension of the Community's antitrust rules to conduct abroad if effects alone occur within the Common Market.[178] Korah provides another interesting explanation in that connection:

> .....the Court did not state, as did the Commission in Zoja, that the subsidiary's acts could be imputed to both subsidiary and parent.....Was the Court merely avoiding a difficult decision, or should one infer from its refusal to state that Article 86 applies whenever an undertaking, within or without the Common Market, causes a dominant position to be abused, that some activities within the Common Market are required? It is thought that this case takes the development of the law a little further than did Dyestuffs.....In Continental Can, although this theory (the principle of territorial jurisdiction - B.B.) was used, the Court also adopted the effects doctrine, but only in relation to 'such transaction', in other words, one into which it caused its subsidiaries to enter and for which it had provided the funds. It has not yet held that a fine can be imposed on a foreign company that merely agrees with another foreign company to keep out of the Common Market. 179

2-64. In the Commercial Solvents Case the Court was again faced with a suggestion, put to it by the Commission in its defence,that the effects doctrine be used as a ground for extraterritorial jurisdiction.[180]

---

176. Malawer, "International Law, European Community Law and the Rule of Reason" 7 J.W.T.L. 43 (1973).

177. Ellis in International Law Association, New York Conference 154.

178. Smit and Herzog, supra note 1, at sec.85-19 (p.3-116).

179. Korah "The Control of Mergers Under Art. 86 of the Rome Treaty: Continental Can" 26 Current Legal Problems 93-94 (1973).

180. The Commission also suggested in its submissions that the economic unit theory is an alternative ground for jurisdiction. On this ground it based its Zoja Decision.

Again the Court avoided any pronouncement on an effects doctrine and preferred to use the attribution of the subsidiary's conduct on the territory of the Common Market to its non-Community parent company as ground for jurisdiction. With regard to this judgment Allen questions why the Court could not have adopted an effects doctrine instead of the economic unit theory, but the Court shed no light on the reason for its choice.[181]

The opinion of Advocate-General Warner in the Commercial Solvents Case implied acceptance of an effects doctrine. However, the Advocate-General found it unnecessary to express a concluded opinion on this doctrine in the circumstances of the Case, since the Commission pleaded it only as a substitute contention.[182]

2-65. The Court's judgments in the EMI/CBS Cases,[183] which were referred to it for a preliminary ruling, could be regarded as confirming a possible application of an effects doctrine. On the details of the cases see 3-56. The Court delivered a broad view of what constitutes a restrictive effect on competition within the Common Market as follows:

> A restrictive agreement between traders within the Common Market and competitors in third countries that would bring about an isolation of the Common Market as a whole which, in the territory of the Community, would reduce the supply of products originating in third countries and similar to those protected by a mark within the Community, might be of such a nature as to affect adversely the conditions of competition within the Common Market. 184.

---

181. See Allen, supra note 58, at 72.

182. Commercial Solvents Case 265.

183. Case 51/75, EMI Records Ltd. v. CBS United Kingdom Ltd. [1976] E.C.R. 811; Case 86/75, The Same v. CBS Grammofon A/S [1976] E.C.R. 871; Case 96/75 The Same v. CBS Schallplatten GmbH [1976] E.C.R. 913 (hereinafter cited as the "EMI/CBS Cases").

184. EMI Records Ltd. v. CBS Grammofon A/S 906, at para. 25.

The concept that the isolation of the Common Market against imports from third countries in the manner described by the Court may impair competition within the Common Market corresponds to the opinion of the Commission on the import into the Community of Japanese products (see 2-54).[185]

2-66. In conclusion it seems correct to state that although some judgments of the Court implied a recognition of an effects doctrine in Community law it is apparent that thus far the judgments, in all the cases which offered the Court an opportunity to rule directly on such a doctrine and consequently to approve the imposition of fines on defendants, were characterized by an intentional avoidance of the use of the doctrine. Instead, the Court decided that the NCES concerned acted within the Common Market by attributing the conduct of Community's subsidiaries to their parent companies.

The reasons for such an approach by Court may be found probably as much in pragmatism as in law. Could it be that the Court interposed the economic unit theory because it read Arts. 85 and 86 as applying only to conduct by enterprises within the Common Market? Such conduct would be present if the parent and the subsidiary in effect formed one enterprise in the sense of the competition rules. However, the Court did not itself equate economic unit with "undertaking" in either of the cases discussed above. Since this would have been so obvious a step,

185. Mr. J Temple-Lang, a Legal Advisor to the Commission, expressed support for the proposition that this pronouncement of the Court in the EMI/CBS Cases approves an "effects doctrine". Mr. Temple-Lang also indicated that the Court's judgment in the United Brands Case could be interpreted to the same effect since it stated that the Commission has power to investigate costs of production outside the Common Market (in a private communication on 2nd October, 1979).

Smit and Herzog infer that the Court deliberately refrained from making it so as to keep its options open for the future.[186]

The Sixth Report on Competition Policy, nevertheless, confirmed the Commission's view, as already published in the Second Report on Competition Policy, i.e. that the Commission and the Court "both considered that the Community had power to act against NCES under the competition rules, wherever the effects of the restrictive practice were felt within the Common Market."[187]

We submit that although the Court will probably choose to apply the economic unit theory in lieu of an effects doctrine the possibility of the Court adopting an effects doctrine in future cases, where the economic unit theory would be unsuitable to support jurisdiction, should not be foreclosed.

There has been a widespread support in literature for interpreting the competition rules as allowing the Community to apply an effects doctrine.[188]

B. Limits on the Application of an "Effects Doctrine" in Community Law as Based on the Intensity of the "Effects" Within the Common Market

2-67. In the following survey we shall examine which effects, from the Community point of view, are so remote from the originating act

186. Smit and Herzog, supra note 1, at sec.85.19 (pp.3-115 to 3-116).
187. Sixth Report on Competition Policy, at point 37.
188. See B. Goldman, European Commercial Law 159 (1973); Riedweg (rapporteur) in I.L.A. Tokyo Conference 478; Oberdorfer, Gleiss and Hirsch, Common Market Cartel Law, sec. 22 (2nd ed. 1971); Kruithof "The Application of the Common Market Anti-trust Provisions to International Restraints of Trade" 2 C.M.L.Rev. 74 (1974); Deringer supra note 127, at sec. 129; Hug, "The Applicability of the provisions of the European Communities Treaties Against Restraints of Competition to Restraints of Competition Caused in Non-Member States, but Affecting the Common Market" in Cartel and Monopoly in Modern Law, vol.2, 653 (1960).

that the Community will avoid exercising its jurisdiction over a NCE. It is proper to examine this question now since we have established the existence of a possible effects doctrine in the law but have not yet indicated what is the scope of that doctrine. A detailed examination of the question of which "effects" on trade and on competition within the Common Market are generally prohibited will be taken at the beginning of the next chapter. However, the question which we propose to examine here is distinct, since if the general tests for prohibited effects in Community law are regarded by the Community as insufficient as a basis for jurisdiction over NCES then the Community would apply different tests only with regard to the latter enterprises. The qualification of "effects" within the Common Market allows one to assume that considerations of international law have been taken into account, but the validity of that qualification under international law is a different matter. See an examination of the meaning of a qualified effects doctrine under international law in 6-13 to 6-14.

2-68. The need to establish some correlation between the action and its effects with regard to NCES was extensively discussed in the submissions of the parties to the Court in the Dyestuffs Cases.

The Commission admitted that it would not do for jurisdiction over NCES to be claimed on the basis of any relationship whatever, however vague and uncertain, with the economy of the place where the effects manifested themselves. At the other end of the spectrum, as stated by the Commission, strict application of the objective territorial principle would scarcely be satisfactory in determining the jurisdiction of a State on the basis of "effects" which are not indissolubly linked to the conduct complained of.[189] The Commission,

189. See I.C.I. Case 628.

therefore, proposed a solution:

> A compromise should be attempted on the basis, first, of a criterion limiting jurisdiction to direct effects.....and, secondly, of the principle of the protection of essential interests, taking into account the fact that every State is highly interested, and quite rightly so, in maintaining the economic structure of the country and in allowing to the forces which go to make up that economy the freedom to act. The defendant asserts that the Community legislation on cartels is a matter of public policy within the Community and that therefore the applicant cannot claim that when it sells its products in the Community it need not take that legislation into account. The recent theory known as that of the connecting link is a means of arriving at similar results. 190

The Commission further stated that the concept of direct consequences covers the visible and normal effects which the conduct adopted has within the Common Market.[191]

2-69. In the parties' submissions to the Court in the <u>Dyestuffs Cases</u> the applicants themselves cited in support of qualified effects the text of Sec. 18(b) of the <u>American Restatement of Foreign Relations Law.</u>[192] According to this section a State has jurisdiction to prescribe a rule of law attaching legal consequences to conduct that occurs outside its territory and causes an effect within its territory, if the conduct and its effects are generally recognized as constituent elements of a crime or tort under the law of States that have reasonably developed legal systems; if the effect within the territory of the State in question is substantial; and if it occurs as a direct and foreseeable result of the conduct in question.[193] For the full text of the section see 5-47. The Commission stated that it would not appear to it that the concept which it itself advanced is wider than the present wording of

---

190. <u>Ibid</u>. at 629.

191. <u>Ibid</u>. at 634.

192. See <u>I.C.I. Case</u> 630.

193. American Law Institute, <u>Restatement (Second) of the Foreign Relations Law of the United States</u>, Section 18(b)(1965).

Sec. 18(b).[194]

In fact, at a later stage in the development of the case law, in its submissions to the Court in the Commercial Solvents Case, the Commission formulated its approach regarding the nature of "effects" by using precisely the wording of the American Restatement: "direct and immediate, reasonably, foreseeably and substantial".[195]

2-70. The opinion of Advocate-General Mayras on the viability of an effects doctrine in the Dyestuffs Cases draws some highly pertinent distinctions on the qualification of "effects":

> .....I think that the first condition lies in the fact that the agreement or the concerted practice must create a direct and immediate restriction on competition on the national market or, as here, on the Community market. In other words, an agreement only having effects at one stage removed by way of economic mechanisms themselves taking place abroad could not justify jurisdiction over participating undertakings whose registered offices are also situated abroad.
>
> I would suggest that the American Restatement of Foreign Relations Law should be interpreted in this way in so far as it states that jurisdiction over conduct occurring abroad may be admitted when the effect occurs as a direct result of that conduct.
>
> Secondly, the effect of the conduct must be reasonably foreseeable, although there is no need to show that the effect was intended.
>
> Thirdly and lastly, the effect produced on the territory must be substantial.....
>
> Would it be right to say that in addition the effect within the territory must constitute a constituent element of the offence? Is it appropriate to borrow this concept from international criminal law and particularly from the judgment of the International Court of Justice delivered in 1927 in the famous 'Lotus' case to which both the applicants and the defendant have referred at length?
>
> In analysing these words one might in fact argue that greater weight is given to the need for effects than to the need for a constituent element of an offence, or even that effects are of themselves enough to justify extra-territorial jurisdiction.

---

194. See Geigy Case 801.

195. Commercial Solvents Case 230.

> However, as I have already said, competition law is not a creature of traditional criminal law, and is it not the case that in competition law the effect of the offence is in fact one of its constituent elements and probably even the essential element? Such is the opinion that I have formed and I think it is the only one that fits an analysis of the facts. 196

2-71. In pursuance of our conclusions on the recognition of an effects doctrine in Community law (see 2-66) it would now be proper to state that in the opinion of the Commission the "effects" which may provide it with jurisdictional basis over NCES should be qualified. The nature of the qualifying conditions, according to that opinion, has already been explained in the preceding paragraphs. In a private communication with Mr. B. Van der Esch, a Senior Legal Advisor to the Commission, it has been reconfirmed that the Legal Service at the Commission considers that the tests for qualified "effects" should be similar to those described by Sec. 18(b) of the American Restatement of the Foreign Relations Law.[197] On the possible interpretation of the qualified conditions see survey in 6-15 to 6-18.

---

196. I.C.I. Case 694.

197. An interview in Brussels on 21st April 1978. Mr. B. Van der Esch represented the Commission before the Court in the Continental Can Case and in the Commercial Solvents Case.

CHAPTER III

Types of Prohibited Arrangements with foreign elements and the various factors for their Assessment

INTRODUCTION

3-1. The primary purpose of the present chapter is to indicate, theoretically and practically, the factors on which the assessment of prohibited arrangements with foreign elements is made in Community law.

Although we have assumed a general knowledge of the substantial competition rules of the Community, it is, nevertheless, essential to begin this chapter with an elaboration of two pertinent requirements of Art. 85(1) and of their elements, i.e. that prohibited practices "may affect trade between Member States" and that they have as their "object or effect the prevention, restriction or distortion of competition within the Common Market". With regard to Art. 86 the corresponding requirements will be examined. These requirements were singled out in the legislative analysis of Arts. 85 and 86 as most pertinent for the study, since they imply a territorial scope for the application of the rules and also indicate the impact of the prohibited practice or of the abuse of a dominant position. The proposed survey of these requirements will rely on decisions of the Commission, the Court's judgments and the literature, in respect of domestic situations as well as situations with foreign elements. Some of the latter situations may, however, be qualified by the special jurisdictional requirements introduced by the effects doctrine, i.e. requirements of certain intensity of the effects in the assertion of jurisdiction over the imposition of fines on NCES having no presence within the Common Market. See 2-67 to 2-71. In fact it is only after studying the background of the general requirements mentioned above, as we do in the first section of this chapter, that we can observe that the operation of an effects doctrine requires a different impact of the prohibited effect within the Common Market than is required in situations where jurisdiction can be based on a basis other than the effects alone.

In Section 2 of the present chapter we examine typical arrangements with foreign elements and the approaches for the assessment of their effects within the Common Market. The assessment of arrangements with foreign elements should also be undertaken in the context of a number of treaties of the Community with third countries which extend the free trade area of the Common Market to various other States, including EFTA countries. We shall, therefore, also examine how far such treaties have widened the territorial scope of the competition policy (this study is undertaken in Section 3).

1. THE FUNCTION AND OPERATION OF THE REQUIREMENTS THAT ARRANGEMENTS "MAY AFFECT TRADE BETWEEN MEMBER STATES" AND HAVE AS THEIR "OBJECT OR EFFECT THE PREVENTION, RESTRICTION OR DISTORTION OF COMPETITION WITHIN THE COMMON MARKET"

A. The Criterion of "May Affect Trade Between Member States"

(1) Scope and Meaning of the Requirement

3-2. The requirement in question is composed of several different qualifications, but first the term "trade" has to be defined.

The term "trade" must be given the broadest possible meaning, and encompasses all incidents of economic life.[1] It includes both the production of goods and the provision of services,[2] such as banking and insurance,[3] and the supply of public utilities.[4] The non-applicability of the rules of competition to sectors which are exempted (see 1-11) cannot be predicated on a narrow reading of the term "trade", but only on the provisions that prescribe exceptional treatment.[5]

---

1. Compare Bellamy, Child and Morris, Common Market Law of Competition, Sec. 2-41 (2nd ed. 1978); Barounos, Hall and James, EEC Antitrust Law: Principles and Practice 27 (1975); A. Deringer, The Competition Law of the European Economic Community, sec. 136A (CCH ed. 1968).

2. See, for example, Second Report on Competition Policy, points 50-53; answer to W.Q. 795/76, O.J. 1977, C 94/12.

3. See, for example, Second Report on Competition Policy, points 54-57.

4. For example: gas and electricity (see Second Report on Competition Policy points 58-60, 65-68); television services (see Sixth Report on Competition Policy, point 163). Military equipment is excluded under Art. 223.

5. For example, notwithstanding Reg. 26/62 of the Council of 4 April 1962, J.O. 1962, 993; O.J. (Special Edition 1959-1962) p.129, Art. 2, anticompetitive agreements that affect interstate trade in agricultural products may violate Art. 85(1) if they have not been concluded by enterprises engaged in production of agricultural products, e.g. by manufacturers of machinery.

3-3. The precise scope of the condition "affect trade between Member States" has been the subject of a lively debate which has led to diverse interpretations. In particular commentators have debated whether the provisions of the Treaty are applicable as soon as the restrictive agreement, or abuse of dominant position, modifies trading conditions between Member States, or whether they are only applicable if this modification is harmful. The significance of this problem depends on the substantive content given to the qualification "affect trade between Member States". The argument mainly rests upon the differences between the four original official versions of Art. 85. Most commentators embrace the view that the article requires the effect on inter-state trade not to be adversely, but only unfavourably affecting.[6] The concept of "unfavourably affecting" has a different meaning from the term "adversely affecting", which includes not only influencing the quantity of goods or services in inter-state trade, but also influencing such trade in a qualitative sense, e.g. poorer quality or higher price for goods or services brought or rendered from one country into the other.

3-4. The present approach in Community law considers whether the agreement is likely to produce any (appreciable - see 3-6) alteration in the natural flow of trade between Member States, or in the words of the Court whether "the agreement in question may have an influence.....

---

6. For references and enumeration see Bellamy, Child and Morris, supra note 1, at 47 in n.42; Oberdorfer, Gleiss and Hirsch, Common Market Cartel Law, sec. 24 (CCH, 2nd ed. 1971); Deringer, supra note 1, at secs. 137, 138 and 183; D.L. McLachlam and D. Swann, Competition Policy in the European Community 175, at n. 9 (1967); R. Graupner, The Rules of Competition of the European Economic Community 14, at n.9 (1965). See also the following articles: Diets "Enforcement of Antitrust Laws in the EEC" 6 Int. Lawyer 747 (1972); Mok, "The Cartel Policy of the EEC Commission 1962-1967" 6 C.M.L.Rev.91 (1968).

on the pattern of trade between Member States".[7] If the flow of interstate trade in the products in question will develop differently from the way in which it would have done without the restriction resulting from the agreement, the agreement will fall under Art. 85.[8] It is immaterial that the agreement in question may favour an overall increase in trade between Member States.[9]

This concept, however, is inconsistent with other pronouncements of the Court which regard the condition as having a substantive content.[10] The Commission, which was an original member of the school according to which the required effect on trade between Member States does no more than delimit the field of application of Art. 85 (the jurisdicitonal theory),[11] was also not consistent in its approach.[12] Nevertheless, the

---

7. See Case 56/65, La Technique Minière v. Maschinenbau Ulm GmbH [1966] E.C.R. 249 (hereinafter cited as the "LTM Case"); Case 71/74 Nederlandse Vereninging voor de Fruit-en Froentenimporthandel and Nederlandse Bond van Brossiers in Zuidvruchten en ander Geïmporteerd Fruit "Frubo" v. Commission [1975] E.C.R. 584 (hereinafter cited as the "FRUBO" Case")

8. See for example: Duro-Dyne/Europair [1975] C.M.L.R. D226; Goodyear Italiana/Euram [1975] 1 C.M.L.R. D31.

9. See Cases 56 and 58/64, Consten S.A. and Grundig-Berkaufs GmbH v. Commission [1966] E.C.R. 341 (hereinafter cited as the "Consten-Grundig Case"); Cimbel [1973] C.M.L.R. D167.

10. See Consten-Grundig Case 341-342, where the Court added that in determining whether trade between Member States was affected it is especially important to know whether the agreement is capable of jeopardising the freedom of interstate trade in such a manner as to prejudice the realization of the objectives of a single market between States. In other judgments the language also implies a requirement for adverse effect, for example: LTM Case 251; Case 23/67, Brasserie de Haecht v. Wilkin (No. 1)[1967] E.C.R. 415 (hereinafter cited as the "Brasserie de Haecht Case (No.1)"; Case 5/69, Völk v. Vervaecke [1969] E.C.R. 302 (hereinafter cited as the "Völk Vervaecke Case"); Case 1/71, Cadillon S.A. v. Firma Höss Maschinenbau KG [1971] E.C.R. hereinafter cited as the ("Cadillon Case").

11. See Grundig-Consten [1964] C.M.L.R. 489 (hereinafter cited as the ("Grundig-Consten Decision"); DRU/Blondel [1965] C.M.L.R. 180; Hummel/Isbecque [1965] C.M.L.R. 242; Jallatte-Voss and Jallate-Bandeputte [1966] C.M.L.R. D1.

12. Following rulings of the Court, as mentioned in note 10 above, the Commission has not consistently adhered to its original formula. See e.g. Cobelaz (No.1)(Usinesde Synthèse)[1968] C.M.L.R. D45; SEIFA J.O. 1968, L173/8.

conclusion which now seems warranted from the recently evolving case law is the one outlined above, i.e. the required effect on trade between Member States is present when the practice involved alters the flow of interstate trade.[13] The Court's judgment in the Commercial Solvents Case may well be read to support this conclusion; instead of repeating the language used in the LTM Case and the Völk/Vervaecke Case the Court made quite clear its intention of giving only jurisdictional and not substantive significance to the requirement of effect on trade between Member States by adding that this requirement cannot be interpreted as limiting the field of the prohibition which Art. 85 contains.[14]

In accordance with that interpretation the condition "affect trade between Member States" should have only jurisdictional significance; it distinguishes between restraints having such effects and restraints which are only locally or regionally important or which are limited to the internal market of a Member State.[15] We consider that interpretation correct, otherwise the very applicability of Art. 85 becomes dependent on some kind of assessment, based on unspecified criteria, of whether an agreement restrictive of competition has on balance an "adverse" or a "beneficial" effect on trade between Member States.[16]

In practice the clearest example of interstate trade "effects" is where the agreement creates an obstacle to the creation of a single

---

13. Cf. Columbia Law School Project on European Legal Institutions: The Law of the European Economic Community, vol. 2, sec. 85.15(e) at p.3-106 (Smit and Herzog eds. 1976)(hereinafter cited as "Smit and Herzog").

14. Commercial Solvents Case 252.

15. See B. Goldman, European Commercial Law 155-156 (1973). See also Oberdorfer, Gleiss and Hirsch, supra note 6, at sec. 27, who argue that the jurisdictional conception embodied in the condition "affect trade between Member States" must be restricted only to a pertinent description of the area of protection and not to an approval of the theory on the competence of the Community, e.g. the Community has to be allowed jurisdiction for granting negative clearance which presupposes jurisdiction over the matter in cases where the prerequisites of Art. 85 are not met.

16. See Goldman supra note 15, at 152-156.

Common Market. The Commission's decisions invariably related to the finding of effects on trade between Member States with undesirable consequences for the Common Market, and spell out the manner in which such undesirable consequences are brought about.[17] The Court's recent judgment in the Hugin Cash Register Case reflects the same approach.[18] It cannot be denied that such an additional requirement is not neutral, but is coloured by the substantive prohibition of Art. 85 which accords a decisive role to the nature of the effect on trade between Member States.

It is important to add here that because of the relations between the requirement of effects "on trade between Member States" and the requirement of effects "on competition within the Common Market" (or "abuse of a dominant position") there is some support, both in the case law and in the literature, for the idea that the application of Arts. 85 and 86 could be conditioned merely on the requirement that the structure of competition within the Common Market is affected. We shall elaborate more fully on that alternative approach to the requirement of interstate effect when examining the interdependence between the requirements mentioned above. See 3-9.

3-5. The jurisdictional function given to the requirement of interstate trade effects does not mean that Art. 85 and Art. 86 encompass only those arrangements which expressly regulate or refer to frontier-crossing trade. Arts. 85 and 86 are designed to promote a regime of actual

---

17. Cf. Barounos, Hall and James, supra note 1 at 26. The inconsistency reflected in the Commission's decisions mentioned in note 12 above may probably be explained in the background of the argument in the text.

18. See Hugin Cash Register Case 47 at para. 7.

competition within the Common Market and, therefore, should be construed to reach all arrangements that have the prescribed effect. The articles cannot leave unaffected all contracual restraints that are not defined by reference to national frontiers between Member States, e.g. a contractual division of a market within, and not coextensive with a territory of a Member State. Within the scope of the articles there is also included a restraint that operates within the whole of the Community, e.g. the contractual designation of the whole Community as the exclusive territory for one of the parties to the contract.[19]

(2) Must the Effect on Trade Between Member States be Non-Negligible?

3-6. The effect on inter-state trade must not be negligible. This has been recognized by the Court in the Vðlk/Vervaecke Case where it ruled:

> .....an agreement falls outside the prohibition of Article 85 when it has only an insignificant effect on the markets, taking into account the weak position which the persons concerned have on the market of the product in question. Thus an exclusive dealing agreement, even with absolute territorial protection may, having regard to the weak position of the persons concerned on the market in the products in question in the area covered by the absolute protection, escape the prohibition laid down in Article 85(1). 20

The Commission and the commentators agree with that condition.[21] The statement that, in view of the weak position of the parties on the

---

19. See Goldman, supra note 15, at 157-158 and references thereof.

20. Vðlk/Vervaecke Case 302, at para. 5/7. See also Case 73/74, Groupement des Fabricants des Papiers Peints de Belgique v. Commission [1975] E.C.R. 1491.

21. For enumeration see Smit and Herzog, supra note 13, at sec. 85.15(f) in p.3-107.

market, the effect of their arrangement on trade between Member States is insignificant, implies that the impact of the effect on trade between Member States should not be measured in relative but in absolute terms (only "effects" that are de minimis should be disregarded). However, it is not necessary that a substantial part of the volume of interstate trade should be affected; the impact of an effect, according to Oberdorfer, Gleiss and Hirsch, need not be of such a magnitude that the economic interests of at least one Member State are influenced as well as the interests of individuals or classses of participants in the market.[22]

(3) Must the Effect on Trade Between Member States be Actual or Can it be Possible?

3-7. According to the terms used in Art. 85 the effect on interstate trade need not be actual: it is sufficient that it be possible. However, this approach leaves undetermined the actual degree of probability required by Art. 85 in that connection. To define it, the Italian text of the Treaty uses the word "possano", the Dutch text the word "kunnen" and the French text the word "susceptible". All of these denote that a mere possibility may suffice. The German text uses the word "geeingnet",which is, perhaps, a little stronger and denotes some degree of likelihood.

Oberdorfer, Gleiss and Hirsch suggest that a heightened degree of probability is not required, but a remote possibility is not sufficient.[23] Deringer's opinion is to the same effect; it is not necessary that the effect be either contained in or aimed at by an

---

22. Supra note 6, at sec. 25.
23. Supra note 6, at sec. 25.

arrangement, or that it be predictable, but it is sufficient if, according to general experience, such effect could occur in the normal course of events.[24] The literature on this point fails to provide certain guidelines, but viewed in the light of its objectives, Art. 85 seems to require at least a preponderance of the probabilities; it should be more probable than not that trade between Member States will be affected.[25] The concept that if a lesser degree of probability is involved, the interest of the Community will be insufficiently affected to warrant its interference was adopted by the Court in the LTM Case:

> .....it must be possible to foresee with a sufficient degree of probability on the basis of a set of objective factors of law or of fact that the agreement in question may have an influence, direct or indirect, actual or potential, on the pattern of trade between Member States. 26

Virtually the same language appeared in the Consten-Grundig Case.[27] See 3-8.

The restraint must, of course, be sufficiently significant to render its actual or potential effect on trade between Member States of some moment.

(4) May the Effect on Inter-State Trade be Indirect?

3-8. Art. 85 does not stipulate explicitly that the effect on trade between Member States need not be direct but may be indirect. The

---

24. See Deringer, supra note 1, at sec. 138.
25. See Smit and Herzog, supra note 13, at sec. 85.16 in p.3-108.
26. LTM Case 249.
27. Consten-Grundig Case 341.

Court, however, stated this in the Consten-Grundig Case, where it referred to the prohibited characteristics of the agreement at issue as being:

> .....capable of constituting a threat, either direct or indirect, actual or potential, to freedom of trade between Member States in a manner which might harm the attainment of the objectives of a single market between States. 28

The approach above corresponds to the view that an agreement between two parties within one Member State which relates to activities wholly within one Member State may still be prohibited. Similarly, an agreement relating to the whole of the Common Market may affect trade between Member States. See 3-5. It will often be difficult to draw a line between a direct (or immediate) effect and an indirect effect; this is done mainly on the basis of existing practice.

B. The Criterion that the "Object or Effect" of the Practice is "the Prevention, Restriction or Distortion of Competition Within the Common Market"

(1) Relations Between the Requirement of Effect on "Trade Between Member States" and the Requirement of Effect on "Competition Within the Common Market"

3-9. It has been stated above that if there is no effect on trade between Member States (and if there is no reasonable probability of any such effect; see 3-7) the agreement is harmless from the point of view of the Community, and in so far as it may contain restrictive provisions these will be solely within the jurisdiction of national law. See 3-4. Indeed, the Court stated in the Consten-Grundig Case:

28. Ibid.

> It is only to the extent to which the agreement may affect trade between Member States that the deterioration in competition caused by the agreement falls under the prohibition of Community law contained in Article 85; otherwise it escapes the prohibition. 29

As a matter of legal logic Art. 85 requires that, in order to decide whether the article applies to an agreement, it should first be determined whether or not the restrictions in the agreement affect or might affect intra-Community trade, and that only upon reaching such a finding would the decision deal with the applicability of the second condition, the restraint of competition. Each of these two conditions for applicability has its own function. The requirement "affect trade between Member States" defines the borderline of Community law in relation to the legal systems of Member States. The existence of anti-competitive effects within the Common Market justifies the application of Community law to restrictive agreements (or to the abuse of a dominant position). Conversely, the absence of any such effects within the Common Market is sufficient to prevent Community law being applied.

This logic must, hwoever, have proved to be difficult to apply in practice as effects on "trade between Member States" presuppose the existence of a restriction of competition causing it. In fact, if the alleged agreement or practice concerns trade between Member States and if its object or effect is anticompetitive, that effect will necessarily be felt within the territory of the Common Market. In each case, therefore, the same result seems to be reached merely by making the application of Community rules conditional upon the affecting of trade between Member States.[30]

---

29. *Ibid*.

30. See Goldman, *supra* note 15, at 160-161.

We have already mentioned that the requirement that the agreement significantly affects the structure of competition within the Common Market may also be an alternative approach in considering whether the agreement affects trade between Member States. If it does so, then that in itself may be a sufficient effect on interstate trade to make Arts. 85 and 86 applicable. Deringer suggests that the more the Common Market takes on the characteristics of an internal market and the national economies become interwoven, the fewer will be the restraints of competition that fail to affect trade between Member States.[31] Bellamy, Child and Morris point out that the precise ambit of this approach, which may be more appropriate to Art. 86 than to Art. 85, remains to be worked out. As an example for such an approach they mention the judgment in the Commercial Solvents Case[32] (see extracts from this case in 3-67) and stress that if an "effect on the competitive structure" is taken to its logical conclusion then there is likely to be little distinction between "restriction upon competition" and "effect on trade between Member States".[33] This line of thinking seems to have been adopted by the Court in the United Brands Case.[34]

(2) "Prevention, Restriction or Distortion of Competition" as an "Object or Effect" of the Prohibited Arrangement

3-10. Prevention of competition occurs when competition, either in whole or in part, is precluded. It specifically covers a situation in

---

31. Deringer, supra note 1, at sec. 136.

32. Commercial Solvents Case 252-253. See also ABG Oil Companies Operating in the Nederlands [1977] 2 C.M.L.R. D1.

33. See Bellamy, Child and Morris, supra note 1, at 47 in n.44. The note mentions, for support of the writers' view, the Vacuum Interrupters Decision ([1977] 1 C.M.L.R. D67) where the Commission treated a change in the structure of competition as itself an "effect" on trade between Member States. See also Smit and Herzog, supra note 13 at sec. 85.18 in pp.3-111 to 3-112.

34. At p.294, para. 201. However, later the Advocate-General Reischl in his opinion in the Hugin Cash Register Case opposed such an interpretation; in his view the elimination of a competitor, albeit as a repercussion on the pattern of competition in the Common Market, does not per se affect trade between Member States (see p.1919).

which potential competition is frustrated. Competition is restricted when existing competition is diminished. Distortion of competition occurs not only when competition is restrained, but also when it is increased or intensified.[35]

The terms "object or effect" in this requirement have been interpreted in the case law as having an alternative nature; the restraint of competition may be either the "object" or the "effect" of the prohibited practice, or both. This was stressed by the Court in the Consten-Grundig Case[36] and previously in the LTM Case;[37] the latter case expressly stressed the fact that, as indicated by the conjunction "or", these are not cumulative conditions. Questions concerning the proper sequence of these terms and other relevant observations will be discussed below.

(a) "Object": A Requirement of Possible Effects on Competition

3-11. The object of an agreement must not always be manifested in its terms.[38] All evidence, in addition to the relevant documents, may be used to show an object. Concerted practices, for example, are not normally regulated by written terms, so that their purpose can be shown only by other, including circumstantial, evidence.[39] It seems immaterial that the prohibited practice also seeks to achieve other ends as long as it seeks the anticompetitive restraint.[40]

35. See Smit and Herzog, supra note 13 at sec.85.26 in p.3-122.

36. At p.342.

37. At 249. See also Brasserie De Haecht (No. 1) Case 415.

38. Accord Deringer, supra note 1, at sec. 130.

39. Cf. I.C.I. Case, opinion of the Advocate-General, 671.

40. The fact that Art. 85(1) is concerned with agreements that have a restriction of competition among a number of objectives is clear from the French text which speaks of "tous accords.....qui ont pour objet ou pour effet". See also Oberdorfer, Gleiss and Hirsch, supra note 6, at sec. 22.

3-12. We have stated above that "object" alone could be sufficient for the application of Art. 85(1)(see 3-10), nevertheless, in practice, for the purpose of application of Art. 85(1) it will generally be insufficient to determine the "object" of the agreement without also taking into account its intended effects.[41] This approach appears to have gradually developed in the Court's judgments. It was debated, but left unconcluded, in the Consten-Grundig Case, however it was adopted in other judgments where the Court emphasized that it is necessary to consider the whole economic circumstances of the agreement.[42] What is meant by that qualification is that the agreement, in addition to its prohibited "object", must also be capable of producing the prohibited effects. One cannot say whether an agreement is apt to produce such effects without examining the likelihood of the (appreciable: see 3-17 to 3-19) effects on competition within the Common Market.[43]

When an agreement has the object or effect of preventing competition it falls within Art. 85(1) notwithstanding that the overall effect may be to increase competition within the Common Market.[44]

3-13. However, an agreement which clearly has the object of restricting competition does not necessarily fall outside Art. 85(1) if it is never put into effect by the parties.[45] This concept was in particular illustrated in the WEA-Filipacchi Decision where the Commission did not accept the defence that an enterprise would not have been able to

---

41. See Bellamy, Child and Morris, supra note 1, at sec. 2-28.
42. See references in note 37 above.
43. Furthermore, it will generally be insufficient merely to consider the "object" of the agreement because of the operation of the de minimis rule. See 3-6.
44. See Smit and Herzog, supra note 13, at sec. 85.24 in p.3-120.
45. See also Barounos, Hall and James, supra note 1, at 41.

enforce prohibitions of an agreement at law and that in consequence they were without effect; it found the object and the likelihood of effects sufficient to prohibit the agreement.[46] But an intent that stands no chance of achieving its goal would not be sufficient, since it would have no possible effect on competition.[47] Such an interpretation of the term "object" not only achieves the desired goal of permitting attacks on incipient or imminent restraints, but also gives proper meaning to the terms of Art. 85(1).[48] Oberdorfer, Gleiss and Hirsch consider, however, that in any case to prohibit an arrangement according to its object without effects on competition would be a sanction against mere anticompetitive attitudes, which is not the task of Art. 85. They demand that in practice such an interpretation of Art. 85(1) will have to be limited, at least where restraint on competition, while intended, is not completed.[49] In view of the recent case law this view seems now too radical.

It could possibly be questioned whether an arrangement that merely intends anticompetitive restraint, without achieving it, can ever have the requisite effect on trade between Member States.[50] However, as already indicated, neither condition need be met (as for the requirement of effects on trade between Member States see 3-7 and for the requirement of effects on competition see 3-11).[51]

---

46. WEA/Filipacchi S.A. [1973] C.M.L.R. D43. Such conclusion is also apparent in the Franco-Japanese Ballbearings Decision and in the French-Taiwanese Mushroom Packers Decision.

47. See References in Oberdorfer, Gleiss and Hirsch, supra note 6 at sec. 22 in n.62.

48. Cf. Smit and Herzog, supra note 13 at sec. 85.24 in p.3-121.

49. See Oberdorfer, Gleiss and Hirsch, supra note 6, at sec. 22.

50. See Deringer, supra note 1, at sec. 131.

51. But see in Smit and Herzog (supra note 13, at sec.85.22) who state that a negative answer is indicated if the effect on interstate trade must be occasioned by the restraint of competition or if such an effect is present only if the anticompetitive factor is itself an element of the requisite effect on interstate trade.

3-14. It must be noted that in defining the concept of concerted practices a particular importance is attached to objective factors, i.e. that such a practice, in order to fall under Art. 85(1), must actually and concretely have had the effect of altering the conditions of competition. In the ACF Chemiefarma Case Advocate-General Gand stated the following view:

> .....although for purposes of the application of Article 85 there is no need to take account of concrete effects of an agreement.....it is no doubt otherwise in the case of a concerted practice which, according to the prevailing view, presupposes that the agreement is actually carried out so that it is necessary to establish the actual conduct of the undertakings concerned and the existence of a link between such conduct and a prearranged plan. 52

(b) Effect on Competition; the Causal Relations Between the Consequence and the Prohibited Practice

3-15. Although the first need is to consider the precise purpose of an agreement, an analysis of all or some of the clauses of the agreement may not reveal that the effect on competition is sufficiently deleterious. The consequences of the agreement themselves should then be considered, or in the words of the Court: "it is then necessary to find that those factors are present which show that competition has in fact been prevented or restricted to an appreciable extent".[53] Moreover while the usual approach requires that the inquiry into the object of the practice must precede that into its effects, it would appear unnecessary to inquire into the object if the effects are clear and forbidden; Art. 85(1) does not warrant a preference. Therefore, it would then be no defence that the restraint of competition was not intended.[54]

---

52. Case 41/49, ACF Chemiefarma NV v. Commission [1970] 2 E.C.R. 714. In the Dyestuffs Cases Advocate-General Mayras expressed the same view but took it further to include consideration of the practice's potential effect (see I.C.I. Case 671-672).

53. LTM Case 249.

54. Cf. Deringer, supra note 1, at sec. 130. Such consideration will, however, be relevant for the imposition of fines in accordance with Reg. 17.

"Object" is, however, still an essential element of the offence in concerted practices since the evidence of actual effects alone is not sufficient. One obviously cannot say that there is a concerted practice merely because common, parallel or similar conduct between enterprises is occurring, and there must be the will on the part of those concerned to act in common.[55]

3-16. In any event there must be a causal relationship between the practice and the restraint of competition. It has been stated by commentators that, in order to come within the terms of this part of Art. 85(1), the anticompetitive effect must have been intended and that careless disregard of possible anticompetitive consequences alone does not suffice.[56] Deringer considers appropriate the application of fairly generally accepted causation doctrines, viz.that only those restraints of competition that are the reasonably forseeable consequence of the prohibited arrangement will be met by the requirements of Art. 85(1).[57] If the restraint of competition occurred contrary to all probability and in contradiction to experience, and if the enterprises concerned were, therefore, unable to see its occurrence, this means that the causal connection was not adequate in the light of the foregoing considerations.[58] The considerations to be taken in such an examination were thus spelt out by Mégret:

> It is sufficient that objectively the agreement should be of a kind capable of restricting competition. But regard must not be had only to effects attributable directly to the provisions of the agreement. If as the result of the performance of the agreement there ensues a factual or legal situation such that the parties are able to restrict competition, the agreement could be forbidden if the parties in fact profit from this

55. See I.C.I. Case 682-683.
56. See Smit and Herzog, supra note 13, at sec. 85.24 in p.3-120.
57. Deringer, supra note 1, at sec. 130.
58. Oberdorfer, Gleiss and Hirsch, supra note 6 at sec. 22.

situation to restrict competition. It is not necessary to prove that the restrictions are the result of concerted practices. It is enough that they should have been made possible by the agreement. [59]

(3) Impact on Competition of the Required Effects

(a) Must the Effect on Competition be Non-Negligible?

3-17. Following the requirement that the effect on "trade between Member States" must be non-negligible (see 3-6) a question is raised whether a similar requirement is applicable with regard to the effect "on competition within the Common Market". A first indication of the Court's approach in that connection is found in the LTM Case where it pointed out that the national tribunal, which asked for a preliminary ruling, must inquire whether the agreement restricts or distorts competition to an "appreciable" extent.[60] In the Völk/Vervaecke Case the Court reconfirmed that an agreement does not fall within Art. 85(1) where it only affects the market insignificantly.[61] Similar statements were repeated in more recent cases and were supported by the Commission.[62]

59. J. Mégret, Le Droit de la Communauté Économique Européenne, vol. 1 - Concurrence 31 (by J. Mégret, J.V. Louis, D. Vignes and M. Waelbroeck 1972); the translation in the text appears in Barounos, Hall and James, supra note 1, at 43.

60. LTM Case 251. The E.C.R. in English use the word "appreciable"; the French text of the Béguelin Case uses the word "sensible"; some writers use the words "noticeable", "perceptible" or "significant".

61. Völk/Vervaecke Case 302, at para. 5/7.

62. See the Cadillon Case 356. See also submissions of the Commission and opinion of the Advocate-General in Case 47/76 De Norre and de Clercq v. NV "Brouwerij Concordia" [1972] E.C.R. 73-74, 103-104.

The question whether an agreement has only an insignificant effect must be considered as much in relation to its capacity to restrict, prevent or distort competition as in relation to its ability to affect trade between Member States.[63]

3-18. Both the Commission and the Court have, as indicated above, consistently taken the view that Art. 85(1) does not reach negligible restraints of competition. However, the concept of what constitutes a negligible restraint has varied.

Initially, the Commission appeared to apply an absolute standard; only if, in absolute terms, the effect on competition was not de minimis, was Art. 85(1) held applicable. As a concequence, even though in relation to the entire market the agreement had only a slight impact it was within the reach of Art. 85(1).[64] However, in more recent times the Commission has appeared to apply a relative standard. The development in the Commission's view is described below.

3-19. The Commission first attempted to give guidelines in that connection in the Communication of 23rd July, 1968, Concerning Agreements, Decisions and Concerted Practices in the Field of Cooperation Between Enterprises. According to this view Art. 85(1) does not apply when the overall market strength of the cooperating enterprises is too small for the cooperation to result in an appreciable restriction of competition.[65]

---

63. See the Béguelin Case 960.

64. For example see the Jallatte-Voss and Jallatte Vandeputte Decision.

65. The Communication was published in J.O. 1968, C.75/3; [1968] C.M.L.R. D5. It applies to the permitted forms of cooperation irrespective of the size of the undertakings (see also Sec. I, 4th para., of the Communication which applies to other forms of cooperation not covered by the Communication).

This principle was further reflected when the Commission tried to reduce the uncertainty surrounding the "de minimis rule" by issuing a Notice on Minor Agreements in 1970, which was reissued in an amended form in 1977.[66] In its view, agreements are not caught by Art. 85(1) if:

> - the products which are the subject of the agreement and other products of the participating undertakings considered by consumers to be similar by reason of their characteristics, price or use do not present in a substantial part of the Common Market more than 5% of the total market for such products, and
> - the aggregate annual turnover of the participating undertakings does not exceed 50 million units of account.

This notice also contains attribution rules to be applied in determining the annual sales of an enterprise and allows excesses of both relevant criteria if these are not more than 10% in two successive book years.

The latter notice, however, is not binding on the Court, which has never referred to it in any of its judgments. Advocate-General Warner pointed out in the Miller Schallpatten Case that the Vðlk/Vervaecke Case had laid down a "de minimis rule" and that the size of the firm's turnover in absolute terms was relevant as well as its market share.[67] Thus there may be circumstances in which the notice has no application (e.g. certain restricted or very special markets) even if the criteria set out in the notice are complied with. Korah points out that the notice is clearly a mitigating factor to be taken into account when imposing a fine on an enterprise that has relied upon it, and it may be relied upon by a civil court (but it is not binding on it) in deciding whether an agreement can be enforced.[68]

---

66. Commission Notice of 27 May 1970, Concerning Agreements of Minor Importance Which do not Fall under Art. 85(1) of the Treaty Establishing the EEC, O.J. 1970, C63/1; [1970] C.M.L.R. D15. This notice was replaced by a notice in 19 December 1977, O.J. 1977, C313/3; [1978] 3 C.M.L.R. 648.
67. See Case 19/77, Miller International Schallplatten GmbH v. Commission [1978] E.C.R. 157-158.
68. V. Korah, An Introduction Guide to EEC Competition Law and Practice 19 (1978).

Although the Commission itself was applying in negative clearances a standard of the impact of the effects on competition similar to that of the notice on minor agreements,[69] it had indicated that Art. 85(1) may apply even in cases where the upper limits given in that notice are not reached; in fact, in such cases restriction of competition may be appreciable.[70] The relative standard which the Commission has appeared to apply in recent decisions is that the effect on competition must be evaluated in relation to the total market for the product and the size of the enterprise involved.[71]

The conclusion is, therefore, warranted that Art. 85(1) should be construed as reaching all restraints of competition except those that are so negligible that they may be disregarded under the adage of"de minimis non curat praetor".[72]

3-20. Finally it has to be stated that in deciding whether an agreement has the effect of preventing, restricting or distorting competition within the Common Market to an "appreciable" extent, it is necessary to consider the whole economic and legal context in which the agreement operates. This principle was clearly stated by the Court in the Brasserie de Haecht (No. 1) Case:

> .....It would be pointless to consider an agreement, decision or practice by reason of its effects if those effects were to be taken distinct from the market in which they are seen to operate and could only be examined apart from the body of effects, whether convergent or not, surrounding their implementation. Thus in order to examine whether it is caught by Article 85(1) an agreement cannot be examined in isolation from the above context, that is, from the factual or legal circumstances causing it to prevent, restrict or distort competition. 73

---

69. See for example, Alliance de Constructeurs Francais de Machines-Outils [1968] C.M.L.R. D23.
70. See for example, the Béguelin Case, observations submitted to the Court (the Commission), 956, and opinion of the Advocate-General p.361.
71. See Commercial Solvents Case, pleas and arguments of the parties 239.
72. See elaboration on that interpretation in Deringer, supra note 1 at sec. 172.
73. See Brasserie de Haecht Case (No. 1) 415.

To survey the relevant factors for the assessment of the effects on competition would involve an examination which cannot be undertaken here. Some of the pertinent considerations will be illustrated in the description of typical cases with foreign elements in section 2, to enable test decisions to be made in similar circumstances. We should only state here that in every case regard must be had first to the relevant market which is the market in which the goods or services concerned are competing; for until this market is identified it may be difficult to say whether there is any appreciable effect on competition or on trade between Member States.[74] In the context of both Arts. 85 and 86 the three principal problems in this area of the relevant market are: first, to define the geographical circumference of the relevant market; second, to determine which goods or services it encompasses; and third, to determine whether separate phases in the marketing process are to be considered separately.

(4) Complementary Comments Relating to Article 86

3-21. In so far as the terminology of Art. 86 resembles that of Art. 85(1) it raises the same problems that have already been discussed, e.g. the limitation of the defined practices being prohibited only "so far as they may affect trade between Member States". But, since we are interested in the impact of the prohibited practices on competition within the Common Market, Art. 86 requires additional attention.

(a) The Requisite Measure of Market Control in the Definition of a "Dominant Position"

3-22. It is necessary to observe that the definition of a "dominant

---

74. See for example, the Consten-Grundig Case 343.

position" relates to the power of the enterprise unilaterally to do what Art. 85(1) calls "prevention, restriction or distortion of competition".

In the United Brands Case the Court defined a "dominant position" as follows:

> .....a position of economic strength enjoyed by an undertaking which enables it to prevent effective competition being maintained on the relevant market by giving it the power to behave to an appreciable extent independently of its competitors, customers and ultimately of its customers. 75

The court reiterated that definition of a "dominant position" in the Hoffmann-La Roche Case[76] and went on to say that dominance does not exclude the existence of certain competition, but that a dominant firm can decide, or at least influence, the conditions under which competition will develop, and that a dominant firm can behave in its market without needing to take account of any competition and without suffering damage as a result.[77]

A "mechanical" standard for finding a dominant position in the context of Art. 86 seems inadequate, for control can be determined only by a factual evaluation of the peculiarities of the structure of the relevant market.

(b) The Requirement that the Dominant Position be "Within the Common Market or in a Substantial Part of It".

3-23. The requirement that "dominant position" be "within the Common Market or in a substantial part of it" would appear to set only

---

75. United Brands Case 277, at para 65.

76. Hoffmann-La Roche Case 520, para. 38.

77. Ibid. at para. 39. In the United Brands Case 283, at para. 113, similar ideas were expressed.

minimum territorial limits rather than define the relevant market. This point is explained by Smit and Herzog in the following paragraph:

> .....for Article 86 to be applicable at all, the dominant position and therefore the relevant market must be within the Common Market or a substantial part thereof. But whether this requirement is met can be determined only after definition of the relevant market in which the dominant position is held. Accordingly, the requirement that the dominant position be within the Common Market or a substantial part thereof is the functional equivalent of the requirement in Article 85 that the competition prevented, restricted, or distorted within the Common Market. 78

Art. 86, therefore, makes clear that it is not necessary that Community-wide competition be affected, as long as the effect be felt in a "substantial" part of the Common Market.

Various territories or whole countries comprising the relevant market have been held to constitute substantial parts of the Common Market in decisions of the Commission on Art. 86.[79] It is, however, not entirely clear whether, in finding that such territories or countries constituted substantial parts of the Common Market, the Commission was comparing their respective territorial areas or whether it was making some form of economic comparison.[80]

(c) "Abuse of a Dominant Position"

3-24. Art. 86 does not prohibit holding or using a dominant position that otherwise comes within its terms; it prohibits only abuse of such a position. The article sets out a non-exhaustive list of examples of what constitutes an abuse of a dominant position. The list of examples

---

78. See Smit and Herzog, supra note 13, at sec. 86.11 in p.3-256.

79. See, for example, Re GEMA (no. 1)[1971] C.M.L.R. D35; the Continental Can Decision; Sugar Cartel [1973] C.M.L.R. D65.

80. See discussion of this point in Barounos, Hall and James, supra note 1, at 153; Smit and Herzog, supra note 13, at 86.11 in p.3-257.

includes both "exploitative" abuses (taking direct advantage of market power to get supra-competitive prices or other benefits) and certain kinds of anticompetitive behaviour (e.g. tying-in, second-line discrimination). The Court in the Continental Can Case and in the Hoffman-La Roche Case held that other kinds of anticompetitive behaviour by dominant firms were unlawful: mergers, refusal to supply raw materials to competitors, and rebates given only to buyers dealing exclusively with the dominant firm. In the Hoffman-La Roche Case the Court, basing itself on Art. 3(f) of the Treaty, gave a definition of abuse covering all forms of anticompetitive behaviour.[81]

In the Continental Can Case the Court held that Art. 86 prohibits a corporation already dominant from merging with or acquiring a competitor. However, Community law at present does not require prior authorization for such acquisitions. Legislation to remedy this weakness has been under discussion for several years.

(d) Is There any "Intent" Requirement in Article 86?

3-25. Art. 86 does not contain a similar requirement to that of "object or effect" to restrain competition, but the general concept of abuse is set forth without further indication. Art. 86 states the decisive criterion for finding abuse: any use that is incompatible with the Common Market is abuse and it is irrelevant whether the perpetrator of the abuse was conscious of the prohibited nature of his activities. Any use of a dominant position which objectively can be qualified as abuse suffices.

---

81. At p.520, para. 38.

2. TYPES OF PROHIBITED ARRANGEMENTS WITH FOREIGN ELEMENTS AND THEIR ASSESSMENT IN COMMUNITY LAW

INTRODUCTION

3-26. In this section the intention is to point to some of the problems that arise with regard to various types of arrangements, to attempt a summary appreciation thereof and to find a basis for foreseeing the legal consequences. Although decisions of the Commission and the Court's judgments do not easily fit into a general pattern, since each case has to be treated according to its particular characteristics, some guidelines can be drawn from a series of cases.

Since the requirements of effects on trade and on competition in Arts. 85 and 86 are only concerned with restraints within the Common Market they seem to have double implications: on the one hand, practices occurring outside the Common Market or initiated by foreign enterprises, but having effects within it, are submitted to the application of the competition rules; on the other hand, practices occurring inside the Common Market but which have only external effects are not affected. The criterion in that respect is therefore the manifestation of repercussions inside the Market. In following this line of argument three main categories of practices are identified: arrangements concerning exports from the Common Market, arrangements concerning imports into the Common Market and other, so-called "international anticompetitive arrangements".[82] These categories of practices are neither specific to NCES in the sense that they are also operated by

82. See similar classification in Åke Skiöld "Antitrust Problems in Connection With Dealings With the Common Market Countries" in the International Bar Association, Ninth Conference Report 192-206 (Edinburgh, 1962).

purely Community enterprises nor are they comprehensive in the sense that the enterprises could or would not also engage in other restrictive practices. These categories have been chosen as a method for classification of prohibited arrangements in the proposed survey because they generally represent special areas of interest for the study and because there seems to be sufficient evidence to demonstrate why they are particularly questionable when operated. Normally, different types of practices are applied together. Therefore, many of the following cases could be brought under two or all of these categories. An attempt has, however, been made to classify cases according to the main restriction operated, including those which were granted negative clearance or exemption under Art. 85(3), even though a certain degree of arbitrariness is unavoidable.

A. Arrangements Concerning Exports From the Common Market

GENERAL

3-27. The business relationships which may give rise to the risk of an application of the competition rules, where selling abroad from within the Common Market is concerned, are mainly agreements of Community enterprises with other exporters within the Common Market and agreements with foreign distributors or buyers. Restrictions on exports may take many forms: they include global bans, prohibitions of exports to specified countries, the requirement of prior approval from the licensor for exports, export quotas, price controls on exports, restrictions of exports to specified products, prohibition of the export of substitute products, permission to export only to or through specified firms, etc.

Export cooperation between Community exporters usually occurs in order to bring about the following desired results: a reduction of the average export sales-cost per firm, a broader operational base improving the ability to supply those foreign buyers who require a continuous and substantial volume of the goods or products, a better bargaining position to compete with or deal with foreign cartels and a possible expansion of the volume of production of each of the members, which may lead to certain economies of scale, such as the reduction of the cost of the products.

The three general types of export organizations that may be used by Community enterprises are as follows: (1) one in which the association serves as a central selling agent for all of the members, taking orders, negotiating sales, and handling shipment of the goods; (2) one in which the association directs the activities of its members and retains certain functions in export trade, but the orders are placed by agents already established by the members abroad (in this case the export department of one member may handle foreign orders for several members); and (3) the export company formed for the purpose of buying the members' products and reselling them abroad at terms agreed upon by the members. The first and second methods of selling may be combined, the members using their established agents for some markets and the association sales office for new markets or those in which the trade is not well developed.

We have also mentioned above the arrangements relating to exports from the Common Market which appear in exporters' agreements with NCES. Such agreements by their terms may, for example, limit a NCE's right to buy Community products it wants, from any one it likes, and at whatever price it can get, and thus limit the opportunity of other Community exporters.

There are, therefore, "pure" export cartels which exclusively cover competition on foreign markets and "mixed" export cartels which cover trade and competition both on foreign and domestic markets. We have already observed that as a general rule "pure" export cartels are normally excluded by definition from the scope of the competition rules. Nevertheless, account must be taken of the fact that the type of the arrangement in question, i.e. a "pure" or a "mixed" export cartel, provides only possible, though by no means conclusive, evidence of the existence of restrictions relating to trade and competition within the Common Market.[83]

(1) National Joint-Selling Agencies for Exports

3-28. On several occasions when agreements between Community enterprises applied both within one Member State and to exports to non-Member States the Commission found, in each case, that the agreement in question did not restrain the freedom of the parties to import and export within the Common Market and that trade between Member States was not affected.[84] All these cases concerned organisations set up as joint-selling agencies, for products manufactured by the participants, to the States in which they were established and to non-Member States. It was essential that the parties (following amendments to the agreements made at the instigation of the Commission) retained their individual freedom to export to other Member States at freely fixed prices. For example,

83. See relevant economic considerations in McLachlan and Swann, *supra* note 6, 110-111.

84. See the following decisions: *Coblaz (No.1)(Usines de Synthèse)* and *Coblaz (No.2)(Cokeriers)*[1968] C.M.L.R. D68 (for Belgium); *Comptoir Francais de l'Azote (CFA)*[1968] C.M.L.R. D57 (for France); *SEIFA* (for Italy); *Supexie* [1971] C.M.L.R. D1.

in the CIMFRANCE Decision the Commission approved an agreement among French cement producers setting uniform export prices and export quotas for the members once the agreement was revised so as not to apply to trade between Member States.[85]

3-29. In commenting generally on prohibited practices in a system of joint-selling for export which is restricted to the national market and to markets outside the Common Market, the Commission pointed out, in the First Report on Competition Policy, that equalization of selling prices in the home markets and export prices to countries outside the Common Market is likely to discourage exports by individual members of the group to countries within the Common Market and cannot, therefore, be allowed.[86]

(2) Division of Export Markets by Bans on Exports to Certain Non-Member States

3-30. An exclusive patent and know-how licensing agreement between a German licensor (Kabelmetal) and a French licensee (Luchaire) included, inter alia, an export ban in respect of countries outside the Common Market.[87] The parties undertook, for the duration of the agreement, not to sell, directly or indirectly, products manufactured using the techniques which were the subject of the agreement in certain countries outside the Common Market: for the German company in Spain and Portugal, and for the French company outside the Common Market and these two countries. However, this undertaking did not apply to imports into these countries of machines or assemblies which incorporated parts

85. CIMFRANCE, EC Bulletine No. 1-72, Part Two, Chap. I, sec. 4
86. First Report on Competition Policy, point 12 (at p.32).
87. Kabelmetal/Luchaire [1975] C.M.L.R. D40.

manufactured under the agreement. Stating which provisions of the agreement were not caught by Art. 85(1), the Commission delivered the following explanation referrring to the export prohibition:

> .....in the case in point this would not substantially affect either competition within the Common Market or trade between Member States, because the products in questions are not suitable for marketing through intermediaries and are therefore unlikely to be reimported into the EEC and subsequently sold from one Member State to another. 88

Other provisions of the agreement were exempted under Art.85(3).

(3) Prohibitions on Exports to All Non-Member States

3-31. The Kodak group adopted new uniform sales conditions for the companies of the group established within the Common Market.[89] For more details of the case see 2-33. On the Commission's request some conditions, which contained a clause whereby the companies forbade their customers to export or re-sell the supplied products for export within the Common Market, were removed. However, contained in the standard conditions of sale of the companies was a prohibition against the purchasers to export outside the Common Market. The prohibition did not seem liable to affect trade between Member States and the Commission reasoned its decision, on this clause, as follows:

> In fact, reimportation into the Common Market of Kodak products previously exported by the resellers would be very unlikely because of the accumulation of profit margins and transport costs and of the obstacle of the common customs tariff on the European Communities. But even if such reimportation could exceptionally be made, it is improbable that it could be followed by a new exportation to another Member State. 90

88. Ibid. at D46, para 32.
89. See the Kodak Decision.
90. Ibid. at D23, para. 20.

3-32. The Omega Decision, which followed the line adopted in the Kodak Decision, dealt with a prohibition on export outside the Common Market imposed on Omega general agents within the Common Market. This, according to the Commission, constituted a restriction of competition which, however, did not seem liable to affect trade between Member States.[91] In the circumstances of the case the Commission held that it was unlikely that products exported outside the Common Market could surmount tariffs on re-entry into the Common Market (other factors to be considered included transport costs and accumulated profit margins). And it would be even more unlikely, the Commission held, that such re-import to an EEC Country would be followed by a further re-export within the Common Market; without such re-export no trade between Member States is involved. The Commission repeated the view which it first expressed in the Kodak Decision that "since the abolition of customs duties within the Common Market, all demand in a Member State can be satisfied directly from another Member State much more comfortably and more cheaply than from a non-Member State to which the requested products have first been exported from the Common Market".[92]

3-33. A further example in this category of cases is the Commission's decision concerning the exclusive-dealing agreement concluded between Goodyear Italia and Euram Italia for the distribution in Italy of plastic film for packing food products bearing the Vitafilm trademark.[93] Euram agreed not to export the products in question outside the Common Market. "This", according to the Commission, "not only prevents Euram from carrying on this business outside the EEC, but, in particular, it

91. Omega [1970] C.M.L.R. D49.

92. Ibid. at D56, para. 5.

93. See Goodyear Italiana/Euram Decision.

also prevents every undertaking outside the EEC from buying the product in question from Euram for resale within the Common Market which results in the distortion of competition within the Common Market."[94] This clause was not, however, regarded as causing an appreciable restraint of competition. Any purchaser whose business is situated within the Common Market is not prohibited from obtaining supplies of Vitafilm directly from other main suppliers of this product (whether their place of business is within or outside the Common Market). With regard to these other sources of supply, there is little likelihood that anybody would wish to sell Vitafilm in the Common Market after it had passed from Goodyear Italiana to Euram and had then been exported from the Common Market. Such sales would be subject to such additional economic factors as the accumulation of consecutive profit margins and transport costs as well as customs duties which would result from the goods passing and repassing through the border controls of the Common Market.

It was explained in the Fourth Report on Competition Policy that at the time of the decision there were no such price discrepancies between the Common Market and non-Member States as would absorb the additional costs involved in such an operation, nor were such discrepancies likely to develop in the foreseeable future.[95]

The agreement was granted exemption under Art. 85(3) after other provisions in it were found contrary to Art. 85(1).

---

94. Ibid. at D35, para.8.

95. Fourth Report on Competition Policy, point 101 (at p.62).

3-34. A further decision concerning bans on exports to non-Member States as part of a selective-distribution system operated in the Common Market by SABA, a manufacturer of radios, television sets and tape recorders was to the same effect.[96] The SABA distribution system was based on a large number of agreements in standard form between the manufacturer and dealers. The latter were, inter alia, obliged not to export SABA products to countries outside the Common Market and not to import the same from outside the Common Market. These provisions were held by the Commission not to cause an appreciable restraint of competition affecting trade between Member States. According to the decision the double customs duties involved in crossing the Community frontier twice discouraged SABA dealers and customers in the Community from obtaining from a non-Member State goods exported there by SABA or by SABA dealers, as SABA did not offer purchasers in non-Member States prices more favourable than those charged in the Common Market. The agreement with its remaining provisions was granted an exemption under Art. 85(3).

The Court dismissed an application from Metro to set aside the Commission's decision on the merits and thus upheld the Commission's practice of authorizing certain forms of selective distribution for specified goods within predetermined limits, provided that the result of the agreement is not to eliminate competiton in respect of a substantial part of the relevant products.[97]

3-35. A prohibition on exports to non-Member States by distributors of clocks and watches was similarly found not appreciably to restrict competition within the Common Market.[98] The company Junghans (a

---

96. SABA [1976] 1 C.M.L.R. D61.

97. Case 26/76, Metro-SB-Grossmärkte GmbH & Co. KG v. Commission [1977] E.C.R. 1875.

98. Junghans [1977] 1 C.M.L.R. D82.

subsidiary of a German company) sold the goods in all Community countries through a network of approved dealers in the Republic of Germany and of sole distributors and retailers in other Member States by way of a uniform distribution system. The fact that customs duties would be levied twice when goods crossed the Community's customs frontier was given, by the Commission, as a reason why the distributors and customers in the Community would, as a rule, have no interest in obtaining from a non-Member State goods exported there by another Junghans distributor.[99]

3-36. The line of decisions described above illustrates the basic approach of the Community regarding restraints on exports to non-Member States. These decisions established the understanding that an effect on trade between Member States may result from prohibitions on exports to non-Member States, since if prices are lower on an export market the exported product might profitably be imported back into the Common Market. Such a source of supply is eliminated by an export prohibition. That approach was reconfirmed recently in the decision of Bulloch and Others v. the Distillers Company Ltd.[100] and in the Davide Compari-Milano Decision.[101] Thus the principle of Art. 85(1) remains applicable in such cases and had the external tariff not been considered prohibitive, the Commission could have found the condition of effect on intra-Community trade satisfied.

(4) Control of Export Quantities by Community Enterprises

3-37. A Decision of the Commission found that, since the common organization of the market in sugar took effect, the biggest sugar

99. Sixth Report on Competition Policy, point 147, (at p.79).

100. A. Bulloch & Co. and Others v. the Distillers Company Ltd. [1978] 1 C.M.L.R. 415, at paras. 72-73.

101. Davide Campari-Milano Spa [1978] 2 C.M.L.R. 408, para. 60.

manufacturers in the Community had been infringing Arts. 85 and 86 of the Treaty.[102] The Community rules stipulated that compensation be paid from time to time for exports to third countries of sugar produced within the maximum quota, the purpose being to allow sugar producers in the Community to sell part of their production in the world market where the price of sugar is generally much lower than that fixed within the Common Market. Since the marketing year 1969/70 a system of invitations to tender had been introduced for obtaining export refunds, whose amounts varied according to the tenders submitted. The various measures taken under the concerted practices engaged in by the sugar producers and their sales organizations in the Common Market were designed to control the sugar trade within the Member States so as to ensure the protection of their respective markets. The deficit situation in certain areas in sugar for human consumption, however, necessitated a number of deliveries between Member States. In order to avoid, as far as possible, the competitive effects of such intra-Community trade, producers (especially the French and Belgian), *inter alia*, made bids, submitted at the auctions organized by the Commission, with a view to granting export refunds. The bids were concerted so that the quantities of surplus sugar remaining within the Common Market could be controlled and would exert no competitive pressure. The Commission decided to impose fines on a number of the undertakings and the Court's judgment essentially upheld the findings as regards the firms' infringement of the rules of competition.[103]

The Court held, for the first time in a case where there were tendering procedures to determine the refunds on exports to non-Member

102. The *Sugar Cartel Decision*.

103. Case 40-48, 50, 54-56, 111, 113 & 114/73, "*Suiker Unie" (Coöperative Vereniging) UA and Others* v. *Commission* [1975] E.C.R. 2010 *et seq*. (hereinafter cited as the "*Sugar Cartel Case*".)

States and where Community firms had engaged in concerted practices, that competition was restricted within the Common Market and trade between Member States might have been affected. If there had been no such concerted action, some firms would have been awarded smaller lots than those actually awarded to them and would thus have been given an incentive to sell more sugar in other Member States. This, the Court decided, could not only change the pattern of trade within the Community, but also intensify competition within the Common Market.[104]

(5) Exclusive-Dealing Agreements with NCES Relating to Exports to Non-Member States

3-38. A negative clearance was granted to an agreement under which the export company Johs. Rieckerman KG, Hamburg, had undertaken to market in Japan the inductive heating, melting and hardening equipment manufactured by AEG-Elotherm GmbH, Remscheid Hasten.[105] Rieckermann was permitted to market AEG-Elotherm equipment in Japan only and was required to purchase equipment of this type for export to Japan exclusively from AEG-Elotherm. AEG-Elotherm was required to market its equipment in Japan through Rieckermann only and to ensure that its other customers did not sell such equipment in Japan.

A theoretical analysis of the agreement produces some interesting conclusions. The prohibition of sale (an obligation not to sell in countries other than Japan) implied that Rieckermann was prohibited from selling within the Common Market and from maintaining an after-sales and guarantee service thereof. Rieckermann was also

---

104. Ibid. 2016 et seq.
105. Rieckermann [1968] C.M.L.R. D78.

obliged by a prohibition of competition (an obligation not to sell in Japan installations competing with those of AEG-Elotherm). Although the latter prohibition places the anticompetitive effects on a person outside the Common Market, this may still be a restraint of trade and competition within the Common Market if there are competitors within the Market who are limited in their freedom by the restriction imposed (which means the foreclosure of distribution through the distributor of products of other Common Market manufacturers). The exclusivity clause (an obligation on AEG-Elotherm to sell to Japan only through Rieckermann and to prevent actions liable to disturb this exclusivity) involved a limitation on other purchasers within the Common Market and might affect trade between Member States. The latter prohibition also implied that a Community manufacturer, who undertakes not to sell to others in the distributor's area abroad, protects other Community manufacturers against competitive sales to others; this aspect of the restraint may not be sufficiently significant to meet the requirements of Art. 85(1) but there is no doubt that competition within the Common Market is to some extent limited.

The Commission, however, considered that such an exclusive-dealing agreement, concluded with an exporting enterprise which was not organized for selling to the Common Market, could not appreciably restrict competition.

The implications and significance of the prohibition on re-export to the Common Market in this case are further analysed with regard to arrangements restricting imports to the Community. See 3-49.

The restriction on AEG-Elotherm with regard to direct sales to Japan was, according to the decision, without repercussion on the level of supply and demand in the Common Market. AEG-Elotherm's freedom was, in the Commission's opinion, limited only on the Japanese market. The restriction with regard to AEG-Elotherm's other customers also did not have an appreciable effect on the levels of supply and demand in view of the fairly large number of manufacturers of the relevant equipment within the Common Market. Even if this clause did not exist, AEG-Elotherm would very probably have recourse to only one promoter of sales, given the highly technical nature of the installations, their high price and the difficulty of selling them to Japan.[106]

The prohibition on Rieckermann not to sell other manufacturers' equipment in Japan seemed to the Commission as only theoretically reducing the level of demand in the Common Market and not materially limiting the other manufacturers' outlets as regards their exports to Japan, so that competition in the Common Market was not appreciably reduced. This prohibition directly restricted Rieckermann's freedom only in its selling to Japan and not within the Common Market. Because of the conditions of competition which prevail in the Common Market and, in particular, of the number of manufacturers of installations and of traders which export them to Japan, it could not be expected, according to the Commission, that the prohibition of competition would have effects on the supply and demand situation within the Common Market liable to be considered as perceptibly affecting competition.[107]

The agreement above had the object of promoting exports from the Common Market, but this fact, the Commission emphasized, did not always mean that the clauses inserted to that end did not aim also at altering the competition within the Common Market.[108]

106. Ibid. D85, para. 15.
107. Ibid. D83, para. 13.
108. Ibid. D82, para. 9.

3-39. In an earlier decision (the Grosfillex Decision), concerning an exclusive-dealing agreement for a non-Member State, prohibitions of similar character to those agreed upon in the Rieckermann/AEG-Elotherm arrangement were undertaken by the parties and granted a negative clearance by the Commission. For an elaboration of the decision in this section, see 3-48. Considering the restriction on the Community enterprise with regard to direct export-sales to a certain territory outside the Common Market, and the prohibition on the NCE of manufacturing or selling articles manufactured by the Community enterprise, the Commission emphasized the following point, which was reiterated in the Rieckermann Decision:

> There exists in the market in plastics, in the groups, 'household' and 'hygiene', a large number of manufacturers which are established in the Member States and which are in a position to compete in the territory of the Common Market. The same applies to the trading stage. 109

(6) Cooperation Agreements Between Community Enterprises in Respect of Exports

3-40. The first Commission decision on an agreement between Community enterprises concerning exports to non-Member States granted a negative clearance.[110] The Community association in that agreement was DECA (Dutch Engineers and Contractors Association), an organization of four Dutch building and construction firms, which also act for their associates and subsidiaries, some of which have their head offices in Belgium, Italy and the Federal Republic of Germany. The firms intended to cooperate on building and construction orders from outside the

---

109. Grosfillex Decision 239.
110. DECA [1965] C.M.L.R. 50.

Common Market in cases where the value of an order exceeds 2 million guilders. They had undertaken to report to the central office on their capacity to undertake contracts and on any intention to submit a tender; where appropriate the firms would cooperate on the submission of tenders and the execution of works.

The following explanation was given by the Commission in support of the decision that Art. 85(1) was inapplicable to the agreement:

> The internal rules of the DECA group have the aim of organising construction and public works carried out outside Europe and the French overseas departements - to which the rules about competition are also applicable under Article 227 of the Treaty. Thus the group only organises the collaboration of its participants outside the territories within which the rules of competition of the EEC Treaty are applicable. The fact that several associated undertakings established in other Member States are also part of the group in no wise changes this, for their activity under the rules is restricted solely to relations with third countries. Therefore the object of the internal rules of the group is not to prevent, restrict or distort competition within the Common Market.
>
> The provisions of the internal rules do not in themselves involve any effects on competition within the Common Market. In addition, in this particular case, the Commission has not hitherto been made aware that the collaboration of these undertakings in this way has such effects within the Common Market. 111

3-41. The V.V.V.F. Decision[112] illustrated that several restrictions which would have been prohibited in respect of exports between Member States, are, however, considered to fall outside Art. 85(1) if they only apply to extra-Community exports. The Dutch Association in question had as its object the defence of the interests of the paint and related products industry, and in particular those of its members (Dutch only). The agreement between the enterprises required the

111. Ibid. at 51-52. See also Eighth General Report 1 April 1964 - 31 March 1965 (June 1965), point 61 at p.57.

112. V.V.V.F. [1970] C.M.L.R. D1.

parties: (1) for exports outside the Common Market, to keep to minimum export prices as they appear in the export programme and to comply with all instructions relating to the conditions of supply fixed by the governing body; (2) to undertake an obligation to appoint only one exclusive concessionnaire or agent per country for the distribution of a given group of products, to inform the secretariat of the group of agreements concluded with the concessionnaires and agents for the distribution on foreign markets, and not to give commissions exceeding the maximum rates authorized by the governing body; (3) to give the secretariat all information requested by the governing body concerning the composition prices and conditions of sale, to let it know every month the exports made during the preceding month and to pass to it a copy of the invoices and export permits.

The only explanation the Commission gave for its decision, that all the provisions above did not have an effect on competition within the Common Market, was the following:

> .....these minimum prices are at present fixed at a fairly low level compared with the effective prices. The possibility of price competition remains real both between the members and with third parties. It should also be emphasised that there exists within the Common Market a strong competition in the paint products sector between the manufacturers of the various Member States. 113.

(7) Specialization Agreements for Promoting Sales Outside the Common Market

3-42. With a view to promoting specialization in their production and sales of thin papers in non-Member States, several French companies concluded an agreement.[114] The companies were to try to increase their

113. *Ibid.* at D5.

114. *French Producers of Fine Papers* [1972] C.M.L.R. D94.

sales outside the Common Market by the following means: coordination of market studies and of distribution methods for those countries; joint participation in tenders in those countries; joint participation, decided jointly, in the cost of travel, publicity, commercial agency, etc., involved in those sales, and in pooling the orders received on the spot in those countries.

The Commission pointed out that cooperation between the principal manufacturers of a product in a Member State to promote export to countries outside the Common Market by the means mentioned above did not distort competition within the Common Market.[115] In this case, a system of division among the participants by quotas and an equalization of profits had been initially abolished (after being objected to by the Commission), and consequently a noticeable restriction of competition only persisted by reason of the specialization of production. Nevertheless, the specialization agreement (whereby each party undertook to restrict its production to certain types and qualities of product) benefitted from exemption under Art. 85(3) so long as there still were adequate competitive conditions on the market.

B. Arrangements Concerning Imports Into the Common Market

GENERAL

3-43. Import cartels, which are also known as "purchase cartels", are founded for the purpose of promoting the joint business of their members on the foreign markets or with the intention of making these

115. *Ibid.* D98, para. 8.

members more competitive than their business rivals in the Common Market. It sometimes happens, however, that an import cartel does not limit its policy to pure purchases on behalf of its mandators, e.g. in order to facilitate the endeavours of a purchase cartel in its bargaining with sellers abroad, the cartel might agree with a foreign party upon sharing markets, so that the foreign party could, in relation to the cartel members, be assured exclusive operations in a certain area. Import cartels also appear in the form of groups of domestic manufacturers who band together, or even cooperate with NCES, to keep out foreign imports or to limit their volume through private rather than governmental regulations.

(1) Voluntary-Import Restraints in Arrangements Between Community and Non-Community Enterprises

3-44. Community case law often relates to certain types of arrangements which deserve a special mention here; arrangements between enterprises or associations of enterprises curtailing imports on the Community Market from non-Member States, or controlling these imports, for example in terms of quantity or price. Such arrangements - known as self-limitation agreements - hamper the Community's commercial and competition policies.[116]

The Commission published an opinion giving a statement of principles, formulated within the framework of the Treaty, with regard to practices which restrain imports of Japanese products into the Community.[117] See 2-54. From the point of view of competition law,

116. See Second Report on Competition Policy, points 15 and 17 (at pp.25-26).

117. See Opinion Governing the Applicability of the Treaty of Rome to the Importation of Japanese Products Into the Community, J.O. 1972, C 111/13.

the opinion recalls that such practices are prohibited under Art. 85 even where some or all of the member enterprises have their principal place of business outside the Common Market, if effects of the agreements extend to that territory.

Consideration of measures concerning voluntary import limitations to the Common Market, notified to the Commission by NCES, has shown that there are various types of measures which should be assessed differently.[118] Art. 85 would not, however, apply to export agreements imposed on enterprises in non-Member States by their governments, unless there was an agreement or concerted practice between the enterprises. See also 4-48. The Commission believes that any import curtailment measures should be part of the commercial policy, a field which must remain in the hands of the public authorities. Hence it feels that in cases where certain imports from non-Member States are causing or are liable to cause grave difficulties to Community manufacturers, such problems should be tackled by the implementation of appropriate commercial policy measures.[119] If an enterprise attempts to rely on various treaties, legislation and regulations as entitling it to require any others to abstain from acts of dumping which are causing it damage, this argument will be objected to by the Commission. The provisions of international treaties which enterprises might attempt to rely upon (Article VI of the GATT and Article 10 of the Paris Convention for the Protection of Industrial Property) do not, in fact,

---

118. See Commission's reply to O.Q. 35/73 concerning agreements between producers of electronic equipment in the Community and Japan; annex to O.J. 1973, 162/31.

119. See Second Report on Competition Policy, point 17 (at p.26); Third Report on Competition Policy, point 20 (at pp.27-28); European Parliament, Doc. 290/74, 1974-75, Report drawn up on behalf of the Committee on Economic and Monetary Affairs on the Third Report of the Commission of the European Communities on Competition Policy (Doc. 118/74), Explanatory Statement, point 9. See also Commission's reply to W.Q. 295/77, O.J. 1977 C 270/10.

constitute a source of positive law directly applicable to enterprises.[120]

3-45. Prohibited agreements in respect of imports into the Common Market were found by the Commission to exist in the flat-glass industry. Community enterprises concluded a number of agreements with their counterparts in non-Member States specifying, among other points, that the latter were not to export to the Common Market. Given the structure of the Community glass market, the exclusion of potential entrants from non-Member States meant, according to the Commission, that conditions of effective competition might not be maintained within the Common Market. Where required, the clauses banning exports were deleted to meet the Commission's objections, so that entry to the Common Market was no longer impeded by these agreements in restraint of competition.[121]

3-46. The Commission's opinion on the importation of Japanese products into the Common Market was actually implemented in the Franco-Japanese Ballbearings Decision. See 2-55. See also the Franco-Taiwanese Mushroom Packers Decision in 2-56. The Japanese and the French trade associations achieved a consensus (in a form of an exchange of letters) that the price of Japanese ballbearings imported into France should be increased so as to align the prices with bearings of French production. The Commission found that practice prohibited. Its decision is interesting in that it illustrates that, although the obvious effect of an increase in import prices to only one Member State could be felt through the French market, there is, however, the additional possibility of effects on trade between Member States which would not have arisen

120. See IFTRA Rules for Producers of Virgin Aluminium [1975] 2 C.M.L.R. D33, para. 26 (hereinafter cited as the "IFTRA Decision").

121. See EC Bulletine, No.8-70, Part II, Ch. I, Sec. 8.

in the absence of such an agreement. A finding by the Commission that the agreement may affect trade between Member States was thus explained in the decision:

> The practical implication of the proposed increase in prices would depend on whether they could have any effect not only on the ballbearings imported directly into France from Japan, but also on those imports of bearings of Japanese origin which were in free circulation in other Member States. It is in this respect that it is significant that the attention of the Japanese producers.....was drawn to the fact that imports of Japanese bearings were brought in via Germany, Belgium and Holland. 122

3-47. A self-limitation practice was also examined by the Commission in the IFTRA Decision. Finding against the agreement in question the Commission decided that the arrangement entitled "IFTRA" (International Fair Trade Practice Rules Administration), between producers of virgin aluminium, constituted an infringement of Art. 85(1).[123] The agreement was signed by enterprises established within the Common Market and by major producers in Austria, Norway, Spain, Sweden and Switzerland. In particular, the parties undertook to refrain from dumping and adopted private rules to this end. By these rules it was sought to discourage price competition in import sales. The provisions in the agreement affected trade between Member States, according to the Commission, even where they related to sales in the Common Market from a third country, as they combined to circumscribe the commercial freedom of producers (Community and non-Community) and consequently to prevent or restrict their sales to other countries. Since the product in question is used in the manufacture of a large number of semi-finished and finished products and is imported into Member States for processing and resale in other Member States, the restrictions in this arrangement

122. Franco-Japanese Ballbearings Decision D17-D18.

123. See IFTRA Decision.

would have, as the decision stated, a serious effect on trade between Member States in those products.[124]

(2) Other Types of Restraints on Imports in Arrangements Between Community and Non-Community Enterprises

3-48. One of the first decisions of the Commission dealt with an exclusive concession for sale outside the Common Market which included, *inter alia*, a prohibition on a NCE to export to the Common Market. See also 2-50. The Swiss company Fillistdorf, undertook, as part of the agreement, to carry on the activity set out in the contract only within the conceded territory (Switzerland); it further undertook neither to manufacture nor to sell any article liable to compete with the articles manufactured by Grosfillex, a French company. For its part, Grosfillex undertook not to make any sale on Swiss territory of articles within the groups covered by the contract other than through Fillistdorf and to take all measures to bring to an end sales of such articles made by third parties on Swiss territories which may be brought to its notice. Furthermore, Grosfillex should pass on to Fillistdorf all orders or correspondence received direct from Switzerland.

Obviously, the re-export prohibition imposed on Fillistdorf was in "restraint of trade" in the literal sense, since Fillistdorf was restricted in its freedom to sell to the Common Market. But the facts of the case were such that this covenant could not, in the Commission's view, have any serious effect on general competitive

---

124. *IFTRA Decision* D37, para. 49.

conditions within the Common Market. A negative clearance was given to the agreement mainly on the following grounds:

> The articles bought by Fillistdorf, having been delivered to it in Switzerland by Grosfillex, would on resale into the Common Market have to cross a new customs frontier. Thereby, they are not liable to enter into competition with the same articles delivered directly in the territory of the Common Market. It would only be otherwise if there were exceptional circumstances and the Commission is not aware of any such. In fact, there is no reason to suppose that the prices of Grosfillex on the Swiss market are lower than those operated by Grosfillex within the Common Market; and this appears to be borne out by the fact that the Swiss purchasers of the products under contract sold by Fillistdorf are not forbidden to resell these in the Common Market. 125

As for the decision with regard to the prohibition on the Community enterprise against direct export-sales see 3-39.

3-49. The Rieckermann Decision, which was previously mentioned in connection with arrangements concerning exports from the Common Market, also concerned a prohibition on exports to the Common Market imposed on the NCE. See 3-38.

The exclusive concession to sell in a non-Member State, in the agreement in question, had indeed as its counterpart a prohibition on selling in other countries, including the Common Market. Such a prohibition, according to the Commission, only excluded a potential selling operation, which in any case was not very likely. Rieckermann was not equipped to sell in the Common Market and the equipment was not readily marketable there. For this, and certain other reasons specified in the decision, the re-export prohibition did not constitute a perceptible restriction of trade and competition. On the basis of global appreciation of the circumstances the Commission reached the conclusion that, even if there were no prohibition of sale, Rieckermann

---

125. Grosfillex Decision 239.

would very probably have no competitive position in the Common Market and so this prohibition had no practical effect on competition within the Common Market.[126]

The following comment on that decision was given in the Second General Report on the Activities of the Communities:

> Through the decision the Commission made it clear that, in respect of most exclusive dealing agreements to which export companies that are not equipped for selling within the Common Market are party, there is no need for notification and no point in applying for negative clearance. The Commission considers that the bulk of the notifications of this type already filed with it can be settled in a simplified procedure. 127

Re-sale control provision which tells foreign buyers, in an arrangement with a Community enterprise, what they can and cannot do with regard to their exports to the Common Market, may, nevertheless, raise some problems. However, although re-sale price or territorial control may affect imports into the Common Market, the possibility of the re-export to the Common Market, in its original form, of a product initially bought from a Community enterprise is somewhat remote.

3-50. A prohibition against exports to the Common Market imposed on exclusive licensees abroad was first examined in a Commission decision which concerned a patent, know-how and utility models licence, granted by the German subsidiary of the French Raymond firm, the biggest firm in this industry in the Common Market, to the Japanese Nagoya Rubber Co., the biggest sub-contractor in the Japanese motor industry, controlled by the Toyota motor company.[128] The licensee obtained the right to apply the grantor's technique and to manufacture in Japan and

---

126. See the Rieckermann Decision D82, para. 11.

127. Second General Report on the Activities of the Communities: 1968 (February 1969), point 28 at p.47.

128. Raymond [1972] C.M.L.R. D45.

sell in the Far East plastic fixing components used in motor construction; the grantor had undertaken to license no other enterprises in any part of the territory covered by the agreement.

Granting negative clearance, the Commission accepted the argument that the exclusive nature of the licence and the export ban - under which the licensee may sell only in his own territory - do not affect the competitive situation within the Common Market, given the special features of the particular case. The exclusive dealing arrangement had as its sole effect the elimination of potential competitors on the Far East market, and, because of the nature of the items concerned, their export from Japan to the Common Market was, in the Commission's view, virtually ruled out. These items were manufactured only to special order in close and constant association with the firm giving the order; if the items covered by the contract were incorporated into the spare parts or the coachwork of Japanese motor vehicles, they could be exported in this state to any country in the world.

An earlier version of the licensing contract provided that any improvements made by Nagoya to the Raymond technique would become the property of Raymond and that Nagoya was required to grant only to Raymond a licence on the ownership rights covering parallel inventions. However, following the Commission's intervention, the parties adjusted these commitments so that Nagoya was only required to grant to Raymond a non-exclusive licence on the patents which it would obtain if improvements or changes were to be made to the Raymond technique.

Nagoya's undertaking not to challenge the validity of Raymond's contractual industrial property rights during the lifetime of the agreement was not found incompatible with Art. 85, since it seemed unlikely that the Japanese licensee would challenge the industrial property rights held by his co-contractor in the Common Market and there was little or no possibility of such action succeeding.

The Commission stated that it must be possible to include quality control and information exchange within the contractual exploitation of the invention and of the know-how. Consequently, the latter did not constitute a restraint of competition covered by Art. 85.

(3) Exclusive Import Agreements Between Non-Community Producers and Community Distributors (for Part of the Common Market or for the Whole of It).

3-51. It is well established in Community case law that arrangements between enterprises within the Common Market and enterprises situated in third countries, which intend to channel in a special way the supply within the Common Market of products originating abroad, are capable of falling within Art. 85. The following cases and decisions concerned such arrangements.

In the Béguelin Case the Court established that an exclusive sales agreement between a producer outside the Common Market and a distributor within a Member State is covered by Art. 85(1) if the distributor is prevented from re-exporting to other Member States or can exclude parallel imports of that product from other Member States to the protected territory. For more details about the factual situation in this case see 2-61.

3-52. In this context it is interesting to note that, provided competition is sufficiently affected, the Commission will prohibit a ban on direct sales to the Common Market even where imposed by a NCE on sellers abroad, in order to protect an exclusive distributorship agreement (or a number of such agreements) within the Common Market. This was the finding in the Watts/Theal Decision which, *inter alia*, considered such arrangements (the non-Member State, *in casu*, was the U.K. between May and December 1972, i.e. after the Treaty of Accession had been signed, but before it came into force).

3-53. The Commission granted an exemption under Art. 85(3) for an agreement under which the American company, Duro-Dyne Corporation (New York) appointed the Belgian company Europair SA (Brussels) as its main exclusive dealer for the importation into the whole Common Market area of a range of parts and fittings intended mainly for use in heating and air-conditioning installations.[129]

The grant of an exclusive dealership for the whole of the Common Market area was regarded as a restriction of competition liable to affect trade between Member States, since it meant that no dealers in the Common Market other than the authorized dealer could obtain supplies of the relevant products directly from the principal for resale in the other Member States:

> The agreement is capable of affecting trade between Member States. Duro-Dyne products have an appreciable share of the EEC market. But for the agreement other dealers in the EEC would have been able to buy, and would have bought, directly from Duro-Dyne for resale in their own or in another Member State .....the flow of inter-state trade in the products in question will, therefore, develop on lines other than those which would have prevailed without the restrictions caused by the agreement.[130]

---

129. See Duro-Dyne/Europair Decision.

130. *Ibid*. at D64-D65 (para. 12). See also Fourth Report on Competition Policy, point 103 (at p.63).

Nevertheless, in order to facilitate trade in goods between Member States, the Commission took the view that under Art. 85(3), concentration by Europair of imports into the Common Market of a whole range of products from a non-Member State would facilitate active sales promotion, continuity of supplies and rationalization of distribution. The decision also noted that the principal exclusive distributor did not enjoy absolute territorial protection, since his principal had not undertaken to refrain from indirect supplies to the Common Market.

(4) Import Prohibitions in Arrangements Between Community Enterprises

3-54. Import prohibitons are often part of various arrangements between Community enterprises concerning distribution within the Common Market where the distributors are also required not to export the same goods from the Common Market. For example, see the SABA selective distribution system in 3-34. In this connection it is obvious that an import prohibition may be permitted by the Commission on the same ground as an export ban, i.e. the fact that the existence of double customs duties involved in crossing the Community frontier twice prevents an interest in obtaining in a non-Member State goods exported there by a Community enterprise.

3-55. A prohibition on direct imports from non-Member States was the subject of an agreement which set up a system of auction-sales in Rotterdam for certain types of fruit imported into the Netherlands.[131]

131. See FRUBO [1974] 2 C.M.L.R. D89 (hereinafter cited as the "FRUBO Decision").

An agreement was concluded between an association of the main Dutch fruit importers and an association of virtually all the Dutch fruit wholesalers (FRUBO). In order to be allowed to take part in auctions, through which most (roughly 80%) of the citrus fruit sold in the Netherlands is handled, dealers had to comply with the conditions imposed by the agreement. The main restriction, apart from a set of technical provisions as to the organization of auction sales, consisted of the obligation for importers and wholesalers to market citrus fruit grown in non-Member States and intended for sale in the Netherlands only through the Rotterdam auction sales. After some modifications the agreement still kept the wholesalers subject to the ban on direct imports from non-Member States and the purchases of citrus fruits from elsewhere in the Community subject to a major restraint, namely customs clearance by another party, thereby compulsorily introducing an additional trading stage. (The fruit had to be purchased from an importer established in another Member State who had previously imported the fruit, cleared it through customs and unloaded it).

The Commission adopted a decision requiring termination of these restrictions. The overall prohibited effect of the restrictions on Dutch wholesalers in their freedom to carry on their business - including the prohibition on importing directly from non-Member States - was thus stated in the decision:

> .....to damage the competitive structure of this sector of the Common Market by weakening the competitive position of these wholesalers in their dealings with the importers and with other wholesalers of the Community. This is capable of affecting the flow of trade between Member States in a manner likely to hinder the establishment of a single market among these States.[132]

Furthermore, the agreement prevented an importer from another Member State from forwarding to a Dutch wholesaler directly, that is

132. Ibid. at D96, para. 18.

without going through the Rotterdam auctions, part of an order of fruit from a non-Member Country when he finds that he will be unable to sell the entire order on his own national market.[133]

The rejection by the Commission of an application for exemption under Art. 85(3) was based on the grounds that, in order to attain the advantages which could be gained from the Rotterdam auction sales, it was not essential to prevent wholesalers from importing directly from the non-Member States or from having access to possibly cheaper or better supplies on other Community import markets.[134]

The Court dismissed an application against the Commission decision and stated that the offending provision, "because it restricts the freedom of members to import direct into the Netherlands.....is liable to interfere with the natural movement of trade and thus to affect trade between Member countries."[135]

(5) The Use of Industrial Property Rights in Arrangements Prohibiting Imports from Non-Member States

3-56. A factual situation which gave the Court an opportunity to clarify its jurisprudence as to the limits imposed by Community law on the exercise of industrial and commercial property rights in relation to the trade between the Community and non-Member States was found in the EMI/CBS Cases.

---

133. Ibid. at D95, para. 17.

134. See Fourth Report on Competition Policy, point 73 (at p.50).

135. The FRUBO Case, 584, para. 38.

The English company EMI Records Ltd., which owned the "Columbia" trademark in all Community countries, relied on its trademark rights in several actions against the American group CBS Inc. CBS had imported into the Community records bearing the same lable manufactured in the United States and distributed through its subsidiaries. Initially the Columbia label was held by an American firm throughout the world. In 1917 it transferred its assets and goodwill in several European countries, together with the trademark rights held there, to its British subsidiary. However, it retained all rights for the U.S. and certain other countries. The American lable has since changed hands several times, and now belongs to CBS, which has no legal or economic link with EMI, the owner of the mark in Europe.

The Court ruled that in cases such as this the applicability of Arts. 85(1) and 86 had to be considered, however, it seemed inclined to reject the idea that Art. 85(1) was applicable in the particular circumstances. It stressed that a restrictive agreement is deemed to produce prohibited effects only if the conduct of the enterprises concerned justifies an inference of concerted action and coordination consistent with the agreement and produces the result intended by the agreement. In the case in question, there had been an agreement between the American and European trademark owners to share world markets in gramophone records but the agreement had been terminated several years before litigation commenced. Therefore no restrictive agreement or practice existed. The Court also held that in the circumstances under consideration the effects did not exceed those normally attached to the exercise of national trade-mark rights. In this connection the Court recalled that the American firm could penetrate the Common Market even without using the Columbia label. The need for the proprietor of an identical trademark would, therefore, be one of the acceptable consequences of the protection given to the trademark. As regards Art. 86 the Court confirmed an earlier ruling to the effect that the trademark right does not of itself confer a dominant position on the proprietor. It further held that to use a trademark to impede imports of products bearing an identical trademark into the protected territory was not to abuse dominant position for the purpose of Art. 86.

In view of this judgment the position of the competition law on the point under consideration was thus summarily explained by the Commission in the Sixth Report on Competition Policy:

> If the exercise of the trademark right served to isolate the whole of the Common Market it could be caught by the prohibition in Article 85 if it were the object, the means or the consequence of a restrictive agreement. The mere fact of a restriction on the supply in the Community of goods originating in a non-member country, but similar to those protected by a trademark in the Community, could adversely affect the conditions of competition in the Common Market. In cases where the owner of the disputed trademark in the non-member country has several subsidiaries established in different Member States of the Community, who can market the relevant goods in the Common Market, the segretation of national markets is also liable to affect trade between Member States. 136

The Court also held that the provisions of the Treaty relating to the free movement of goods, and notably the prohibition of measures having an equivalent effect to quantitative restrictions (Art. 30), normally apply only to trade between Member States. The exercise of a trademark right in order to block sales under an identical trademark of goods imported from a non-Member State is without effect on intra-Community trade since it does not jeopardize the unity of the Common Market.

---

136. Sixth Report on Competition Policy, point 25 (at p.26).

There is no need, according to the judgment, to consider whether the trademarks share a common origin with an identical trademark registered in a non-Member State.[137] This would be significant only if it were necessary to consider whether there was the possibility of partitioning markets within the Common Market. The question does not arise where a single owner has the same trademark rights for the same product in all Member States.[138]

3-57. It has been seen in the case above that the provisions relating to the free movement of goods have no application in relation to products being imported from third countries. Similarly in Minnesota Mining & Manufacturing Co. v. Geerpres Europe Ltd.[139] the High Court in England in effect ruled, without considering it necessary to obtain a view from the Court of Justice, that the exercise of patent rights to prevent imports into England of patented products sold by a licensee in the U.S., holding a licence from a company in the same group as the plaintiff, did not contravene the provisions of the Treaty as to the free movement of goods.

---

137. The principles applicable to trademark rights of common origin which have evolved for the Common Market were formulated in Case 192/73 Van Zuylen Freres v. Hag AG [1974] E.C.R. 745: "to prohibit the marketing in one Member State of a product legally bearing a trademark in another Member State for the sole reason that an identical trademark, having the same origin, exists in the first is incompatible with the provisions for the free movement of goods within the Common Market".

138. This conclusion is not invalidated by the provisions of the Treaty relating to the free circulation of goods coming from non-Member States (Arts. 9(2) and 10), nor by the rules on the common commercial policy (Art. 110 et seq). But the Court did not consider the question of whether these principles also apply where the trademark rights are not held by the same person in all the Member States. Here the exercise of the trademark right would tend, in the Commission's opinion, to divide the Common Market into separate national markets (see Sixth Report on Competition Policy point 24 (at p.26).

139. Minnesota Mining & Manufacturing Company v. Geerpres Europe Ltd. (in the High Court of Justice; Chancery Division)[1973] C.M.L.R. 259.

C. International Restrictive Business Arrangements

GENERAL

3-58. International cartels, which are the subject of the present survey,are, according to traditional interpretation, cartels with partners in different nations[140] (in the context of the study, with partners in Member States and in countries outside the Common Market). In fact although the preceding investigation focussed to some degree on the phenomenon of international cartels, those arrangements were classified only in accordance with the main relevant restriction operated by them, ie. whether the restraint concerned exports or imports. International cartels relevant to the present study are formed by Community and non-Community enterprises for the purpose of regulating competition by using traditional cartel methods, such as allocation of markets or customers, specialization in production between the members, limitation of out-put as per quotas fixed for each member, limitation of productive capacity, joint participation and cooperation in plans including exchange of information, price fixing, etc.

Such arrangements are facilitated by the possibility in many third countries of legalizing certain types of cartels in which subsidiaries of Community enterprises may participate and which may serve as the nucleus for an international system of restrictive agreement.[141] Patent licensing agreements are frequently used as a

140. See H. Kronstein, The Law of International Cartels 41 (1973).

141. See OECD, Committee of Experts on Restrictive Business Practices, Restrictive Business Practices of Multinational Enterprises, sec. 57 (1977).

vehicle to achieve international market and product allocation, price discrimination and other restrictions. In this connection the dividing up of market territories is the essential factor, and when each member thus gets his own exclusive area the price agreement loses its significance.

(1) World-Wide Market Sharing Agreements (Including the Use of Industrial Property Rights)

3-59. Although there are no special rules in the Treaty for international cartels as such, that does not mean that these operations are not opposed by the Community if they have effects on trade and competition within the Common Market. The Nichols Frères/Vitapro Decision[142] concerned an international cartel, but granted the partners a negative clearance.

The facts of the case were as follows:

Nicholas Frères, a French firm, had acquired the assets of Vitapointe Laboratories which held various patents, trademarks and designs in the hairdressing line. Vitapointe had a licensing and exclusive dealership agreement with Vitapro, a British corporation, for the distribution of Vitapointe products in Great Britain (before the accession of the U.K. to the EEC) and other territories outside the Common Market. The agreement was one by which Nicholas sold to Vitapro part of the assets bought from Vitapointe, *viz.*, the clientele of Vitapointe in third countries (especially the countries of the

142. Nicholas Frères/Vitapro [1964] C.M.L.R. 505.

Commonwealth), and the right to use the Vitapointe trade-name in that area as well as various patents, trademarks and designs registered in these countries in the name of Vitapointe. This sale of business and goodwill contained several restrictive covenants: Vitapro agreed not to use the trade-name "Vitapointe" outside the assigned territory; Nicholas undertook on his part to refrain from using the same trade-name in the assigned territory of the other party. Moreover, both parties were committed not to manufacture or to sell for five years any other product used for hairdressing in the territory reserved to the other. This undertaking, however, did not cover products bought from a third party or manufactured and sold pursuant to a licensing agreement with a third party.

That arrangement might have been analysed as disguising a division of markets between Vitapro and Nicholas. The Commission found that the main purpose of the arrangement was to sell the assets of Vitapointe for exploitation in third countries. This purpose in itself was, of course, lawful. But the Commission went on to look at the effect of the transaction. Two provisions - the two imposed on the British corporation - seemed on the face of it restricting the ability of this firm to compete within the Common Market. First, Vitapro was prohibited from manufacturing and selling hairdressing products within the Common Market. But this prohibition, the Commission observed, was limited to a five-year period, and products bought from third parties, or manufactured under a licence from a third party, were excepted. The second provision prevented Vitapro, with no limitation of time, from using or permitting the use, within the Common Market, of the ceded trademarks. However, according to the decision, this provision was agreed to on the occasion of the partition of the old

Vitapointe enterprise, a partition which was carried out in such a way that Nicholas retains all the assets attached to the territory of the Common Market and especially the trademarks registered there, while ceding to Vitapro the whole of the Vitapointe assets in various third States, without the Common Market being divided into separate zones. The prohibition imposed on Vitapro had, in the Commission's view, only the effect of preventing the sale under the same trademark, within the Common Market, of the products hitherto manufactured by an enterprise having its centre there, as well as by an enterprise whose centre is in a third State.

Furthermore, with regard to each of the two contractual provisions mentioned above, the hairdressing products which they concern are in competition with a very large number of similar products available in the Common Market. Nicholas, according to the information at the disposal of the Commission, was not among the largest enterprises in this field, and was in lively competition with numerous enterprises manufacturing or selling hairdressing products in the Common Market.[143]

In the same category of world-wide market-sharing agreements we can also include various exclusive-licence agreements for territories outside the Common Market, discussed under previous headings, and the conditions they imposed on the parties. See, for example, Raymond Decision 3-50.

---

143. Ibid. at 508.

(2) International Cooperation Between Community and Non-Community Enterprises

3-60. The Transocean Marine Paint Association Decisions[144] dealt with activities of an association of twenty medium-sized marine paint manufacturers established in as many countries both inside and outside the Common Market. The aim of the association was to enable its members to compete effectively on the world market in marine paint. This means that standard-quality paints must be offered for sale in as many ports as possible. Consequently, the members undertook to manufacture marine paint of identical quality, using a single formula, and to sell it under a common Transocéan trademark. A territory was assigned to each member, namely the country in which that member was established. In addition, other territories were allotted to members in which they were to concentrate their sales efforts.

In the first decision the Commission authorized for a launching period the flexible system of geographical division which provided each member with a priviliged competitive position, since deliveries to countries where other members were established could only be made by means of a system of reciprocal compensatory commissions.

The exemption period allowed by the first decision (under Art. 85(3)) was extended for a further six years, subject to certain conditions. In particular the Commission took the view that certain export restrictions on the members could no longer be regarded as

144. Transocean Marine Paint Association [1967] C.M.L.R. D9; [1974] 1 C.M.L.R. D11; [1975] 2 C.M.L.R. D75. See also Case 17/74, Transocean Marine Paint Association v. Commission [1974] E.C.R. 1063.

indispensable to the attainment of the association's justifiable objectives. On the imposition of additional conditions which brought the Association to appeal against the decision see 4-38.

An exemption under Art. 85(3) was not, therefore, excluded where such an international cooperation agreement resulted in an appreciable restriction of competition. The Commission found on the whole that the arrangement was justified on economic grounds. See also 3-75.

3-61. International arrangements, prohibited under Community law, do not include only coordination directly concerning market behaviour. This would be too limited an approach. Such arrangements also include indirect effects upon the market behaviour of the parties concerned as, for example, in agreements concerning pricing information or joint development work.

As a result of representations from the Commission, Community manufacturers of metal and plastic paper machine wires used for draining water from pulp, who were organized in national associations in Germany, France and the U.K. and in the International Association of Paper Machine Wire Manufacturers (OFITOMEP), deleted a number of restrictive provisions from an information agreement entered into at the end of 1972.[145]

Under the agreement in its original form the members undertook to send the following documents, through any existing national association, to the OFITOMEP Secretariat-General:

---

145. See Sixth Report on Competition Policy, points 134-136 (at pp.73-74).

(1) lists of prices and discounts and terms of delivery and payment, to be sent two to three weeks from the submission of these documents to the customer or from their entry into force. The Secretary-General was authorized to distribute these lists to other members;

(2) copies of invoices for delivery to all countries, except the U.S., within ten days of issue, giving the name of the customer, the type of wire, the measurements and price of the wire, and any discount or favourable terms. Subsequent discounts or favourable terms were similarly to be notified as soon as they were granted.

The OFITOMEP Secretariat-General was authorized to use this information to prepare market statistics and, at the request of a national association or a member firm, to inform it if a particular price had been paid by a particular customer for a given type of wire, in order to prevent users of paper machine wires from playing one supplier off against another.

Such a system, in which the data needed for independent price formation are not compiled individually by firms, but are supplied collectively to the firms concerned, established links of commercial solidarity and interdependence with regard to prices which would not have existed in a genuinely competitive market. After hearing the Commission's objections to the agreement, the enterprises involved agreed to stop informing each other of price lists, discounts and terms of sale, to send their copies of invoices to OFITOMEP or to the national association without giving the name and address of the customer and to use these copies in future solely for the preparation of statistics.[146]

(3) Mergers Between Community and Non-Community Enterprises

3-62. Extraterritorial application of the competition rules can be of crucial importance when an enterprise whose headquarters are outside the Common Market has exercised its dominating power within this market, e.g. by acquiring one of its competitors domiciled within the Common Market. The inverse situation where a market-dominating Community enterprise acquires a company outside the Common Market which is also a competitor in the Common Market may also be critical. A mere acquisition of a foreign company by a Community enterprise may, however, affect the foreign trade of the Community as a whole, but it will rarely do so with respect to trade between Member States.

The Continental Can Case is a good example for the application of the Community competition rules (Art. 86) to a merger situation with international implications. Since the facts of this case have been stated before, there is no place for repetition here. See 2-5. The question of mergers, including international mergers between Community and NCES, may, in the future, find solution in a special Community regulation outside the framework of Art. 86. See 3-74.

---

146. For illustration of the Commission's approach to open price systems in the context of domestic arrangements see Third Report on Competition Policy, point 55.

D. The Nature of the Limitations on the Application of the Competition Rules to Arrangements with Foreign Elements with Regard to the Type of the Arrangements Concerned

(1) Are the Limitations a Result of Strict Interpretation of the Rules or of Philosophy Behind the Law?

3-63. Following the review of various arrangements with foreign elements the question contained in the above title seems now warranted.

The fact that "interstate character" is absent where trade between outside countries and the Community area as an economic bloc is concerned, has been argued by commentators to have significant consequences and to leave beyond the reach of Arts. 85 and 86 many restraints of competition. For example Oberdorfer, Gleiss and Hirsch take, on this point, the view that a German producer may bind his Swedish or Japanese customer not to export the goods supplied to him (or other goods) to the Common Market, since what is involved is only trade between one Member State and a third country which is not protected by the competition rules. Likewise, the producer may prohibit his Swedish or Japanese customer from importing competing products from the Common Market or from a Member State since again trade between Member States is not involved. These commentators consider the combination of that prohibition against import with a re-export prohibition on the customer in a third country permissible. If the German producer has given the Japanese customer an exclusive distribution franchise for the latter's country, he furthermore may in their view export his products to Japan in order to protect his right.[147]

147. See Oberdorfer, Gleiss and Hirsch, supra note 6 at sec. 130.

Commentators have also argued that the Commission has displayed no urge to find that arrangements by Community enterprises concerning their conduct outside the Common Market had (appreciable) restrictive effect within the Market.[148] For example, if the accepted revised distribution schemes in the Kodak and the Omega decisions, which preserved a ban on export outside the Common Market, did not affect trade within the Market, why did the enterprises insist on retaining the meaningless clauses? Thus one may fairly conclude, according to this view, that there has been little attempt at true extraterritorial enforcement of the competition rules against activities by Community enterprises outside the Common Market, and that the Commission has only limited jurisdiction in this area since "trade between Member States" must be affected and an effect on the foreign commerce of a Member State is not sufficient.[149]

The Grosfillex Decision is mostly criticized as an example of the application of the competition law to situations outside the Common Market being substantially limited by the Commission's approach. Kirschstein notes in this connection that the Commission disregarded some possible restraints of competition of this arrangement. He points out that the export prohibition imposed on the Swiss sole distributor, Fillistdorf, could, under certain conditions, also serve the purpose of preventing the enterprise from offering the contract-goods within the Common Market.[150] Deringer remarks that this criticism shows how unforeseeable the results can be if the actual effects are not taken into consideration when determining the restrictive purpose.[151]

---

148. See Dietz, supra note 6, at 762-763.
149. Ibid.
150. Kirschstein WRP 65. 77, mentioned in Deringer, supra note 1, sec.164.
151. Deringer, supra note 1, sec. 164.

In 1970 Rahl, an American commentator, remarked that in practice the Commission had been quite conservative in its approach to extraterritorial situations, in particular in the DECA, Grosfillex and Rieckermann Decisions:

> Adverse secondary effects on competition within the Common Market.....are not readily presumed, and small effects will evidently be tolerated. Even where the arrangement on its face explicitly bars sales in, or re-export to the Common Market it may escape in the absence of positive proof that it will produce significant adverse effects. 152

3-64. Referring to the decisions in the examples above (with the addition of the Raymond Decision) Jacquemin opines that it is tempting to conclude as Rahl did above.[153] However, Jacquemin emphasizes that such a straightforward conclusion may be premature. He mentions that, granting a negative clearance in the DECA Decision, the Commission stated that if the restraints outside the Common Market would produce secondary effects within the Market, such conduct could have been reached by the rules of competition. He also mentions the European Sugar Industry Case which suggested that, although the Commission will not apply the competition provisions to theoretical or minor effects, it will do so to indirect secondary effects of restrictive practices as well as to direct effects.

Although the decisions which were subject to criticism above gave too narrow a scope to the competition needing to be protected by Arts. 85 and 86, Smit and Herzog stress that in none of them did the Commission hold the rules inapplicable on the ground that interstate trade was not at all affected.[154]

---

152. J. Rahl, Common Market and American Antitrust; Overlap and Conflict 106 (1970).

153. Jacquemin "Application to Foreign Firms of European Rules of Competition" 19 Antitrust Bulletin 159 (1974).

154. Cf. Smit and Herzog, supra note 13, at sec. 85.63(k) in p.3-198.

3-65. Perhaps some of the earlier decisions of the Commission can be explained by its unwillingness to prohibit, at an early stage of the development of Community antitrust law, arrangements that produce their principal effects outside the Common Market. Since the decisions which were criticized are of a date when the Commission was still making its first tentative steps in the antitrust arena they have perhaps little precedential value.

A good example in which to find such an approach is the Nicholas Frères/Vitapro Decision which dealt with an agreement clearly dividing the world into two markets - one of which was the Common Market - and which should have been, therefore, forbidden. Nor could the restrictions imposed on Vitapro be argued to be merely inherent in the industrial property rights Nicholas retained within the Community, for these rights could not prevent Vitapro (a British enterprise) from selling its products within the Common Market without or under different trademarks and brands. However, even though it would be difficult to maintain that the prohibition preventing Vitapro from selling its non-trademarked products within the Common Market satisfied the prerequisites of Art. 85(3), exemption rather than negative clearance could then have provided the proper solution. Since the entry of Ireland and the U.K. into the Community fundamentally altered the situation with regard to the Nicholas Frères agreement and the latter became capable of partitioning the englarged Common Market the Commission reopened the case. Even so, it was found unnecessary to take further action under Art. 85, since in the meantime the interest of both parties in Vitapointe products had been brought together in the hands of one British company, Fisons Ltd., so that the potential barriers to trade between Member States created by the 1962 agreement had been eliminated.[155]

Nevertheless, of major importance to the present discussion is the comment which followed the note about the reopening of the Nicholas Frères/Vitapro Decision in the Sixth Report on Competition Policy:

> .....just as the Community has in general grown more outward-looking over the last decade, so in particular has the Commission's attitude changed towards agreements of this type which have the effect of isolating the common market from imports from outside the Community. 156

(2) The Change of Approach Through the Case Law

3-66. The development in the Commission's approach, as admitted in the Sixth Report on Competition Policy (see 3-65), was well reflected in the Transocean Marine Paint Association Decision of June 27, 1967.[157] For details on the background of the decision see 3-60. In that decision the Commission, before granting an exemption, required elimination of a provision which it previously allowed allocating foreign markets between members of the association. But the Commission still permitted the substitution of a provision requiring payment of a commission on exports to foreign States reserved to another party. Of course, the latter provision might restrain competition within the Common Market and if produces the requisite effect on trade between Member States is forbidden.

3-67. Very strong evidence for the Commission's gradual change of attitude from its early decisions can be found in the Zoja Decision

---

155. See Sixth Report on Competition Policy, point 168 (at. p.87).

156. Ibid. at point 169 (at p. 87).

157. See supra note 144.

which was confirmed by the Court. The decision related Zoja's foreign trade to Zoja's trade between the Member States by saying that Zoja could not economically manufacture for the Common Market area only, and that Istituto's refusal to supply Zoja with the necessary material would lead to Zoja having to shut down its ethambutol plant. The Commission, therefore, obliged Istituto to supply intermediary products to Zoja in quantities calculated on Zoja's trade throughout the world. See details of the case in 2-7.

Relying on the earlier Commission's position as had been evidenced, inter alia, by the DECA and the Rieckermann decisions, Istituto and its foreign parent company, Commercial Solvents Corporation (CSC), argued before the Court that the real markets for anti-tuberculosis drugs are the developing countries, where tuberculosis is still rampant. The argument, according to the original file of the case before the Court,[158] went as follows:

> What, then, would have been the rule if Zoja would have exported its entire production to third countries? We submit that in that case this business of Zoja would not be covered by the Treaty's rules on competition.
>
> Taking this one step further: if Zoja sells 10% of its production in the EEC and 90% outside, does this bring the whole of Zoja's world-wide trade under the EEC rules on competition? We submit that it does not, and that CSC's offer to Zoja to supply quantities based on Zoja's expected sales in the EEC was entirely in line with the Treaty's rules on competition.
>
> The Commission did not agree. The Commission claims that the Applicants had to respect Zoja's identity as a world-wide trader. This we contest, as we find this thesis irreconcilable with the text of the Treaty's rules on competition, including the basic principle laid down in Article 3(f).

The Court, referring expressly to Art. 85 as well as to Art. 86, said that the condition about the effect on trade between Member States

158. The content and wording of these arguments, although not fully reported with the judgment, were made available to us by the Legal Service of the Commission in its Brussels office.

should be applied, in this case, in the light of Art. 3(f) of the Treaty and Art. 2:

> The Community authorities must therefore consider all the consequences of the conduct complained of for the competitive structure on the Common Market without distinguishing between production intended for sale within the market and that intended for export. When an undertaking in a dominant position within the Common Market abuses its position in such a way that a competitor in the Common Market is likely to be eliminated, it does not matter whether the conduct relates to the latter's exports or its trade within the Common Market, once it has been established that this elimination will have repercussions on the competitive structure within the Common Market. 159

It is noteworthy that the Commission also referred to patent situation in Korea and Japan, in its submissions to the Court, in order to give indication of the value of Zoja's patents and hence of its competitive strength.[160]

Referring in particular to the applicants' argument that the Commission's order should have been quantitatively related to Zoja's trade between Member States and not with third countries the Court ruled:

> .....it cannot be inferred from the expression "in so far as it may affect trade between Member States" that only the effects of a possible infringement on trade within the Community must be taken into account when it is a question of defining the infringement and its consequences. Moreover, the rather limited measure that the applicants suggested would have resulted in the production and sales outlets of Zoja being controlled by CSC-Istituto and in Zoja being in a position where its cost price would have been affected to such an extent that its production of ethambutol would have been in danger of being unmarketable. In these circumstances the Commission could well consider that the maintenance of an effective competitive structure necessitated the measures in question. 161

3-68. In the FRUBO Case (see 3-55) the applicants contended before the Court that the fact that an agreement makes different provisions for

---

159. Commercial Solvents Case 252, para. 33. According to Korah this all embracing statement almost read the interstate trade condition out of the competition rules (see supra note 72, at sec. 212 in p.16).

160. Commercial Solvents Case, submissions and arguments of the parties, 239.

161. Ibid. at 256, para. 48.

imports according to whether they have been brought in from a third country or from another Member State does not justify the conclusion that trade between Member States is affected.[162]. The Commission argued that the agreement makes it difficult for, e.g. French importers of Spanish oranges to supply direct to Dutch wholesalers and for the latter to act as direct importers; these restrictions certainly affect trade between Member States. It stated that such an effect is an example of the indirect prejudice which was the subject of the judgment of the Court in the Commercial Solvents Case. See 3-67. There is no relevance, according to the Commission, in a reference to the general scheme of the Treaty as suggested by the applicants to object the application of Art. 85; on the contrary, by virtue of Arts. 9(2) and 10 of the Treaty, free circulation also applies to products coming from third countries if import formalities have been complied with. Finally the fact that vertical integration has been made difficult for potential competitors undoubtedly reduces their competitiveness.[163] In the Commission's view trade between Member States is affected by the attempt to distort the course normally followed by direct imports and thus to ensure that they are not proceeded with.[164] The Court rejected the appeal of the applicants.

3-69. A further example in the line of cases which reflect a stricter Community approach in relation to agreements concerning trade with third countries is the Commission's attack in the course of an issue submitted to the Court for a preliminary ruling on world-wide market sharing agreements. At the Commission's invitation the Court

---

162. FRUBO Case, submissions and arguments of the parties, 574.
163. Ibid. at p.575.
164, Ibid.

recognized in its judgment in the EMI/CBS Cases that:

> .....a restrictive agreement between traders within the common market and competitors in third countries that would bring about an isolation of the common market as a whole which, in the territory of the Community, would reduce the supply of products originating in third countries and similar to those protected by a mark within the Community, might be of such a nature as to affect adversely the conditions of competition within the common market. 165

3-70. As to the Commission's approach regarding export cartels, a remark in the First Report on Competition Policy indicated a readiness to examine rather strictly export cartels even if restricted to the national market and to markets outside the Common Market. See 3-29. The so-called "pure export cartels" frequently also restrain domestic competition, even if there is an explicit clause in the cartel contract that no internal effects are intended. The Commission's remark, thus, falls in line with the guidance on this point given by the OECD Committee of Experts on Restrictive Business Practices:

> It is easy to conceive that the efforts to achieve a common export policy and the exchange of information on prices, costs, production lines, capacities, sales policies, etc., may influence the domestic competitive conduct of the participating firms. Thus, the 'side effect' of most pure export cartels may be a restraint of domestic competition mainly through conscious parallelism. This is all the more likely when it is realised that many export agreements probably impose a cost on the parties concerned in the form of exports foregone. Not only will the price rigidity imposed by an export agreement tend to prevent member firms from meeting foreign competition but the agreed price level itself will tend to reflect some average of the costs of all members rather than those of the most efficient members. If the more efficient firms incur losses in export markets the assumption must be made that they obtain compensating advantages on the domestic market by means of the restraints of competition. 166

---

165. EMI/CBS 906, at para. 25. See also elaboration on this point in the Cases in Hay and Oldekop "EMI/CBS and the Rest of the World; Trade Mark Rights and the European Communities" 25 A.J.C.L. 150-151 (1977).

166. OECD, Committee of Experts on Restricitive Business Practices Export Cartels, sec. 140 (1974).

(3) Interpretation of the Competition Rules as if Having a Qualified "Foreign Trade" Clause

3-71. By adopting a wide concept of "effect" on trade between Member States the Commission has significantly removed part of the important qualification that the Community competition rules do not contain a "foreign trade" clause. Nevertheless, each case must be determined according to its circumstances and in line with the purpose of the competition rules. For example, the interplay of supply and demand within the Common Market are affected, but not where an enterprise restricted in competition wholly outside the Common Market by an agreement has its seat within the scope of application of the competition rules.[167] However, if the agreement, for example, prevents enterprises in non-Member States from becoming suppliers or competitors within the Common Market it may fall under Art. 85(1)[168].

3-72. The view that arrangements previously discussed, which are mainly intended to affect Community trade with foreign countries, do not affect trade between Member States cannot, on the face of it, be accepted. The better construction is that practices that have an appreciable effect on the competitive position of enterprises within the Common Market (especially if located in different Member States) will ordinarily also be likely to affect inter-state trade, for they will affect the competitive strength of these enterprises in markets within the Common Market. See 3-9 and 3-67.

Smit and Herzog consider proper the following analysis of agreements which seem to affect only trade between Community and third

167. See Deringer, supra note 1, at sec. 127 (but see different opinions cited thereof in n.99).

168. Ibid. at sec. 551.

countries:

> .....agreements that relate in terms only to commerce between one or more Member States and a foreign country and that have an appreciable effect on the Community's foreign commerce ordinarily also affect inter-state commerce. For agreements of this nature are likely to affect inter-state commerce indirectly, and it is well established that an indirect effect on inter-state commerce meets the requirements of Article 85(1). 169.

3-73. The view defended above gives an expansive interpretation to the phrase "may affect trade between Member States". This interpretation is required fully to effectuate the policy of promoting competition within the Common Market in accordance with the Treaty provisions. Such an approach is the more defensible in our view because Art. 85(3) offers ample opportunity for awarding relief in cases in which anticompetitive practices in the foreign trade of the Community may be deemed in its interest. It is appropriate that this relief be granted under the flexible provision of Art. 85(3) rather than by an interpretation of Art. 85(1) that would amount to an inflexible blanket exemption. As Art. 85(1) should be construed to reach all arrangements that have the prescribed effect, frequently irrespective of whether the person placed at the anticompetitive disadvantage or the place of the conduct are within or outside the Community, it has to prohibit the type of anticompetitive arrangements under consideration.

(4) Comments on the Application of Article 86 in Situations with Foreign Elements

3-74. A few additional comments relating to the application of Art. 86 in situations with foreign elements are applicable here.

---

169. Smit and Herzog, supra note 13, at sec. 85.15 in p.3-110.

(1) It is worth noting that, as a general rule, in determining whether an enterprise has a dominant position in the Common Market, the Commission has often taken account not merely of the enterprise's market share in the Common Market, but of its entire economic power.[170]

(2) An abuse occurring within the Common Market, but vis-à-vis third countries, can be deemed to have an indirect effect on trade and competition within the Common Market. This interpretation may go too far, however, except where a third party is only a tool and the measures are actually aimed at a competitor or customer within the Common Market, e.g. indirect discrimination by differential treatment of foreign customers for the purpose of affecting a competitor located within the Common Market;

(3) We have already commented on the use which the Commission made of Art. 86 to prevent merger situations. See 3-62. From a teleological point of view it is generally admitted that a consistent policy against restraints of competition cannot meaningfully concern itself solely with cartels and abuses of dominant position. For it goes without saying that mergers and acquisitions may bring about anticompetitive effects which, because of their stability, are perhaps even more dangerous than a mere cartel arrangement or abuse of dominant position. The crucial question is, therefore, whether concentration itself may be checked within the framework of the Community competition policy. The proposed regulation for control of mergers, which is still under consideration by the Community institutions, may influence the future direction in which the Commission and the Court might proceed in that connection. The Draft Regulation of the EEC Council Concerning Control

---

170. See, for example United Brands Decision D49, at para. 83.

of Mergers Between Undertakings[171] provides that:

> Any transaction which has the direct or indirect effect of bringing about a concentration between undertakings or group of undertakings, at least one of which is established in the Common Market, whereby they acquire or enhance the power to hinder effective competition in the Common Market or in a substantial part thereof, is incompatible with the Common Market in so far as the concentration may affect trade between member states. 172

It has to be noted that the draft means that mergers of enterprises established in third countries (foreign mergers) are excluded regardless whether such mergers have effects on interstate trade, e.g. where the only two competing exporters of a product not manufactured in the Common Market merge. Although this is not in line with the practice regarding Arts. 85 and 86 Markert considers that the exclusion of foreign mergers in the draft is acceptable for practical reasons.[173] Community law should, however, remain applicable where a foreign merger involves enterprises established in the Common Market, for example if two foreign enterprises merge and one or both have subsidiaries in the Common Market.

(5) Is the Law Applicable to Foreigners Different?

3-75. The Commission and the Court have, in their practice, generally considered the same conduct as violating the competition rules whether or not the parties were Community enterprises. The principle of "full, uniform and non-discriminatory application of Community law on competition.....regardless of where the head office is situated" was

---

171. Draft Regulation (EEC) of the Council on the Control of Concentration Between Undertakings, O.J. 1973, C 92/1; [1973] C.M.L.R. D205. This draft was submitted to the Council by the Commission on 20 July 1973.

172. Ibid. at [1973] C.M.L.R. D207.

173. See Markert, "EEC Competition Policy Towards Mergers" in Competition Policy in the United Kingdom and the EEC 78 (Eds. K.D. George and C. Joll, 1975).

stated by the Commission at an early stage of the development of the law[174] and the same test of safeguarding the Common Market was always applied.[175] This practice answers the question whether Art. 85(1) takes on a special significance in the event of foreign elements. That question may follow from arguments that Art. 85(1) contains a "rule of reason".[176] However, not only is it uncertain what that "rule of reason" could mean, but its meaning, in any event, is unclear because of the exemptions of Art. 85(3). Although the Commission may be urged to be more lenient with foreigners in some circumstances than with Community enterprises (on the grounds of comity or because of reasons explained in Chapter VI) there is no statutory basis and no clear judicial precedent as yet for that effect.

However, it has been argued that the competition policy must be such as to enable Community enterprises to combine for the purpose of competition on foreign markets or to compete with foreign giants in their own market.[177] Such a defensive aspect of the competition policy exists and can be observed, in our view, in decisions enabling cooperation between medium-sized enterprises for effective competition on the world market. With regard to the first Transocean Marine Paint Association Decision the Commission explained that it approved of the purpose of the agreement "to tap a world-wide market and to compete from a stronger position with the big international marine paint manufacturing group".[178] Similar observations were made with regard to the French Producers of Fine Papers Decision[179] and the Prym-Beka Decision.[180]

174. See Third Report on Competition Policy, point 16.
175. Cf. Diets, supra note 6, at 755.
176. See for example Joliet, R. The Rule of Reason in Antitrust Law: American, German and Common Market Laws in Comparative Perspective (1967).
177. See H. Hermann and C. Jones, Fair Trading in Europe 60-61 (1977).
178. First General Report on the Activities of the Communities (Feb. 1968), point 48. See also explanations in Third Report on Competition Policy, points 61-63.
179. Commission Decision published in O.J. 1972, L182/24. See Second Report on Competition Policy, point 37.
180. Prym/Beka [1973] C.M.L.R. D250. See Third Report on Competition Policy point 60.

3. THE EXTENSION OF THE TERRITORIAL SCOPE OF THE COMPETITION POLICY IN AGREEMENTS BETWEEN THE EEC AND THIRD COUNTRIES

A. The Free Trade Area Agreements

(1) Structure and Principles of the Agreements

3-76. Competition clauses appear in the Community treaties with Austria,[181] Sweden,[182] Switzerland,[183] Portugal,[184] Iceland,[185] Norway,[186] and Finland,[187] which set up free trade areas between the Community and those countries. The text of the provision concerning restrictive business practices is identical in all of those agreements; these practices are treated together with the subject of public aid, which appears as a sub-article in the special clause.

The competition clause provides:

> The following are incompatible with the proper functioning of the agreement in so far as they may affect trade between the Community and [the specific country].
> (i) all agreements between undertakings, decisions by associations of undertakings, concerted practices between undertakings which have as their object or effect the prevention, restriction or distortion of competition as regards the production of or trade in goods;
> (ii) abuse by one or more undertakings of a dominant position in the territories of the contracting parties as a whole or in substantial part thereof.....
>
> Should a contracting party consider that a given practice is incompatible with this article it may take appropriate measures, under the conditions and in accordance with the procedure laid down in article.....

---

181. Treaty of 22nd July, 1972, Arts. 23, 27. See also Art. 20.
182. Treaty of 22nd July, 1972, Arts. 23, 27. See also Art. 20.
183. Treaty of 22nd July, 1972, Arts, 23, 27. See also Art. 20.
184. Treaty of 22nd July, 1972, Arts. 26, 30. See also Art. 23.
185. Treaty of 22nd July, 1972, Arts. 24, 28. See also Art. 21.
186. Treaty of 14th May, 1973, Arts. 23, 27. See also Art. 20.
187. Treaty of 5th October, 1973, Arts. 23, 27. See also Art. 20.

3-77. Some of the existing EEC agreements with less developed countries for the establishment of free trade areas contain the same provisions as those which are applied with the developed countries of EFTA. Examples of such less developed countries are Portugal[188] and Israel.[189]

3-78. The competition clauses are, as to substance, comparable with those on competition in the EEC Treaty. Accordingly, the Commission has stated that it would assess restrictive or improper practices incompatible with the competition rules of the free-trade agreements (hereinafter "FTA") by referring to the criteria deriving from the application of Arts. 85, 86, 90 and 92 of the EEC Treaty.[190]

The significant differences in wording between Arts. 85 and 86 of the Treaty and the relevant provisions in the FTA are the following: (1) the FTA contain the same principles without the elaboration of provisions for exemption contained in Art. 85(3); (2) Arts. 85 and 86 of the Treaty both provide that the practices in question "shall be prohibited as incompatible with the Common Market", whereas the provisions of the FTA provide that the practices "are incompatible with the proper functioning of the agreement"; (3) the FTA's provisions are restricted to the trade in goods but cover production as well, whereas Art. 85(1) extends to services but relates only to trade and not directly to production; (4) Art. 85(1) requires prevention etc. of competition within the Common Market, whereas the FTA's provisions refer only to prevention etc. of competition.

---

188. Treaty of 22nd July, 1972, Art. 26. See also Art. 30.

189. Treaty of 11th May, 1975, Art. 12. See also Art. 16.

190. It is not clear from the text if the free trade agreements also refer to public enterprises, since they are not mentioned specifically as in the Treaty of Rome (Art. 90), or the Stockholm Convention which established the ERTA (Art. 14(2)).

3-79. An important feature which the EEC Treaty and the FTA have in common is that in both there is no reference to the "nationality" of the enterprises. It is apparent from the text of the FTA that national, regional or international cartels whose object or effect are in third countries outside the States party to the agreements, are permitted. Nevertheless, according to the Commission's approach which has been illustrated in the previous section, it is likely that practices which have an effect on the trade between the parties to the agreements may also be carried out in countries other than those States.[191]

(2) Implementation Arrangements

3-80. The procedure following an infringement of the competition clauses in the FTA is the following:

(1) either Contracting Party may refer the matter to the Joint Committee;

(2) the Contracting Parties shall provide the Joint Committee with all relevant information and shall give it the assistance it requires in examining the case and when the Joint Committee recommends the elimination of the practice objected to.

If the other Contracting Party fails to put an end to such a practice within three months from the date when the matter was referred to the Joint Committee, the Contracting Party concerned may adopt as a safeguard any measures it may consider necessary to deal with the serious difficulties resulting from that practice. In particular, it may withdraw tariff concessions. It should be mentioned

191. Cf. Rom "Restrictive Business Practices in EEC Agreements With Less Developed Countries " 12 J.W.T.L. 41 (1978).

here that the pertinent provision also stipulates that in the selection of measures priority must be given to those which least disturb the functioning of the agreement. The Joint Committee should be immediately notified of the safeguard measures which would subsequently be subjected to periodical consultations.

3-81. Neither the Community nor the other parties to the agreements concerned have as yet taken any internal regulatory measures to enforce sanctions on infringements of the competition clauses,[192] and it is doubtful whether such infringements are actually forbidden or void in the respective laws. See 3-82 and 3-83. It could well be that it is politically undesirable to extend the Community's powers in respect of the practices of Community enterprises in trade with third countries through regulation, and it is also not clear what measures could be decided in that respect by the Council. Would Art. 110 or Art. 155(1) of the Treaty really be adequate for that purpose? There is no example so far of the Commission or the Council following this course. Some writers argue that it is very difficult to find any proper legal basis for such acts as required here without relying on the direct effect of the FTA. See 3-82. The Commission interprets the procedure following an infringement, as provided for in the FTA, to mean that it will be for the Contracting Party involved to take, autonomously, appropriate measures to ensure termination of the infringement. Each Contracting Party must, therefore, ensure that it is in a position to bring about the elimination of incompatible practices, for it cannot invoke the lack of proper powers in order to oppose the implementation of the safeguard clauses.[193] It is because

192. Information provided to the writer by the Commission, updated to January 1980.

193. See Second Report on Competition Policy, point. 6.

of this reason, i.e. that the competition clauses must be applied by each party on the basis of its own law, that the Commission declared that it will assess any practices on criteria arising from the respective provisions of the Treaty.

(3) The Legal Consequences of the Competition Clauses

(a) Are the Competition Clauses Directly Applicable?

3-82. The legal status of the competition clauses in the FTA have been the subject of a lively debate.

It has already been indicated above that the concept prevailing at the Legal Service of the Commission is that the FTA bind only the parties to the FTA and not the individual enterprises, and consequently the only implementing measures the Community can take are those provided for by the FTA.[194]

Bellamy, Child and Morris state that while there is no direct authority to that effect, the relevant provisions of these agreements may well be "directly applicable" within the Member States, i.e. give rise to individual rights and duties enforceable in national courts.[195] If this is correct, agreements which affect trade between the Community and these countries and which restrict competition as regards production

---

194. This was confirmed in a private interview with Mr. J. Temple-Lang, Legal Advisor to the EEC Commission, Brussels, 2nd October, 1979.

195. Bellamy, Child and Morris, supra note 1, at sec. 2-50. The authors refer to the following cases: Case 181/73, Haegeman Sprl v. Belgium [1974] E.C.R. 449; Case 87/75 Bresciani v. Administrazione Italiana Delle Finanze [1976] E.C.R. 129; Case 51/75, EMI/CBS [1976] E.C.R. 847, paras. 18-19.

of or trade in goods, may be unenforceable in national courts. The authors, therefore, reach a practical conclusion that the safest course is to regard these countries as part of the Community for the purpose of Arts. 85 and 86.

The argument of direct applicability has been advanced in a series of articles by March Hunnings who, in an elaborate and interesting analysis, tries to indicate that there would seem to be a clear tendency of the Court to regard international treaties to which the Community is a party as in principle directly effective in international law, depending on the specific nature of the treaty in question.[196] In other words, the argument is that Community law relationship with international law is monist and, therefore, the FTA are self-executing, and some specific provisions,including the competition clauses, have a force which is very similar to that of their equivalents in the EEC Treaty. In consequence of this, March Hunnings submits that in various cases it would be open to an affected private person to bring or defend proceedings, before the local courts within the Community or before the Commission, directly on the basis of the applicable provisions of the FTA.[197]

In a detailed reply to March Hunning's submission Waelbroeck agrees that the FTA are capable of producing domestic effects and that a number of their provisions are directly applicable within the Community legal order and the legal order of the Member States. However, he does not share the opinion that the competition clauses in the FTA are directly applicable.[198]

---

196. See March Hunnings "Enforceability of the EEC-EFTA Free Trade Agreements" 2 Eur. L. Rev. 173-179 (1977).

197. Ibid. at 188.

198. Waelbroeck "Enforceability of the EEC-EFTA Free Trade Agreements: A Reply" 3 Eur. L. Rev. 27-31 (1978). There was also a rejoinder by March Hunnings in 3 Eur. L. Rev. 287 (1978).

3-83. The Supreme Court of Switzerland had an opportunity to rule on the question whether Art. 23 of the EEC-Switzerland Free Trade Agreement is self-executing, in a Swiss case which is described later (see the Adams Case in 3-86).[199] It ruled that the agreement in question is "purely a trade treaty", and Art. 23:

> .....does not go on to create any right of action for private persons; it merely lays down that practices are incompatible with the proper functioning of the Agreement, but it does not prohibit them or designate them as unlawful nor, in contrast to Article 85 and 86 of the EEC Treaty, does it declare them void or lay down sanctions; Article 23 merely authorises the contracting parties to take suitable measures in accordance with the conditions and procedures laid down in Article 27..... If Article 23 does not constitute a prohibition it cannot be contravened. 200

It would go beyond the scope of the study to explore the various legal agruments as to whether or not the competition clauses in the FTA are directly applicable, particularly since the Commission has already formed its view on this point.

(b) The Utility of the Competition Clauses in View of the Weakness of the Implementation Arrangements and the Absence of National Legislation to that Effect

3-84. The competition clause in the FTA is more flexible and has less coercive power than those of the EEC Treaty. This is evident from several considerations mentioned by Rom: (1) the provision only refers to the trade in goods (and not services); (2) the complaint is handled through the governments of the Contracting Parties without direct

199. The Swiss Supreme Court Proceedings were reported in [1978] 3 C.M.L.R. 480.

200. See ibid. at 486, para 10. Another attempt to argue that the competition clauses in the FTA (in this case the EEC-Sweden Agreement) are self-executing was made in Sweden, but the case was later settled between the parties and the proceeding before the civil courts and before the Antitrust Commissioner have been withdrawn (see Hans Hauenschild Chemische Fabrik KB v. AB Kemiska Byggnadsprodukter [1976] 1 C.M.L.R. D9).

contact between the enterprises and a higher authority; (3) the authority of the Joint Committee is weak and conditioned by the cooperation of all member countries in the Committee; (4) the possibilities of sanctions seem to be rather limited as much depends on the authority of the Joint Committee and on the ability and/or desire of the concerted Member State to take measures regarding its own enterprises (which depends, among other factors, on the degree that internal legislation allows for such measures); (5) the threat of the injured party to take counter measures as the last resort may be the determining factor; (6) there exist no external institutions to examine the complaint and give a reasoned opinion; (7) even if a ruling against a restrictive practice has been given, it does not make the agreement void, neither from its inception nor from the time of the ruling; the agreement continues to be valid in spite of possible negative decisions of the Joint Committee.[201]

3-85. In the associations for the establishment of free trade areas between the EEC and less-developed countries the competition clauses, even though identical to those in the agreements with EFTA countries, provide less meaningful protection than the latter. It may be argued that in the agreements between the EEC and EFTA countries the interests of all sides to the agreement are more balanced and that within the countries different pressure groups may force acceptable solutions for fear of counter measures. The possibility of taking appropriate measures within the Joint Committee against restrictive practices which are harmful only to the less-developed countries is, therefore, less certain.[202] Not only has a threat of sanctions by the

201. Rom, _supra_ note 191, at 42-43.
202. Cf. _ibid._ at 48.

Community much greater weight than similar threats by the less-developed countries but in many cases the latter's dependence on foreign markets as potential sources of capital investments, transfer of technology and know-how, etc., is likely to prevent any resistance in that respect. In fact some restrictive practices are allowed by less-developed countries' legislations and justifiably from their point of view. This is of course due to the differences in the level of economic development of those countries. See discussion in 6-39.

3-86. In the absence of efficient implementation procedures for the competition clauses in the FTA the utility of these provisions must be doubted.

The Commission and Switzerland were on a collision course in respect of the agreement with that country in connection with evidence necessary for the Hoffmann-La Roche Case. A former employee of Hoffmann-La Roche, Stanley Adams, was arrested by the Swiss authorities on suspicion of industrial espionage, because he passed information on the vitamin sector to the Commission. He was then released on bail paid by the Commission and later sentenced, in his absence, to one year's suspended imprisonment and banned from entering Switzerland for five years. An appeal was dismissed. Nevertheless, the Commission stated that it feels entitled, as in this case, to use any information it receives concerning alleged infringements once it is satisfied that the information is well-founded. See 4-53.

In the present context this incident is interesting as the agreement in question seemed to have produced an undertaking which was clearly in conflict with the domestic law of Switzerland.[203] After

203. See European Parliament Debates, January 12, 1977, at pp.109 and 110.

the arrest of Mr. Adams, but before his trial, the Community delegation raised that question in the EEC-Switzerland Joint Committee.[204] As a result a procedure has been laid down for the exchange of information between the Commission's departments and the Swiss mission, which the Commission considers should ensure that there will be no repetition of similar incidents. The mutual obligation of the parties to assist each other does not seem to go so far as to require alteration of laws on secrecy.[205]

March Hunnings remarks that the Commission did not, however, claim in the Adams affair that its investigations were aimed at implementing the FTA:

> .....it was merely using the FTA as a politico-legal argument that the Swiss prosecuting authorities should refrain from enforcing a human rights provision (in so far as industrial espionage is a branch of the law of privacy as opposed to industrial property) to enable it (the Commission) to take action under purely domestic law (Art. 86 EEC) which had nothing to do with Switzerland except for the residence of the firm. It is indeed a typical illustration of the well-known phenomenon in international treaty relations in which the application of a treaty by one of the High Contracting Parties in relation to another remains on a fairly confidential, low key, quiet diplomatic level and only breaks out into public demands for enforcement if there are serious political issues involved. Consequently, in the absence of internal legislative implementation, a treaty, such as the Free Trade Agreement could, apart from the tariff provisions, be regarded as merely a series of pious wishes with no legal consequences of political importance. [206]

---

204. Ibid. at p.111 per Vice-President Haferkamp. See also reply to W.Q. 54/75, O.J. 1975, C161/15.

205. However, we have been informed that following a bill which was introduced to the Swiss Parliament on 25th September, 1978, some changes in the rules regarding secrecy are now proposed in order to make the law compatible with the Free Trade Agreement concerned. See Rapport Concernant le Project de Revision de la Loi sur les Cartels of 20.12.78 (points 14.33.4, at pp.53-55).

206. March Hunnings, supra note 196, at 171. March Hunnings further remarks (in n.24) that there is no mention of the Free Trade Agreement in the Commission decision or even that Hoffmann-La Roche was situated in a country having a Free Trade Agreement with the EEC. In particular the Commission did not find that there was any effect on "trade between the Community and Switzerland".

(c) The Implications of the Competition Clauses in the Free-Trade Agreements for the Application of the Community Competition Rules

3-87. As for the consequences which the FTA have had for the application of Arts. 85 and 86 of the Treaty, it has been observed by the Commission that it is now systematically requiring enterprises to delete from their marketing agreements restrictions or prohibitions on exports to the FTA's countries.[207] Such was the case in the SABA Decision (see 3-34) which dealt with an agreement by which SABA's sole distributors and specialist retailers were obliged by that firm not to export SABA products to countries outside the Common Market nor to import the same from outside the Common Market. SABA gave the Commission an undertaking to lift these prohibitions once the relevant products were no longer subject to customs duties in trade between the Community and EFTA countries, as was later the case.[208]

In the Junghans Decision (see 3-35), a case relating to the wholesale and retail distribution of a German manufacturer of clocks and watches, the Commission held that a prohibition preventing that manufacturer's dealers from exporting out of the Common Market "does not at present have any appreciable effect on competition within the meaning of Article 85(1).....it has the object of restricting competition in non-Member Countries". However, the decision continued:

> .....while at present the Commission sees no reason to object to this export prohibition, this will not necessarily be the case after 1 July 1977 as regards those States with which the EEC has a free trade agreement. After that date there will be no customs duties on trade between the Community and the countries in question. 209

---

207. See Sixth Report on Competition Policy, point 147.

208. See the SABA Decision at para. 11; see also para. 35.

209. Junghans Decision, at para. 24.

3-88. While there are no sanctions which the Commission can impose for breach of the FTA's provisions as such, an agreement affecting trade between the Community and those countries and restricting competition in the relevant respect may in many cases fall within Art. 85(1). Cf. 3-71 to 3-73. Furthermore, all the FTA (and other commercial agreements with third countries mentioned in 3-77) contain provisions corresponding to the rules on the free movement of goods in the EEC Treaty, in particular Art. 36.[210] How far such treaty provisions themselves affect the enforceability of agreements which restrict imports and exports between the Community and the relevant countries is still an open question, but they may very well prevent industrial property rights being exercised to prevent the importation of goods into the Common Market originating in a country which is party to a relevant Community treaty.[211]

Where appropriate the competition rules of the Treaty and the corresponding clauses in the FTA can be applied together. For example, when the Commission opened an inquiry into the conduct and position of the Hoffmann-La Roche pharmaceutical group, whose head office is in Switzerland, in connection with the possible abuse of its dominant position in the vitamin sector, it initiated two concurrent, but quite separate procedures. One was under Reg. 17 and one under the agreement with Switzerland in respect of repercussions on trade between the Community and Switzerland. As already has been mentioned the Community delegation referred the matter to the joint EEC/Switzerland Committee under the procedure laid down in Art. 27 of the agreement.[212]

---

210. See list of examples in Bellamy, Child and Morris, <u>supra</u> note 1, at sec. 2-50 in n.90.
211. <u>Ibid.</u> at sec. 9-30.
212. See Commission reply to W.Q. 152/75, O.J. 1975, C 209/15.

B. Partial Free Trade Agreements, Association Agreements and Cooperation Agreements

3-89. Although in agreements for partial free trade areas or for the creation of custom unions through association the Community ignored completely the specific subject of restrictive business practices (e.g. the interim agreement towards the association with Cyprus[213] and Malta[214] or the agreements with Tunisia,[215] Algeria[216] and Morocco[217]), some agreements still include an arrangement for that purpose. For instance Art. 51 of the Association Agreement with Greece[218] - now a potential Member State - stipulates that the contracting parties recognize that the principles established by Arts. 85, 86, 90 and 92 of the EEC Treaty must be applied in the relations of the association. Art. 52 stipulates that, within two years of the entry into force of this agreement, the association's Council will determine the conditions and details of the principles mentioned in Art. 51. In the Association Agreement with Turkey the relevant provision is less clear. Art. 16 of the original Turkish Association Agreement[219] speaks of the recognition, in principle, by the Contracting Parties that Part III Title I of the Treaty of Rome (which contains the competition rules) should be applied within the Association Agreement. However, there are no specific instructions for the implementation of Art. 16, since the interim agreement in the initial stage only requires Turkey to strengthen her economy. These types of provisions raise the question of what will be the specific content of the provisions when they are agreed upon.[220]

213. Treaty of 19th December, 1972, with Cyprus.
214. Treaty of 5th December, 1970, with Malta.
215. Interim Agreement with Tunisia of 25th April, 1976.
216. Interim Agreement with Algeria of 26th April, 1976.
217. Interim Agreement with Morocco of 27th April, 1976.
218. Treaty of 9th July, 1961 with Greece.
219. Treaty of 12th September, 1963 with Turkey.
220. We have no knowledge of specific provisions worked out in line with the framework of those clauses in the treaties.

3-90. But even the agreements which do not have specific provision to the same effect include a general provision which may perhaps be invoked in cases of serious restraints of competition. Thus the agreements with Malta and Cyprus stipulate in Art. 3(3) Title I that "the contracting parties shall take all appropriate measures, whether general or particular, to ensure fulfillment of the obligations arising out of the agreement. They shall refrain from any measure likely to jeopardize the achievements of the aims of the agreement". An identical provision appears in Arts. 35, 36 and 37 of the agreements with Algeria, Tunisia and Morocco. These general provisions do not refer to a specific obligation of one of the parties to prevent restrictive business practices. Because of this, and on the ground that there are marked differences in the aims of the agreements, various interpretations are possible. Rom, elaborating on some possible explanations in that respect reaches the following conclusion:

> If one notices that the general provision also appears in the association agreements, and in the agreements for the establishment of industrial free trade areas with less developed countries in addition to the specific provision, one must perhaps see the exclusion of the specific reference to restrictive business practices. Thus, it becomes more reasonable to assume that the general provision does not cover the subject of restrictive business practices. 221

3-91. Another example of a general competition clause appears in the Agreement for Economic and Commercial Cooperation with Canada.[222] Article II(2) and (3) provides:

> 2. The Contracting Parties shall use their best endeavours to discourage, in conformity with their legislation, restrictions of competition by enterprises of their respective industries, including pricing practices distorting competition.
> 3. The Contracting Parties agree, upon request, to consult and review matters in the Joint Cooperation Committee referred to in Article IV.

221. Rom, supra note 191, at 49.

222. See Agreement for Economic and Commercial Cooperation with Canada of July, 1976.

In view of what has been said above, the limited practical significance of such a clause is obvious. Informal consulations with other third countries have now been established by the Commission on a regular basis. See 6-46.

CHAPTER IV

The Enforcement Jurisdiction of European Economic Community in respect of Non-Community Enterprises and Conduct Abroad

INTRODUCTION

4-1. In the preliminary observations to this study we have noted that a particular aspect of the general legal competence of State jurisdiction under international law is concerned with enforcement jurisdiction. See 1-16. The rule in that respect is that even when a State has jurisdiction to prescribe rules, such jurisdiction does not give it the right to engage in extraterritorial enforcement of its rules in the territory of another State.[1] Extraterritorial enforcement is generally regarded as a violation of international law, except in certain limited situations (e.g. enforcement action on a vessel of one State in the territorial waters of another), unless the territorial State consents.[2] The limits on enforcement jurisdiction are concerned both with the exercise of physical force in the territory of another State and with the peaceful performance of acts of authority therein, e.g. whether police investigations and search may be mounted, orders for production of documents may be exercised, summons may be served, orders may compel an action abroad and persons may be arrested in the territory of another State.

It is apparent that the reach, purpose and content of the Community enforcement measures are of major importance to any evaluation of

---

1. See Jennings "General Course on Principles of International Law" 121 Recueil (1967-II) p.522; Mann, the Doctrine of Jurisdiction in International Law" 111 Recueil (1964-I) p.13.

2. See Oppenheim, International Law, vol. 1, 327-328 (8th ed., Lautherpacht, 1963): Research in International Law Under the Auspices of the Harvard Law School, Jurisdiction With Respect to Crime 29 Am. J. Int. L. Supp. 435 et seq (1935). The scope of the concept of State's consent or the question whether it has been granted by implication may leave room for controversy.

substantive extraterritoriality. On the one hand, these elements may give practical breadth to broad substantive rules, while on the other hand, doubts about the ability of the authorities to issue orders under threat of penalties may seriously limit otherwise fairly far-reaching substantive provisions. It is, therefore, important to examine how far enforcement jurisdiction has been extended, and whether it will prove to be less than, or co-extensive with, the Community jurisdiction on the subject-matter (legislative and judicial jurisdiction).[3]

In the present chapter we shall only examine the existing practice of the Commission and the Court, including the guidelines which they are likely to follow in the course of future developments due to their notions of justice and not because of the rules which they ought to follow as superior principles of international law. Once we have determined by what rules and limitations the Commission and the Court consider themselves bound, we will be able to examine that practice against the background of international law (in Chapter VI).

---

3. These aspects of "jurisdiction" have been explained in 1-16.

1. THE REQUIREMENTS OF PERSONAL JURISDICTION

GENERAL

4-2. In the present account the term "jurisdiction", which is susceptible of several different meanings, is used in the sense that a court has power to hear and determine an issue upon which its decision is sought.[4] This aspect of "jurisdiction" is distinct from other aspects of the term in that it relates to the jurisdiction over the subject of the law enforcement. In all legal systems there are requirements for a form of proceeding which must be followed in a court for the purpose of giving compulsory effect to its jurisdiction; this is called "process". For example, the process of the Supreme Court of Judicature in England consists of writs, originating summonses, motions and petitions. As the requirements for personal jurisdiction must be distinguished from the requirements for subject-matter jurisdiction, the Community, in our view, ought to have practical, clear and reasonable rules for the service of process in the context of NCES.[5]

A. The Community Rules of Service of Process in Competition Matters

(1) The Commission's Procedure

4-3. Community Law does not distinguish between service to a Community enterprise and to a NCE. When a case comes to the Commission's notice

4. See Cheshire's Private International Law 77 (9th ed.,North, 1974).,

5. In accordance with the wide definition of the term "enterprise" in Arts. 85 and 86 (see 1-29) the question of service of process holds true for natural persons and legal entities alike.

it holds an informal investigation, then commences proceedings against the enterprise involved, while continuing further investigations until the drafting of the indictment.[6] The decision to commence procedures against an enterprise is in practice communicated to the enterprise involved (and to the pertinent national cartel authorities).[7] Merely acknowledging receipt of a notification does not commence the procedures.[8]

A subsequent step taken by the Commission is the communication of a notice to "inform undertakings and association of undertakings in writing of the objections raised against them" (Art. 2(1) of Regulation 99/63 [hereinafter Reg. 99]; see also Art. 19 of Reg. 17). The same article (of Reg. 99) permits publication in the Official Journal "if from the circumstances of the case this appears appropriate.....", however, a fine or periodic penalty payment may be imposed on the enterprise only if the objections were notified in the manner provided for in para. (1)(Art. 2(2)). Without prejudice to the method of notifying the parties of the objections, in the Official Journal, Art. 10 (of Reg. 99) provides that information and summonses from the Commission "shall be sent to the addressees by registered letter with acknowledgement of receipt, or shall be delivered by hand against receipt".

The enterprise concerned replies to the Notice of Objections in writing and an oral hearing usually follows.[9] After the hearing, and

---

6. For detailed discussions of the Commission's procedure in antitrust matters see the following articles: Graupner "Commission Decision-Making on Competition Questions "10 C.M.L.Rev. 291 (1973); Temple-Lang "The Procedure of the Commission in Competition Cases" 14 C.M.L.Rev. 155 (1977).

7. On commencement of the Commission's procedure the national cartel authorities lose jurisdiction over the alleged Treaty infringement; see case 127/73 Belgische Radio en Televisie (BRT) and Société Belge des Auteurs Compositeurs et Éditeurs v. SV SABAM and NV Fonior [1974] E.C.R. 51.

8. See Case 48/72, Brasserie de Haecht S.A. v. Wilkin (No.2)[1973]E.C.R.77.

9. The Commission is obliged to hold an oral hearing if it proposes to impose a fine or periodic penalty payment (Art. 7(1) or Reg.99/63).

consultations with the Advisory Committee, the Commission considers and formulates the final decision. Art. 191 of the Treaty (second para.) states that the decisions shall be notified "to those to whom they are addressed", but does not lay down any particular form in which service of a decision is to be effected. Nor does Art. 3 of Reg. 17 which concerns decisions terminating infringements; it only states that a decision shall take effect upon such notification.

(2) The Court's Procedure

4-4. The Rules of Procedure of the Court of Justice lay down specific and detailed orders for service of process.[10] Competition cases will come before the Court only on appeal and it is, therefore, important that a written application of the applicant shall state, for the purpose of the proceedings, an address for service in the place where the Court has its seat; it shall also give the name of a person who is authorized and has expressed willingness to accept service (Art. 38(2)). If the application does not comply with the requirements of Art. 39(2) to (6) and the applicant fails to put it in order within the period prescribed for him, the Court shall, after hearing the Advocate-General, decide whether to reject the application on the ground of want of form (Art. 38(7)). The provisions of Art. 38(2) to (5) apply in a corresponding manner to the defence (Art. 40(1)).

Service of process, for proceedings before the Court, is maintained in accordance with an express provision in Art. 79(1) of the Rules of Procedure: "Where these rules require that a document be

10. See Rules of Procedure of the Court of Justice, adopted on 4th December, O.J. 1974, L 350/1 (hereinafter cited as "Rules of Procedure").

served on a person, the Registrar shall ensure that service is effected at that person's address for service either by the dispatch of a copy of the document, by registered post with a form for acknowledgment of receipt or by personal delivery of the copy against a receipt". Further detailed orders concerning service are contained in the Court's Instructions to the Registrar (Art. 3).[11]

B. Service of Process to Non-Community Enterprises In Community Case Law

(1) Practice in the Service of Notices of Objections

4-5. In the Dyestuffs Decision the Commission claimed not only substantive jurisdiction over the actions of the foreign parent companies, but also authority to impose penalties upon them, levying fines upon each. The Commission's final decision stated that the enterprises concerned were "heard", but it did not explain how compliance was made by the Commission with Article 2(1) of Reg. 99. From the material before the Court it appeared that registered letters, containing both the Commission's decision to commence proceedings and Notices of Objections, were sent to the producers of dyestuffs, established both inside and outside the Common Market, and to their subsidiaries and representatives established within the Common Market.[12]

4-6. I.C.I. received the registered letter, mentioned above, in its London office. The board of I.C.I. gave its answers to the Commission's objections before representatives of the Commission and of the Member

11. The instructions to the Registrar are annexed to the Rules of Procedure; see note 10.

12. See I.C.I. Case, Statement of the facts, 623.

States. According to a statement issued by I.C.I. to the press the company had provided the Commission with information and other assistance, in the course of the investigations, but had contended, from the outset, that the Commission had no jurisdiction over it.[13] From the material before the Court it seems that I.C.I. submitted arguments which concentrated mainly on the illegality of the service of the Commission's final decision and on the lack of substantive jurisdiction on the part of the Community.

The case with Geigy was, however, different. A registered letter was sent to its office in Switzerland, but the Swiss firm, acting on instructions from its national authorities returned the letter to the Commission and did not take part, as such, in the hearing.[14] On appeal Geigy argued that such an act of the Commission constituted an official measure of coercive character by a foreign authority; it emphasized that Swiss Law, the law of the place where the Notice was served, does not allow such a measure to be carried out on the territory of the Confederation, except where there is a reciprocal agreement or where the Swiss authorities have granted permission.[15] Geigy also observed that Switzerland, by refusing to sign the Hague Convention of Civil Procedure of 1905, had already made it clear that as regards civil and commercial matters it did not permit notifications to be served by post on its territory,and that the invariable practice of the Swiss Federal Authorities follows this approach.[16] Professor Huber, who

13. Financial Times, 2nd August, 1969.

14. See Geigy Case, submissions and arguments of the parties, 805; I.C.I. Case, opinion of the Advocate-General, 669. It has to be mentioned again that the issues of fact and of law and the grounds of judgment in the Geigy Case are similar to those in the Sandoz Case (concerning another Swiss company involved in the affair).

15. See Geigy Case, judgment, 823, at para. 10.

16. Ibid. submissions and arguments of the parties, 804-805.

submitted a legal opinion on behalf of the applicant, pointed out that international law permits a sovereign State to refuse acceptance of notification by post if it constitutes an expression of the sovereignty of a foreign State.[17] The applicant, therefore, argued that since the notice was effected in disregard both of Swiss Law and of the general principles of international law, it was void and of no effect.

4-7. The Commission objected to Geigy's arguments that the service of the Notice of Objections by post constituted the exercise of a coercive administrative power. It stressed that the applicant could have elected domicile in one of the Member States of the Community if it had wished the Commission to respect the provisions in force in Switzerland.[18]

The opinion of the Advocate-General in the Dyestuffs Cases followed the line which the Commission had advocated, and emphasized the absence of compelling sanctions connected with the Notice of Objections by spelling out its particular purposes:

> The Notice of Objections does not of itself have any coercive force; it is intended simply to enable the undertakings concerned, first to take cognizance of the basic facts held against them, and secondly to express their point of view during administrative proceedings which may lead to the imposition of a fine. 19

The Court seemed to agree with the latter remarks and its judgment on this point largely expanded the reasons:

> The purpose of the notice of objections for which Article 2(1) of Regulation No. 99 makes provisions is to enable those concerned to put forward their arguments in the context of proceedings initiated against them by a decision adopted by the Commission in the exercise of the powers which Articles 3 and 15 of Regulation No.17 confer on it.

---

17. Ibid.

18. Ibid. at 805.

19. I.C.I. Case 699.

> Since there is no convention on the matter between the Community and the Swiss Confederation, the question how this notice is to be served on interested parties established outside the territory of the Community depends on International practice and must be resolved with mutual regard to the spheres of jurisdiction both of the Community and of the third State concerned.
>
> It appears from the file that the authorities of the third State in question do not for the present envisage any practical possibility of service, considered by them to be valid under internal law, on the territory of the State.
>
> Therefore international law cannot be invoked in order to deny the Community the power to take the necessary steps to ensure the effectiveness of measures taken with a view to curtailing conduct adversely affecting competition which has arisen in the Common Market, even if the registered office of the undertaking responsible for such conduct is situated in a third country.
>
> Furthermore, the main purpose of the notice in question is to ensure that those concerned may exercise the rights which they enjoy under the Treaty and Community legislation.
>
> Therefore a notice served in accordance with Community rules cannot be considered to invalidate the subsequent administrative procedure if it must be served in a third country, once it is established that by enabling the addressee to take cognizance of the objections held against him it has achieved its purpose. 20

4-8. In the Continental Can Case the non-Community parent company concerned argued before the Court that a Notice of Objections was addressed solely to its non-Community subsidiary (Europemballage) and served upon it (the subsidiary operated an office in the Common Market), but that the decision challenged specified Continental Can. The Court reiterated the broad guidelines from its judgment in the Dyestuffs Cases that the primary consideration in each case is whether the defendant in the course of the administrative proceedings had received sufficient opportunity for placing its position on record. In this case, the Court concluded, the Commission had not violated Continental's rights of the defence.[21]

---

20. Geigy Case 823-824, at para. 11.

21. Continental Can Case 239-240, at paras. 3-4.

4-9. In the Commercial Solvents Case Notices of Objections were sent by registered letters both to the American company concerned and to its subsidiary in the Common Market.[22] Such procedure preceded a decision by which both companies were found liable and were fined by the Commission. Both companies submitted oral comments to the Commission, but on appeal argued before the Court about alleged general infringements of the rules of procedure. However, there was no direct reference in the judgment to the point concerning the service of the Notices of Objections.

4-10. In subsequent decisions relating to NCES the Commission pursued a practice of sending the Notice of Objections by a registered letter directly to the companies suspected liable for the infringement wherever they were situated.[23] The principle which has developed in that respect is that as long as the notice reached the knowledge of the defendant this method of service appeared to agree with the requirement that the fundamental rights of the defence are observed, because "the Commission in its decision shall deal only with those objections raised against the undertakings in respect of which they have been given the opportunity of making known their views" (Art. 4 of Reg. 99). In the Dyestuffs Cases the Court similarly held that "to safeguard the rights of the defence in the administrative procedure, it is sufficient if the undertakings are informed of the essential matters of fact on which the objections are based ",[24] and in the Continental Can Case that "the statement of objections fulfils this requirement (of Art. 4 of Reg. 99-B.B) as it indicates the essential facts on which the Commission bases

22. See Commercial Solvents Case 245 at para. 2.

23.. It has been confirmed in a private communication with the Head of Inspection Division at the Directorate-General for Competition, Mr. A. Pappalardo, (in 2.10.79) that this is the current practice of the Commission.

24. I.C.I. Case 650, at para. 22.

its case in an admittedly concise but nevertheless clear form."[25]

(2) Practice in the Service of the Commission's Final Decisions

4-11. With regard to the service of its final decision in the Dyestuffs Cases the Commission avoided the practice of direct posting outside the Common Market which it had adopted with regard to the Notices of Objections and, instead, attempted to present service on the parent-companies through service on the subsidiaries established within the Common Market.

I.C.I. argued, on appeal, that its German subsidiary, to which the decision was notified by the Commission, had not been given any authority by the parent company to accept notification, and that under German law it was under no duty to bring the documents in question to the attention of the parent company.[26]

The Swiss applicant, Geigy, argued that the service of the contested decision was irregular in that it attempted to alter Art. 191 of the Treaty which provides notification to the addressee of the decision.[27]

4-12. The Commission in its defence, in the I.C.I. Case, gave a detailed explanation why it had selected this particular method for the service of its decision:

> Since the Ambassador of the Government of the U.K. refused to convey the decision through the normal diplomatic channels to the British parent company, the Commission, taking the view that

25. Continental Can Case 240, at para. 5.
26. I.C.I. Case 635.
27. Geigy Case 825 at paras. 16 and 17.

for reasons of international relations it ought not to have recourse to service by post, concluded that notification through a subsidiary established within the Community was the means of notification best suited to the interest of the undertakings concerned. 28

Identical considerations were expressed in the Geigy Case, where the Commission revealed that the Swiss Ambassador refused to forward notification of the decision by a dimplomatic channel. "It was for reasons of courtesy in international relations , and taking into account in particular the position of the Swiss Government", as the Commission explained "that the contested decision was not sent by post."[29]

4-13. Whatever were the "reasons of international relations" which the Commission argued for not sending the decision through the post, the Dyestuffs Decision indicated that the Commission considered service correct when the decision entered the "internal sphere", of the addressee, even if the subsidiary is a separate legal personality.[30] In the circumstances of this decision service was based on the economic unit theory, which on appeal was argued by the Commission, with appropriate variations, as an alternative ground for its substantive jurisdiction. The application of the concept of "internal sphere" (or "internal structure" as sometimes used by the Commission) was, however considered irrelevant by Advocate-General Mayras who argued that as long as the applicants had full knowledge about the decision they

---

28. I.C.I. Case 635.
29. Geigy Case 803.
30. Dyestuffs Decision D33, at para. 29; see also I.C.I. Case , submission and arguments of the parties 635. The Court had found service to the "internal sphere" of the addressee proper in Case 8/56, A.L.M.A. v. High Authority [1957] 3 Rec. 179 (a matter in the context of the E.C.S.C. Treaty) but see argument of the applicant in the Geigy Case (pp.802-803) that according to the A.L.M.A. judgment due process reaches the internal structure of the addressee upon duly reaching the registered office of the enterprise in question and not of its subsidiary.

were not prejudiced in their rights.[31]

Most important in that respect are, of course, the Court's judgments. These did not pay much attention to economic considerations relating to the issue of service, i.e. the "internal sphere" concept, but settled the question of the service of the Commission decisions along the line of the Court's observations on the service of the Notices of Objections. Having established that the applicants had had full knowledge of the text of the decision, and that they had exercised their rights to institute proceedings within the proper period, the Court concluded that "irregularities in the procedure for notification of decision are extraneous to that measure and cannot therefore invalidate it."[32]

The Court admitted that under certain circumstances a notification of a decision as described above may prevent the period within which an application for the annulment of a decision must be lodged from starting to run.[33] The last observation is based on Art. 173 of the Treaty, according to which the relevant period for such an application (to annul a decision), in the absence of notification to the plaintiff starts to run from the day on which it came to the knowledge of the latter. The article, in fact, applies the concept of "knowledge" as a substitute for actual service for the purpose of the relevant limitation period. The Court, however, rejected a suggestion of the Commission that in competition law it is appropriate to consider that service at the registered place of business of the subsidiary, which is part of the economic unit, takes effect simultaneously with regard to the parent company.

31. I.C.I. Case 697.
32. I.C.I. Case 652, at para. 39; Geigy Case 825, at para. 18.
33. I.C.I. Case 652, at para. 40; Geigy Case, ibid.

4-14. In the Continental Can Case the Commission sent its decision through the post to both the parent company and its subsidiary (which operated an office within the Common Market).[34] The applicants argued that the decision should have been notified to them through diplomatic channels. Continental, which was later found the only liable company, had even returned the letter it had received on the advice of its lawyers. The Court concluded on this point as follows:

> A decision is properly notified within the meaning of the Treaty if it reaches the addressee and puts the latter in a position to take cognizance of it. This was so in the present case, because the contested decision actually reached Continental and the latter cannot make use of its own refusal to take cognizance of the decision in order to render this communication ineffective. 35

4-15. In the Zoja Decision the Commission posted the decision to the non-Community parent company abroad and to its subsidiary within the Common Market; both were held liable for carrying-out prohibited arrangements in the Common Market.

In the Hoffmann La-Roche Decision the Commission posted its decision directly and solely to the Swiss multinational in Basle, although the enterprise controlled subisidiaries within the Common Market by which it infringed the competition rules. The subsidiaries were not held liable for the offence.

In the Franco-Japanese Ballbearings Decision, the first incident where a NCE having no place of business within the Common Market was ordered (together with its Community partners) to terminate infringements

---

34. See Continental Can Case, issues of fact and of law, 220. However, the decision as published in the Official Journal, was addressed to Continental Can Company Inc. of New York.

35. Continental Can Case 241, at para. 10.

of the Treaty, the Commission posted its decision directly to the enterprise outside the Common Market. In subsequent similar circumstances - e.g. the French and Taiwanese Mushroom Packers Decision - the same practice was again adopted.

In the United Brands Decision the Commission proceeded against an American company which had appointed one of its Community subsidiaries as its representative in the proceedings. Therefore, notice of the Commission's final decision was given to that subsidiary.[36]

In the Lipton Cash Registers Decision, where both the non-Community parent company and the subsidiary within the Common Market were found jointly and severally liable, the practice adopted in the Commercial Solvents Case was repeated, i.e. the decision was posted directly to the Swedish parent company abroad and to its English subsidiary.

In none of the cases mentioned in this paragraph (i.e. 4-15) had the NCES concerned complained about lack of personal jurisdiction. The practices of previous cases took precedent through having established procedural rules for the service of progress.

(3) Service by "Knowledge"; Scope of the Requirement

4-16. The judgments of the Court, for all practical purposes, settled the question of international service of process. Nothing can prevent the Commission from taking advantages of ordinary mail transportation

36. See explanation on this point in the United Brands Decision D59, at para. 131.

if this way of communication is correct, i.e. complies with the requirement for "knowledge". If a refusal of acceptance of the communication is immaterial (cf. 4-14), then furthermore no enterprise outside the Common Market will be able to avoid the impact of the Common Market antitrust standards by merely taking refuge in the technicalities of service procedure.[37]

However, the Commission for various reasons, e.g. courtesy in international relations, may still resort to the method of service to a subsidiary or an agent of the non-Community parent company within the Common Market.[38] In this context we have to remember that the Court did not directly follow the line according to which service to the subsidiary is equivalent to service to the non-resident parent company, but instead stressed the need of "knowledge" of the latter company so that irregularities of service would become immaterial.

It is also important to note that in its judgment in the Continental Can Case the Court emphasized that the "knowledge" which the defendant, in proceedings before the Commission, must have in order to satisfy proper service should be "actual". Cf. 4-14. In its pronouncement on this point the Court seemed to agree with an observation which the Commission made in the Geigy Case that, once the decision has reached the "internal sphere" of the addressee, it is still not proved that the latter must have the required actual notice of it.[39] Relying on a letter, sent by Geigy to the Commission, the

37. Compare Koppensteiner, "International Enterprises Under the Antitrust Law of the European Economic Community" 9 J.W.T.L. 316-317 (1975).

38. In the Geigy Case (submissions and arguments of the parties 802) the Commission stressed that the principle of service to a subsidiary established in the Common Market, on behalf of its non-Community parent company, must also apply to the notification of measures during the course of purely administrative procedure.

39. Geigy Case, submissions and arguments of the parties, 802. The Commission interpreted the A.L.M.A. judgment (see note 30) as expressing such a view.

latter argued that the obligation for a proper notification was fulfilled a fortiori because the contested decision did indeed come to the notice of the addressee.[40]

The "presence test",i.e. service to the subsidiary within the territory for the purpose of obtaining personal jurisdiction over the parent company, as advocated by the Commission in the Dyestuffs Cases, may not be as strict as the tests for establishing liability for an economic unit. The latter tests are listed in 2-11. It would probably be sufficient to comply with the purpose of this test if the business done in the Common Market is of such a nature and character as to warrant the inference that the enterprise has subjected itself to the local jurisdiction and is by its duly authorized officers and agents (subsidiaries) present within the Common Market, where service is attempted. Everything, according to this view, would depend on how the relationship is organized in a concrete situation. Taking into account the Court's approach attention will be also focussed on whether the relationship enables the transfer of "actual knowledge".

4-17. In view of the requirement for "actual knowledge" a certain paradox has been mentioned in some of the applicants' arguments in the Dyestuffs Cases. For example I.C.I. argued that German law concerning limited liability companies does not allow notification addressed to the parent company to be made to its subsidiary established in Germany.[41] The Commission did not solve the difficulty which is imposed by a national legal barrier and which could prevent the existence of "actual knowledge". In fact the Commission ignored the national legal provisions which objected to its practice. It therefore remains

---

40. Ibid.
41. See I.C.I. Case 635.

to be seen in future cases to what extent parent-subsidiary relationship as such can be decisive on questions of service.[42]

4-18. The same requirements for a proper service are applicable for the service of a Notice of Objections and for the service of the Commission's final decision. These requirements for a proper service as have been developed in the case law seem to be in line with the concepts of fair play and orderly administration of the laws. These concepts take properly into account the interests of the plaintiff and the defendant. The interest of the Community has been particularly emphasized in the Continental Can Case where the Court ruled that the NCE could not, in the circumstances of the case, make use of its own refusal to take cognizance of the decision. This statement illustrates a consideration of the interest of the plaintiff which, thus, balances the interest of the defendant in that its knowledge about the process must be "actual". However, in view of the requirement for "actual knowledge", a total disregard by the Commission of "unawareness" of service on the part of a NCE may result in an injustice; the "actual knowledge" may, in such cases, become constructive knowledge. No such cases have yet reached the Commission and its reactions are as yet unpredictable; the difficult cases on this issue are likely to be where a NCE, having no affiliate within the Common Market, firmly refuses to take any notice of the Commission's letters to it.

4-19. Could publication of the content of process be regarded as proper service and thus satisfy the requirement for an "actual knowledge" of the enterprise concerned?

---

42. See Steindorff, "Annotations on the Decision of the European Court in the Dyestuffs Cases of July 14, 1972" 9 C.M.L.Rev. 504 (1972).

The Commission is obliged to publish in the Official Journal, inter alia, decisions terminating an infringement of Arts. 85 or 86 of the Treaty (Art. 21 of Reg. 17) and it may also publish other decisions, such as those which impose fines. But it appears that no regulation exists for the substitute of service by way of publication. This view is also apparent from the Commission's approach in the Geigy Case that the only thing that matters is the notification of the decision; it is the date of that notification which counts in calculating the period within which an appeal must be lodged and it is the text which is notified to the addressee which alone is authentic.[43] In this connection attention should also be paid to the duty upon the Commission that information for reasons concerning the protection of business secrets must be omitted from any publication. In the Geigy Case the applicant commented on the inadequacy of publication as a method of service by saying that notification must not only take place in fact, but also in law.[44]

It has already been stated that the mere publication in the Official Journal of a Notice of Objections, without service, may prevent the imposition of a fine or periodic penalty payment (Art. 2(3) of Reg.99).

(4) What is the Proper Connection Between Service and Jurisdiction in Community Law?

4-20. The question of whether there is a proper connection between service and the Community's substantive jurisdiction can be formulated

43. Geigy Case, submission and arguments of the parties, 802.
44. Ibid. at 803.

as follows: does the Community jurisdiction depend on the ability to serve process or does the ability to serve process depend on the jurisdiction?

The present development of Community law has reached the point that personal jurisdiction extends as far as the Community's jurisdiction over the subject-matter.[45] Since "actual knowledge" and other measures of "fairness" (see 4-21) are the ultimate issues for a proper service there is no mechanical or quantitative formula which can be counted on in questions of service. Furthermore, contrary to requirements in other legal systems, Community Law does not require, for purpose of service of process, any nexus with the territory of the Common Market, e.g. assets, subsidiary or other ways of doing business within the Common Market.[46] See distinctions in the comparative study with American antitrust law in 5-61.

4-21. The test for a proper service of process places jurisdictional determination primarily on a case-to-case basis and many situations will be sufficiently different from preceding ones to make prediction difficult, but certain factors of fairness will obviously be relevant. The general rule laid down by the Court is that "a person whose interests are respectively affected by a decision taken by a public authority must be given an opportunity to make his point of view known".[47] Art. 173 of the Treaty permits a decision of the Commission to be annulled on the grounds that it infringed an "essential procedural requirement"; some requirements are set out in Reg. 17 and Reg. 99, but the Court may rule

---

45. Cf. Kruithof "The Applicability of the Common Market Antitrust Provisions to International Restraints of Trade" 2 C.M.L.Rev. 92 (1964). The writer also anticipates such a development in the approach of the Community authorities in the future.
46. In the Community legal system there is, therefore, no need for an additional requirement of "venue".
47. See the Transocean Marine Paint Association Case 1080.

that there are others. In the Nold Case[48] the Court stated that fundamental rights are in principle an integral part of Community law. These fundamental rights may be held by the Court in the future to include procedural rights, which could be read into Art. 173 or "procedural due process" to use convenient U.S. terminology.[49]

The difficult cases will occur in the enterprise's non-appearance, following a refusal to acknowledge service. We may assume that the Commission would make sure that all reasonable steps have been taken to make the defendant aware of the decision issued against him, but it would be going too far to say that it should never proceed without proof of such "awareness" by the defendant, because this might unfairly deprive the Community of a remedy. The question is further discussed in the context of the section dealing with remedies available to the Commission against absent NCES. See 4-73.

4-22. It is important to note that the Rules of Procedure of the Court permit judgments by default "if a defendant on whom an application originating proceedings has been duly served fails to lodge a defence to the application" (Art. 94(1)). The rules lay down the procedure for such judgments and for applications to set them aside (Art. 38 of the Statute of the Court; see also Art. 94(3) to (6)).

---

48. Case 4/73, Nold v. Collission [1974] E.C.R. 491.

49. See Temple-Lang, supra note 6, at 169. It has to be observed in that connection that for the purpose of reinforcing the protection of fundamental rights at Community level, the Commission has recently proposed that the Community formally adhere to the European Convention for the Protection of Human Rights and Fundamental Freedoms of 1950 and to the protection mechanisms which it contains. See Commission Memorandum, Accession of the Communities to the European Convention of Human Rights, Bull. E C Supp. 2/79.

2. EXTRATERRITORIAL DISCOVERY ORDERS AND INVESTIGATIVE MEASURES

GENERAL

4-23. The Commission has extensive powers of investigation which are set forth in Arts. 11 tб 14 of Reg. 17 and sanctioned by fines set forth in Arts. 15 and 16 of the same regulation. The Court is empowered by specific provisions to require various documents and information and to pursue investigations (Art. 21 of the Statute of the Court of Justice and Art. 45 of the Rules of Procedure of the Court of Justice). Taking these powers into account the main question in the following survey concerns orders to gather information from abroad relating to conduct both within and outside the Common Market. Such information is required in different stages of the Commission's initial investigation and in subsequent proceedings, both before the Commission and the Court.

Without examining the question yet of whether the general rule under international law for ordering the production of documents from abroad is the same as that for ordering the carrying out of other conduct abroad, it will become apparent in this section that the extraterritorial discovery orders have some distinctive features which warrant a separate examination. As to the applicable international law see 6-28.

The problem of discovery of foreign documents or records has in practice two main principal difficulties: (1) determining whether the documents are in the control of the individual or company from which discovery is sought; (2) determining whether foreign legal prohibitions to such discovery exist and would be recognized by the Commission or by the Court.

4-24. Some solutions to difficulties in requests for information from abroad may well turn upon the position of the parties concerned; whether they have notified the agreement to the Commission and would like further to cooperate with it, or whether they would partially or completely oppose the discovery orders. Therefore, before any examination of the exercise of the discovery and investigative powers of the Commission with regard to NCES, we have to take notice of the three ways by which the Commission's procedure against any one or more enterprises may begin:

(1) Where the enterprise discloses the agreement, decision or practice to the Commission, in a request for a negative clearance or for an exemption under Art. 85(3)(Arts. 2 and 4 of Reg. 17)(hereinafter "notification");[50]

(2) As a result of a complaint, which may be made by any natural or legal person with a "legitimate interest"; normally a person injured by the acts complained of, such as a supplier, a customer, or a competitor of the enterprises concerned (Art. 3 of Reg. 17);

(3) _ex officio_, the Commission can take the initiative, whether as a result of a general inquiry into the economic sector involved (Art. 12 of Reg. 17), or information obtained by the Commission (Art. 11 of Reg. 17), or of an investigation by the Commission (Art. 14 of Reg. 17) or by the authorities of Member States at the request of the Commission (Art. 13 of Reg. 17), or

50. Usually this filing is referred to by writers loosely as a "notification" rather than an application and notification; the procedure in these matters have been joined (Form A/B) since most firms in practice request negative clearance and failing this an exemption.

by less formal inquiries.

A. Notification

(1) The Application of the Notification Provisions to Non-Community Enterprises

4-25. At an early stage of the operation of Reg. 17 it seemed to international lawyers "unreasonable to require that foreign organizations and foreign firms should observe from abroad these formalities [of notification - B.B.]".[51] However, the first regulation implementing Reg. 17, Regulation 27/62[52] (hereinafter "Reg. 27"), made it clear that any enterprise, which is a party to an agreement, decision or practice, may submit an application for negative clearance or a notification in request of which the enterprise seeks application of Art. 85(3) of the Treaty (Art. 1 of Reg. 27). The possibility of the use of such a procedure by a NCE was approved by the Court where a question of the validity of an agreement between a NCE and its Community partner, which had not been notified to the Commission, was discussed in the Béguelin Case. For details of the case see 2-61. "Since the nullity for which Article 85(2) of the Treaty provides is absolute" the Court ruled that "the agreement concerned has no effect as between the contracting parties and cannot be set up against third parties."[53] Thus the

51. Cf. Åke Skiöld "Antitrust Problems in Connection with Dealings with Common Market Countries" in International Bar Association, Ninth Conference Report 199 (Edinburgh 1962).

52. Regulation 27/62 of the Commission, First Regulation Implementing Council Regulation 17/62, J.O. 1962, 35/1118; O.J. (Special Edition 1959-1962) p.132.

53. The Béguelin Case 963, at para. 4.

notification provisions have been interpreted by the Court as equally applicable to Community enterprises and NCES.

The procedure of notification as it affects NCES was mentioned in the Commission's Opinion Concerning the Applicability of the Treaty of Rome to Importation of Japanese Products Into the Community.[54] Referring to enterprises which have their head offices outside the Community and to their conduct, partly autonomous and partly in concentration with corresponding Community industries, the Commission recommended that those concerned notify in good time such arrangements, as stipulated by Reg. 17 in the implementation of Arts. 85 and 86. The content of this opinion and the recommendation for notification of the arrangements involving NCES were reiterated by the Commission in the Franco-Japanese Ballbearing Decision and in the French and Taiwanese Mushroom Packers Decision, where similar practices had been examined.[55]

The opportunity to notify arrangements suspected of being contrary to Art. 86 is as well equally applicable to the Community and to NCES. The Commission expressed an explicit opinion on this point in the Continental Can Case:

> Community law offers undertakings the possibility of making sure about the Commission's verdict on any intended behaviour as they can apply for a negative clearance under Article 2 of Regulation No. 17. 56

---

54. Opinion Concerning the Applicability of the Treaty of Rome to the Importation of Japanese Products into the Community, J.O. 1972, C111/13. For details about the content of the Opinion see 2-54.

55. Cf. Franco-Japanese Ballbearings Decision D15, at para. 16, and D90 at para. 43; French and Taiwanese Mushroom Packers Decision D90, at para. 21.

56. Continental Can Case, pleas and arguments of the parties, 228.

(2) Notification as a Discovery Technique

4-26. There is a certain "power" in the content of the competition rules to impel the notification of restrictive business arrangements of the kind described in Arts. 85(1) and 86, and it has been employed effectively as a technique which somewhat decreases the need for extraterritorial discovery orders. Art. 85(2) of the Treaty reads: "any agreements or decisions prohibited pursuant to this Article shall be automatically void". Accordingly, an agreement falling under Art. 85(1), which has not been declared inapplicable under Art. 85(3), is null and void; a declaration under Art. 85(3) may only be obtained after notification, except if the agreement is exempted from notification by being in a special category of agreements. The inducement for enterprises to notify such arrangements is that there will be no punitive fine for a notified agreement or practice, unless it is pursued after being ruled illegal.

4-27. The importance of notification in the event of foreign documents should not be underestimated. Art. 1 of Reg. 27 requires that where the application or notification is submitted by some, but not all of the enterprises concerned, they shall give notice to the others. Form A/B (Annex to Reg. 27) further requires that those who notified the agreement state what steps have been taken to inform the other enterprises not associated in submitting the notification (Sec. 2 in the Form). Therefore, not only does the notification procedure enable the Commission to obtain information about NCES from those associated with them, but it also puts the NCES concerned in a position of having "knowledge" about the proceedings and gives them an opportunity to intervene.

If notification is actually made by a NCE or by its participation with a Community enterprise, it may indicate the NCE's voluntary submission to supply correct information under a threat of a fine. Such notification may also entail decisions by the Commission which will eventually involve the NCE itself in the proceedings.[57] For example, the Commission has power under Art. 16(6) of Reg. 17 to warn enterprises which have notified an agreement that, after a preliminary examination, it considers that Art. 85(1) applies and that Art. 85(3) does not. This ends the immunity from fines which notification confers and it also ends the agreement's provisional validity.[58] Such a note or warning has legal effects. It constitutes a decision, unlike a normal Notice of Objections. It must, therefore, give reasons justifying the decision and may be annulled by the Court.[59] The Commission accepts that before sending a decision under Art. 15(6), it should send a preliminary Notice of Objections to the enterprises, and give them a chance to comment.[60]

---

57. This situation, with proper distinctive qualifications, resembles a submission to jurisdiction as recognized in some legal systems; the enterprise could be seen to submit to the personal jurisdiction of the Commission in respect of the agreement notified to it. For example, in English law it is possible for a person to contract, either expressly or implicitly, to submit to the jurisdiction of a court to which he would not otherwise be subject, see Cheshire's Private International Law, supra note 4, at 83.

58. See Case 10/69, Portelange S.A. v. Smith Corona Marchant International S.A. [1969] E.C.R. 317; Brasserie de Haecht Case (No.2) 77.

59. See joined Cases 8-11/66, Cimenteries v. Commission [1967] E.C.R. 75.

60. On the use which the Commission makes of Art. 15(6) of Reg. 17 see Second Report on Competition Policy, point 31; Sirdar/Phildar [1975] 1 C.M.L.R. 378; Bronbemaling/Heidemaatschappij [1975] 2 C.M.L.R. D67. On the right to a hearing (but not necessarily to an oral hearing) which exists before a preliminary decision under Art. 15(6) of Reg. 17 see the Cimenteries Case, supra note 59.

(3) Information and Documents Relevant to Notification and in Pursuance of It

4-28. Enterprises are obliged to transmit to the Commission information as to facts and circumstances in support of their notification. For this purpose Form A/B spells out the content of the information required (see also Art. 4 of Reg. 27). At any stage after notification the Commission may ask for further information; such powers are implied in Art. 11 of Reg. 17 which provides that the Commission, in carrying out the duties assigned to it by the Treaty and subsequent provisions, may obtain all the information it needs. In an Explanatory Note to Form A/B the Commission stresses that in their own interests, enterprises should give the completest possible survey in order to avoid requests for additional information (see Annex to Reg. 27). The note also explains that Form A/B makes provision for further information to be supplied; in particular it is possible to send later on either supporting documents or actual answers to the questions listed in it.[61]

4-29. Section V of Form A/B stresses expressly that the information in the notification must be correct and obliges enterprises to sign a declaration that they are aware of the provision in Art. 15(1)(a) (Reg. 17) which enables the imposition of fines for incorrect information. Nevertheless, one may legitimately refuse to comply with requests for additional information or may comply only partially, until the Commission, acting under paragraph (5) of Art. 11 (Reg. 17), issues

---

61. See Information Requested Under Heading No. V. in Explanatory Note (annexed to Regulation 27/62);the explanation given there concerns the information requested for exemption under Art. 85(3).

a formal request for the relevant information. In this connection it is important to note that Art. 15(1)(b)(Reg. 17) provides for the imposition of fines on enterprises which intentionally or negligently supply incorrect or misleading information in response to a formal request made by the Commission, or which refuse to supply information within the time limit fixed by the formal request under Art. 11(5) (Reg. 17). For the purpose of obtaining complete and correct information which it has requested by formal decision under Art. 11(5) the Commission may also impose periodic penalty payments.

4-30. In an exemption under Art. 85(3) of the Treaty, following notification of an agreement, the Commission is entitled to impose conditions and obligations on the parties. Some of these conditions may provide for the supply of information with regard to changes in basic acts concerning the making of the decision, etc. (Art. 8 of Reg. 17).

Examples in the case law on how notification was used as an initial discovery technique, and in particular on the practice of attaching conditions providing for the future supply of information with regard to exemptions under Art. 85(3), will be examined later in this chapter. See 4-38 and 4-39.

B. Measures of Discovery and Investigation Other Than Notification and Their Extraterritorial Application

(1) The Relevant Rules and Their Scope

4-31. The extensive powers of the Commission to request information are not limited to the procedure of notification. In all other cases by which the Commission may begin a procedure against an enterprise (see 4-24) it is permitted to send the enterprises concerned requests for information which must, inter alia, state that sanctions may be imposed if the information supplied is not accurate (Art. 11(3) of Reg. 17). There is, however, no penalty for non-compliance with this informal request. If incomplete information, or none is given, the Commission may adopt a formal decision ordering specified information to be supplied within a specified time, warning of the penalties for incomplete or inaccurate information and for delay, and mentioning the right to challenge the decision before the Court. Such a decision must state its reasons (in accordance with Art. 190 of the Treaty).

Acting under Art. 12 of Reg. 17, which gives the Commission authority to investigate an entire economic sector, the Commission may request every enterprise concerned to communicate to it information and agreements which are exempted by virtue of Art. 4(2) and Art. 5(2) of Reg. 17; it shall also request enterprises, whose size suggests that they occupy a dominant position within the Common Market, or in a substantial part thereof, to supply particulars about their structure and behaviour necessary for an appraisal of their position in the light of Art. 86 of the Treaty. Art. 12 does not state that a formal decision of the Commission is required before such a particular request for information is made to an enterprise; it only states that in the course of an inquiry into sectors of the economy the Commission may request that information. If the information supplied is incorrect, the Commission may impose fines (Art. 15(b) or Reg. 17), but not periodic penalty payments. It appears, however, that unless a formal decision for information is addressed to the enterprise, in this context (in accordance with Art. 11 of the regulation), a refusal would not be illegal.

The Commission's principal investigatory powers are set forth in Art. 14 of Reg. 17 which authorizes the Commission to conduct all necessary investigations into the affairs of enterprises and particularly empowers the Commission, in conducting such investigations, to examine and copy books and other business documents, to ask for verbal explanations and to have access to premises, land and vehicles of the enterprises being investigated; penalties may be imposed for non-compliance. Art. 14(3) requires enterprises to submit to investigations when ordered by a decision of the Commission. If the enterprises refuse to submit to an investigation ordered by a decision or produce incomplete books or other business records, the Commission may impose fines on them (Art. 15(1)(c)) and periodic penalty payments in order to compel them to submit to such investigations (Art. 16(1)(d)).

4-32. In accordance with Reg. 17 the decisions concerning requests for information or investigation do not require the Commission to give the enterprises concerned an opportunity of being heard on the matters to which the Commission has taken objection. Such an obligation rests on the Commission with regard to other decisions, and in every case where it proposes to impose fines or periodic penalty payments (Art. 19).

4-33. The Court is allowed, in accordance with its Statute, to require the parties before it "to produce all documents and to supply all information which the Court considers desirable" (Art. 21). The Statute requires that formal note shall be taken of any refusal. The Rules of Procedure of the Court of Justice also provide for several modes of inquiry which the Court is permitted to pursue; in addition to the request for information and the production of documents the rules mention an inspection of the place or thing in question (Art. 45(2)).

4-34. Reg. 17 does not state in so many words that the discovery orders and the investigative powers may be exercised only with regard to Community enterprises or to information located within the territory of the Common Market. But there are various requirements in the regulation that the authorities of Member States be notified or consulted about investigations to be conducted in their territory. May an inference of territorial limitation be drawn from such requirements?

It is important to note that the mention of an enterprise's place of business does not appear in Arts. 12, 13 or 14, thus supporting an inference that investigations may be made into the affairs of NCES. Art. 11, dealing with "requests for information", however, states that a copy of the request must be sent to the "competent authority of the Member State in whose territory the seat of the undertaking.....is situated". Strict compliance with this clause by the Commission seems to be impossible in the case of a NCE. This would be true even though the NCE had furnished the name of an agent in connection with an application under Arts. 2, 4 or 5 of Reg. 17, since appointment of an agent would not amount to establishing its seat in the territory of the Common Market.[62] Nevertheless, in view of the broad discovery powers which are essential for the enforcement of competition policy, an inference of territorial limitation seems unwarranted.[63] It is, of course, important that the Commission should

62. Such a conclusion is expressed in an article, from an early stage of the development of Community Law; see Nebolsine "Foreign Enterprises Under the Common Market Antitrust Rules" 38 N.Y.Un. L. Rev. 486-487 (1963). The writer argues that the participation of Member States in the exercise of such power constitutes a functional part of the investigatory power and that the requirements in the regulation are not solely for the Member States' benefit, but can be invoked by the non-Community enterprise itself.

63. Deringer, The Competition Law of the European Economic Community, sec. 2207 (CCH Ed. 1968); Hug "The Applicability of the Provisions of the European Community Treaties Against Restraints of Competition to Restraints of Competition Caused in Non-Member States, But Affecting the Common Market" in Cartel and Monopoly in Modern Law, vol 2, 632 (1961).

be able to order the custodian or a party in control of any documents to produce the relevant information. When a court of administrative authority has jurisdiction over a case, it must have power to order the defendants to produce documents relevant to the case, even though the defendants are foreigners and the documents are situated abroad. If this were not so, a foreign corporation could transact business within a State and defeat all attempts by the authorities of that State to investigate whether the business was being carried on in accordance with local law, by keeping its business records in another State. As in the constitutional law of the U.S. and the law of international organizations, the existence of an express power carries with it such implied powers as are necessary to enable the express power to be effectively exercised. See also 6-28.

As the key questions in compelling the movement of documents from abroad into the Common Market and the scope of orders to NCES do not appear to be capable of resolution by resort to the language of Reg. 17 they will have to be settled by the case law.

(2) The Extraterritorial Scope of Discovery Orders in Community Case Law

4-35. The following survey of the scope of discovery orders in the case law is illustrative of the Community's approach to discovery orders in various situations which involve foreign elements; the examples given are not conclusive, but they reflect relevant and typical incidents. Thus we shall point out the scope of information required by the Commission with regard to the operations of a Community and NCES outside the Common Market; such information may be found in documents which could be either within the territory of the Common Market or outside that territory. In particular we shall examine whether the Commission and the Court would require that documents located abroad - under the control of a Community or a NCE - be submitted for investigation. These requirements may follow, as has already been stated, an initial investigation taken by the Commission or in its pursuance of observance of a conditioned exemption under Art. 85(3). The survey of the case law will concentrate only on the factual description of cases while the legal issues involved will be examined in subsection (3) under appropriate headings.

4-36. The Dyestuffs Decision reveals very little about the Commission's view of its powers to engage in discovery of information located outside the Common Market. It states simply that the Commission undertook a series of investigations in the Member States. While this may imply that no investigation outside the Common Market was attempted, it does not necessarily prove this.

4-37. In the Commercial Solvents Case the Court put questions to the applicants and required Commercial Solvents Corporation, as well as Istituto, to reveal information about their activities on a world scale; these concerned supplies to customers outside the Common Market, export policies towards third countries and even sources of supply of the applicant's competitors. Commercial Solvents Corporation answered the questions while emphasizing that the nature and extent of its sales outside the Common Market were irrelevant to the proceedings.[64]

---

64. See Commercial Solvents Case, questions put to the parties by the Court, 242.

It has already been pointed out that in determining whether a NCE has a dominant position within the Common Market the Commission has taken account, inter alia, of the enterprise's entire economic power within the Common Market. See 3-74.

4-38. A wide scope of discovery was requested by the Commission in the Transocean Marine Paint Association Decision.[65] The decision, relating to individual exemption pursuant to Art. 85(3) of the Treaty, was scrutinized by the Court on appeal. However, the Court avoided judging the scope of the discovery order and, in line with the Association's main arguments, concentrated on safeguarding the rights of the applicant for a fair trial.

The Association's membership comprised eighteen manufacturers each established in a different country, only five being Member States of the EEC. The joint marketing arrangements which initially qualified for a conditioned exemption under Art. 85(3) of the Treaty[66] related to cooperation between those small and medium sized enterprises with a view to organizing on a world-wide scale a system of distribution for marine paints. In October 1972 the Association applied for the simple renewal, for a period of ten years, of the exemption granted in 1967, but the Commission did not follow this course. It considered, just as it had done in 1967, that the agreement was covered by the provisions of Art. 85(1) of the Treaty and that exemption on the basis of Art. 85(3) was justified, but in view of some changes which had occurred since 1967 in the competitive situation, such exemption must be subject

65. Transocean Marine Paint Association [1974] 1 C.M.L.R. D11.
66. See Transocean Marine Paint Association [1967] C.M.L.R. D9.

to stricter conditions than those imposed by the original decision. In this connection, the Commission put forward the following additional matters to be informed to it: "any links by way of common directors or managers between a member of the Association and any other company or firm in the paints sector or any financial participation by a member of the Association in such outside companies or vice-versa, including all changes in such links or participation already in existence".

An action was brought before the Court by the Association for the purpose of annulling the last provision.[67] The applicant alleged an infringement of the Treaty's provisions, in addition to infringements of procedural rules, and in particular of Art. 8(1) of Reg. 17, in that the obligation imposed upon it was wider in scope than anything which may be imposed upon it. The contention that the Commission acted ultra vires, because in formulating the obligation it had failed to distinguish between the marine paint market and the markets for paint in general and between links which are relevant to the Common Market and those which are not, was advocated in court by the Association's counsel. The latter explained that the obligation is one to which the Association would not be able to adhere and which, without good reason, would harm its members' interests due to the following facts:

(1) the information available at the central office pertained only to activities in the marine paint field. The members, particularly those in Asia and in the U.S., tend to cover themselves in "clouds of secrecy of varying density" with regard to activities in other fields;

---

67. The Transocean Marine Paint Association Case.

(2) NCES in the Association might regard the provision of the information required by the Commission as too high a price to pay for the retention of the Community members in the Association; (3) members who are remote from Europe might in fact fail to supply the information and so place the other members in danger of being fined.[68]

The Court's judgment, which was mainly concerned with a breach of procedural requirements (lack of opportunity for the members of the Association to submit observations or suggestions on the matter under consideration), held that the decision at issue be annulled and the case be remitted to the Commission. The only pronouncement of the Court, on the arguments of the applicants mentioned above, was that the Commission enjoys a large measure of discretion in relation to the detailed rules to which it may subject the exemption, while at the same time it has to act within the limits imposed upon its competence by Art. 85 of the Treaty. The exercise of such discretionary power is linked, according to the judgment, to a preliminary canvassing of objections which may be raised by the enterprises.[69] The Commission, therefore, issued a revised monitoring requirement to replace the provision in its previous decision (after giving the Association opportunity to submit observations).[70] The obligation imposed by the Commission to supply information was limited to links with such enterprises as carry on business within the Community in the paint sector, that is to say those which do business in one or several Member

---

68. Ibid. at 1085; the arguments are expanded in a letter sent to the Commission (annex 1 to the Defence) and mentioned in the submissions of the Advocate-General.

69. Ibid. at 1080, para. 16.

70. See Transocean Marine Paint Association [1975] 2 C.M.L.R. D75.

States, directly or through subsidiary undertakings or by means of a joint venture (where the link is in the form of a 25 per cent financial participation or an interlocking directorship or management). The obligation was not limited to the marine paint sector alone and it extended to links with enterprises in the paint sector as a whole. The reason given for such a wide scope of discovery was that a paint manufacturer is capable of extending his production in a relatively short time to the marine paint sector.[71]

The latter decision was taken in the Commission's capacity to impose conditions in an exemption pursuant to Art. 85(3). The possibility of notification, either for a negative clearance or for an exemption, has already been mentioned as a discovery technique used by the Commission to obtain information from NCES. This has also been manifested in the case law.

4-39. In the Henkel-Colgate Decision[72] the Commission held that the prohibition in Art. 85(1) could apply to a joint research by two large enterprises with world-wide markets. The agreement between the enterprises was given exemption in accordance with Art.85(3) on the condition that the enterprises will inform the Commission of their policy relating to patent licensing and know-how, and also notify any links or participation established between the enterprises of both groups, and all interests acquired by the enterprises of both groups in non-member enterprises. The decision was not limited to the Common Market territory, but required discovery on a world-wide scale of activities.

71. Ibid. at D77, para. 6.
72. Henkel/Colgate, J.O. 1972, L14/14.

Subsequent decisions of the Commission adopted a similar approach.[73]

4-40. In scrutinizing the operation of the Dutch nitrogenous fertilizers selling agency (Centraal Stikstof Verkoopkantoor BV-CSV), the Commission asked for information on its business activities and on its relations with manufacturers whose products it was selling.[74] The information was needed for an assessment of the effect of the joint sales in the Netherlands and outside the Common Market on individual exports to Community countries by CSV member manufacturers. The information, according to CSV, was under the control of a company based in Zürich, Switzerland (for more details see 4-52); when CSV refused to comply, the Commission ordered it, by a decision issued under Art. 11(5) of Reg. 17, to provide the information within a certain period on pain of periodic penalty payments for delays. CSV then complied with the decision and provided the information.

4-41. The Commission adopted another decision in respect of documents located abroad by which the German Vereinigung Deutscher Freiform-Schmieden (hereinafter called "the Union") was required to submit to an investigation and to allow requisite business records to be examined.[75] Among the records of the Union the decision in particular mentioned those "concerning the joint office in Zürich including details of any payments made to that office". Such information relating to activities abroad seemed "necessary" to the Commission, after its inquiry established sufficient grounds for suspecting that restricted agreements were being applied on the Common Market for heavy forgings

73. See, for example, De Laval/Stork, O.J. 1977, L215/11.
74. CSV, O.J. 1976, L192/27.
75. Re the Business Records of Vereinigung Deutscher Freiform-Schmieden [1978] 1 C.M.L.R. D36.

weighing over four tonnes. Prior to the decision, the Director-General for Competition gave orders that investigations would be made at several enterprises and associations of enterprises pursuant to Art. 14 of Reg. 17. The checks which were due to be carried out at the Union, in the presence of a representative of the competent German authorities, could not be carried out because the Union refused to submit to the investigation unless it was authorized by a formal decisision of the Commission. Therefore, the decision above was adopted.

4-42. The scope of information required in the Commission's inquiries into sectors of the economy is as wide as in the other types of investigations and may touch upon matters external to the Common Market. This is evident from the following paragraph in the conclusions of the Commissions' Report on the Behaviour of the Oil Companies:

> The Commission's investigative powers extend to all Member Countries, but the inquiry also produced important information relevant to matters outside the Community, notably the formation of crude oil process in producer countries and also the transfer prices charged by oil companies in respect of crude oil sold to their refineries and refined products sold to their distributing subsidiaries. 76

C. Legal Considerations of the Commission in Issuing Extraterritorial Discovery Orders

(1) The Range of Situations in Which Extraterritorial Discovery Orders May be Issued

4-43. If documents are located within the Common Market, access may be had to them; they may be copied and oral explanation of them may

76. Fifth Report on Competition Policy, point 9.

be required. In one case the Commission took advantage of its wide investigative powers and sent inspectors to search for information on the premises, within the Common Market, of an American enterprise suspected of instructing its Community concessionaries to operate an arrangement of discriminatory pricing policy.[77] However, the absence from the Common Market area of the principal office of an enterprise, with its corporate records and managerial staff, may be significant if the Commission is interested in documents located abroad under the control of a NCE. This will have a direct effect upon the investigatory powers of the Commission as explained in subsequent paragraphs.

4-44. Suppose, however, that a Community-based enterprise has a subsidiary located outside the Common Market which possesses a document, a copy of which is desired by the Commission, the issue concerning the compulsion of the Community enterprise to produce such records is whether the enterprise actually exercises control of the business of its subsidiary abroad or has power to control its actions. Since Community law has adopted the principle of "economic unit" for the solution of issues, both of substantive and of procedural matters (see 2-11 _et seq_. and 4-14 _et seq_. respectively), it seems appropriate that in issues of foreign discovery the Commission will investigate the corporate entity to confirm control of the records which is free from the necessity of securing the consent of others. The test of "control" may, therefore, be followed in all cases in which the issue of extraterritorial discovery is raised where a Community enterprise does business abroad through a branch or a controlled subsidiary.[78]

---

77. The _Pittsburgh Corning Europe Decision_.
78. When using the economic unit theory here, a distinction should be made between the liability to compel the production of documents from abroad by a subsidiary and the substantive liability for the subsidiary's acts; the latter issue may require application of stricter guiding principles for the exercise of control (see also 4-16).

As a Community parent company may be held accountable for the way it exercises its powers over its foreign affiliates, perhaps not too much will ever depend on whether or not the foreign subsidiary itself can be made subject to direct discovery orders of the Commission, simply because it is owned by a parent that is itself subject to Community jurisdiction. This question seems largely theoretical and it may not often be fully tested.

4-45. If the liability for the infringement of the competition rules rests on a non-Community parent company, and on its subsidiary within the Common Market, it seems likely that the subsidiary, by being an integral part of the "economic unit" and equally responsible for this unit's operations, may be directly requested to submit the relevant information from abroad.

In a case where a Community subsidiary alone is liable for the infringement,[79] it is not clear yet how far the Commission would be willing to accept the arguments that, in the absence of an "economic unit", the subsidiary cannot comply with the discovery order of documents under the parent company's control. Inferences may be deduced from cases which did not concern parent subsidiary relations at all but where the Commission relied on a presumption that the corporation is capable of "possession" of the relevant documents in spite of some alleged barriers; e.g. Transocean Marine Paint Association Decision (in 4-38). Nevertheless, the assessment that a corporation is capable of obtaining "possession" of documents located abroad must be made in the circumstances of each case.

---

79. This may be the case, for example, where a NCE, although it has the majority of the stock of the Community subsidiary, is not in a position of an actual control (see 2-12).

4-46. Documents required by the Commission may be outside the Common Market in the possession of a foreign-based enterprise which is alone suspected of committing the infringement without a branch or subsidiary in the Common Market. Although the Commission has no power (or right) to send its representatives to conduct an investigation abroad, it possibly may, by virtue of its discovery and investigative powers, and in accordance with public policy considerations (cf. 4-34), order the documents, or copies, to be produced inside the Common Market. The request for information may be sent directly to the enterprise's address abroad.

Such a request does not seem in our view incompatible with the competition policy, for if the Commission has substantive jurisdiction over the enterprise the location of records, theoretically, would be irrelevant to the practice of service of the discovery order. However, there are no, as yet, precedents to that effect in the case law. Deringer states that the Commission may address requests for information to firms outside the Common Market and attach assets inside the Common Market by way of penalizing such firms.[80] Community law may provide many other examples for the use of various techniques to obtain compliance by NCES with such discovery and investigative provisions. See 4-67 to 4-75. However, it is unlikely, in our view, that the Commission will succeed in obtaining documents from abroad by asking Member States to issue letters rogatory to foreign courts, as has been suggested by writers.[80a] The information required by the Commission is

80. Deringer, supra note 63.

80a. See McCoy "The United States Parent Corporation-European Subsidiary Relationship Under the European Antitrust Regulations" 8 Va. J. Int. L. 65 (1963); Hollmann "Problems of Obtaining Evidence in Antitrust Litigation; Comparative Approaches to the Multinational Corporation" 11 Texas Int. L.J. 470 (1976).

needed for the purpose of criminal proceedings and foreign courts are, therefore, likely to accept defences of self-incrimination based on their own law and public policy. See for analogy arguments of the defendants in the Westinghouse Uranium Contracts Litigation in 5-17.

(2) Defences Available Against Discovery Orders

(a) Discovery Orders with Excessive Scope

4-47. A most likely defence in the context of defences against excessive scope of discovery orders is that the information is not necessary to investigate the case. Art. 11(1) and Art. 14 (of Reg. 17) state that both the information requested and the investigation should be "necessary".[81] The change in the obligation imposed by the Commission on the Transocean Marine Paint Association in connection with such a defence (see 4-38) indicates that "necessity" is evidently the criterion which must govern the scope of requests for information. According to J. Van Damme, a former Commission investigations official, "it is generally accepted that the information requested must be more than merely useful for the investigating staff."[82] The investigation itself, states J. Van Damme, should be considered as "necessary" if the Commission is in the possession of facts establishing a "presumption" of violation of Arts. 85 and 86 of the Treaty; "a preventative investigation therefore seems impossible in this connection."[83] The existence and the importance of the "presumption" are questions of fact.

---

81. See for an analogy Case 31/59, Acciaieria di Brescia v. High Authority [1961] 5 Rec. 151, which referred to the investigatory powers of the High Authority of the E.C.S.C. It indicated that the necessity of information required by the High Authority must be clearly apparent from the decision demanding the information.

82. J. Van Damme, Rechtskundig Weeklad 1630 (1965).

83. Ibid.

In a case where the Commission opened an investigation of suspected violations of Art. 85 within a certain industry it ordered search of premises of Fides.[84] The enterprise was independent, not part of a certain industry, but suspected of performing services on behalf of firms in that industry. It refused to submit to investigation since; (1) procedure initiated by the Commission did not concern it; (2) it was not involved in manufacturing or marketing the product of the industry in question. A third contention concerned secrecy. The Commission, nevertheless, ordered the enterprise to submit to investigations at its premises stating that it had serious reason to believe that Fides performed services directly for manufacturers in the industry in question. The decision which relates to a domestic situation implies the wide discretion the Commission has in considering whether the investigation it requires is "necessary".

4-48. Subsequent to a possible reply by an enterprise that the information formally requested is not "necessary" the Commission may impose a fine (for refusal to supply information), but it will first hear the enterprise involved and decide with due regard to its contentions. It must, however, be taken into account that an appeal to the Court on this point can take several months and that, until the formal decision requesting the information is overruled by the Court, it is binding on the enterprise in question. The appeal does not suspend the Commission's decision unless the Court specifically orders it suspended (see Art. 36 of the Statute of the Court of Justice and Art. 83 of the Rules of Procedure) and this of course may frequently make the appeal practically academic.

---

84. Re the Business Records of Fides SpA [1979] 1 C.M.L.R. 650.

4-49. The preparation and documentation of a case for trial in the Common Market may be vastly more difficult for a NCE than for an enterprise which does most of its business in the Common Market and the Commission must, inter alia, give appropriate weight to such cases of hardship. The Commission is, therefore, expected not to violate requirements of "reasonableness". For example, if documents, of which a copy is in the Common Market, are physically located abroad the copy may be supplied; if no copy is in the Common Market, the orders should apply only to those documents located in the principal office or offices of the parent company under the order, maintained by it in each foreign country by or for any affiliate corporation. The scope and burden of antitrust extraterritorial discovery must also be reasonable with regard to the expenses of selecting the documents called for, the cost of photostating and translating them and the expense of the transfer. It is therefore interesting to note that the Court's Rules of Procedure, which require that supporting documents expressed in a language different from the language of the case must be accompanied by a translation, provide that in the case of long documents translations may be confined to extracts (Art. 29(3)).

(b) Claims of Privileged Rights to Refuse Disclosure

4-50. Under Community law there is no express right for the enterprise to refuse to give privileged information or documents to the Commission or the national authorities acting under Reg. 17.[85] Correspondence between an enterprise and its legal advisers, which is in the possession

---

85. See the decision mentioned in note 84 above. A requirement for the disclosure of information would not be regarded as a violation of business secrets under the law of any Member State (see Commission's reply to W.Q. No. 152/72, O.J. 1975, C209/15, and the decision of the English High Court, Chancery Division, British Leyland Motor Corporation Ltd., British Leyland U.K. Ltd., Pressed Steel Fisher Ltd. and British Leyland (Austin Morris) Ltd. v. Wyatt Interpart Company Ltd. [1979] C.M.L.R. 83, at para. 12).

of the enterprise, is also not expressly protected from disclosure. However, the Commission must have regard to the legitimate interests of enterprises in the protection of their business secrets (Art. 19(3), Art. 21(2), Art. 20 of Reg. 17) and the Commission may not use for other purposes information obtained under Reg. 17 (Art. 20).[86]

As to lawyers' professional privilege, the Commission has recognized, in a decision issued in the course of an investigation of an international cartel to fix prices and sales conditions for zinc, that it may not use as evidence strictly legal documents written with a view to seeking or giving opinions on points relating to the preparation or planning of the defence of the firms concerned.[87] Under present Community practice it is the Commission's own inspector who determines in the first instance whether a document is privileged or not.[88] The Commission will recognize as privileged only documents written to or by a lawyer in his capacity as legal adviser, and would not regard as privileged documents written to or by a lawyer who was helping his client to do something which was clearly contrary to Community law. The extent to which salaried lawyers in the Community are subject to rules of professional ethics and discipline comparable to those of independent lawyers in private practice still has to be cleared up, and until it is, the question of privilege for their documents is in suspense. The whole question of privilege is being actively considered by the Consultative Commission of European Bars and Law Societies.

The Court's Rules of Procedure allow agents, advisors and lawyers to enjoy the privilege that their papers and documents relating

86. The judgment in the Hoffmann-La Roche Case indicated the Court's awareness of some deficiencies in the law regarding business secrets and confidential information (see pp.510-513), although the Court's opinion offers little guidance as to how those deficiencies will be corrected.
87. See Re An Investigation at Am & S. Europe Ltd. [1973] 3 C.M.L.R. 378, at para. 14-17.
88. Ibid.

to the proceedings shall be exempted from both search and seizure (Art. 32(2)(a)). There are detailed rules in the event of a dispute and also an option for the Court to waive such immunity.

(c) Disclosure by Enterprises Which are not Parties to the Infringement

4-51. The Commission may request information from enterprises which are not parties to any violation of the Treaty (Art. 11 of Reg. 17). Penalties for non-compliance with such requests are in accordance with Art. 15 of the same regulation. However, the Court's powers to request information and documents from non-parties to the case are limited and confined only to the Member States and the Institutions (Art. 21 of the Statute of the Court). Nevertheless, information may be obtained from witnesses who are called to give evidence. The Court is empowered to impose a pecuniary penalty if a witness who has been duly summoned fails to appear or refuses, without good reason, to give evidence (Art. 48 of the Rules of Procedure).

The fact that the enterprises or the witnesses required to discover documents are not parties to the case may give rise to difficulties in the production of documents from abroad. Such an order can be served on the local branch of a foreign corporation which itself is called as a witness. However, it is doubtful whether the Commission would directly order a foreign witness to produce documents if either the witness or the documents are not in the State at the time when the order is made. This case resembles the situation of liability for omission under criminal law; in the absence of a voluntary undertaking on the part of the witness, it is submitted that a positive duty to act can be imposed by the Commission only if an individual is present or carrying on business within the Common Market (in the case of an enterprise) at the time when action is called for.

(3) Foreign Legal Obstacles To the Disclosure of Documents

(a) The Existing Practice of the Community

4-52. The most relevant decision in the context of foreign legal obstacles to disclosure is the CSV Decision. See 4-40. CSV had justified its refusal to produce documents on the ground that some of the information requested concerned exports made by CSV outside the Common Market under an agreement combining all European manufacturers of nitrogenous fertilizers under the control of Nitrex AG, a company formed in Zürich, Switzerland, to supervise the application of the agreement. According to CSV's legal advisers it was quite possible that if officers of CSV, who were also directors of Nitrex, provided the Commission with the documents requested they would be regarded by the Swiss authorities as having committed an offence punishable by imprisonment and possibly fines under Article 273 of the Swiss Criminal Code. The enterprise's concern related to the general prohibition in Swiss law on the disclosure, by both national authorities and private enterprises, of State, manufacturing or business secrets or any other kind of information obtained for a specific purpose, e.g. competition, fiscal or companies legislation.[89]

89. Article 273 of the Swiss Criminal Code reads: "A person who endeavours to discover a manufacturing or business secret in order to pass it on to a public or private foreign organization or to a foreign company or to their staff, and a person who reveals a manufacturing or business secret to a public or private foriegn organization or to a foreign company or to their staff, shall be guilty of an offence punishable by imprisonment, or, in serious cases, by imprisonment with hard labour. The court may also order payment of a fine."(Translation given in Sixth Report on Competition Policy, page 96).

In its decision the Commission stated that it needed the information it had asked for to appraise the effects of CSV's conduct on competition within the Community and that the information was available within the Community. Both the Commission as an authority and individual members of its staff were required by the Treaty itself and by Reg. 17 to refrain from divulging confidential information. The fact that some of the information requested had been communicated to a cartel domiciled in Switzerland and governed by Swiss law did not, according to the decision, deprive the Commission of its right to receive it. CSV complied with the decision by providing the relevant information.

The CSV Decision was thus explained in the Sixth Report on Competition Policy:

> This, then, establishes the principle that where information obtained or requested by the Commission under Article 85 and 86 of the Treaty is regarded by the law of a non-member country as a business secret, this is no reason for preventing the Commission from enforcing the rules on competition within the Community. 90

However, the CSV Decision did not provide sufficient ground for inferences as to the many possible types of conflicts with foreign laws since it concerned only the particular issue of secrecy, for which the Community has its own solution.

4-53. It was mentioned in Chapter III that the application of the Swiss Code regarding economic espionage to cases which the Commission investigated had resulted in a collision course between the Community and Switzerland over the Hoffmann La-Roche Decision. See 3-86. Mr. Stanley Adams, a senior employee of Hoffmann La-Roche, was sentenced by a court in Basle to one year's suspended imprisonment and banned from

90. At point 190.

entering Switzerland for five years for supplying internal company documents to the Comission (an appeal on the judgment was dismissed). This affair illustrated the private law consequences which may follow a disclosure of documents prohibited by foreign law. However, the Commission acted in the Joint Committee with Switzerland to lay down procedures to prevent the repetition of such a situation, which it had seen as incompatable with the EEC-Switzerland Free Trade Agreement. In relation to the interference in the course of the Commission's investigation it was stated in the European Parliament that:

> .....the Commission will not hesitate to take the necessary steps if the future application of Article 273 of the Swiss penal code were to prevent or obstruct the provision to the Commission of information on practices detrimental to the competition, particularly under the terms of the free trade agreement. 91

It is interesting to note here that Mr. Adams who was initially convicted and imprisoned in Basle was released on bail paid by the Commission. In reply to accusations of its using industrial espionage in that matter the following statement of the Commission is also noteworthy:

> The Commission has no need to resort to industrial espionage. It is empowered by Council Regulation No. 17 to carry out investigations, and it also receives unsolicited information from very varied sources. Since its duty is to ensure that the rules of competition are observed in the general interest of the Community, the Commission feels entitled to use any information it receives concerning alleged infringements once it is satisfied that the information is well-founded. The Commission does not regard this as industrial espionage. 92

(b) Anticipating the Difficulties in Future Disclosure Orders Conflicting With Foreign Law

4-54. Extraterritorial discovery orders may be barred and frustrated

91. European Parliament Debates, Jan. 12, 1977, at p.111 per Vice President Haferkamp.
92. See Reply to W.Q. No. 54/75, O.J. 1975, C161/16.

with regard to documents and records located abroad if the foreign country forbids their production or transfer outside its borders. The reasons for such foreign resistance may vary: they may stem from foreign distrust and resentment of the Community's efforts to enforce its competition law on NCES or from foreign objection and resistance to what is sometimes regarded as intrustion upon foreign sovereignty by the Community.

As in the case of CSV, a foreign government may use existing "business secrets" or "espionage" legislation to frustrate Community discovery orders. In other cases existing foreign corporation legislation may be interpreted to prevent disclosure as a matter of company law. For example, foreign statutes or administrative rulings relating to management responsibilities for corporate activity or an obligation to act in the corporation's best interest, may override any stockholder's legal power and permit minority stockholders to block the publication or discovery of corporate documents. Such barriers can operate even where a Community enterprise is a majority stockholder in a NCE of which discovery is required. Even if no statutory barriers exist, the articles of association may still forbid production of such documents at the request of one stockholder without the consent of all.

The possibility exists that foreign governments would react to the Community's discovery orders by passing legislation specifically forbidding access to or removal of local records of corporations doing business within their jurisdiction. These prohibitions may appear in the law itself or may take the form of a specific government order prohibiting enterprises from disclosing to foreign authorities information on their activities as a result of an antitrust action abroad (see examples in the case of counter legislation concerning the U.S. anti-trust discovery orders in 5-63). It may well be that such government orders will also include subsidiaries of Community enterprises in foreign countries.

4-55. Calling for the disclosure of documents is a procedural matter. However, even if the rule is that the "lex fori" governs the law of procedure, substantive law in another State's jurisdiction may be affected. Thus, promulgation of certain procedural order by the Commission may even impose serious criminal penalties on the enterprise concerned under foreign substantive law and we may face a situation where an enterprise is forbidden by one law to do an act which is required by other law. One of the difficulties involved in predicting and assessing such a foreign reaction, or the imposition of fines, arises from the fact that many of the legal barriers can not fully be determined in advance. It is therefore for the Commission to decide, in each case where foreign law opposes its discovery orders, whether to modify an order or refrain from enforcing it where compliance with the order will result in legal sanctions against the enterprise concerned.

On the one hand the Commission may give effect to foreign legal requirements, when such a result seems called for by the "act of State" doctrine (see discussion in 4-80), but, on the other hand, it can be strongly argued that the public policy of Community law requires the overriding of such considerations in the interest of the enforcement of competition. What is required, here as elsewhere, is a balancing by the Commission of the relevant factors involved in each situation to minimize foreign resentment and to recognize the interests of both jurisdictions. See also 6-51 and 6-52. The precondition for the imposition of fines by the Commission for non-compliance with a request for information is "an intentional or negligent act" (Art. 15(1) or Reg. 17) and this may, in our opinion, provide some escape-clause for enterprises confronted by foreign law prohibiting discovery. It can only be assumed that the Commission will indicate its willingness to enforce such orders, notwithstanding foreign law, where the enterprises have failed to produce convincing evidence that they have tried in good faith to gain the foreign sovereign's consent to remove the required documents (or copies) and have been refused the necessary permission.

3. ANTITRUST REMEDIES AGAINST NON-COMMUNITY ENTERPRISES: ISSUES OF ENFORCEMENT

INTRODUCTION

4-56. In any legal assessment of situations which involve NCES there lies the awareness of the possible enforcement difficulties which may arise if the arrangement is found illegal. The essence of the matter with regard to the assertion of extraterritorial enforcement jurisdiction is whether, if personal and substantive jurisdiction exist, the Community would not (or would not only) enforce its laws against the Community branch or subsidiary of a NCE to implement Community orders outside the Common Market. Such issues may also be discussed in relation to the subject of extraterritorial discovery orders, e.g. if a fine is imposed to obtain broader discovery, the fine's execution, if it cannot be carried out within the Common Market, may raise similar problems to those raised by the enforcement of a fine for violating Arts. 85 or 86.

These comments should not, however, be interpreted to mean that difficulties have always arisen. The following survey of the extraterritorial enforcement measures of the Community will be confined only to the latter's existing practice and will not, at this stage, question the legality of such practice under international law. We shall first examine with particular reference to NCES the types of remedy available to the Community according to its rules and only then describe the case law in that respect. We shall later discuss general considerations pertinent to the effectiveness of the Community's extraterritorial enforcement measures.

A. Measures of Relief Generally Available Against Non-Community Enterprises

(1) Informal Settlements and Recommendations

4-57. Any discussion of measures of relief against NCES must draw heavily on the many and various informal settlements.

The Commission has power to make an initial recommendation to the enterprises involved requesting them to terminate their agreement or practice (Art. 3 or Reg. 17). Such a recommendation is a formal act of the Commission, but is not legally binding. Many cases are thus dealt with by the Commission without formal proceedings. Enterprises can approach the Commission officials informally for advice on whether the Commission will object to a particular agreement or clause, or to discuss the modification or abandonment of an agreement to which the Commission has objected. However, if the parties are not willing to abandon all the arrangements to which the Commission, after discussion, continues to object, the Commission cannot substitute an informal procedure for the procedure laid down by the regulations. The parties may still approach the Commission informally, even after receiving the Notice of Objections, to seek an informal settlement or a favourable decision, after the proper procedure has been carried out (Art. 7 of Reg. 99).

The importance of informal arrangements in ending infringements applies both to the NCES concerned and the Commission, because of antitrust's inherent uncertainty, jurisdictional doubts, litigation, expense and harassment; all may be increased by the foreign situs of many facts and witnesses. Furthermore, the litigious scrutiny of the foreign interests or contractual relationships of the NCES' businesses makes it necessary for the enterprises to negotiate a settlement. And, of course, negotiation permits greater bargaining power than legal power. The Commission, for its part, clearly takes advantage of such arrangements if it foresees difficulties in exercising its enforcement jurisdiction.

(2) Fines and Periodic Penalty Payments

4-57a. A Commission decision may impose a fine on a NCE for deliberate or negligent violation of the Treaty. The amount of the fine depends on the gravity of the infringement and the duration of the infringement (Art. 15(2)(b) of Reg. 17). Periodic penalty payments may be imposed to compel enterprises to act in accordance with a decision (Art. 16 of Reg. 17). The appropriate circumstances for the imposition of fines or periodic penalty payments on NCES and possible methods for their execution are discussed later in the present section. In particular see 4-59 and 4-70.

(3) Commission's Orders

4-58. The Commission may simply order the infringement to be ended. However, additional orders of the Commission may be even more significant to the foreign businessman, e.g. injunctions which may impose special burdens and upset vested contractual or ownership rights and expectations with regard to persons or properties. The scope of Community orders to NCES and their nature are topics for a detailed examination in some of the following paragraphs. In particular see 4-60 to 4-61 and 4-63 to 4-65.

B. Measures of Relief Against Non-Community Enterprises in Community Case Law

(1) Scope of Orders and Relief Measures Against Non-Community Enterprises

4-59. The orders issued to NCES in the Dyestuffs Cases to pay fines were, in a sense, orders to do something abroad, i.e. the payment of fines normally would have to be accomplished by the headquarters of those enterprises in their respective countries.[93] There may be a difference between this relatively simple act, however, and a requirement that the foreign enterprises obey orders seeking to govern aspects of their business conduct abroad. Such a conclusion is implied in the Commission's submission to the Court in the I.C.I. Case. After referring to far-reaching court orders in the U.S. which included injunctions to enterprises established abroad or which ordered that amendments be made to contracts or articles of association the terms of which had been agreed between foreigners abroad, the Commission concluded on the possibility of limitations on its own orders:

> .....this problem does not arise in the present case because the contested decision does not go further than to state that the practices complained of constitute an infringement of Article 85 of the Treaty and impose a fine because of this. The simple fact of imposing a fine should not be considered as exercising an enforcement jurisdiction. 94

Nevertheless, I.C.I. denied the interpretation above and argued before the Court that the imposition of a fine is a means of putting competition law into effect and that the purpose of it is to influence

93. See J. Rahl, Common Market and American Antitrust: Overlap and Conflict 139(1970).

94. I.C.I. Case 628.

the applicant's conduct.[95] The Commission, in its rejoinder to the Court, reiterated the observations it had previously stated in a more detailed manner:

> The fact of declaring that the conduct of the applicant is illegal under the Treaty and of inflicting a fine on it should not be confused with the stage of effective coercion, that is to say, with putting that declaration into effect and enforcing those fines by issuing injunctions or effecting confiscations. That is the distinction between jurisdiction to prescribe and jurisdiction to enforce. By virtue of the former a public authority draws up provisions in relation to its own territory and these apply even if the act has been committed abroad. On the other hand, in exercising its jurisdiction to enforce, the authority in question will sometimes attempt to control the acts which are to be carried out abroad. 96

Advocate-General Mayras followed the same distinction between the imposition of fines on the one hand and the exercise of coercive enforcement measures on the other hand as relied on by the Commission:

> .....it must be recognized that those same authorities are competent to prohibit an agreement or practice which produces direct, foreseeable and substantial effects inimical to competition on their own territory and thus, in this case, in the Common Market, and that they are even competent to impose sanctions, even pecuniary ones, by judicial or administrative decisions.
>
> Might it not nevertheless be objected that to impose a fine is ipso facto in the nature of an enforcement jurisdiction?
>
> I think not, for two reasons:
> - The imposition of a pecuniary sanction, the purpose of which is to suppress conduct interfering with competition, and also to prevent its continuance or renewal, should be distinguished from the recovery of a fine imposed which could only be effected, should the undertaking penalized refuse to pay, by means of forcible execution.
>
> - It is also necessary to distinguish, I think, between the imposition of a fine and a true injunction which would result, for the production, under pain of periodic penalty payments, of certain documents, or which would constitute a means of applying pressure to obtain the revocation of certain clauses considered illegal.
>
> In my opinion the Commission was competent to take the contested decision in relation to the undertakings outside the Common Market, without its being necessary to consider the fact that there are no legal means available to it to ensure that its decision is in fact implemented. 97

95. Ibid. at 630.

96. Ibid. at 633-634.

97. Ibid. at 695.

4-60. The Continental Can Decision did not impose fines on the enterprises involved, but required Continental Can Corporation to put an end to the violation of Art. 86 of the Treaty, and for that purpose to present proposals to the Commission within a certain period. On appeal the order was annulled on grounds irrelevant to the subject discussed here, but without the Court commenting on the legality of the relief sought by the Commission. The Commission's order meant in fact that a dissolution of a merger was to be carried out by a holding company situated abroad.[98] Although the order primarily entailed activities in the Netherlands stock-exchange it also required some activities to be carried out abroad.

4-61. In the Zoja Decision the Commission, in addition to imposing a fine on the parent company and its subsidiary, ordered the foreign parent company to supply certain quantity of raw-material (60,000 kg) to an enterprise within the Common Market, at a price not exceeding the maximum price charged for those products: all this under the threat of penalties for delay. The Commission also ordered the NCE concerned to submit proposals for subsequent supplies under additional penalties for delay.

The relevant issue in that connection was whether or not the Commission and the Court would have sufficient jurisdiction not only to impose fines, but also to order some positive action to be taken by a foreign corporation largely outside the territory of the Common Market, for Commercial Solvents Corporation would surely need to take appropriate production measures.[99] The applicants in the Commercial

98. Cf. Continental Can Decision D35.

99. Cf. Allen "The Development of European Community Antitrust Jurisdiction Over Alien Undertakings" 2 Legal Issues of European Integration 74 (1974).

Solvents Case apparently did not raise this question, although it challenged the competence of the Commission under Reg. 17 "to issue specific orders for delivery of products and for submitting..... proposals for further supply, both sanctioned by a daily penalty for non-compliance". The Court held that the Commission did not exceed its discretion according to Art. 3 of Reg. 17, as it may order certain acts or provide certain advantages which have been wrongfully withheld, as well as prohibit the continuation of certain actions, practices or situations which are contrary to the Treaty.[100]

4-62. In the Franco-Japanese Ballbearings Decision the Commission was for the first time faced with a situation in which it could have directed an order to NCES having no establishment within the Common Market. However, it avoided either fining the parties or even ordering them to terminate the agreement, but only declared the arrangement to constitute an infringement of Art. 85(1) of the Treaty and notified its decision to those involved. In its Fourth Report on Competition Policy the Commission explained that it did not enjoin the parties to terminate the agreement since the parties had made a formal statement that they were no longer bound by it.[101]

In the subsequent French and Taiwanese Mushroom Packers Decision, where similarly neither of the NCES had an establishment within the Common Market, the Commission ordered all parties to terminate the agreement, but fined only the French partners. The reason for the distinction between the Community and NCES with regard

---

100. Commercial Solvents Case 255, at para. 45.

101. See Fourth Report on Competition Policy, point 75 (at page 51).

to fines for the same infringement was, as stated in the decision, the "unawareness" by the NCES of the scope of the competition rules. Nevertheless, the Commission's avoidance of imposing a fine on the Taiwanese Mushroom Packers might have well resulted from considerations relevant to its enforcement jurisdiction.

(2) Summary of Guidelines Concerning Relief Measures Against Non-Community Enterprises and Their Scope

(a) The Limits on the Reach of Orders to be Carried Out Abroad

4-63. Although the Commission admits its inability, or its lack of right, to pursue effective coercive measures abroad (see 4-59) it is, nevertheless, apparent from the case law that remedies which are regularly required for the protection of competition within the Common Market may, when directed to NCES, involve at least a modicum of action in foreign countries, although for the most part the orders can be carried out in the Common Market.

4-64. It is not yet completely clear from the case law what the Commission would still consider as permitted orders to carry out some activity abroad and which are the exact proper measures available within the Common Market to enforce the carrying out of some activity abroad. We submit that the question of how much action is required abroad in order to comply with such orders by NCES depends on the circumstances in each particular situation. Some orders, which may be readily accepted by the Commission, may require the performance of acts within the Common Market which will, however, affect persons or things outside it. The distinction is not easy to maintain between the latter type of orders and orders enjoining acts outside the territorial limit of the Common Market, or even the enjoinment of acts within the Common Market, even though the enterprise, to comply therewith, must take affirmative acts outside the Common Market. However, it is very difficult, at this stage of our enquiry, to conclude whether the Commission would affirmatively and directly order NCES to perform acts abroad. The examination of this issue in the context of international law may throw some light on the possible approach. See 6-30 to 6-32.

4-65. The Commission's power to impose fines and penalties and to order enterprises to terminate an infringement are wide and flexible. The general terms of the judgment in the Commercial Solvents Case indicate that the Commission is in an advantageous position with regard to NCES in that it can on the one hand require enterprises to bring an end to an infringement, without telling them specifically what to do,[102] while on the other hand it may, if it so wishes, order specific actions to be taken by the enterprise (within the exercise of its powers and in a way appropriate to the nature of the infringement in question). Although in many cases the difference in the final result would not be material, the semantic change in the language of the order may allow the Commission to enjoy better relations with third countries. Some leeway may be allowed in permitting particular accomodations in orders directed to NCES, e.g. if it is clear that an action abroad is required the order can include a direction to the NCE to terminate and conceal the agreement, with the alternative of modifying it.

(b) Effectiveness of Relief Measures Against Non-Community Enterprises

4-66. The case law, as yet, does not contain precedents concerning

102. On this background Advocate-General Warner stressed that requesting the enterprises to submit general proposals to end the infringement would have placed them in an intolerable position (see Commercial Solvents Case 272).

the ineffectiveness of measures which the Community has taken against NCES. As in the incidence of requests for information from NCES, the enforcement of remedies seems to depend on the various relationships of the NCE with the territory of the Common Market, i.e. whether the NCE is a subsidiary of a Community parent company, whether the NCE is a parent company of a Community subsidiary or controls a branch or an office within the Common Market, or merely has assets thereof, or whether the NCE sells to the Common Market without internal affiliations with Community enterprises (its business may be carried on by itself alone, in conjunction with other NCES which do not themselves do business in the Common Market, or through legally distinct Community agents). Each of these relationships may allow an opportunity for a separate discussion on the effectiveness of the Community enforcement jurisdiction. From this point of view the problems of enforcement, as treated in the case law and as examined in detail below, can be simply described as the problems of applying and adjusting the proper remedy.

C. Practical and Legal Considerations in the Enforcement of Orders Against Non-Community Enterprises

(1) Problems of Applying and Adjusting the Proper Remedy

(a) Sanctions Imposed Jointly and Severally on Non-Community Parent Companies and on their Subsidiaries Within the Common Market

4-67. In the *Zoja Decision* the Commission required that the applicants, jointly and severally, would pay the fine and resume supplies, under certain conditions, to a Community enterprise. The decision was approved by the Court which also confirmed the liability of both the parent company and its subsidiary for the prohibited conduct. The legal reasoning for such an order may possibly be based on the concept of an "agency theory" (see 2-26). Nevertheless, such a wide scope of liability was also intended to assist the Commission in creating a threat to the whole of the economic unit if it does not abide by the order. In fact the way in which the Commission had used the concept of an "intelligent agent" for the imposition of fines jointly and severally was not even clear of misunderstanding. The decision was criticized by the applicants who pleaded before the Court that even on the hypothesis (rejected by both applicants) that Istituto was a dependent subsidiary of Commercial Solvents Corporation, and that its behaviour in the market had to be imputed to the latter, "the Commission's own theory has not been consistent because if the Commission is right in alleging that Commercial Solvents Corporation dictated Istituto's conduct, then the latter cannot be considered as liable for the former's decision."[103]

4-68. The possibility of fining both the foreign parent company and its subsidiary within the Common Market as a method of facilitating enforcement must be supported by substantive legal reasons and, therefore, is not readily available in every case where parent-subsidiary relations exist. Only particular circumstances may lend themselves to the application of the "intelligent agent" concept which provides the ground on which both companies can be held jointly and severally liable. See 2-27.

---

103. Commercial Solvents Case, pleas and arguments of the parties, 229. See also Koppensteiner, supra note 37, at 311 in n.99; the commentator states that in upholding the conviction of Istituto the Court's position was manifestly illogical and obviously unsound.

In the Dyestuffs Cases where the economic unit theory supported the Court's judgment neither the Court nor the Commission proposed that the parent companies and the subsidiaries involved were equally liable for the infringement. In the Continental Can Decision the Commission ordered only the parent company to put an end to the infringement of Art. 86, and to submit proposals for this purpose. The Court, which annulled the orders, confirmed, however, that the transaction under issue was to be attributed first and foremost to the parent company, Continental Can.[104]

4-69. In the Hoffmann-La Roche Decision and in the United Brands Decision the Commission imposed fines only on the non-Community parent companies and exculpated their subsidiaries within the Common Market. That approach, in both cases, was approved by the Court. However, the Commission acted differently in the Lipton Cash Registers Decision where it imposed a heavy fine for which the Swedish parent company and its English subsidiary were jointly and severally liable. Both companies were ordered to bring the infringement to an end, but only Hugin Register Ltd. (U.K.) was requested, under the threat of periodic penalty payments for delay, to submit proposals for the resumption of supplies of spare parts to an English company which had complained about the practice.[105] (See 2-9). The Commission had probably found the English subsidiary an "intelligent agent", although the decision did not elaborate this point. The precautions the Commission had taken for ensuring an effective and enforceable order were therefore the

104. Continental Can Case 242, at para. 16. The appeal, however, was lodged both by the subsidiary and the parent company as the case was entitled, in the Journal Official of 8th January, 1972, "Europemballage Corporation", and likewise the letter accompanying the decision was served on Europemballage and there too the case was called "Europemballage Corporation". The Court stated that the heading of the contested decision was a formal error which can not effect the validity of the contested measure.

105. See Lipton Cash Registers Decision D37 at para. 75, and D40-D41.

imposition of operative-positive orders mainly on the subsidiary within the Common Market. The Lipton Cash Registers Decision was overruled by the Court on a different ground.

(b) Seizure of Foreign Assets or Property Within the Common Market

4-70. If the NCE which is found liable for infringing the competition rules and is fined has a place of business or assets within the Common Market then the Commission, as in the case of a Community enterprise, can insist on the application of Art. 192 of the Treaty for the purpose of enforcing the decision. Art. 192 provides as follows:

> Decisions of the Council or of the Commission which impose a pecuniary obligation on persons other than States shall be enforceable.
>
> Enforcement shall be governed by the rules of civil procedure in force in the State in the territory of which it is carried out. The order for its enforcement shall be appended to the decision, without other formality than verification of authenticity of the decision, by the national authority which the Government of each Member State shall designate for this purpose and shall make known to the Commission and to the Court of Justice.
>
> When these formalities have been completed on application by the party concerned, the latter may proceed to enforcement in accordance with the national law, by bringing the matter directly before the competent authority.
>
> Enforcement may be suspended only by a decision of the Court of Justice. However, the courts of the country concerned shall have jurisdiction over complaints that enforcement is being carried out in an irregular manner.

Seizure of foreign assets within the Common Market, as an enforcement technique in the context of decisions against NCES, was proposed by several writers. Honig, Brown, Gleiss and Hirsch state that by calling in the aid of Art. 192 the Commission would be able "to call upon the national authorities of the Member State, in whose territory the assets of the NCE are situated, to levy execution against those assets to the extent of the fine or penalty imposed."[106] The danger to parties, both of whom are outside the territory of the Common Market may be, in these writers' opinion, a very serious one in law. We have already mentioned suggestions by Hug and by Deringer, in the context of requests for information from NCES, that the Community may in a case of refusal seize assets inside the Common Market by way of penalizing such enterprises. See 4-46. Kruithof states that it seems logical that the authorities of the Community have the power to seize all property which the foreign company owns in the Community in order to obtain payment of fines and penalties.[107] A leading official of the Commission stated at an early stage of the operation of the competition policy, that the idea that penalties may be imposed and enforced on NCES by distraint on property inside the Common Market belonging to them was not ruled out by the Commission.[108]

4-71. The Commission has not as yet been in a situation that actually required the application of Art. 192, which it cites in each decision as the basis for enforcement, against the property of a NCE within the Common Market.[109] From observations of the Commission in the Dyestuffs

---

106. Honig, Brown, Gleiss and Hirsch, Cartel Law of the European Economic Community 14-15 (1963).

107. Kruithof, supra note 45, at 12.

108. Statement by Mr. G. Linssen (Office of Competition, Commission of the EEC) in The Application of Articles 85 and 86 of the Treaty in the Antitrust Structure of the European Common Market (a penal debate) 153 (J. Growley ed., Fordham University Press, 1963).

109. In 1975 the Commission replied to a W.Q. which, inter alia, wanted to know the number of competition cases where the fines had been fully paid up and inquired whether the Commission had ever followed the enforcement procedure when a fine was not paid up in due course. The Commission replied that so far it had had to resort to the enforcement procedure under Art. 192 on one occasion only. This was the case of ACF Chemiefarma NV (a Community enterprise) which paid the fine after the procedure had been initiated (see answer to W.Q. No.542/74, O.J. 1975, C40/16). In correction to this answer (which was published as an answer to W.Q. 584/76, O.J. 1977, C27/16) the Commission admitted that at that time Boehringer Mannheim GmbH (a Community enterprise) still owed it 80,000 units of account (this happened as a matter of error and the Commission took immediate steps to collect the amount).

Cases it may be deduced that there may be legal limits (as distinct from practical limits) to the seizure of property if it involves coercive measures which oblige a NCE to carry on certain activities abroad (see 4-59); this issue is to be further discussed in context of international law (see 6-31). Here we only emphasize that a seizure of foreign property can be a weapon in the Commission's anti-trust arsenal and may prove to be of considerable value at times as a lever to compel NCES to consent to its orders. While the seizure of property method may not be used often it is always a potential threat against NCES. A point which supports a forfeiture system as an enforcement method is that the imposition of a fine or a penalty by the Commission would otherwise normally be a futile gesture, because foreign courts are very likely to refuse to give effect to the Commission's decision. See 4-76.

4-72. If a forfeiture method were used the Commission would then have to decide what is the legal right of the NCE concerned in assets within the Common Market. Where the assets belong to the economic unit which has been found to act in infringement of the competition rules then their location within the Common Market and the legal right of the foreign parent company in such assets are relatively easy questions. In other cases, where there is no liability of the subsidiary or other interests of the NCE within the Common Market, identification of the assets and the legal right in them can be based on information in Form A/B if the arrangement has been notified. Form A/B for application for a negative clearance and notification in pursuance of Art. 85(3) requires enterprises, established or having their seat outside the territory of the Common Market, to state the name and address of their representative or branch established in the territory of the Common Market (Instructions 1.6). Nevertheless, since the absence of a place of business within the Common Market is not a condition for accepting the notification by the Commission[110] and since the Commission does not require in such instances a designation of an agent within the Common Market, tracing the location of assets belonging to the foreign NCE concerned may become more difficult. Furthermore, in many cases infringements are found without any notification being made at all.

The question of the legal right of a NCE in the assets within the Common Market also concerned the relevant time.[111] This question for example depends on the law to be applied to the transaction; import goods become the property of the purchaser already on conclusion of the contract of sale, the contract for work, labour and materials or the contract for work and labour (Latin system) or only through transition (system of German law). In the latter case, too, transfer of possession can be effected by selecting the place of performance outside the territory of the Treaty and delivering the imported goods there to an agent of the purchaser, for instance, a carrier.[112]

(c) Measures Against the Absent Co-Conspirator

4-73. It seems likely that, if the requirements for personal and substantive jurisdiction are satisfied, the Commission may pursue proceedings in the absence of a non-Community partner. See 4-21. The question then is how effectively the decision can influence the absent co-conspirator. Such proceedings would inevitably place a practical

---

110. See Kruithof, supra note 45, at 93.

111. See Hug, supra note 63, at 666.

112. It has been indicated in a private communication with Mr. J. Temple-Lang, a Legal Adviser to the Commission, that a forfeiture method in the present context is regarded by the Legal Service of the Commission as a practical possibility; the assets concerned must be defined as exclusively owned by the enterprise, but they do not have to be related to the subject of the proceedings.

limitation upon the effectiveness of any enforcement measures if these are required by the Commission.

A decision about the illegality of an arrangement would only be of a declaratory nature, as it is in accordance with the Treaty provisions that arrangements of the kind described in the Treaty are prohibited and automatically void, no prior decision to that effect being required (Art. 85(1) and (2) and Art. 1 of Reg. 17). But this may mean, at least, a public examination of the absent enterprise's conduct in the light of antitrust standards. At most, it may mean the reorganization of the ownership of properties in which the non-resident enterprise has a crucial commercial interest, and the dismantling of arrangements with Community enterprises on which it had counted.

The legal consequences of the Commission's decision will have effects on the co-conspirator's business abroad (even if only effects of the illegality of the arrangement are recognized abroad; see 4-77) and, of course, within the Member States of the Community. For instance, the NCE or its assignee would not be in a position to complain in national courts within the Common Market, or to argue the contract's legality to enforce it in a territory of a national court. This is a necessary measure of protection so that the Community party in such a case does not continue to perform a contract which the Commission has attacked under the competition laws.[113]

4-74. The absence of foreign associates will not, however, prevent the Commission from finding a violation if the facts warrant it, and

113. Cf. Oberdorfer, Gleiss and Hirsch, Common Market Cartel Law, sec. 22 (CCH 2nd ed. 1971) See also discussion in 1-22. The writers furthermore state that a foreign judgment validating an agreement that violated the Community competition rules could not be enforced inside the Common Market since it would be a breach of the ordre public.

from restraining those within the reach of its mandate from continuing a restrictive business practice. For example, where a cartel arrangement for a division of markets stipulates that each party will stay within its own territory, and that the NCE, accordingly, may refrain from shipping to the Common Market, the only defendants before the Commission may be the Community partners to the arrangement; the NCE, if absent because of various reasons, will merely be named as a co-conspirator. For those who are within the jurisdiction this may involve disadvantages, since they may by decision of the Commission be forced into the awkward position of having to renegotiate agreements with an enterprise which may not be subject to any antitrust inhibition.[114]

A Community enterprise might, however, be held liable in a damage suit in a foreign court for its failure to perform the agreement enjoined by the Commission, but the foreign court could probably try to avoid a direct conflict with Community law.[115]

(d) Enforcement Measures Against Non-Community Enterprises and Limitation Periods in Community Law

4-75. Since fines imposed on an absent co-conspirator can be realized from its assets within the Common Market they can present a threat to the enterprise, in case of non-compliance, in respect of any future contacts with the territory of the Common Market. This legal situation is referred to in various legal systems as "entry

---

114. It would be interesting to see whether injunctions may be granted by the Commission binding defendants not to perform contracts with parties not before the Commission.

115. In the U.S. the Attorney General's Committee recommended that in such situations (where an American enterprise is prosecuted abroad for infringing an agreement ruled prohibited by a U.S. court) the U.S., through the Department of State, should use its offices to assist the American party in defending the foreign suit (see Report of the Attorney General's National Committee to Study the Antitrust Laws 76 (1955).

after jurisdiction", i.e. where the State must wait until the offender enters its territory. "Entry after jurisdiction" may be a precise label as to the moment when jurisdiction can be exercised, but it is a system of enforcement, not a criterion of jurisdiction.[116] The OECD Committee of Experts on Restrictive Business Practices observed, in this connection, that the fact that the Common Market (as well as the United States) constitutes an important market which multinational enterprises are obliged to enter sooner or later must be an incentive for them to comply with decisions imposing fines for anticompetitive behaviour.[117]

The latter observation is particularly significant in view of the possibility that a case may be pending for several years if the foreign defendant refuses to appear in court; this may exert an influence on NCES to appear and, eventually, to comply with the decision taken. In this connection Regulation 2988/74[118] provides for limitation periods not only as regards the power to impose fines or penalties, but also as regards the power to enforce decisions and fines, penalties or periodic penalty payments (with a limitation period of five years). The Commission may even use permitted legal excuses to interrupt the limitation periods which will then start the time running afresh, e.g. by notification of a decision which increases the original amount of the fine or periodic penalty payments.[119] The regulation,

---

116. See Baxter "Extraterritorial Application of the Domestic Law" 1 Un. of Brit. Col. L.R. 333 (1959).
117. OECD, Committee of Experts on Restrictive Business Practices, Restrictive Business Practices of Multinational Enterprises 53, at sec. 180 (1977).
118. Regulation 2988/74 of the Council of 26 November 1974, Concerning Limitation Periods in Proceedings and the Enforcement of Sanctions Under the Rules of EEC, Relating to Transport and Competition; O.J. 1974, L319/1.
119. Interruption of the limitation periods could possibly be by a decision imposing periodic penalty payments on a NCE with the hope to compel it, eventually, by occasionally increasing the sums, to comply with the decision (Art. 16(a) or Reg. 17).

however, lacks a special provision for the interruption of limitation periods in the particular situations under consideration here.

(2) Would the Community Antitrust Decisions and Judgments be Enforced or Recognized in Non-Member States?

4-76. The enforcement of the antitrust provisions of the Treaty becomes somewhat doubtful where the NCE, which is responsible for the restraint of trade and competition within the Common Market, has neither a branch nor a permanent agency nor any assets in the territory of the Common Market.[120] The question arises whether the Community can achieve its aim of enforcing Community law, in the absence of treaties to that end, by invoking the assistance of the foreign State's courts. In other words, is it open to the Community to bring proceedings, in the courts of another State for an injunction, for example, which restrains the defendant from following certain restrictive practices?

The answers to these questions require the elaboration of concepts of private and public international law, as has been considered elsewhere in the study. For example see 1-21. However, a few brief guidelines will be given here. A direct reply to these questions could be found in the following explanation by Mann:

> .....merely to put these questions should be sufficient to make it obvious that the answers can only be in the negative. The reason is to be found in the broad principle of international law according to which a State has no right to enforce in a foreign court any claim which in substance involves the direct or indirect enforcement of a prerogative right of the enforcing State, which is made by virtue of sovereign power. 121

120. See Hug, supra note 63, at 668-696.

121. Mann, supra note 1, at 141-142. See also Cheshire's Private International Law, supra note 4, at 134. For references to sources on the unenforceability of penal claims in many countries see Mann "Pregogative Rights of Foreign States and the Conflict of Laws" 40 Transactions of the Grotius Society 28, in n.8 (1955).

4-77. A question distinct from the issue of enforcement of judgments is whether the penal laws of one country will be taken notice of in another. According to Cheshire a negative reply is not true, for subject to the possible intervention of the doctrine of public policy, such a law must be regarded as operative in the proceedings if it is part of the foriegn legal system which, according to the relevant rule for the choice of law, governs the transaction that is sub judice.[122]

In the present context it should be stressed that the enforcement of a foreign penal law must be distinguished from its application or recognition. Although enforcement will not be allowed, "it is going too far to assert that the penal laws of one country cannot be taken notice of in another".[123] The illegality of a contract, though springing from an offence according to Community competition laws, cannot be entirely ignored in a foreign country. The distinction between the enforcement and the application of foreign laws has been developed both in the Civil Law and in the Common Law; in England it was primarily emphasized by Sir A. McNair.[124] The distinction is a fruitful one provided the term "enforcement" is understood in a narrow sense; the peculiar enforcement envisaged by this concept, as explained by Mann, presupposes that it is a foreign State or one of its instruments that asserts before the court the authority conferred upon it by its own law.[125] The rule so established is, in all probability, not subject to any exception if a foreign law is of a penal, revenue or political character.[126]

---

122. Cheshire's Private International Law, supra note 4, at 139.
123. See Ibid.
124. See A. McNair, The Legal Effects of War 359 (3rd ed. 1948).
125. Mann, supra note 121, at 27.
126. See Mann "Illegality and the Conflict of Laws" 21 M.L.Rev. 131 (1958).

Both the recognition of foreign public law and the exceptions to this rule are derived from the public policy consideration of the country concerned. Since it is obvious that the Community would not be able to enforce its competition laws abroad, the question of the recognition, either of its public law or of some effects of its decisions abroad, remains particularly important in relation to the application of the competition rules in the private law sphere. Further examination of this issue is beyond the scope of the subjects under consideration in this study (see 1-11).

(3) Enforcement Measures Conflicting with Foreign Law

4-78. In the incidence of orders addressed to NCES an important question is whether the Commission will order enterprises to terminate an infringement or an abuse in a way which will compel the carrying out of an act, outside its territory, contrary to the laws of the country in which it is to be performed. As to this problem with regard to extraterritorial discovery orders see 4-52 and 4-53. The familiar problem with such orders or injunctions is that they sometimes place the NCE in a difficult position, because the authorities of the foriegn country or the countries where the decision has to be carried out may give these enterprises conflicting orders. We have noticed with regard to extraterritorial discovery orders that there are no rules of Community law to settle such conflicts and it seems mainly a political question whether the Community will use all its powers and influence to force NCES to comply with its decisions. See discussion in 4-55.

4-79. There are at least four situations where there is little chance that a Commission decision will conflict with obligations imposed upon the defendant by foreign States. First, if foreign and Community law coincide , the problem of any conflict is avoided. Such a coincidence of laws is however unlikely in the antitrust field. See survey in 1-3. Second, although foriegn law may permit a particular type of agreement which the Commission would consider illegal, the problem may possibly be resolved by the unenforceability of the agreement abroad, not for antitrust reasons, but as a result of the contract law of the foreign state (i.e. lack of contractual requirements), or because of the existence of a termination clause which the defendant has a right to invoke (e.g. termination for reasons beyond the control of the parties). Third, an agreement, even though it is enforceable abroad, may not result in a conflict of obligations because the only parties aggrieved by the termination are close associates or subsidiaries of the defendant and thus are not likely to bring a suit. Finally, a foreign statute may be designed to give certain benefits to the defendant, but not to impose any duties upon him; thus, an order by the Commission that the defendant shold refrain from taking advantage of such a statute would be incompatible with foreign legislative policy, but could not result in conflicting foreign judgments against the defendant.

In other instances the problem of a decision conflicting with obligations imposed upon the defendant in a foreign State will be somewhat greater than in the situations above, but still may not deter the Commission from exercising properly its quasi-judicial task. This would be the case when the relevant foreign law is concerned only with the protection of private rights generally created by agreements enforceable in foreign courts. In such cases it is likely that foreign courts, by invoking generally accepted doctrines of illegality, will treat the Commission decision as effectively terminating the contract (see 4-77). Similarly the foreign court may regard the Commission decision as stating the "proper law of the contract"; finding the "proper law of the contract" constitutes the English approach to problems of enforcing private international agreements.[127] It is also possible that, if a foreign court views the Commission's proceedings as penal, it may hesitate to issue a judgment or decree which is likely to subject the defendant to punishment by the Community.

4-80. Decisions designed to change the behaviour or the structure of foreign enterprises are expected to raise the greatest enforcement difficulties. They may give rise to real conflicts of sovereignty between States, particularly in cases where it is a foreign law which has required the enterprises to engage in the restrictive activities complained of. In this connection there are two limited defences which may be invoked by enterprises whose extraterritorial conduct would otherwise be subject to prosecution under Community competition laws. The first defence is that such conduct is interrelated with the public acts of a foreign sovereign within its territory, i.e. the defence of "act of State" which means that the real and primary cause of the injuury to competition was a sovereign act of a foreign executive within its territory, performed as a matter of policy in the course of its relations with another State, including its relations with the subjects of that State. The second defence is that such conduct is compelled by a foreign sovereign.[128]

---

127. Cheshire's Private International Law, supra note 4, at 229 et seq. The defence of illegality exists also in non-Common Law countries, e.g. Code Civil Articles 1131, 1133 (54th Ed., Dalloz,1955). This approach may also apply to the issue of whether a Community enterprise may be confronted by a foreign judgment, compelling it to carry action abroad which has previously been prohibited by the Commission (e.g. if such action abroad is required by a foreign enterprise which resorted to his own national courts for redress).

128. Both defences must be disentangled from the defence of sovereign immunity.

The defence of coercive foreign legislation in competition proceedings has not yet actually been applied in proceedings before the Commission. However, the Commission has taken a stand in respect of such a defence, at least in so far as it involves Art. 85 proceedings, in two pronouncements which deserve elaboration. The Commission first announced its position in the Third Report on Competition Policy when it stated that "Article 85 would not apply to export agreements imposed on firms in non-member countries by their governments, unless there was agreement or concerted practice between the firms".[129] Pertinent conclusions may also be inferred from guidelines the Commission gave in the Franco-Japanese Ballbearings Decision, on the question of which measures taken in Japan, at either government or private level, with a view to controlling exports of Japanese products to the Common Market (either by restricting them or by regulating them as regards price, quality or in any other respect) are outside the scope of Art. 85:

> Four types of measures can be distinguished and should be differently assessed:
>
> (a) measures taken in pursuance of trade agreements between the Community and Japan. These are acts of external commercial policy, which as such are outside the scope of Article 85 of the EEC Treaty.
>
> (b) measures imposed on Japanese undertakings by the Japanese authorities. These measures are also outside the scope of Article 85.
>
> (c) measures resulting from agreements or concerted practices between undertakings which are merely authorized by the Japanese authorities under Japanese law. Such authorization, while required for the measures to be lawful in Japan, would in no way alter the fact that the undertakings concerned were free to refrain from entering into an agreement or engaging in concerted practices.

---

129. Third Report on Competition Policy, page 27.

(d) measures resulting solely from agreement, concerted practices, or decisions by associations of undertakings, entered into or engaged in either unilaterally by Japanese undertakings or in concert with the appropriate European undertakings. These measures of a private nature may also come within the provisions of Article 85. 130

Although the "Japanese authorities" were not involved, the Franco-Japanese Ballbearings Decision gave the Commission an opportune moment to clarify the principle as it applies to proceedings at the Commission level. This pronouncement established the point that mere authorization of the defendant's conduct under foreign law, as opposed to conduct compelled under foreign law, is not a defence to the application of Community competition law. The defence that an act is compelled by a foreign sovereign may, however, be limited to incidents where the defendants had not solicited and obtained foreign legislation to facilitate their restrictive arrangements, while the foreign governmental interest in compelling the act is being viewed as merely incidental. If it had been otherwise, then the NCE would presumably be held to be intentionally infringing the competiton rules within the framework of Art. 15(1) of Reg. 17 and any defence would be denied to it. Merely petitioning a democratic government seems apparently to be permissible and in line with the regulation.[131]

The Franco-Japanese Ballbearings Decision limits the application of the principle in question here to "Japanese undertakings". This

130. Franco-Japanese Ballbearings Decision D14-D15, at para. 16.

131. These views are currently held by the Legal Service of the Commission and are based on the relevant American experience. It is thought at the Legal Service that the Commission may recognize a defence of coercive foreign legislation only in exceptional circumstances, e.g. if the foreign legislation protects vital interests of the foreign State like security, etc. In most cases the Commission will first attempt to deal with such matters through the political negotiations. (private information given by Mr. J. Temple-Lang in 2.10.79).

distinction may be more than academic if an inference can be drawn from it that the defence of foreign governmental coercion would not be available to Community enterprises doing business in the Common Market as well as in a foreign State, while a NCE which is doing business in the Common Marekt could take advantage of the defence enunciated by the Commission in regard to "measures imposed" by such foreign State.[132]

It is interesting to note that the general policy of States in matters of sovereign immunity may supply analogous precedents for the defence of foreign compulsion. This line of reasoning implies that one of the results of coercive foreign legislation is that, for jurisdictional purposes, the foreign sovereign and the enterprise are one and the same.

It can also be observed that the economic unit theory as recognized by the Community would seem to be equally applicable as a test for a foreign-based enterprise acting under the compulsion of a foreign sovereign; the necessary inference being that a firm coerced by a foreign government has not really made an agreement because of its lack of free will - a general principle of contract law applied to both competition law and foreign relations.[133] This suggestion further indicates that because of the absence of free will the conduct of the foreign enterprise which would otherwise be a violation of Art. 85(1) falls outside the prohibitions of that article. If it does the question

---

132. See Preston "The Defence of Coercive Foreign Legislation in Competition Proceedings Before the Commission of the European Economic Community" 11 The Int. Lawyer 625 (1977).

133. Ibid. at 626.

of being "null and void" under Art. 85(2) does not arise, and there is no use whatever for the escape provisions of Art. 85(3) and the implementing of Reg. 17.[134]

Although the exact circumstances in which the Commission may recognize a defence of sovereign immunity have not yet been fully laid down in the case law the Commission has indicated its intention to apply the competition rules to enterprises in a State-trading country. In one case the Commission examined an agreement of two firms in the German Democratic Republic (G.D.R.) with a West German firm. The parties reached a compromise settlement so that the agreement became compatible with the Common Market.[135]

Where defences are raised in objections to orders by the Commission alleged to be contrary to foreign law it is expected that the Commission's response to the assertion of such defences is likely to turn to the principles of comity. Particular attention has been given by international law specialists to this subject, which has often been discussed at international conferences, and such expectations are in line with their conclusions. See discussion in 6-48 to 6-52.

(4) Double Fines; the Question of Setting Off a Fine Imposed by a Foreign State Against a Fine Imposed by the Commission

4-81. The very fact that one and the same restrictive agreement can be the subject of two parallel procedures, namely the Community and

134. Ibid.

135. Re Pentacon Dresden/Elbe Kamera/Carl Hostert, Bull. E C 10-1978, point 2.1.41.

a third country one, raises the problem of the imposition of double fines. In the Boehringer Mannheim Case[136] the Court dismissed an application by an enterprise which had been fined by the Commission for the fine to be reduced by the amount of a fine imposed on it by an American court for an offence arising out of the same cartel agreement. The Court's judgment emphasized that the question whether the Commission is under a duty to set off against a fine it imposes the amount of a fine imposed by the authorities of a non-Member State only arises if the acts in the two cases are identical. This will not be the case where the acts, although they arise out of the self-same agreements, are in essence distinct from one another as regards both their purpose and their territorial impact, for the problem lies not in the cartel agreement itself, but in the execution of its terms.[137] The judgment only took into account such acts done in the execution of the cartel agreement as were likely to affect trade between Member States and the applicant argued nothing that could support the view that the conviction in the U.S. extended to acts done outside that country in execution of the cartel agreements and to its effects in such places. It is, however, apparent that the Commission is under a duty to take into account the sanctions already imposed on the enterprise for the same act in cases before the courts of Member States.[138]

D. The Need For a Community Manual of Powers and Procedure

4-82. It has been the purpose of this chapter to suggest some clarification of the extraterritorial enforcement measures of the

---

136. Case 2/72, Boehringer Mannheim GmbH v. Commission (No. 2) [1972] E.C.R. 1281.
137. Ibid. at 1289 (see in particular para. 6).
138. Ibid. at 1289, para 3. See also Case 14/68 Wilhelm v. Bundeskartellamt [1969] E.C.R. 1.

Community by drawing evidence from various Community sources. For that purpose the writer arranged a series of meetings with officials from both the Legal Service of the Commission and the Directorate-General of Competition. The advice and suggestions which were given on those occasions are embodied in the relevant sections of this chapter and for reasons of simplicity do not always include references to the names of officials.

One general conclusion which was repeatedly emphasized in those interviews was that a compilation of a comprehensive antitrust manual by the Commission would be very desirable in view of the uncertainty inherent in the topics discussed above and the few adjudicated cases. The Head of the Inspection Division at the Directorate-General of Competition, Mr. A. Pappalardo, indicated (in an interview on 17 January 1978) that important decisions in the process leading to the Commission final decisions in competition matters are the result of a beaurocratic consultations and are based on the general goals of the competition policy and on pragmatic considerations of efficacy but often lack the background of academic reasoning. In stressing that a manual, as suggested above, is generally necessary and even urgently required for the foreign businessman, Mr. Pappalardo referred to the American example. Both the Federal Trade Commission and the Antitrust Division of the U.S. Department of Justice have prepared general manuals for attorneys.[139] In 1977 the U.S. Department of Justice published an Antitrust Guide for International Operations.[140] A similar guide for the Community would enable foreign businessmen to

139. See BNA, Antitrust & Trade Reg. Rep. Oct. 21, 1975.

140. Antitrust Division, U.S. Dept. of Justice, Antitrust Guide for International Operations (1977), reprinted in BNA, Antitrust & Trade Reg. Rep. No. 799 (1977), and Trade Reg. Reports (CCH) No. 266, pt. II (1977).

consult in a relatively accessible manner the regulation by the Community of the topics which we have discussed in the preceding sections. Asssuming that the predictability and certainty of law is desirable, and assuming further that legal principles are available as a guide, we join the call for prompt compilation of the proposed manual.

CHAPTER V

A Comparative Study of the Jurisdiction of Community Member States and of the United States in Antitrust Matters involving Foreign Elements

INTRODUCTION

5-1. The proposed comparative study of legislative, judicial and enforcement aspects of antitrust laws will concentrate on restrictive trade legislation which has some connection with the Community. First the important laws and practice presently found within the Common Market (namely, the laws of Belgium, France, Germany, the Netherlands and the United Kingdom) will be briefly examined. Then we shall refer to the U.S. legislation which in particular operates on a comparable basis to that of the Community.[1]

A survey on the scope of those laws is important in the context of the present study, *inter alia*, becuase of the following reasons:

(1) To study and compare the systems of the Member States in order to arrive at a synthesis of the national concepts and to promote them into Community concepts adapted to the needs and interests of the Community. In the same manner the authors of the Treaty had undoubtedly

---

1. The texts of primary antitrust laws of the Member States and the United States, with explanatory notes, can be found in the OECD, *Guide to Legislation on Restrictive Business Practices* (loose leaf; the Guide is kept up to date)(hereinafter cited as "OECD, *Guide to Legislation*"). Another valuable source for texts of specific antitrust laws is the OECD, Report of the Committee of Experts on Restrictive Business Practices, *Export Cartels* (1974)(hereinafter cited as "OECD, *Export Cartels*").

relied on their national antitrust background in framing the legislation, and the present administrators of the Treaty are likewise accustomed to and influenced by the laws in their own countries.[2] It must also be observed that the States which constitute the EEC have to a certain extent delegated sovereign powers to the authorities of the Community. Here the general principle applies: Nemo plus juris in alium transferre potest quam ipse habet. International law sets limits to what any State can do by way of extraterritorial application of national laws. These same limitations hold good for the extraterritorial application of Treaty law by the authorities of the Community. The States constituting the EEC cannot set aside the international limitations of their national jurisdiction by entrusting this national jurisdiction in certain matters to a Community authority. Cf. 6-2 to 6-4.

(2) To study the foreign concepts of the U.S., which for long was the sole originator of extraterritorial application of antitrust laws, and either reject them as incompatible with the common European legal tradition and philosophy and the present economic and social realities, or receive, adopt and transpose them into the existing general and special legal framework of the Community.

---

2. Cf. Schapiro "The German Law Against Restraints of Competition: Comparative and International Aspects (Part I)" 62 Col. L. Rev. 3 (1962).

1. THE EXTRATERRITORIAL SCOPE OF MEMBER STATES' ANTITRUST LAWS

A. Belgium

5-2. Sec. 1 of the Act of 27th May, 1960, which provides for measures against abuses of economic power, applies to national persons and bodies incorporate acting in concert to exert a dominating influence "within the territory of the Kingdom, through industrial, commercial, agricultural or financial activities".[3] This law, which is a very narrow statute substantively, has been interpreted by the authorities to require that "effect" must be felt within the nation.[4] This "effect" is interpreted by Reepinghem and Waelbroeck as the exercise, in Belgium, of preponderant influence which serves as a jurisdictional link with Belgian law; the nationality of the holders of the economic power and the place of the conclusion of the cartel agreement or the seat of the central organs of the cartel are irrelevant in this respect.[5]

Import cartels and other import restrictions exercising dominant influence inside Belgium could be reached by the law. There is,

3. Act of 27th May, 1960, on Protection Against the Abuse of Economic Power; see OECD, Guide to Legislation Vol. 1, (Belgium 1.0)(Loi du 27 Mai 1960 Relative à la Protection Contre l'Abus de Puissance Économique).

4. See Business Regulation in the Common Market Nations (Blake ed. 1969), Vol. 1 (Ginsburg ed.) pt. 1, Belgium (by de Keyser & Suetens) 69, 160. See also del Marmol and Fontain, "Protection Against the Abuse of Economic Power in Belgium; the Law of May 27, 1960" 109 U.Pa.L.R. 931 et seq (1961); Suetens "Belgium Antitrust Law in Action" 2 C.M.L.Rev.338-339 (1964); Smit, Belgian and Dutch Antitrust Law, in Hearings on International Aspects of Antitrust Before the Subcomm. on Antitrust and Monopoly of the Sen. Comm. on the Judiciary, 89th Cong., 2nd Sess. 402, 403 (1966)(hereinafter cited "hearings").

5. P. Van Reepinghen and M. Waelbroeck "La Legislation Belge Concernant les Pratiques Restreignant la Concurrence" in Rapports au Colloque International de Droit Européen (Brussels 1962) pp.179, 182: a reference to this source appears in the opinion of the Advocate-General in the Dyestuffs Cases [1977] C.M.L.R. 596.

however, no specific legislation with regard to export cartels, which would apparently be generally beyond the scope of the law although the Act may be applicable in appropriate circumstances.[6]

It is interesting to note that Belgian law provides for a special procedure for notification of acquisitions and mergers which involve foreign interests and, any public offer for the purchase or exchange of securities in that respect must have prior authorization.[7]

In so far as enforcement jurisdiction is concerned it has been argued that the scope of the Belgian law "is academic if the head-quarters of an economic power and all of its property are situated in another country" as enforcement would then be completely "ineffectual".[8]

B. France

5-3. The French regulations of competition do not constitute a special body of laws; they are integrated in the general system of price regulations. The Price Ordinance of 30th June, 1945, as amended, makes a distinction between dominant position and the prohibition of cartels which does not involve any abuse of dominant position.[9]

The law seems to deal explicitly with territorial coverage in certain aspects. Art. 61 of the Price Ordinance provides that the

---

6. Cf. OECD, Restrictive Business Practices: Comparative Summary of Legislation in Europe and North America 33, 39 (1964).
7. See Art. 36 of the Law of 30th December, 1970, as amended by the Law of 17th August, 1973 (B.S.G. of 8th September, 1973) as interpreted in CCH, Common Market Reporter: Doing Business in Europe (Belgium) sec. 21, 522 (hereinafter cited as "CCH, Doing Business in Europe").
8. See Marmol and Fontain, supra note 4, at 931.
9. See Price Ordinance No. 45-1483, 1945: see in OECD, Guide to Legislation, Vol. 3 (France 1.0)(Ordonnance No.45-1483, 30th June 1945, C. PEN, 628, 644 (1966)).

antitrust provisions, Arts. 37 and 59, are applicable to transactions carried out in metropolitan France and its territorial waters, to CIF prices of imported goods, and to imports from all countries. Art. 62 exempts "exports direct or through an agent"; it follows from this article that export cartels are exempted in so far as they relate exclusively to exports and do not distort competition in the internal market.[10]

In the Dyestuffs Cases (Community cases which we have described in 2-2) Advocate-General Mayras' opinion expanded, for the purpose of comparative analysis, on the fact that the applicability of French law depends on the localization in the French market of the effect inhibiting competition or economic freedom. Examples were given in the opinion to illustrate the application of the law on this basis to foreign enterprises.[11]

It is not clear, however, to what extent the French antitrust laws reach conduct which is merely carried out abroad, but which has effects within the nation. Some writers opine that the effects within the country are all that is required.[12] In that respect Advocate-General Mayras stated that the Technical Commission on Cartels, which the Minister of Economic and Financial Affairs must consult before commencing legal proceedings, "is careful never to state the place where the agreement is made, and this implies that it does not consider

10. Cf. OECD, Export Cartels sec. 33; C. Edwards, Control of Cartels and Monopolies; An International Comparison 44 (1967)(with explanation of the method for appraisal of export cartels in France).

11. See I.C.I. Case 689.

12. See Business Regulation in the Common Market Nations (Blake ed. 1969), vol. 2 (Perillo & Blake eds.), pt. 1, France (by Bergsten) 310; Plaisant in I.L.A., Helsinki Conference 89.

this to be a determining factor". In this connection Mr. Mayras mentioned the second opinion of the Committee, dated 22nd April, 1966, on the electric lamp cartel, whereby the conduct of the Dutch company Phillips on the French market was held to be an abuse of a dominant position, even though the conduct was necessarily determined, in essence, in Holland. However, the contrary has also been stated, i.e. that the law is limited in its application to conduct which actually takes place in France.[13]

Criminal prosecution of a French national located outside France and exporting to France would apparently depend not only upon effects in the French market, but also whether they were unlawful under the law of the State where the sale was made. Bregsten states that apparently foreign nationals could not be prosecuted criminally for acts which merely have effects in France, but some civil consequences are possible.[14]

C. Germany

5-4. The German Act Against Restraints of Competition provides (sec. 98(2)):

> This Act shall apply to all restraints of competition which have effect in the area in which this Act applies, even if they result from acts done outside such area. 15

This section has been interpreted as applying to all restraints of competition which have effects in the domestic market without regard

13. See Riesenfeld, statement in Hearings, supra note 4, at 403, 406.
14. See Business Regulation in the Common Market Nations, supra note 12, at 306-307.
15. Act Against Restraints of Competition, of 27th July, 1957, as amended, see in OECD, Guide to Legislation, Vol. 2 (Germany 1.0) (Gesetzgegen Wettbewerbsbeschränkungen (GWB) of 27th July, 1957) (the German law was consolidated in 1973).

to where the enterprises concerned or the acts causing the restraints have been committed.[16] Before further elaboration of this interpretation other sections of the Act deserve attention.

The general principle of Sec. 98(2) is supplemented or modified by several special provisions. Export cartels of domestic enterprises are subject to the control of the Act regardless of whether they affect domestic competition or not. Where they only restrain competition on foreign markets they are valid upon mere notification (Sec. 9(2)) but remain under the abuse control of the Federal Cartel Office (Sec. 12).[17] Export cartels having domestic effect are subject to Sec. 1 of the Act, but may be exempted under Sec. 6(2) and (3), if they are necessary to carry out "desired regulation of competition in markets outside" Germany, and if they do not violate German treaty obligations or lead to a substantial restraint of domestic competition where "there is a predominating interest in preserving competition".[18] "Voluntary" export cartels, i.e. arrangements without an obligatory character, are not export cartels in the legal sense.

---

16. Such an explanation was given to Sec. 98(2) by the Bundestag Committee for Economic Affairs which proposed the formula which finally became the relevant provision in its report (Bundestagsdrucksache 3644, Annex at 40)(translation into English is found in Markert "The Application of German Antitrust Law of International Restraints on Trade" 7 Va. J. Int. L. 52 (1967). See also CCH, Doing Business in Europe (Germany) sec. 23.521; I. Schwartz "Applicability of National Law on Restraints of Competition to International Restraints" in Cartel and Monopoly in Modern Law, Vol. 2, 703-704 (1961); a survey by R. Müller in I.L.A., Tokyo Conference 447-448.

17. However, the Supreme Court has held that "pure" export cartels (i.e. cartels having no impact on the domestic market) need not be registered with the Federal Cartel Office (Judgment of 12th July 1973, Case No. KRB 2/72, "Mannesmannröhern-Werke"). Consequently that Office has no power to check whether those cartels entail abusive practices.

18. For a survey of the appropriate appraisal of the domestic impact of export agreements by the Federal Cartel Authority see Edwards, supra note 10, at 184.

The German Act does not contain special provisions for international cartels. Therefore, Sec. 6 applies not only to agreements between German enterprises but also to the participation of German enterprises in international cartels.[19]

Import cartels (Sec. 7) are permissible if the German importers are faced with monopolistic or oligopolistic competition on the foreign suppliers' side. The import agreement must not relate to transactions on the domestic market, but indirect domestic effects necessarily arising out of its performance do not prevent authorization.

Sec.15 dealing with vertical agreements on resale prices and conditions with respect to "goods or commercial services relating to markets located within the area to which this Act applies" is merely a confirmation of the principle of Sec. 98(2). Under this rule, vertical agreements on prices and conditions are void if they limit the competitive choice of domestic buyers. The same rule applies to measures against vertical agreements covered by Sec. 18.[20]

As to private law, Sec. 98(2) constitutes a conflict rule of German private international law, requiring the application of German law to all restrictive agreements that affect the German market. Consequently, an agreement which is ineffective under German cartel law has to be treated as such by all German courts and administrative authorities, regardless of where it was concluded, or of which law is

19. Export cartels are also subject to other restrictions of the German Act, see OECD, Guide to Legislation, supra note 15: OECD, Export Cartels, sec. 12.

20. Cf. Markert, supra note 16, at 58-60.

applicable according to the intentions of the parties, or of whether it is permitted or even - as in the case of a compulsory cartel - legally required abroad.[21] The Act further provides for enforcement by private parties: (a) by permitting, to a certain extent, the intervention of private parties in proceedings before the cartel authority; (b) by giving, in certain cases of the violation of provisions of the Act, the aggrieved party the right to take legal proceedings against the violator for an injunction, damages or other appropriate relief.

5-5. As to agreements on patents and similar industrial property rights, Sec. 20(1) applies both to domestic and foreign patents and designs; this is firmly established in the Federal Cartel Office practice.[22] Sec. 20(1) provides:

> Agreements concerning the acquisition or use of patents, utility models, or protected seed varieties shall be ineffective in so far as they impose upon the acquiror or licensee any restrictions on his business conduct which go beyond the scope of the protected right; restrictions pertaining to the type, extent, quantity, territory or period of exercise of such right shall not be deemed to go beyond its scope.

Sec. 20(2), No. 5, provides that the prohibition of Sec. 20(1) does not apply to "obligations of the acquiror or licensee relating to restraints of competition in markets outside the area to which this Act applies". Whether this foreign market clause automatically exempts all restrictions imposed on German licensees pertaining to foreign markets or merely those relating to the protected right is, according to Markert, still an open question.[23] The Federal Cartel Office has

21. See Ibid. at 59; Schapiro (Part II of the Article), supra note 2, at 238; OECD Guide to Legislation, Vol. 2 (Germany 2.0), 19.
22. See Markert, supra note 16, at 60.
23. Ibid.

interpreted this limitation as applying only to restrictions relating to the protected matter, i.e. restrictions which exceed the scope of the patent are invalid.[24] This interpretation of the foreign market exemption could be criticized as not being in harmony with the principle of domestic effects established in Sec. 98(2).[25]

Export restrictions imposed on domestic licensees in respect of other matters (not relating to the protected right) are, therefore, subject to the general rule of Sec. 20(1). The same applies to restrictions on foreign licensees having effects on the business opportunities of domestic enterprises.[26] As to the impact of the "effects" required in this case, see below 5-6. An obligation not to compete which was imposed by a German licensor on a foreign licensee has been held to be still related to the protected matter and, therefore, exempted by Sec. 20(2), No. 5.[27]

5-6. In view of the extraterritorial reach of the German antitrust law the question of what constitutes an "effect in the area in which this Act applies" has not yet been clearly defined. The prevailing view is that this requirement includes only direct effects on the competitive process or on the economic freedom of enterprises on domestic markets, but not other indirect economic effects.[28] However, a difference of opinion remains as to whether any direct influence or

24. See BKA decision of 14th December 1960, WuW/E BkartA 331, 334-336 11 WuW 297 (1961); Federal Cartel Office, Activity Report, 1962, p.72.
25. See Buxbaum "The Applicability of German Cartel Law to Licenses of Foreign Patents" 8 Antitrust Bull. 934 (1963).
26. WuW 1960, 815, BKartA 251, and 1961, 217 BKartA 317.
27. WuW 1964, 345, BKartA 741.
28. See OECD, Guide to Legislation, supra note 21. The explanations in the Guide cite the following for this view: Rehbinder, Extraterritoriale Wirkeungen des Deutschen Kartellrechts 112-153. Markert (supra note 16, at 53) also cites Rehbinder's contribution and Würdinger "Exportkartell und EWG" 10 WuW 313, 315 (1960). However, it is noted that some German commentators support a broader view "that any effect on the domestic economy is sufficient".

effect is sufficient or whether a substantial infleunce is also required.

The explanatory notes in the OECD Guide to Legislation indicate that the strength of the influence on the German market is irrelevant, but emphasize that according to a decision of the Federal Supreme Court this influence must be "perceptible" (Spürbar), thus excluding purely hypothetical influences on the market conditions.[29] Markert mentioned, with regard to international licence agreements, that the effects required are effects upon the territory in which the act applies and they must already be provable or at least recognizable as imminent, at the time of the review of the agreement under antitrust criteria. Licence agreements between foreign enterprises affecting German territory have to be judged by the same rules, i.e. by their adverse effects on the position of competitors or suppliers and customers on German territory. Whether in such a situation a substantial adverse effect upon the domestic competition is required is still an open question, at least where the parties are not doing business in Germany.[30] American commentators opine that the German act concerned apparently relies upon substantially the same territorial principle as is embodied in Sec. 18(b) of the Restatement (Second) of Foreign Relations Law of the United States (a direct, substantial and foreseeable effect).[31] For the text of Sec. 18(b) see 5-47.

---

29. See OECD, Guide to Legislation, supra note 21, at 2 (sec. 5). See also Müller, supra note 16, at 448 (with the following references: WuW/E BGH 486; Reimer (Gemeinschaftskommentar)(2nd ed. 1963) (note 14 to Sec. 20 GWB).

30. See Markert, supra note 16, at 62.

31. Cf. J. Rahl, Common Market and American Antitrust; Overlap and Conflict 111 (1970); Business Regulation in the Common Market Nations (Blake ed. 1969), Vol. 3 (K. Ebb. ed.) West Germany,(by Juenger, Markert, Pfeifer & Steckhan) ch. 6; Günther, in Hearings on Economic Concentration; Concentration Outside the U.S., Before the Subcomm. on Antitrust and Monopoly of the Sen. Comm. on the Judiciary, 90th Cong. 2d. Sess., pt. 7, at 3484 (1968); Günther Remarks, Panel on Conflicts Between, and the Extraterritorial Application of, the Antitrust Laws of the United States, the Common Market and Member States, in Proceedings, ABA, Antitrust Section Conference on Antitrust and the European Communities 189 (Brussels and Luxembourg, Sept. 23-26, 1963).

5-7. A far reaching interpretation by the Federal Supreme Court of the extraterritorial jurisdiction of the Federal Cartel Office has recently been brought to our attention. The Federal Supreme Court (BGH) ruled on an obligation to notify the Cartel Office when a German company's foreign subsidiary makes a foreign acquisition.[32] The case concerned the acquisition of Allied Chemical Corporation, Morristown, New Jersey (ACC) by Harmon Colors Corporation, Trenton, U.S. (HCC). HCC is completely owned by the Rhinechem Corporation of New York and this in its turn is completely owned by Bayer (International Finance) in the Netherlands which is a completely owned subsidiary of the West German chemical giant. The Cartel Office ordered Bayer to notify it of the acquisition. Bayer's appeal against the order was defeated in the Berlin Appeal Court and a further appeal asking for a review of the main legal issue brought the matter before the BGH.

The BGH approved the view of the Berlin Appeal Court that Sec. 23 of the German Competition Act, calling for notification of acquisitions by companies of certain magnitude, is part of the substantive law and as such quite independent of Sec. 24 which lays down the conditions for the prohibition of a merger. The only important consideration, the Court said, was whether the acquisition had a direct effect on the German market and it was of no importance whether this effect did or did not create conditions for banning the acquisition. But the BGH went even further. Embracing the U.S. doctrine of "potential entry" it held that though the share of ACC in the German pigment market was only 0.23 per cent in 1976, this American company was a potential

32. <u>Bayer v. Federal Cartel Office</u>, BGH judgment of 29th May, 1979, KVR 2/78.

competitor which, had it not been acquired by Bayer's American subsidiary, could have entered the German market and competed with Bayer and the other producers. This too represented a direct effect on competition in Germany. The Federal Cartel Office was not concerned with events taking place abroad, the BGH said, only with the domestic effects of these events. The ruling concluded that there was no legal possibility of absolving a German enterprise from its duty to notify an acquisition because it touched only on the interests of its foreign subsidiary and on those of the acquired American company. This ruling indicates the scope of interpretation of the term "effect" in German law.

5-8. Referring now to the scope of extraterritorial enforcement measures of the Federal Cartel Office we consider the following short statement by Rahl fully exhaustive in that respect:

> .....though not containing an explicit "foreign commerce" clause, the German law theoretically can have a very substantial extraterritorial scope. In practice, however, it has been applied cautiously in so far as restraints occurring outside Germany are concerned. Its actual extraterritorial operation being largely confined to an administrative practice of narrowly construing the export and international licence exemptions. 33

Rahl adds that, on the one hand, court and administrative jurisdiction to apply substantive rules to acts occurring outside Germany is evidently as extensive as the rules themselves, but that, on the other hand, the German Government's view of its investigatory and enforcement powers is rather strictly territorial.[34]

The OECD Guide to Legislation also explains that the enforcement of such public law provisions in Germany is strictly limited to the

---

33. Rahl, supra note 31, at 113.

34. Ibid. at 112. See also Markert, supra note 16, at 63-66.

territory. For example, the participants of a foreign export cartel, which affects exports to Germany, could be subjected to an administrative or quasi-criminal proceeding in Germany, but the sanctions imposed could not be enforced outside Germany.[35]

Müller points out that the Federal Cartel Office has not yet used extreme measures to prohibit the action or to fine the foreign party, while it has modified submitted agreements or caused German parties to such agreements to withdraw or else has applied the law against the German party only, or moved the EEC Commission to proceed against a non-German party under Community competition law.[36]

5-9. The theory of personal jurisdiction and the method of service of process in German antitrust law are of particular interest for a comparison with Community practice. Schwartz explains the German theory as follows:

> .....under a doctrine of German international law of administrative procedure the exercise of personal jurisdiction depends upon venue, at least where venue is founded on reasons of substantive law, that is on the most important local relationship of the case.....There could hardly be a more important point of contact from an antitrust angle than the place where a particular restraint of competition takes effect.....The personal jurisdiction of the cartel authority would thus extend as far as its jurisdiction over the subject matter in respect of which Sec. 98, para (II) of the Act.....provides.....No personal relationship of the foreign corporation to the national territory would be required. 37

35. OECD, Guide to Legislation, supra note 21, at 19. See also Jaenicke, I.L.A., Helsinki Conference 93.

36. Müller, I.L.A., Tokyo Conference 448.

37. Supra note 17, at 703-704. (It is emphasized by Schwartz that the theory of personal jurisdiction in Germany has been developed by Karl Neumeyer). See also Kruithof "The Application of the Common Market antitrust Provisions to International Restraints of Trade " 2 C.M.L.Rev. 87 (1964); OECD, Committee of Experts on Restrictive Business Practices, Restrictive Business Practices of Multinational Enterprises, secs. 176-177 (1977)(hereinafter cited as "OECD, Restrictive Business Practices of Multinational Enterprises").

The only legal difficulty in administrative proceedings against a foreign enterprise without domestic representatives in Germany is that the affected party must be given an opportunity to be heard before the decision is rendered. It seems, however, that notice of the proceeding by ordinary mail would be sufficient, at least where the abuse in question has had substantial domestic effects.[38]

Administrative proceedings involving the imposition of fines do not require service of a complaint. However, the defendant must be given an opportunity to be heard before a fine is imposed.[39]

D. The Netherlands

5-10. Sec. 1 of the Dutch Economic Competition Act defines the agreements regulating economic competition which are to be registered and subjected to administrative authority and it gives no territorial limitation.[40] The definition of "dominant position" in the same section is confined to predominant influence in some market in the Netherlands. The scope of the law has been interpreted, in the light of the *travaux préparatoires*, as follows: "to avoid any misunderstanding it is to be noted that the nationality of the members of a cartel operating in Holland or of those who hold a dominant position on the Dutch market is of no importance".[41]

Administrative proceedings to invalidate an agreement may be taken only if the agreement is contrary to the "public interest" (Sec.

---

38. See Markert, *supra* note 16, at 65.
39. See *Ibid*.
40. Economic Competition Act of 28th June, 1956, as amended (by the Act of 16th July, 1958, the Act of 18th February, 1971 and the Act of December 1971); see in OECD, *Guide to Legislation*, Vol. 5, (Netherland 1.0)(*Wet Economische Mededinging* of 28th June, 1956, as amended). The Act is to be revised again soon.
41. See Mulder and Mok, *Kartelrecht* (1962) cited in the *Dyestuffs Cases*, opinion of the Advocate-General, 689.

19). This phrase has been interpreted as precluding the Act's application to a cartel in a foreign market merely because it raised prices in that market.[42]

The Economic Competition Act has no special provisions relating to import cartels. It may, however, be applied when the import cartel is considered to be contrary to the public interest. The act also does not contain provisions for regulating export cartels; "pure" export cartels are exempted from notification and registration under an order implementing Sec. 4(1), requiring the Minister responsible to "grant exemption as to any regulations of economic competition not regulating competition in the Netherlands."[43] However, the act may be applied when the export cartel is considered to be contrary to the "public interest". The exemption mentioned above applies to both national and international export cartels.

Rahl concludes that, despite what he calls "technical and practical limits", Dutch law seems to be nearly:

> .....as broad as the American law in theoretical extraterritorial scope, if not broader. It clearly may apply to conduct abroad by both Dutch and foreign firms, where the Dutch public interest is affected. Not only are effects in the domestic market within this concept, but agreements which inhibit either Dutch exports or imports may also, according to extant administrative interpretation, infringe the public interest, thus giving the act a "foreign commerce" application. The penal requirement of an "act" in the Netherlands has apparently been broadly interpreted, and while this is a limitation on enforcement, it does not necessarily remove jurisdiction over all of the civil consequences which may attach to extraterritorial violation."44

---

42. See Business Regulation in the Common Market Nations (Blake ed. 1969) Vol. 1 (Ginsburg ed.), pt. 2, The Netherlands (by Silbiger) 470.

43. Decree of the Secretary of Economic Affairs and Ministers of Finance, Traffic and Agriculture, Official Gazette of 3rd June, 1960, No. 107 ([1960] Netherlandse Staatscourant No. 107, at 9); see in CCH, Doing Business in Europe (Netherlands) sec. 27,007. See also OECD, Export Cartels, sec. 44.

44. Rahl, supra note 31, at 114. But attention must be paid to the scope of enforcement of the law as territorial (see 5-11).

5-11. The scope of operation of the Dutch law has been described by Ellis as territorial.[45] He makes references to statements by the Government when the bill was before Parliament in which it was said that no application of the law was envisaged beyond the limitations imposed by international law and by the limitation in international matters imposed by Netherlands law itself (e.g. Art. 2 of the Criminal Code provides: ".....to be possible to apply the Netherlands law there must.....have been concrete conduct on Netherlands territory").

In practice the law does not appear to have been applied to any other than Dutch nationals and then only for activities in the Netherlands.[46] Moreover, although Ministerial decrees must be complied with by all the enterprises concerned, whether foreign or domestic, they do not have extraterritorial effect in the sense that Dutch enterprises outside the Netherlands will not be bound by them.[47]

In this connection it is interesting to note that one feature of the law is a provision designed to counteract the efforts of foreign authorities (mainly the U.S.) to obtain information about restraints of trade and to enforce orders relating to measures applicable in Dutch territory (Sec. 39).[48]

---

45. See Ellis, International Bar Association, Report of the Eighth Conference (Salzburg 1960) 491, and in I.L.A., Tokyo Conference 459.

46. See Business Regulation in the Common Market Nations, supra note 42, at 470.

47. See Doing Business in Europe, Netherlands, sec. 27,009.

48. For a detailed survey of the Economic Competition Bill as submitted to the State-General of the Netherlands in 1953 see Antitrust Law; A Comparative Symposium 265 et seq. (Friedmann ed. 1956).

E. The United Kingdom

5-12. The substantive competition law of the U.K. is now consolidated principally in the Restrictive Trade Practices Acts 1976 and 1977 (restrictive agreements relating to goods and services), the Restrictive Practices Court Act 1976, the Resale Prices Act 1976 (prohibition of resale price maintenance) and the Fair Trading Act 1973 (control over monopoly and mergers).[49] The 1976 statutes consolidate earlier legislation; they repeal and reproduce, without modification, provisions which were previously contained in a number of different Acts.[50] In addition to legislation there is a substantial body of common law principles relating to restraint of trade. Under this legislation the competition authorities in the U.K. comprise the Director General of Fair Trading, the Restrictive Practices Court, the Monopolies and Mergers Commission and the Secretary of State for Prices and Consumer Protection.

Sec. 6(1) of the Restrictive Trade Practices Act 1976 provides the following framework for the application of the law:

> This Act applies to agreements (whenever made) between two or more persons carrying on business within the United Kingdom in the production or supply of goods, or in the application of goods of any process of manufacture, whether with or without other parties, being agreements under which restrictions are accepted by two or more parties in respect of any of the following matters-.....

---

49. See OECD, Guide to Legislation, United Kingdom 1. A new Competition Act has come into force when this chapter has already been given for typing. This act does not change in any substantial way our conclusions with regard to the extraterritorial aspects in the application of the law. The recent Protection of Trading Interests Act 1980 is discussed in 5-18.

50. In the following discussion references will be made to literature which relates to the legislation before consolidation in so far as this material is relevant.

It can be noted from this section that the parties who accept the restrictions need not be the same as those who carry on the business in the U.K.[51] The two parties carrying on the business in the U.K. must do so in the course of certain activities , but it is immaterial whether the parties to an agreement carry on the same or different classes of business (sec. 6(2)).

Edwards states that at first glance the wording of sec. 6 appears to be designed to confine the scope of the act to the British domestic market. However, the effect of the limitation is to place beyond the reach of the statute various types of restriction that might bear upon British markets for goods.[52] Korah gives the following example in that respect: if a monopolist in the U.K. adheres to an international cartel which ensures that the foreign members will not sell in the U.K., in return for his promise not to export to their home markets, the act does not apply to it provided that none of the other parties carry on business in the U.K.[53]

The condition of carrying on business in the U.K. of sec.6(1) must be read together with sec. 43(4) which provides that a person shall not be deemed to carry on business within the U.K. by reason only of the fact that he is represented for the purposes of that business by an agent within the U.K. The interpretation of that condition, i.e. whether it introduces a narrow test for jurisdiction, is evidently an arguable one.[54]

---

51. Cf. Korah, Competition Law of Britain and the Common Market 86 (1975).

52. See supra note 10, at 442.

53. See supra note 51, at 85. Korah has explained in a private communication that in her knowledge this result of the law was intended.

54. See discussion on this point in Wilberforce, Campbell and Elles, The Law of Restrictive Trade Practices and Monopolies, sec. 556 (2nd ed. 1966 and Supplements in 1969 and 1973)(relating to the earlier version in sec. 36(6)). See also Lever "The Extraterritorial Jurisdiction of the Restrictive Practices Court," in Int. & Comp. L.Q. Supplementary Publication No. 6, 121 (1963).

5-13. Agreements with export or overseas operations (whether involving goods or services) stand in a special position and must be treated separately. By virtue of sec. 28 of Schedule 3, para. 6(1) of the Act of 1976 such agreements can be divided into two calsses: those which apply to exports from the U.K. and those which operate outside the U.K. Para. 6(1) of Schedule 3 reads:

> This Act does not apply to an agreement in the case of which all such restrictions as are described in sec. 6(1) above, or all such information provisions as are described in sec. 7(1) above, relate exclusively -
> (a) to the supply of goods by export from the United Kingdom;
> (b) to the production of goods, or the application of any process of manufacture of goods, outside the United Kingdom;
> (c) to the acquisition of goods to be delivered outside the United Kingdom and not imported into the United Kingdom for entry for home use; or
> (d) to the supply of goods to be delivered outside the United Kingdom otherwise than by export from the United Kingdom;
> and subsections (2) and (4) of sec. 8 above do not apply in relation to recommendations relating exclusively to those matters.

It can be seen that this section deals specifically with the question of "effects" in the U.K. by enumerating the cases which are not regarded as having "effects" in the U.K. It does not leave it open to argument before the Restrictive Practices Court whether a particular agreement has effects or not; if the agreement is of the kind listed, then it is exempt; if not, it is not.[55]

Similarly, by virtue of sec. 28 and Schedule 3, para. 9(1), of the Act of1976 agreements with export or overseas operations are excluded from control if all the relevant restrictions relate to the supply of services to persons or to property outside the U.K. "Pure"

---

55. See R. Wilberforce and A. Drucker in I.L.A., Tokyo Conference 433.

export agreements do not, however, entirely escape the net. Although they are exempt from registration and reference to the Restrictive Practices Court, if they contain restrictions which would be registerable should they relate to the U.K. market, their particulars must be furnished to the Director General of Fair Trading (secs. 24 and 25 of the Act of 1976). The particulars of such agreements are not placed on the register of the Director General of Fair Trading and so are not available for public inspection.

The law therefore covers only "mixed" export cartels. Such cartels are subject to the same rules as domestic cartels - registration with the Director General of Fair Trading (sec. 24 of the Fair Trading Act 1973) and examination by the Restrictive Practices Court, except that this Court would not be concerned with the overseas element.[56]

The following paragraph is broadly a summary of the foregoing as formulated by Lever:

> .....the Act covers restrictive agreements, two or more of the parties to which carry on or are deemed to carry on business within the United Kingdom. Where these conditions are satisfied and restrictions are accepted by two or more parties neither of whom need himself have any connections with the United Kingdom, the agreement falls within.....the Act unless its subject-matter is entirely extraterritorial. If, however, the United Kingdom market as such is directly affected by the agreement, then even though nothing is to be done within the United Kingdom in pursuance of the agreement, the agreement will be registrable. 57

Other statutes in the U.K. determine their field of application very widely, particularly the Resale Act 1976 which applies to agreements

56. Cf. Wilberforce, Campbell and Elles, *supra* note 54, at sec. 558.
57. Lever, *supra* note 54, at 128.

or other practices aimed at imposing a minimum price for the resale of goods in the U.K., irrespective of the place where the production enterprises carry on their activity, and which incontestably adopts the criterion of "effect" on the British market.

5-14. The Fair Trading Act 1973 deals with merger situations qualifying for investigation (sec. 64(1)). In this connection it is noteworthy that only one of the enterprises need have any connection with the U.K. Korah mentions that it is surprising that a reference may be made to the Commission by the Secretary of State, when the only connection with the U.K. is that one company was created under the laws of England, Scotland or Northern Ireland, a connection with the U.K. that does not seem relevant to economic policy.[58]

The Fair Trading Act 1973 describes in sec. 8 the monopoly situation in relation to export of goods. It is obvious that these provisions may well extend to and cover restrictive agreements made outside the U.K. by foreign individuals or companies. They must, however, have effect in relation to the export of goods produced in the U.K. to other markets.[59] In relation to services there is nothing equivalent to sec. 8 which defines a monopoly situation in relation to exports of goods: sec. 7(3) deals with export of services, but in a different way. Nevertheless, sec. 7(1)(d) may provide a wide interpretation in that respect.

5-15. The reach of the U.K. law which covers certain agreements external to the U.K. which directly affect the domestic market and to

58. Supra, note 51 at 62.

59. See J. Cunningham, The Fair Trading Act 1973; Consumer Protection and Competition Law, sec. 8-16 (1974).

which foreigners outside the jurisdiction may be parties is, however, limited in respect of the Court's orders. The jurisdiction claimed in respect of persons not carrying on business in the U.K. in the ordinary sense of that term is very much more limited than that exercised in respect of persons found within the jurisdiction. It is true that under the Restrictive Practices Court Rules service may be effected on persons outside the United Kingdom whether or not they carry on business there. The real limitation of the Court's jurisdiction over foreigners is to be found in sec. 2(3) which provides that where the Court finds restrictions of the sort described to be contrary to the public interest the agreement shall be void in respect of those restrictions and the Court may, upon the application of the Registrar, make such order as appears to the Court to be proper for restraining all or any of the persons party to the agreement "who carry on business in the United Kingdom" from giving effect to the agreement in respect of the condemned restrictions or making any other agreement to the like effect.

In sec. 90(3) the Fair Trading Act of 1973 qualifies the reach of orders which are provided for by the act:

> Nothing in any such order shall have effect so as to apply to any person in relation to his conduct outside the United Kingdom unless that person is
> (a) a citizen of the United Kingdom and Colonies, or
> (b) a body corporate incorporated under the law of the United Kingdom or of part of the United Kingdom, or
> (c) a person carrying on business in the United Kingdom, either alone or in partnership with one or more other persons, but, in the case of a person falling within paragraph (a), paragraph (b) or paragraph (c) of this subsection, any other order may extend to acts or omissions outside the United Kingdom .....

Where a British firm is party to an international cartel, it may be ordered to resign, but no orders can be made against foreigners, even if they are restricting competition within the U.K.; the orders are, as provided in the law, limited by the nationality and territorial doctrine.[60]

5-16. In the last few years particular attention in the international antitrust field has concentrated on questions of discovery in the U.K. for the purpose of foreign antitrust suits. A new statute, the Evidence (Proceedings in Other Jurisdictions) Act[61] (hereinafter the "Evidence Act") sets forth the procedures by which the British courts may order compliance with foreign discovery requests. The act applies only to discovery pursuant to letters rogatory, whereby one country requests another country, acting through its own courts, to assist the administration of justice in the former country. Sec. 1(a) of the act explains which is a proper foreign court to request the discovery, but the status under the act of an administrative proceeding, if it arguably involves rule making or investigation rather than adjudication, is unclear. In addition, the evidence must be requested "for the purposes of civil proceedings which either have been instituted before the requesting court or whose institution before that court is contemplated."[62] Sec. 5 of the Evidence Act does provide for obtaining evidence for a criminal proceeding at the request of a foreign court. Here, however, the powers of discovery under the statute are much narrower. The foreign criminal proceeding must have been

60. Cf. Korah, supra note 51, at 31; Cunningham, supra 59, at 155.

61. The Act replaced the provisions previously contained in the Evidence by Commission Act,1885. 48 and 49 Vic., c.74; the Evidence by Commission Act 1859, 22 Vict., c.20; and the Foreign Tribunals Evidence Act 1856. 19 and 20 Vict. c.113, and added new provisions conforming to the Convention on the Taking of Evidence Abroad, Mar. 18, 1970, 23 U.S.T. 2555, T.I.A.S. No.7444 (the Hague Convention).

62. Sec. 1(4) of the Evidence Act. The term "civil proceedings" is defined in section 9(1) as "proceedings in any civil or commercial matter".

"instituted" - precluding the granting of evidence for use by a grand jury investigation[63] - and the range of discovery is limited to the examination of witnesses and the production of documents.[64] In addition no evidence can be obtained "in the case of criminal proceedings of a political character".

5-17. The recent Westinghouse Uranium Contracts Litigation, which is concerned with antitrust actions, has been the first case in which the English Court of Appeal and the House of Lords considered the Evidence Act.[66] Because of the international aspects of this litigation we elaborate here to some extent on its relevant facts. This litigation, encompassing at least 27 separate suits, involved contracts made in the 1960's and 1970's by Westinghouse Electric Corporation to provide a number of American utilities with uranium for nuclear reactors at a fixed price, subject only to adjustments for inflation. Between 1972 and 1975 the price of uranium on the world market rocketed from about $7 to about $42 a pound, and in 1975 Westinghouse announced that it could not fulfill its contracts because performance had become "commercially impracticable". Thirteen federal actions in the U.S., brought by the purchasing utilities were consolidated in the Eastern District of Virginia,[67] and the case went to trial on 12th September, 1977. Four suits brought in State courts were settled, and three suits were brought in Sweden.[68] In 1976

63. A grand jury investigation is just an investigation in the U.S., not a trial. A government attorney presents both testimony and documentary evidence to the grand jury, but the grand jury alone decides whether to bring an indictment on accusation against those suspected of crime.

64. Sec. 5(1)(b) to (c) of the Evidence Act.

66. In re Westinghouse Elec. Corp. Uranium Contracts Litigation [1978] 2 W.L.R. 81 (H.L. 1977), aff'd [1977] 3 W.L.R. 492 (C.A.), rev'g on add'l facts [1977] 3 W.L.R. 430 (C.A.).

67. In re Westinghouse Elec. Corp. Uranium Contracts Litigation, 405 F. Supp. 316 (J.P.M.D.L. 1975).

68. See Cheeseright, "RTZ Stands in the Shade", Financial Times (London) 8th November, 1977, at 14, col.3.

information was made public indicating the existence since 1972 of a uranium cartel involving a number of multinational corporations and the governments of Australia, Canada, France and South Africa.[69] Westinghouse brought an antitrust suit in Illinois against 29 foreign and American uranium producers.[70] The U.S. Department of Justice confirmed that it was conducting a criminal investigation of the cartel[71] and the House Oversight and Investigations Subcommittee began its own investigation.[72]

Discovery of evidence concerning the existence of a cartel was relevant to Westinghouse's "commercial impracticability" defence in the contracts litigation and was essential to Westinghouse's antitrust action. Much of this evidence, however, was located abroad. In October 1976, a federal court in Virginia issued letters rogatory to the Supreme Court of Ontario in Canada, to the Supreme Court of New South Wales in Australia, and to the High Court of Justice in England. The discovery sought in England included documents which were according to the allegation possessed by Rio Tinto Zinc Corporation (RTZ), an English company thought to be a member of the cartel, and oral testimony from certain RTZ officials.[73] An appeal was brought against this request. The English Court of Appeal in the Westinghouse Case upheld the letters rogatory under the Evidence Act, but at the ensuing depositions RTZ officials refused both to testify, asserting the American fifth amendment privilege against self-incrimination, and to produce

---

69. See International Uranium Supply and Demand: Hearings Before the Subcomm. on Oversight and Investigations of the House Comm. on Interstate and Foreign Commerce, 94th Cong. 2d. Sess. 56-62 (1976) (testimony of Jim Harding).

70. Westinghouse Elec. Corp. v. Rio Alsom Ltd., Antitrust and Trade Reg. Rep. (BNA) No.786, at A-3 (N.D. Ill., filed Oct. 15, 1976).

71. Ibid. at A-4.

72. Ibid. No. 818, at A-12 (1977).

73. In re Westinghouse Elec. Corp. Uranium Contract Litigation [1978] 2 W.L.R. 81, 97-99 (H.L. 1977).

documents, asserting the English privilege against self-incrimination.[74] The U.S. Department of Justice then granted immunity to the RTZ officials in order to obtain evidence for its grand jury investigation of the cartel. The appeals from the Court of Appeal judgments were heard in the House of Lords amid intense diplomatic pressure from the governments of Australia, Canada, France and South Africa to prevent the British Government from allowing the discovery.[75] The Law Lords ruled that, because of the grant of immunity by the Department of Justice, the testimony could not be compelled under the Evidence Act.[76]

In fact, when the Department of Justice granted immunity in the litigation, it openly stated that its goal was to obtain evidence for a grand jury. The Lords were divided on the question whether the letters rogatory were valid before the grant of immunity, but they were unanimous in finding that after the grant of immunity the letters could not be enforced. Lord Viscount Dilhorne stated: "It cannot be right for a State to seek to avail itself for the purpose of securing evidence for criminal proceedings, of the obligations accepted by another state in respect of the furnishing of evidence for civil or commercial proceedings."[77] Lord Wilberforce went so far as to conclude that "the making of the order.....is a matter of government policy, and not related to the civil proceedings in Richmond (Virginia)."[78]

---

74. In re Westinghouse Elec. Corp. Uranium Contracts Litigation [1977] 3 W.L.R. 492, 494-496 (C.A.), aff'd, [1978] 2 W.L.R. 81 (H.L. 1977). There was reasonable ground for the belief that, if RTZ were compelled to disclose the documents which were required by the U.S. courts, there was a risk of the documents being used against them; they might be brought to the knowledge of the EEC Commission and used in support of grounds for a fine.
75. See The Times (London), 26th July, 1977, at 17, col. 7.
76. In re Westinghouse Elec. Corp. Uranium Contracts Litigation, supra note 73, at 116.
77. Ibid. at 107.
78. Ibid. at 94.

The substance of Westinghouse's case in the U.S. will not be tried on its merits until the other defendants - those who have accepted jurisdiction - come to court in late 1981.[79] Meanwhile, on 4th November, 1979, a Federal Court in Chicago began the hearing on damages which, according to Westinghouse's request, is directed against the "defaulting" defendants (among them Britain's Rio-Tinto Zinc and RTZ subsidiary).[80] The sums involved are enormous - with treble damages, possibly as high as $6 billion, to be recovered, if the judge decides for Westinghouse.

5-18. The Westinghouse Litigation is one major reason for Britain to adopt the Protection of Trading Interests Act 1980.[81] The act has four major components: (1) it provides means by which the Secretary of State may counter measures taken or proposed under the law of another country which would damage the trading interests of the U.K.; (2) it provides that the Secretary of State may prohibit compliance with certain requirements of a court or authority in an overseas country seeking commercial documents or information located outside that country; (3) it provides that judgments for multiple damages given in civil proceedings by courts of overseas countries shall not be enforceable in the U.K. It also provides that judgments given in overseas countries, based on certain competition laws, which the Secretary of State may specify by order, shall not be enforceable in the U.K.; (4) it enables companies and individuals carrying on business in the U.K. to recover through the U.K. courts sums paid under multiple

---

79. The Economist, November 15, 1979, p.65.

80. The Economist, September 15, 1979, p.80.

81. The Protection of Trading Interests Act 1980 (c.11) became law on March 20th, 1980. Another major cause for the introduction of this act is a case involving shipping companies, see supra note 79, and in New L.J., 8th Nove. 1979, pp.1095-1096.

damage judgments given in overseas countries. The sums recoverable are those in excess of the compensation for the actual loss suffered.

The act repeals and supersedes the Shipping Contracts and Commercial Documents Act 1964. It has been reported that when the bill for the new act was introduced to Parliament the U.S. sent diplomatic notes to the U.K. expressing its concern in particular over what is described in clause (4) above.[82]

Although the discussion of the Protection of Trading Interests Act, as well as the discussion of the Evidence Act and the Westinghouse Uranium Contracts Litigation, are not directly concerned with the description of the extraterritorial reach of the U.K. competition law, these issues are, nevertheless, indicative of the U.K. approach on related matters. We, therefore, found it proper to include these discussions here while relevant references to them will be included in other connected issues.

---

82. The Times, 5 December, 1979.

2. THE EXTRATERRITORIAL SCOPE OF THE UNITED STATES ANTITRUST LAWS

Any analysis of an antitrust system, particularly the American one, must be defective if it is made without a comprehensive knowledge of the country's political, legal, economic and cultural history; of its contemporary political, economic and legal institutions; and of the whole range of relevant government policies.[83] Therefore, the following survey of the extraterritorial reach of the U.S. antitrust laws will be preceded by a very brief description of a few of the fundamental differences between the Community competition law and the U.S. antitrust laws.

A. Fundamental Differences Between the EEC and the United States Antitrust Systems

(1) Basic Philosophy

5-19. Whilst Community antitrust law is generally patterned on U.S. antitrust law, the law of the Community was certainly born from a totally different kind of parent. A principal purpose of the Treaty was to eliminate the national barriers which have divided Europe for centuries by removing import duties and restrictions on goods and by increasing the flow of persons, services and capital across the frontiers. In the U.S. such barriers were largely eliminated at the creation of the U.S. as a republic in the Federal Constitution.[84]

---

83. See the author's preface in Edwards, supra note 10, at p.III.
84. Cf. A. Crotti Trading Under EEC and United States Antitrust Laws 14-15 (1977). For further elaboration on the distinctive philosophies behind both bodies of law see Temple-Lang, The Common Market and Common Law: Legal Aspects of Foreign Investment and Economic Integration in the European Community, with Ireland as a Prototype 378-379 (1966); Riesenfeld "The Protection of Competition" in American Enterprise in the European Common Market; A Legal Profile, vol. 2, 323-324 (E. Stein and T. Nicholson eds., 1960); Fugate, "The Common Market and the U.S. Antitrust Laws" 38 N.Y.U.L.Rev. 460-464 (1963).

This distinction results in substantial differences in specific antitrust laws. For example, practices such as export bans, which have the effect of partitioning the market along national boundaries, constitute perhaps the clearest violation of Community law.

(2) Substantive Law

5-20. A fundamental difference between the U.S. and Community antitrust law is the concept of the "reasonableness" of a restraint, and that of a restraint being illegal in itself (i.e. *per se*, irrespective of its actual effect on competition). This distinction, which will become clear in the following survey, does not exist in Community law.

(3) Exemptions

5-21. Art. 85 of the Treaty is more generous than the U.S. laws. Under certain conditions, showing generally an actual benefit to the public, the otherwise illegal act may be declared exempt from the sanctions of violating the law (Art. 85(3)). There is no such generosity in the U.S. law; if an act unreasonably restrains trade there is no escape from punishment. However, the recently developed "balancing" approach in the U.S. encourages the same consideration as is required under Art. 85(3). See 5-50.

(4) Judicial and Enforcement Agencies

5-22. The greatest institutional contrast between U.S. and EEC antitrust is the high degree of centralization present in the EEC where the Commission plays a pervasive role in both the formulation and execution of not only competition policy but also general economic policy in the Common Market (subject, of course, to Member States control). This highly centralized system contrasts vividly with the proliferation of statutes, enforcement bodies and fora in the U.S., all charged, to an overlapping and sometimes inconsistent degree, with "antitrust" policy.[85] The judicial and enforcement agencies in the U.S. are listed below (in 5-23) in the context of actions which are available in the U.S.

(5) Types of Remedies and Types of Action

5-23. A very important difference between the EEC treaty rules and American practice is the range of their respective sanctions. U.S. antitrust rules carry with them many sanctions which have no counterpart under the Treaty. A remedial approach shows the great number and variety of both actions and remedies available in the U.S. and that the maintenance of competition in open markets is promoted by a system of public and private enforcement.[86] In comparison, the number and variety of actions and remedies available in Community law and the private law function of that law are considerably different. On the private law consequences of Community law see 1-22.

To handle the remedial aspects of the U.S. law requires first the classification of the remedies into civil, criminal and regulatory

85. To a limited extent an approach towards an explanation of the foundations of American antitrust laws on the basis of which institutions are empowered to instigate proceedings is found in Oppenheim & Weston, Federal Antitrust Laws 826 et seq. (3rd ed. 1968). For a concise synopsis of the enforcement agencies see W. Fugate, Foreign Commerce and the Antitrust Laws, sec. 4.14 (2nd ed. 1973); J. Van Cise, The Federal Antitrust Laws 39, 40, 41 et seq. (rev. ed. 1955).
86. See a survey of historical sources of American antitrust laws with a particular reference to the development of remedies in H. Zwarensteyn, Some Aspects of The Extraterritorial Reach of the American Antitrust Laws 14-36 (1970).

(administrative) and then the inspection of them in that order. According to an often-used classification remedies are civil where the government litigates in the same manner as a private litigant, but only the government can avail itself of a criminal action (aiming at punishing) or of a regulatory action (aiming to correct a situation.)[87]

The civil remedies available in the U.S. antitrust laws are the (treble) damage suit (a tort action) and the (temporary) injunction (an equity action). The criminal sanctions consist of either a fine or imprisonment, also forfeiture of property is a possibility (even though rarely used).[88] Regulatory remedies consist of the following:[89]

(1) dissolution, divestiture and divorcement (regulation of structural relationships between enterprises).

(2) the Department of Justice consent judgement and decree (a procedural device involving an agreement by the litigating parties). Approval of the court is necessary for the agreement to become binding upon the parties as if it were a judgment or a decree in a litigated case .

(3) the Federal Trade Commission stipulation (presently an informal settlement reached by an assurance of voluntary compliance).

---

87. These guiding principles for the classification of remedies are used by Zwarensteyn, supra note 86, at 46 et seq. See also Carlston "Antitrust Policy Abroad" 49 Northw. U.L.Rev. 573 (1954). Such classification is, of course, an arbitrary one, because some of the remedies which may be qualified as civil, could just as well be classified as regulatory while some of the remedies which are still qualified as criminal could just as well be classified as civil.

88. On 21st December, 1974, the Antitrust Procedures and Penalties Act (APPA) 15 U.S.C. para. 16, was enacted. This raised criminal antitrust penalties under the Sherman Act to $1 million for corporations and $100,000 for individuals. Maximum prison sentences for such antitrust violators were extended from one year to three years, thereby raising price fixing and other criminal antitrust activities to the status of felonies, whereas prior to this Act they were only misdemeanors.

89. See a concise synopsis of the various remedies in the antitrust laws in Oppenheim & Weston, supra note 85, at 22-27.

(4) the Federal Trade Commission administrative treatment (a device for disposing of an investigation or an adjudicative proceeding on an informal non-adjudicatory basis).

(5) the Federal Trade Commission consent order (a procedure similar to the one followed by the Department of Justice in (2) but with some slight differences).

(6) the cease and desist order (which can be issued after a consent or after a hearing).

(7) advance clearance by the Federal Trade Commission (an advisory opinion).

(8) the Federal Trade Commission trade practice conference (rules drafted and submitted to the members of a certain industry to be adopted in conferences between such members and representatives of the Federal Trade Commission). The Federal Trade Commission now very rarely holds trade practice conferences, although this practice was used in earlier times.

A classification of the remedies available in the U.S. according to the bodies or agencies which seek to apply them indicates that proceedings can be initiated by the following : (1) the Department of Justice through civil and criminal actions; (2) the Federal Trade Commission, through administrative procedures, encouraging voluntary compliance; (3) other regulatory agencies, through a system of miscellaneous sanctions; (4) injured individuals, through private actions seeking injunctive relief and/or treble damage.

The remedial approach as described here confirms the statement above that it can determine both the relief asked for and the character of the proceedings (types of action).

B. Legislative and Judicial Efforts in the U.S. to Control Transnational Restrictive Business Practices

(1) The Legislative Aspect: Applicable American Statutes

5-24. The commerce clause of the U.S. Constitution, Sec. 8 of Article I, provides that Congress shall have power ".....To regulate commerce with foreign Nations, and among the several States, and with the Indian Tribes....." . It is noteworthy that in the constitutional provision "commerce with foreign Nations" is mentioned before commerce "among the several States".

Various arrangements which concern foreign enterprises and/or conduct external to the U.S. are subject to scrutiny by the American antitrust enforcement agencies, if for no other reason than that the pertinent provisions of the American antitrust laws make specific reference to the trade or commerce with foreign nations.[90]

5-25. Of the legal provisions having a "foreign commerce" clause the Sherman Act is, of course, the pre-eminent antitrust law.[91] The Act provides in Sec. 1:

> Every contract, combination in the form of trust or otherwise, or conspiracy, in restraint of trade or commerce among the several States or with foreign nations, is hereby declared to be illegal.....

---

90. With regard to the U.S. antitrust laws only the Federal laws will be considered. It would go beyond reasonable expectations to include a discussion of antitrust laws of the several States. Moreover, although it is becoming of increasing importance, the substantive provisions of State law nearly all follow closely the provisions of federal law and are concerned with applying similar legal principles to cases of local rather than national importance.

91. Act of 2nd July, 1890, 15 U.S.C. (1964).

Sec. 2 makes it a crime to monopolize or attempt to monopolize, or combine or conspire with any other person or persons, to monopolize any part of "the trade or commerce among the several States, or with foreign nations.....".

5-26. The Clayton Act is also applicable to both interstate and foreign commerce. Sec. 1 of this Act defines "commerce" to include "commerce with foreign nations".[92] Other provisions of the Clayton Act are of narrower applicability. Section 2(a) condemns price discrimination in the sale of goods within the U.S.[93] This provision would apply to discriminatory prices charged by foreign sellers in American import transactions, but would reach export situations in only a limited number of complex cases.[94] However, the brokerage allowances and services in subsections (c), (d) and (e) of Sec. 2[95] contain no limitation of application regarding the type of transaction, and evidently may apply directly to export transactions.[96] Sec. 3 of the Clayton Act, in general, makes it unlawful to sell or lease goods, patented or unpatented, for use or resale in the U.S., on condition that the vendee or lessee will not deal in the goods of a competitor where the effect may substantially lessen competition, or tend to create a monopoly in any line of commerce.[97] This section contains the same limiting language as Sec. 2(a).

The Clayton Act Sec. 7 applies to the acquisition by a corporation, engaged in commerce, of the whole or part of the capital

92. Act of 15th October, 1914, 15 U.S.C. s.12 (1970).
93. Ibid. at § 13(a). Formerly this section was § 1 of the Robinson-Patman Act of 1936.
94. See theoretical examples in Rahl, supra note 31, at 52. In fact no decided cases in point have been found.
95. 15 U.S.C. §§ 13(c), (d), (e) (1970).
96. See, for example, Baysoy v. Jessop Steel Co., 90 F. Supp 303 (W.D.Pa. 1950).
97. 15 U.S.C. § 14 (1970).

stock or assets of another corporation also engaged in commerce.[98] This section has a different kind of limitation in that the acquisition concerned may occur anywhere, but the required adverse effect on competition must be found "in any line of commerce in any section of the country". The Act appears to cover mergers of American and foreign companies where there is a specified effect within the U.S.[99]

5-28. "Unfair methods of competition" in Sec. 5 of the Federal Trade Commission Act embracing potential as well as full-blown Sherman Act violations, applies to "commerce.....with foreign nations or..... between.....any State or foreign nation."[100] It must be observed that the limitations on the scope of the Clayton Act control actions by the Justice Department and private litigants, but do not necessarily prevent the Federal Trade Commission from proceeding against similar types of activities under Sec. 5 of the Federal Trade Commission Act.[101] The Commission may treat conduct of the type prohibited either by the Sherman Act or the Clayton Act as a violation of Sec. 5 and may also use the same section to reach "incipient" violations of either Act.[102]

5-29. In addition other antitrust statutes include provisions relating to foreign commerce. The Wilson Tariff Act[103] in effect applies the Sherman Act to importers. Sec. 73 of this Act[104] declares that "Every

98. 15 U.S.C. § 18 (1970).

99. See possible interpretation of few cases on the application of §.7 to foreign commerce in Fugate, supra note 85, sec. 10.8: the author states that, while as yet there have been no merger cases in which a substantial lessening of competition was predicted on an export effect, this is quite possible.

100. 15 U.S.C. § 44 (1970).

101. 15 U.S.C. § 45 (1970).

102. For example FTC v. Motion Picture Advertising Serv. Co. 344 U.S. 392 (1953); FTC v. Brown Shoe Co., 384 U.S. 316 (1966); FTC v. Texaco Inc. 393 U.S. 223 (1968). Moreover Sec. 5 of the Federal Trade Commission Act may be used to fill gaps in the language of the Clayton Act sections, see Atlantic Refining Co. v. FTC 381 U.S. 357 (1965): Grand Union Co. v. FTC, 300 F. 2d 92 (2d Cir. 1962).

103. 15 U.S.C. §§ 8-11 (1970).

104. 15 U.S.C. § 8 (1970).

combination, conspiracy, trust, agreement, or contract" made by or between two or more persons, "either of whom.....is engaged in importing any article from any foreign country into the U.S......" is illegal and void, when intended to operate in restraint of lawful trade or to increase the market price of any imported article in any part of the U.S., "or of any manufacture into which such article enters or is intended to enter". Sec. 76 of the Act,[105] seldom invoked, provides for seizure of articles "imported into and being within" the U.S., "owned under any contract or by any combination, or pursuant to any conspiracy" in restraint of trade. This follows a similar provision contained in Sec. 6 of the Sherman Act, but in the latter section the property must be "in the course of transportation" from one state to another, or to a foreign country.

Sec. 337 of the Tariff Act of 1930,[106] which is administered jointly by the Tariff Commission and the President, proscribes:

> .....unfair methods of competition and unfair acts in the importation of articles in the United States.....the effect or tendency of which is to destroy or substantially injure an industry, efficiently and economically operated, in the United States, or to prevent the establishment of such an industry, or to restrain or monopolize trade and commerce in the United States.....

Although Sec. 337 has been applied previously against imports which infringe an American patent, the breadth of its language may be sufficient to encompass traditional antitrust violations in the import trade.[107]

5-30. The Webb-Pomerence Export Trade Act makes an exception to the Sherman Act with respect to an association entered into for the sole

---

105. 15 U.S.C. § 11 (1970).

106. 19 U.S.C. § 1337 (1970).

107. See for example Tractor Parts, Tariff Comm'n Publ. No.401 (June 1971).

purpose of engaging in export trade under certain conditions.[108] For a more detailed discussion of this Act see 5-33.

Other acts relating to foreign trade which have antitrust provisions include regulatory statutes like the Shipping Act of 1916;[109] the Revenue Act of 1916[110] (antidumping provisions); the Merchant Marine Act of 1920, Sec. 29;[111] the Federal Communications Act;[112] the Federal Aviation Act;[113] and the Panama Canal Act.[114] The Defence Production Act[115] has also been of importance in the antitrust foreign trade context. The Atomic Energy Act[116] provides for advice or licences by the Attorney General under the Act for the prevention of situations inconsistent with the antitrust laws in foreign as well as domestic trade.

(2) Scope and Content of "Foreign Commerce"

5-31. The great majority of situations in American antitrust cases which have involved foreign activities have also involved restraints of competition in American domestic, interstate commerce, so that the law would have reached them without a "foreign commerce" clause. In the following paragraphs we shall concentrate on the question: when is there "commerce with foreign nations"?

---

108. 15 U.S.C. (1970).
109. 46 U.S.C. §§ 801-42 (1970).
110. 15 U.S.C. §§ 71-77 (1970).
111. 46 U.S.C. § 885 (1970).
112. 47 U.S.C. §§ 202, 203, 309, 313-314 (1970).
113. 49 U.S.C. §§ 1302, 1378(b), 1381, 1382 (1970).
114. 15 U.S.C. § 31 (1970).
115. 50 U.S.C. § 2158 (1970).
116. 42 U.S.C. § 2135 (1970).

The phrase "commerce with foreign nations" at least comprehends all commerce conducted between any point in the territory of the U.S. and any point in any other nation's territory.[117] A transaction between two places in a foreign territory may also affect some other transaction in American foreign commerce and thereby be drawn within the statute's reach. The language of the cases has, however, been rather general in respect of what constitutes U.S. foreign commerce and what acts or contracts abroad affect it for jurisdictional purposes; some references in the cases are made to acts "included in" the "foreign commerce" and some mention acts "affecting" or "directly and materially affecting" such commerce. In the following paragraphs we shall briefly explore these references in respect of possible types of restriction.

(a) Import Restrictions

5-32. Whenever competition in the domestic market is restrained through a restriction on imports, there is an effect on interstate commerce which merges with the effect on foreign commerce.[118] There are a number of cases involving restrictions (e.g. price-fixing or territorial limitations) upon distribution in the U.S. of products imported from abroad. These for the most part involve U.S. domestic commerce, although, to the extent that a foreign manufacturer seeks to limit distribution in the U.S., such restrictions may also be considered import restraints. It is theoretically possible, however, to have an illegal restraint on imports which does not at the same time

117. See Rahl, supra note 31, at 60.

118. For a detailed survey of various import restraints see Fugate, supra note 85, sec . 2.14.

illegally restrain interstate commerce, e.g. where the domestic effect of an import restraint is confined to one State.

A different type of import restriction is that resulting from the control of foreign supply, and thereby of U.S. imports, by combinations of U.S. and foreign enterprises or by solely foreign combinations. Some of the most difficult questions of jurisdiction are raised by the effects on U.S. imports of entirely foreign combinations. See 5-41 _et seq._

(b) _Export Restrictions_

5-33. Problems of outright interference with foreign commerce are more clearly isolated from interstate commerce when they occur in export transactions.[119] There are few decided cases of this kind as export restraints are carefully guarded by exemption in the _Webb-Pomerence Export Trade Act_ of 1918. This Act provides a specific exemption from the antitrust laws which permits firms within an industry to establish export associations, but the associations must register with the Federal Trade Commission and file periodic reports. The immunity conferred by the Act is restricted by the requirement that the export association must not interfere with competition in domestic commerce or restrain the export trade of any domestic competitor. The Act provides further:

> .....that such association does not, either in the United States or elsewhere, enter into any agreement, understanding or conspiracy, or do any act which artificially or intentionally enhances or depresses prices within the U.S. of commodities of the class exported by such association, or which substantially lessens competition within the United States or otherwise restrains trade therein (Sec. 2).

119. Cf. Rahl, _supra_ note 31, at 70; K. Brewster, _Antitrust and American Business Abroad_, sec. 2.2 (1958).

Therefore, there is no provision for the authorization of domestic restraints connected with export cartels as in Germany. Cf. 5-4. "Mixed" export cartels are subject to the same rules as domestic cartels.

The Webb-Pomerence exemption does not apply to international export cartels (i.e. agreements which divide world markets and fix international prices).[120] In addition, various types of prohibited conduct have been found to be beyond the scope of the Webb-Pomerence exemption.[121]

(c) Restraints in Foreign Commerce (or in the Course of it) Which Do Not Directly Interfere With Imports or Exports

5-34. It has already been mentioned above that a distinction has been made in the cases between interference with, or restriction of, foreign commerce (i.e. restraints on the freedom of export or import) and restriction of competition in the course of foreign commerce (i.e. restrictions on competition which occur in foreign transactions without interferring physically with the trade itself). See 5-31. More specifically the difference is between prevention or redirection of a line of foreign commerce, on the one hand, and regulation of the prices, terms, customers, sales territories or other business aspects in a line of foreign commerce, on the other hand.[122]

---

120. See United States v. United States Alkali Export Assn. Inc., 86 F. Supp. 59 (S.D.M.Y. 1949). International Export cartels are not legitimate activities "in the course of export trade", as defined in the act, in view of its legislative history whose emphasis was upon furthering competition between domestic and foreign concerns and not the elimination thereof.

121. See OECD, Export Cartels, sec. 24.

122. See Rahl, supra note 31, at 76.

Some Sherman Act cases have involved restraints of competition committed in connection with transportation in foreign commerce, which are very much like the restraints of competition of the second type described above carried out in the course of engaging in business transactions in foreign commerce.[123]

(d) Summary: Scope of "Foreign Commerce"

3-35. Nearly all the decided foreign commerce cases have dealt with imports or exports of goods or transportation of goods to or from U.S. ports. Thus the outer contours of "trade or commerce.....with foreign nations" have not been charted by judicial decisions. The relevant antitrust statutes may, however, be interpreted as broadly in determining the scope and content of "foreign commerce" as they have been in determining the scope and content of "interstate commerce". Thus, the American antitrust statutes regulating foreign commerce may reach all types of activities covered by domestic antitrust laws, including the export and import of commodities; direct investments and acquisitions abroad; transportation and communication services; financial activities; and transactions in industrial property rights, such as patents, know-how, trademarks, and copyrights.[124]

---

123. For example, see United States v. Pacific Arctic Ry. & Nav.Co. 228 U.S. 87, 33 Sup. Ct. 443, 57 L. Ed. 742 (1913); Thomsen v. Cayser, 243 U.S. 66, 37 Sup. Ct. 353, 61 L. Ed. 597 (1917).

124. For references for what "commerce", for antitrust purposes, comprehends, see Report of the Attorney General's National Committee to Study the Antitrust Laws 77-80 (1955)(hereinafter referred to as "Report of the Atty. Gen. Comm"); Gibbons v. Ogden 22 U.S. (9 Wheat) 1, 189-190 (1829).

(3) The Required Impact and Effect on U.S. Commerce

(a) Effects of Local and Foreign Activities on the U.S. Domestic Commerce

5-36. We now propose to examine the impact of the "effect" which is required within the U.S. to allow for the exercise of jurisdiction on the basis of the federal laws. The "effect" in the present context is on the domestic interstate trade and not on the foreign trade of the U.S. In this context an effect on interstate trade or commerce, which relates to the flow of goods or services across State boundaries, is the effect necessary for the application of the jurisdiction under the *Sherman Act* or, indeed, any federal antitrust law.[125] However, restraint of competition can occur in commerce without causing provable changes in its volume, but it can still change the pattern of interstate trade. It is clear from the American case law that such restraint is, nevertheless, subject to the *Sherman Act*.[126] Therefore, restraints which increase the volume of commerce as well as those which do not alter it at all may be equally within the jurisdictional scope of the law.[127]

It becomes obvious that the effect on interstate trade in the U.S. laws is a jurisdictional issue separate from other questions of substantive jurisdiction. See in analogy a similar requirement in

---

125. See Crotti, *supra* note 84, at 81.

126. A primary purpose of the *Sherman Act* is to cover agreements among competitors to restrict competition, although it contains a different formula. The act's draftsmen connected the phrase to the constitutional language giving power to Congress to regulate commerce, by creating an awkward combination of two quite distinct concepts ("restraint of competition in" or "affecting commerce"); to avoid error, these must be analytically separated.

127. See Rahl, *supra* note 31, at 62-63.

EEC law in 3-5. The questions of substantive jurisdiction also involve inquiry into effects, but of a different kind. The effects in the latter connection are on competition and must be shown to be unreasonable for the Sherman Act purposes, or to amount to a substantial reduction of competition for most Clayton Act purposes. The latter type of effects must, therefore, be "adverse", but it is an "adverse" effect on competition (or in affecting commerce), not an "adverse" effect on the volume of commerce which must be shown.[128] See in analogy the requirement of effects on competition in EEC law in 3-9.

5-37. Fugate explains that in the interstate commerce cases, the courts have used two concepts; one that the acts are in the "flow of commerce", and the other that acts, while essentially local, substantially affect interstate commerce.[129] In other words, a business practice under Sherman Act scrutiny must either occur in the flow of interstate commerce or, if the practice takes place wholly in one State it must substantially affect interstate commerce. The condition that business activity which takes place solely within one State must substantially affect interstate commerce is the only qualification of the requirement stated above that the amount of interstate commerce which is involved is not relevant.[130]

5-38. It is interesting to note that the cases which have been the subject of the greatest controversy, concerning the application of

---

128. For example Timken Roller Bearing Co. v. United States, 341 U.S. 593 (1951); Mandeville Island Farms, Inc. v. Crystal Sugar Co. 334 U.S. 219 (1948).
129. Fugate, supra note 85, at 71. See also United States v. Women's Sportwear Mfg. Assn., 336 U.S. 460, 69 Sup. Ct. 714, 93 L. Ed. 805 (1949); Burke v. Ford and Kune 389 U.S. 320, ss. Sup. Ct. 443, 19 L. Ed. 554 (1967).
130. See Crotti, supra note 84, at 82-83.

the laws to foreign activities, included interstate commerce allegations. In most of the antitrust cases involving foreign activity the acts and agreements partially took place in the U.S. and partially abroad. Certainly where a good part of the activity in question is in the U.S. there will be little question of the effect on U.S. trade, but it may be different in other cases.

Where effects of foreign activity were examined in the U.S. Supreme Court, considerations of effects on U.S. commerce often found expression in a formula which stated that the restraint must be shown to have "direct and substantial effect on the foreign or interstate trade."[131] However, a list of extracts from leading foreign commerce cases, collected by Fugate, suggests that the majority have not considered it necessary to find both "direct" and "substantial" effect.[132] It would probably be more accurate to say that the restraints must have either a "direct" or a "substantial" effect, as Rahl advocates very convincingly; the directness and substantiality may be viewed as expressing different ways of asking whether the facts rise to the level which requires regulation.[133] The less "direct" the restraint is, the more important it would become to convincingly show that it produces a substantial effect. On the basis of the classification which is being made in purely domestic interstate commerce

131. For example see Continental Ore Co. v. Union Carbide and Carbon Co. 370 U.S. 69, 82 Sup. Ct. 1404, 8 L. Ed. 2d 777 (1962); Timken Roller Bearing Co. v. United States 341 U.S. 593, 71 Sup. Ct. 971, 95 L. Ed. 1199 (1962); United States v. National Lead Co., 332 U.S. 319, 67 Sup. Ct. 1634, 91 L. Ed. 2077 (1947); United States v. Sisal Sales Corp. 274 U.S. 268, 47 Sup. Ct. 592, 71 L. Ed. 1042 (1927); Thomsen v. Cayser, supra note 123; United States v. Pacific & Arctic Ry. & Nav. Co., supra note 123; United States v. American Tobacco Co. 221 U.S. 106, 31 Sup. Ct. 632, 55 L. Ed. 663 (1911).
132. See Fugate, supra note 85, at sec. 2.20.
133. Rahl, supra note 31, at 64-67, 77 et seq. See also Timberg "United States and Foreign Antitrust Laws Governing International Business Transactions" in A Lawyer's Guide to International Business Transactions 622 (Surrey & Shaw eds. 1966).

cases, between restraints which occur in commerce and restraints which cannot readily be said to be "in" commerce, but, nevertheless, have an effect on it (see 5-37), Rahl further suggests that a proper formula for the test of "effects" of foreign activity is "in-or-substantial effect". Thus a case qualifying as "in" commerce meets the "directness" test; a restraint which is not "in" commerce is indirect and must meet a "substantial effect" test.[134] The category of cases involving foreign activities, but which can rest upon "effects" on domestic interstate commerce contain cases of both types of the "in-or-substantial effect on commerce".

For reasons of convenience we shall analyse the meaning of the terms "direct"and "substantial" (which arealso used in other legal systems) elsewhere in the study. See 6-18 and 6-19.

(b) Effects on the Foreign Commerce of the U.S.

5-39. In the present context a comment is first required. There is no distinction in the terms of the Sherman Act as to U.S. citizens and non-nationals. However, the courts are more likely to find effects on U.S. trade in the activities of U.S. citizens.[135] Fugate mentions that this basis of jurisdiction may swing the balance when there is a question of whether acts or contracts abroad affect U.S. foreign trade.[136]

5-40. The theory "in-or-substantial" by which we tested the "effects" of foreign activities on the domestic commerce of the U.S. is argued

---

134. Rahl, *ibid*.

135. See Fugate, *supra* note 85, sec. 2.9.

136. See examples *ibid.*

by Rahl to support also the test required to identify "effects" on foreign commerce. The argument has been considered by Rahl that interstate commerce doctrines (such as those mentioned in 5-37) do not necessarily suit the kinds of restrictive agreements in foreign commerce, because of different trade conditions, and because of problems of possible conflicts with foreign law and sovereignty. Nevertheless, among the many good reasons to adopt the concept explained above, Rahl emphasizes the fact that the foreign commerce cases seem to fit the "in-or-substantial effect on commerce" formula. (The indication where a restraint is "in" or not "in" foreign commerce is given in 5-31 to 5-34).

No case has been found holding that proof of substantiality is required where the restraint operates directly to interfere with a line of export commerce by cutting it off, or by rechannelling it to different markets or customers, or into different products.[137] Brewster draws an inference, from the import cartel cases, that restraints which explicitly govern U.S. foreign trade have been "vulnerable" even if imports or domestic production were not proved to be seriously curbed or extortionately priced.[138] Following this inference Rahl adds that an explicit restraint on exports without evidence that exports have been curbed is equally vulnerable; cases applying to situations of interference with exports the same substantive doctrines that are used in domestic cases.

The question as to the impact in an export situation of a restraint upon the foreign commerce would not usually be at issue,

---

137. See United States v. United States Alkali Export Assn., 325, 69 U.S. 196 (1945).

138. Brewster, *supra* note 119, at 28 and 81.

since normally only U.S. enterprises and U.S. activity would be involved. Accordingly, the parties would not raise such a question if such an agreement were proved.

In summary, a restrictive agreement which interferes with the movement of either imports or exports is likely to be regarded as falling within the "foreign commerce" jurisdiciton of the Sherman Act, without regard to how much actual effect there has been, either upon the parties, or upon trade generally. The question "how much effect?" could play an important role in determining the legality of the agreement under the rule of reason, if the restraint present is not of the *per se* variety, but this question would not seem to have much bearing upon the applicability of the act in so far as effects on commerce tests are concerned. The same rationale would apply to restraints upon exports or imports under Sec. 5 of the Federal Trade Commission Act.

Therefore, restraints in the course of foreign commerce, or in transportation in foreign commerce, all fit the "in" commerce test. Such restraints of competition "in" foreign commerce are subject to the law regardless of how much effect on trade, if any, can be shown. If the restraints are not "in" foreign commerce the effects required must be substantial.

(4) Jurisdiction in Antitrust Cases Merely on the Basis of Effects on Commerce of Foreign Conduct in Foreign Markets

5-41. Despite a line of authority which has illustrated the formula "direct and substantial effect on commerce", the basis for jurisdiction on foreign conduct abroad has continued to be a subject of very lively interest, highlighted by the discussion and criticism of the judgment in the Alcoa Case.[139]

That effects within the U.S. or upon the U.S. commerce with foreign nations would bring wholly foreign conduct within the Sherman Act's reach was not propounded until Judge Learned Hand, in discussing Aluminium Ltd.'s participation in the European aluminium cartels of the thirties, said:

> .....it is settled law - as "Limited" itself agrees - that any State may impose liabilities, even upon persons not within its allegiance, for conduct outside its borders which has consequences within its borders which the State reprehends; and these liabilities other States will ordinarily recognize. 140

5-42. In the Alcoa Case the Aluminium Company of America (Alcoa), an American corporation, and Aluminium Limited, a Canadian company (a wholly owned subsidiary of Alcoa), were charged with having entered into an unlawful conspiracy in restraint of interstate and foreign commerce, particularly in the manufacture and sale of "virgin" aluminium ingot. From the facts of the case it appears that a Swiss corporation had been created (the "Alliance"), in pursuance of an agreement, the signatories to which would issue shares to be taken up by the signatories. This corporation was from time to time to fix a quota of production for each share, and each shareholder was to be limited to an amount in proportion

139. United States v. Aluminium Co. of America, 148 F. 2d 416 (2 Cir. 1945).

140. Ibid. at 444. A particularly enlightened discussion of these points in the Alcoa Case with interesting information drawn from Aluminium's Trial Brief in the District Court appears in C. Oliver's survey "Range of Effect of the Antitrust Laws of the United States" in I.L.A., Tokyo Conference 518-519.

to the number of shares it held. Later the system of unconditional quotas was replaced by a system of royalties; if a shareholder exceeded his quota, he was to pay a royalty; those royalties the "Alliance" divided among the shareholders in proportion to their shares. Although the trial court had found that the agreement did not materially affect the foreign trade or commerce of the U.S., the Court of Appeals did not accept this finding. The end result was that the Court found the agreement to be in violation of Sec. 1 of the Sherman Act.

It is important to stress here that the Court of Appeal accepted the findings that Alcoa (the American corporation) was not itself party to the international "Alliance". The American party had, nevertheless, admitted awareness of what was going on, its prior active participation in foreign cartels, and the close identity of the American and the foreign cartel participant, Limited. There was common control of Alcoa and Limited, which the court disregarded, as well as the fact that Limited itself, although chartered in Canada, had its effective business headquarters in New York. Emphasis on such facts makes the case less like a situation where the foreign conduct of a foreigner, without any American conspirators, is complained of.[140a] However, the literature on the case adopts a strict interpretation of the findings in the judgment.

5-43. As mentioned above the Alcoa Case is significant in two respects. For the first time the Court relied upon an effects test alone rather

---

140a. See Brewster, supra note 119 at 72-73; Note 69 Harv. L. Rev. 1456 (1956).

than on the fact that some of the conduct took place within the U.S. In addition, Alcoa was, as interpreted in subsequent cases and in the copious literature on this particular case, the first application of U.S. antitrust laws to conduct effected abroad solely by foreign corporations. The standards advanced by the case were: (1) that the acts or agreements were intended to affect U.S. imports and exports; and (2) that performance of the acts or agreements did have some effect upon imports and exports. The full theoretical implications of this case were obviously considerable. Any conduct, anywhere, by any body which was intended to and did restrain American import, export, or interstate trade or commerce in a manner unlawful by domestic standards would be within reach of the law.[141]

5-44. An "intent" to affect U.S. commerce was stated by Judge Learned Hand in the Alcoa Case as a special condition for jurisdiction over foreign companies. There is no indication that Judge Learned Hand did not have in mind the usual rule that persons are presumed to intend the normal consequences of their acts. The Alcoa statement was so interpreted in the later Incandescent Lamp Case.[142]

The rule as to the reqirement of "intent" is thus formulated by Fugate:

---

141. Cf. Brewster, supra note 119 at 72.

142. United States v. General Electrical Co., 82 F. Supp. 753, 884, 885 (D.N.J. 1949). The court referred to evidence indicating one of the defendant's, Philips, awareness of the U.S. antitrust laws, but further stated that a specific intent to violate the antitrust laws was not required (at 891). Other approaches regarding intent, such as "a conspiracy intended to restrain (foreign) trade" (see United States v. Sisal Sales Corp., supra note 131, at 1045) and conspiracies "aimed at obstracting the foreign commerce of the United States " (United States v. United States Alkali Export Assn. supra note 137) also appear to have been used with the same meaning.

> .....the necessary intent is merely a general intent to affect U.S. commerce and may be satisfied by the rule that a person is presumed to intend the natural consequences of his actions. Thus, if effects are demonstrated, proof of intent would not appear to be a great problem. On the other hand, if there is a contract abroad which on its face indicates an intent and purpose to affect U.S. trade, the burden appears to be upon the participants to show that there has been no effect. The rule in both instances would seem to be little different from that in the interstate commerce cases. 143

5-45. There are many arguments in the literature on why Alcoa cannot be expected to yield firm predictions of future judgments and why in the words of Brewster "factual distinction might open the door to advocacy in an attempt to trim the breadth of Hand's language".[144] See also second paragraph in 5-42.

The extraterritorial scope of the U.S. antitrust law is, of course, most doubtful when the restraints concerned are carried out solely in foreign market transactions.[145] There has not been any reported case since Alcoa involving activities in which jurisdiction was based solely on "effects" on trade of activities of foreigners abroad. Each decided case involving acts abroad has been concerned primarily with the conduct of American corporations or, when concerned with the conduct of foreign defendants, has found and emphasized the existence of restraints by the defendants of American domestic (interstate) commerce within the U.S.[146]

5-46. The Report of the Attorney General's National Committee, which is an important milestone in the historical development of the American

---

143. Fugate, supra note 85, sec. 2.10.

144. Brewster, supra note 119, at 72-74.

145. Cf. Rahl, supra note 31, at 80-89.

146. See e.g. United States v. Imperial Chem. Indus. Ltd., 100 F. Supp. 504 D.N.Y. (1951); United States v. Timken Roller Bearing Co., supra note 131; United States v. General Elec. Co., supra note 142; United States v. National Lead Co., supra note 131.

antitrust laws,[147] gave the following directives on how to deal with foreign defendants and conduct abroad:

> (1).....the Sherman Act applies only to those arrangements between Americans alone in concert with foreign firms, which have such substantial anticompetitive effects on this country's 'trade or commerce with foreign nations' as to constitute unreasonable restraints.
>
> (2).....conspiracies between foreign competitors alone should come within the Sherman Act only where they are intended to, and actually do, result in substantial anticompetitive effects on our foreign commerce. 148

These directives have ever since been the subject of new proposals for changes and modifications. Before we examine more recent developments it is important to refer to a short summary of the extra-territorial reach of U.S. antitrust laws made by Brewster in 1958:

> a. The Sherman Act is presumptively territorial in its application to foreign corporations and trade and commerce with foreign nations.
> b. In spite of the territorial presumption, foreign acts are within reach if they are interwoven with domestic conduct initiating or carrying out a restraint of American interstate or foreign commerce.
> c. Proven effects on American commerce which were intended may subject wholly foreign conduct to jurisdiction, although all cases have involved some activity within U.S. territory, either initiating or carrying out the restraint complained of. 149

5-47. Although it has been the subject of much debate, the Alcoa Case was the principal support for Sec. 18(b) of the Restatement (Second) of Foreign Relations Law of the United States,[150] basing extraterritorial jurisdiction, as a matter of international (or foreign relations) law, over acts or conduct abroad upon domestic "effects":

---

147. Both the literature and the judicial decisions make many references to the report.

148. Report of the Atty. Gen. Comm. 76.

149. Brewster, supra note 119 at 74.

150. Restatement (Second) of Foreign Relations Law of the United States § 18(b) (1965) (hereinafter cited as the "Restatement").

§ 18 Jurisdiction to Prescribe with Respect to Effect within Territory

> A state has jurisdiction to prescribe a rule of law attaching legal consequences to conduct that occurs outside its territory and causes an effect within its territory, if .....(b)(i) the conduct and its effect are constituent element of activity to which the rule applies; (ii) the effect within the territory is substantial; (iii) it occurs as a direct and foreseeable result of the conduct outside the territory; and (iv) the rule is not inconsistent with the principles of justice generally recognized by states that have reasonably developed legal systems.

The Restatement does, however, circumscribe the jurisdictional aspects of Alcoa regarding "effects" in that it requires as prerequisites to the assumption of jurisdiction that there be a close connection between proscribed conduct and its effect and that the effect be a "substantial", "direct and forseeable" result of the conduct.[151] (For interpretation of the main features of Sec. 18(b) see 6-17 to 6-20).

The approach in the Alcoa Case also differs from that suggested in the Restatement in that the latter speaks of an "effect within [the] territory of the nation", while in the Alcoa opinion, Judge Learned Hand, spoke of effect on imports ("foreign commerce"). A mere theory of "effect" on export or import sufficient to satisfy Sherman Act commerce tests would not, therefore, automatically qualify under the Restatement, but something more than effect on the foreign commerce would be required. A second difference is that the Restatement specifies no "intent" requirement, although it has been suggested that its "direct and foreseeable result" amounts to such requirement. Compare 5-44.

---

151. The Restatement also modifies the impact of Sec. 18(b) by establishing rules of forebearance which must be read in conjunction with that section. Those rules do not negate jurisdiction but temper its exercise; see Restatement Part IV (Responsibility of States for Injuries to Aliens), at § 40.

5-48. An important development in the application of the law to foreign operations was the "updating project" of the 1955 Report of the Attorney General's National Committee by the Section of Antitrust Law of the American Bar Association (completed in 1968).[152] With regard to the relevant aspect of the extraterritorial reach of the American antitrust laws the findings of the Committee were summarized as follows:

> The assumption of jurisdiciton over the subject matter involving foreign conduct of alien defendants is limited to cases involving the deliberately engaging in conduct the natural and probable consequences of which is restraint of trade or monopoly. 153

This statement purports to harmonize the apparent difference between the guideline contained in the 1955 Committee Report and the corresponding provision in the Restatement.

(a) Recent Developments

5-49. It has already been indicated that the extraterritorial scope of the U.S. antitrust law, particularly if pushed to its outer limits, is a very controversial issue.[154] In practice, the Department of Justice does not go to the limits of the theories discussed above.[155] Partly because of many foreign complaints in the past over the extra-territorial application of American law, and lately because of concern

152. American Bar Association, Antitrust Developments 1955-1968, A Supplement to the Report of the Atty. Gen. Comm. (Chicago 1968) (herinafter cited as "Supp. to Atty. Gen. Nat. Comm. Antitrust Report")
153. Ibid. at 49.
154. For additional material on the controversy of extraterritorial jurisdiction of U.S. laws see: Caudy, Note, "Sherman Antitrust Law; Applicability to Foreign Commerce" 37 Cornell L.Q. 821 (1952); Fugate, "Antitrust Jurisdiction and Foreign Sovereignty" 49 Va.L.Rev. 925 (1963).
155. Fugate, supra note 85, at sec. 2.19.

that overzealous enforcement could hurt American business abroad, the Department of Justice has emphasized that it does not seek to push matters to possible extremes.[156] A high Department of Justice official Donald Baker, stated that the government is not interested in application of the law to activities in foreign markets, either by foreign or by U.S. firms, where the U.S. interests are not substantially affected.[157] Baker has also said that the Sherman Act should not be applied even to substantial restraints of competition in the course of U.S. export commerce, or by U.S. firms in foreign countries, if the only victims of the restraints are foreigners.[158]

5-50. The current doctrinal approach of the U.S. Antitrust Division has been stated in 1977 in the Antitrust Guide For International Operations. The scope of the laws is indicated in the guide in general terms:

> U.S. law in general, and the U.S. antitrust laws in particular, are not limited to transactions which take place within our borders. When foreign transactions have a substantial and foreseeable effect on U.S. commerce, they are subject to U.S. law regardless of where they take place.....to use the Sherman Act to restrain or punish an overseas conspiracy whose clear purpose and effect is to restrain significant commerce in the U.S. market is both appropriate and necessary to effective U.S. enforcement. 158a

---

156. See Address by Donald I. Baker, Director of Policy Planning, Antitrust Division, before the New York State Bar Ass'n, New York City, Jan. 24, 1973, reprinted in 5 CCH Trade Reg. Rep. para. 50,161, at 55,283 (1974); Address by Keith I. Clearwaters, Special Asst. to the Asst. Attorney General Antitrust Division, before the Ass'n of General Counsel, Hot Springs, Virginia, May 1973, reprinted in 5 CCH Trade Reg. Rep. para. 50,169, at 55,300 (1974).

157. Baker, "Antitrust and World Trade: Tempest in an International Teapot"? 8 Cornell Intl. L.J. 31 (1974).

158. This view is however not sustained by the case law; see Rahl, "American Antitrust and Foreign Operations: What is Covered?" 8 Cornell Int. L.J. 8 (1974) and "A Rejoinder" 8 Cornell Int. L.J. 43-44 (1974).

158a Antitrust Division, U.S. Dept. of Justice, Antitrust Guide for International Operations 6-7 (1977), reprinted in BNA, Antitrust & Trade Reg. Rep. No. 799 (1977), and Trade Reg. Reports (CCH) No. 266, pt. II (1977).

5-51. A certain change of approach by the courts has been discerned in the case law in 1976 when the Court of Appeals for the Ninth Circuit, in the context of an antitrust suit with international ramifications, declined to apply any form of the "direct and substantial" test in asserting its jurisdiction and instead substituted a balancing approach incorporating multinational, as well as domestic, considerations.[159]

The Timberlane Case arose out of the allegations by the plaintiff, an American partnership and its two recently acquired Honduran subsidiaries, that the Bank of America and others[160] had conspired to prevent the plaintiffs from exporting lumber from Honduras to the U.S. The defendants were accused of using outstanding claims against Timberlane to obtain a court-ordered attachment of the assets of the subsidiaries in Honduras. The appointment of a judicial officer to take charge of the property resulted in the shut down of the plaintiffs' milling operations in Honduras. In their complaint, the plaintiffs also charged other forms of harassment, including the false arrest of their regional operations manager in Honduras. By effectively eliminating the Timberlane partnership as a competitor, only individuals financed and directed by the Bank of America remained in control of the Honduran export lumber business.

The federal district court granted a motion to dismiss the plaintiffs' complaint on the grounds that the act of State doctrine prevented the court from examining the acts of the Honduran Government

159. Timberlane Lumber Co. v. Bank of America, 549 F. 2d 597 (9th. Cir. 1976).
160. The named defendants also included a wholly owned subsidiary of the Bank and several employees of the Bank named individually.

in question, and that, in any case, the court lacked subject-matter jurisdiction over the dispute in the absence of a direct and substantial effect on U.S foreign commerce.

The holding of the lower court, as it related to a consideration of the applicability of the act of State doctrine in the instant situation, was overruled by the court of appeals. In considering the extension of subject-matter jurisdiction of a U.S. court over the alleged acts, the court of appeals criticized the view that a direct or substantial effect on American foreign commerce only could support the assertion of jurisdiction by an American court over events occurring in a foreign country. The "direct and substantial" effects approach was deemed inadequate because it ignored the interests of the other country and the relationship of the actor to the U.S. The court noted the confusion between the use of an effects test to establish jurisdiction over foreign acts (which it did not apply) and the requirement of "substantial effects" necessary to prove a Sherman Act violation. In applying a two-tier analysis to the instant case, the court of appeals found that the effect on foreign commerce was substantial enough to make the restraint cognizable under the Sherman Act. Then, in balancing the factors required by the second inquiry, the court noted that while the actions took place in Honduras and had the most substantial effect on that country, there was no indication of conflict with any Honduran law or policy. Therefore, dismissal of the plaintiffs' complaint could not be sustained because of the asserted inability of an American court to assume jurisdiction over the action.

We have reserved our view on the question whether the change in the jurisdictional tests as described above adopts a better approach to the jurisdictional questions concerned for a later stage in the study. See 6-48 to 6-50.

(5) The Scope of the United States Extraterritorial Enforcement Measures

(a) Courts' Orders Involving Some Activity Abroad

5-52. Fugate points out that U.S. orders and decrees have included injunctions against acts abroad which would violate its antitrust laws, for instance the divestiture of stock holdings in foreign corporations, the ordering of the transfer of foreign patent and trademark rights, and the enjoining of the exercise of foreign patent and trademark rights. Although for the most part the orders can be carried out in the U.S. they involve some action abroad.[161]

The general rule in that respect has been stated in the Restatement (Second) of Conflict of Laws (1971) as follows:

> A state has power to exercise judicial jurisdiction to order a person, who is subject to its judicial jurisdiction, to do an act or to refrain from doing an act in another state. 162

The only barrier which the U.S. at present recognizes, in some circumstances, is legislation in the foreign country which renders illegal what the American judgment commands the defendant to do (see below).

---

161. Fugate, supra note 85, at sec. 3.16. For further discussion on the compulsion of conduct abroad by aliens see I.L.A., Tokyo Conference 328, 407-415, 522-524.

162. Restatement (Second) of Conflict of Laws § 53 (1971).

(b) Courts' Orders Conflicting with Foreign Law

5-53. At one time the American rule was said to be that a court in one State could order an act to be done in another State only if the act were not contrary to the law of the State in which it was to be performed.[163] A good example for that rule is the decree relating to the alien defendant in the United States v. General Elec. Co.[164] which carefully specified that condition.[165]

5-54. In recent years the American courts have assumed that they have the power to order conduct abroad even though such conduct would violate foreign law. However, the courts also exercised discretion to avoid placing a party in a position where he must violate foreign law. Thus, in the Du Pont-I.C.I. Case[166] the enforcement of provisions, governing the British corporate defendant's ownership and use of British patent rights, was abandoned by the court only after British courts enjoined compliance with them.

Du Pont, an American corporation, and Imperial Chemical Industries (I.C.I.), an English corporation, had made extensive manufacturing and marketing agreements, pursuant to which Du Pont had licensed and later assigned to I.C.I. its English nylon patents. I.C.I. had in turn granted exclusive and irrevocable licences of these patents

163. See Note "Limitations on the Federal Judicial Power to Compel Act Violating Foreign Law" 63 Col. L. Rev. 1441 (1963).

164. 115 F. Supp. 835 (D.C.N.J. 1953).

165. Ibid. at 878.

166. United States v. Imperial Chemical Industries Ltd. 105 F. Supp. 215, 229; British Nylon Spinners Ltd. v. Imperial Chemical Industries Ltd. [1953] I Ch. 19 (C.A. 1952)(interlocutory appeal); British Nylon Spinners Ltd. v. Imperial Industries Ltd. [1954] 3 Weekly L.R. 505 (Ch.)(final appeal).

to British Nylon Spinners (B.N.S.), an English corporation in which I.C.I. had a half interest. In United States v. Imperial Chemical Industries Ltd., an antitrust suit brought against Du Pont, I.C.I. and others, the district court decreed that I.C.I. should refrain from exercising its rights under the English patents to prevent importation into England of the patented products for resale, and ordered I.C.I. to licence the patents to all persons desiring them. To prevent such a curtailment of its rights as an exclusive licensee, BNS, which had not been a party in the American proceedings, successfully sued I.C.I. in an English court for specific performance of the licensing agreement. Since no further action was taken in any American court, I.C.I. was thus able to escape the mandate of the American decree. The English court which granted specific performance relied expressly on the saving clause in the American decree, which in its view precluded conflict.

5-55. In the Holophane Case[167] the court's order to an American defendant to use "reasonable efforts" to promote the sale and distribution of its products in foreign markets in violation of contract obligations, which were lawful in the foreign countries concerned, was subsequently tempered. A letter from the Solicitor General to the Supreme Court interpreted the order as requiring only acts which do not violate a "foreign statute, regulation or ordinance, or the valid judgment of a competent foreign court."[168] The order was then affirmed by the Supreme Court in an equally divided court.

---

167. Holophane Co. v. United States 119 F. Supp. 114 (S.D. Ohio 1954).

168. Quoted in Supp. to Atty. Gen. Nat. Comm. Antitrust Rep. 53 (1968).

5-56. In the Swiss Watchmakers Case[169] the sweeping injunction concerning Swiss and American defendants abroad was finally modified to provide exemption for acts required by the foreign law, or for failure to act where action would be illegal.[170]

The Swiss Watchmakers Case involved a civil suit by the U.S. against a number of Swiss and American defendants, alleging that the defendants had unreasonably restrained the American trade in Swiss watches, watch parts, and watch machinery. All of the Swiss defendants were parties to a "Collective Convention" regulating the production, sale, and export of watches and watch parts. The Swiss defendants were ordered to amend their "Collective Convention". The order required the virtual reorganization of the Swiss watch industry in Switzerland, in a way which was contrary to long-established Swiss Government policy and the latter vigorously protested.

On the basis of this case a distinction has since been made between what conduct a foreign government authorizes and what it requires, implying that normally authorized conduct is no defence.[171]

(c) Discovery Orders for Foreign Located Documents

5-57. The approach of the courts in the U.S. has been that "calling for the disclosure of documents is a procedural matter and it has long been the rule that the 'lex fori' governs the law of procedure".[172]

169. United States v. The Watchmakers of Switzerland Information Center, Inc. (S.D.N.Y. 1962), 1963 Trade Cas. para. 70,600 at 77,457.
170. See 1965 Trade Cas. para. 71,352 at 80,491.
171. See a very detailed examination of this case in Rahl, supra note 31, at ch. 6.
172. In re Investigation of World Arrangements etc., 13 F.R.D. 280; 286 (D.D.C. 1952). See also Societé Internationale etc. (I.G. Chemie) v. McGranery, 14 F.R.D. 44, 53 (D.D.C. 1953); Beale A Treatise on the Conflict of Laws, Vol. 3, § 584.1 (1935); Nussbaum, Principles of Private International Law 187 (1943).

This approach was in fact moderated in the Oil Cartel Grand Jury Investigation when the court ruled against the companies subpoenaed, with respect to the argument that the subpoena (directed by the grand jury) called for documents located within the territorial jurisdiction of foreign governments which prohibited the removal of these papers. The court, nevertheless, concluded that substantive law may be affected in one jursidction when procedural law operated in another, and went on to say that it did not want to promulgate a "procedural order" imposing serious criminal penalties under foreign substantive law. To avoid any harsh circumstances, the court reserved its view on this matter pending the companies showing: (1) an endeavour in good faith to gain consent from the foreign sovereign to remove the required documents; (2) the interest, if any, that the foreign sovereign has in the companies concerned or in the investigation; and (3) proof of the foreign law.[173]

The opinion did not resolve the question of non-production by reason of foreign law, leaving this for a later decision. This proved unnecessary since the grand jury was dismissed upon the filing of a civil case.

5-58. The Courts have supplied a variety of solutions to the problem of conflicting foreign law. In the Application of Chase Manhattan Bank[174] the subpoena was modified to require only that the company cooperate with the U.S. by applying to authorities of foreign government for permission to produce the documents. In Ings. v. Ferguson[175]

173. In re Investigation of World Arrangements etc., ibid.
174. Application of Chase Manhattan Bank, 297 F. 2d 611 (2d Cir. 1962).
175. Ings v. Ferguson, 282 F. 2d 149 (2d Cir. 1960).

subpoenas issued by the district court were modified and letters rogatory were issued to officials of foreign governments to determine whether production would violate foreign law.

5-59. In United States v. First National City Bank[176] production of documents located in a bank branch in Germany was ordered under penalty of contempt. The court balanced the substantive terms of the statute allegedly prohibiting production, the nature of the sanctions for violation of the statute and the probability of prosecution against the interest of the plaintiff in gaining access to the documents in question. It found that the U.S. interests in enforcing its antitrust laws ".....considered the corner stones of.....[that].....nation's economic policies"[177] outweighed the interests of Germany and any hardship that might ensue to the defendant. The German division of First National City Bank was required to produce its documents.

5-60. Following recent developments on the issue of production of documents, which is resisted by a foreign government, it is possible to conclude that while foreign government compulsion, in the absence of inducement of such compulsion by the defendants, may be immune (see also 5-62), interference by a foreign government with enforcement procedures by U.S. courts will sometimes be resisted. Thus an American court has ordered persons under its jurisdiction to produce documents located in the Canadian Province of Quebec, despite a Quebec statute prohibiting this.[178] In the Ampicillin Case, the U.S. court ordered a British parent company to answer interrogatories[179] and

---

176. United States v. First National City Bank 396 F. 2d 897 (2d Cir. 1968)

177. Ibid. 903.

178. American Industrial Contracting, Inc. v. Johns-Manville Corp. 326 F. Supp. (W.D.Pa. 1971).

179. In re Ampicillin Antitrust Litigation, Civil No. 822-870 (D.DC., filed Mar. 19, 1970).

when the British Government ordered the company not to answer, the U.S. court stated that it would deprive the company of the right to advance defences in the case. Ultimately, the British order was modified and the U.S. court rescinded its penalizing order.

There are more implications for the reach of the U.S. discovery orders to be learnt from the recent developments in the Westinghouse Uranium Contracts Litigation. See 5-17.

(d) The Basis for Personal Jurisdiction and Service of Process

5-61. American law cannot be applied to any company unless "personal jurisdiction" is obtained over that company through valid service of process. In general, there must be enough contact on the part of the company with the U.S. to satisfy constitutional requirements of "due process of law" in serving the company with process and ordering it to submit to the American court.[180]

Sec. 12 of the Clayton Act is the basic provision governing in personam jurisdiction in antitrust litigations. Its function is to fix a venue, or place of suit in antitrust cases, and determine where the defendant may be served with process in such suits. Sec. 12 provides that "any suit, action, or proceedings under the antitrust laws against a corporation may be brought.....in a judicial district wherein it may be found or transacts business".

---

180. Cf. Int'l Shoe Co. v. Washington 326 U.S. 310, 319 (1945), the test in this case also provides that the maintenance of the suit does not offend the U.S. traditional concept of fair play and substantial justice.

The leading Supreme Court case in that matter is United States v. Scophony Corp.[181] The court in interpreting the venue provision of Sec. 12 found the term "transacting business" to mean "the practical, every day business or commercial concept of doing or carrying on business of any substantial character....."[182]. An agent in the U.S. will generally be sufficient for this. As to the presence of a U.S. subsidiary of a foreign parent as a basis for jurisdiction, the courts have said that mere ownership is not enough, but that the parent might be found to control the subsidiary in such a way as to make it an agent or the alter ego of the parent.[183] In practice, unless the foreign parent gives the subsidiary almost full autonomy, it is likely to be subject to American antitrust control.

A foreign company having no U.S. subsidiary and no agent in the U.S. may be immune from service of process unless it carries on business activities of some substantial kind in the U.S. Selling and administering an insurance contract in an American State by mail has been held sufficient in an analogous case.[184]

Actual service of process may be made in various ways, including sometimes by registered mail, or directly in the home country of the foreign firm if this is acceptable to the foreign government. In the Hoffman Motors Corp. v. Alfa Romeo S.p.A.[185] the defendant was properly served in Italy by registered mail and by personal service

---

181. 333 U.S. 795 (1948).

182. Ibid. at 818.

183. Dobbins v. Kawasaki Motors Corp. 362 F. Supp. 54 (D. Ore. 1974).

184. See McGee v. International Life Ins. Co. 355 U.S. 220 (1957).

185. Hoffman Motors Corp. v. Alfa Romeo S.p.A., 244 F. Supp. 70 (S.D.N.Y. 1965).

on the Italian company's general manager by court appointed Italian attorney (in addition to Sec. 12 mentioned above, use was made of Rule 4 of the Federal Rules of Civil Procedure to perfect service abroad in a manner prescribed by the foreign State statute).

(e) Defences of "Act of State" and "Sovereign Immunity"

5-62. The defence of "foreign government compulsion" was recognized in the Inter-American Refining Co. Case[186] to create an exception where the company is required by the foreign law to pursue the course of action which has resulted in the U.S. antitrust suit. It is, however, not clear what kinds of compulsion will suffice and in certain cases the U.S. courts might not permit U.S. law to be undermined. A further qualification may exist as to this defence: where a company in a foreign country persuades the foreign government - through simply lobbying, or through agreement, or even possibly through "gifts" or bribery, to issue an order compelling firms to engage in conduct that restricts competition affecting U.S. commerce, the company is not protected.[187] There are, however, U.S. Supreme Court decisions holding that persuasion of American government officials by U.S. corporations is immune.[188]

Another type of restraint in this connection is restraint committed by government owned enterprises. While an American court granted sovereign immunity to a foreign corporation which is primarily a government-run organization organized primarily for the purpose of

---

186. Inter-American Refining Corp. v. Texaco Maracaibo, Inc., 307 F. Supp. 1291 (D. Del. 1970).

187. See Occidental Petroleum Corp. v. Buttes Gas & Oil Co., 331 F. Supp. 92 (C.D.Cal. 1971), aff'd per curiam, 461 F. 2d 1261 (9th Cir. 1972), cert. denied, 409 U.S. 950 (1972).

188. Cf. California Motor Transport Co. v. Trucking Unlimited, 404 U.S. 508 (1972).

serving governmental needs, no such immunity was granted to foreign corporations whose way of doing business and whose purposes are primarily of an everyday commercial nature, merely because the foreign government is the dominant stockholder.[189]

The American approach in matters of sovereign immunity, which corresponded for a long period to the 12th May, 1952, Letter of the Acting Legal Advisor of the State Department to the U.S. Attorney General Concerning Sovereign Immunity of Foreign Governments,[190] has recently been changed. New enforcement policy in the U.S. relies upon a formulation of the principle of sovereign immunity recently incorporated in the U.S. Foreign Sovereign Immunities Act of 1976.[191] This formulation is narrower than either that enunciated in the letter mentioned above or the "restrictive" theory of sovereign immunity applied by many States. The new act provides that "the commercial character of an activity shall be determined by reference to the nature of the course of conduct.....rather than by reference to its purpose."[192] Since the U.S. act looks at the nature, not the purpose, of the conduct, it would make no difference that a foreign government had acted for a clearly governmental purpose, e.g. maintaining the viability of a vital resource or manufacturing industry. The fact that it had acted in a commercial context would preclude immunity. It appears that a similarly restrictive approach will govern the application of the act of State doctrine.[193]

---

189. See United States v. Deutsches Kalisyndikat Gesellschaft, 31 F. 2d 199 (S.D.N.Y. 1929)(French owned company held amenable to antitrust action because not acting in government capacity). See also Brewster, supra note 119, at 61.
190. Letter from Jack B. Tate to Philip B. Periman (May 19, 1952) reprinted in 26 Dep't of State Bull. 984 (1952).
191. Pub. L. no. 94-583, 90 Stat. 2891 (codified at 28 U.S.C. §§ 1330, 1332(a), 1602-1611, 1391(f), 1441(d)(1976).
192. 28 U.S.C. § 1603(d)(1976).
193. See Alfred Dunhill of London, Inc. v. Republic of Cuba 425 U.S. 682 (1976).

(6) Protests and Counter Legislation

5-63. Not all of the diplomatic protests against the extraterritorial application of U.S. antitrust laws have been published, but there are published protests from fourteen States: Canada, Denmark, Finland, France, India, Ireland, Italy, Japan, the Netherlands, Norway, Sweden, Switzerland, the United Kingdom and Yugoslavia.[194] Representations were also raised by foreign governments in U.S. courts in cases in which they questioned the jurisdiction of the U.S. courts over their nationals or over the activities of their nationals outside the territorial boundaries of the U.S.[195]

A number of States have enacted legislation in order to block the extraterritorial application of the laws to acts performed within their territory, namely the Netherlands, the Canadian Provinces of Ontario and Quebec, Belgium, Denmark, Finland, France, India, Norway, Sweden and the U.K.[196] In this connection it is also important to refer to the Protection of Trading Interests Act 1980 recently adopted in the U.K. (see 5-18).

194. For compilations and summaries of protests see Brewster, supra note 119, at 46-51; National Security and Foreign Policy in the Application of American Antitrust Laws to Commerce with Foreign Nations 12-15 (1957) a preliminary report by the Special Committee on Antitrust laws and Foreign Trade of the Association of the Bar of the City of New York. See also I.L.A. Tokyo Conference 565-592 (including extracts from some published material on official protests, directives, prohibitions, comments, etc.); Supp. to Atty. Gen. Nat. Comm. Antitrust Rep. 52-55.

195. The most notable cases are the Int'l Oil Grand Jury Investigation (In re Investigation of World Arrangements, supra note 172; the Swiss Watchmakers Case, supra note 169; the Shipping Industry, 186 F. Supp. 298 (D.D.C. 1960); and the Incandescent Lamp Case (United States v. General Electric Co. 82 F. Supp. 753 (D.N.J. 1949). See an extensive discussion of these cases in this connection in I.L.A. The Hague Conference 213-221.

196. Information about particular enactments is given in D. Swann, Competition and Consumer Protection 250-251 (1979); OECD, Restrictive Business Practices of Multinational Enterprises sec. 157; Rahl supra note 119, at 121-122; I.L.A. Buenos Aires Conference 339 and 360-369 and New York Conference 143-145 (the Canadian legislation) Brewster supra note 119, at 483 (legislation in Ontario); I.L.A. The Hague Conference 178-180.

Fourteen maritime nations have taken joint action against proposed extraterritorial application of U.S. laws against the international shipping industry.[197]

197. See information as to the actual controversies and protests in that respect in I.L.A. Tokyo Conference 403-407; Buenos Aires Conference 385-387 (legislation in the Scandinavian countries).

CHAPTER VI

The Extraterritorial Scope of the EEC Jurisdiction in Antitrust Cases from the perspective of International Law and the Methods for the Resolution of International Conflicts

6-1. In the preliminary comments on the limits of the jurisdiction of the Community in antitrust matters at the outset of the study we observed that the assumption of Community jurisdiction over enterprises and arrangements external to the Common Market is subject not only to Community law but also to the principles of international law. See 1-12 et seq. The present chapter is concerned with the impact on the Community of those limitations which international law generally imposes on the extraterritorial reach of a State's legislative and enforcement jurisdiction.

1. THE INTERNATIONAL LEGAL PERSONALITY AND CAPACITY OF THE EEC IN RELATION TO THE EXTRATERRITORIAL REACH OF THE COMPETITION RULES

6-2. The special position of the legal personality and capacity of the EEC with reference to the exercise of extraterritorial jurisdiction in antitrust matters raises questions of the law of international organization in particular and of international law in general. A first aspect may be put in this way: to what extent can a treaty establishing an international organization or regime bind States which are not parties to it and their nationals? A second aspect concerns the question of the extent to which the Community can claim to have rights and powers comparable to those of a State.[1]

It is not the purpose of the present study to seek to answer fully these questions of international law whose implications go far beyond the scope of the study. We shall, therefore, only state the issues involved and approaches which have been suggested in answering them. It should be emphasized at the outset that such issues of international law have not yet loomed large in the life of the Community.[2]

6-3. It has to be observed that legal personality and capacity have been given to the Community to the degree which is necessary to enable it to carry out its functions on the international as well as on the national plane. The attribution of such rights and powers to the Community may be inferred from the nature of the Community as an

---

1. Those questions are raised by Mann in the article: "The Dyestuffs in the Court of Justice of the European Communities" 22 Int. & Comp. L.Q. 42-43 (1973).
2. The only case known to us in which such issues were discussed is the I.C.I. Case (see submissions and arguments of the parties, 625-626 and 629.)

international legal person.[3] The Court of Justice has expressly confirmed the attribution of functional rights and powers to the Community in the judgment in Re ERTA, E.C. Commission v. EEC Council.[4] Are these rights and powers of the Community comparable to those of a State exercising extraterritorial jurisdiction in antitrust matters? Advocate-General Mayras in the Dyestuffs Cases, after he had cited the Treaty provisions attributing legal personality to the Community, said:

> .....all this does not turn the Community into a State, but there are many other bodies amenable to international law which differ from States in the nature and extent of their powers, in so far as these are necessarily adapted to the aims and particular purposes assigned to such bodies.
>
> The same is true of the European Economic Community, whose legal personality and capacity are determined in relation to the objectives and functions defined by the Treaty of Rome.
>
> Thus it cannot exercise all the powers that a State possesses, but only those powers vested in it which are necessary for it to carry out its tasks. Where such powers have been granted to it - and this includes the field of cartels - the Community possesses just as much power as a State provided that cartels affecting competition in the Common Market are concerned. 5

6-4. The question whether the Community powers are comparable to those of a State seems, in view of the explanation by the Advocate-General, related to the notion of "power"; it is important to know what the Community may do in an international context rather than whether it has an abstract quality of "statehood". The powers of the Community

---

3. See generally Arts. 210-240 and the Interim Committee Documents 167-176.

4. Case 22/70, [1971] E.C.R. 263. See also Case 3/76, Kramer [1976] E.C.R. 1279. References to literature on the point under consideration in the text can be found in L. Collins, European Community Law in the United Kingdom 3-4 (1975); Costouis, "Treaty Making Powers of the EEC; Art. 238 and Association Agreements" 15 European Year Book (1967) 31.

5. The I.C.I. Case 692-693. The Treaty provisions which the Advocate-General mentioned in the opinion are Art. 113 and 114 (negotiation of commercial agreements), Art. 228 and 238 (conclusion of international agreements in general) and Art. 210.

to establish and to enforce rules of law are limited to specific matters, namely those matters which are provided for in the Treaty. Thus, the Community, as a subject of international law, may have within that framework, like a State, a material, territorial, temporal and personal jurisdiction in those matters.[6] The idea of the functional character of the powers of an international organization was strongly asserted by the International Court of Justice in its Advisory Opinion in the Reparation for Injuries Case.[7]

The idea of the functional powers of the Community on the international plane can be substantiated, inter alia, by the extent of recognition which is granted to the Community in practice by non-Member States. States are not prohibited from recognizing or treating as a State an entity which for some reason does not qualify as a State.[8] A fortiori States are not prohibited from treating an organization as if it were a State in some respects. It is necessary only to refer to the very many treaties concluded by the Community with non-Member States. The Community legislation receives recognition in foreign countries comparable to that accorded the legislation of its Member States. For example, recognition by the U.S. of the Community as an entity acting on the international level is contained, inter alia, in the Trade Expansion Act of 1962, which authorized the President to negotiate tariff agreements with the EEC.[9]

---

6. See Hug "The Applicability of the Provisions of the European Community Treaties Against Restraints of Competition to Restraints of Competition Caused in Non-Member States, But Affecting the Common Market" in Cartel and Monopoly in Modern Law, vol. 2, 649, (1961).

7. I.C.J. Reports (1949) p.174.

8. See Crawford "The Criteria for Statehood in International Law" 48 Brit. Y.B. Int. L. (1977) p.142. See also note 9 below.

9. 76 Stat. 872 (codified in scattered sections of 19 and 26 U.S.C.A. (Supp. 1962)). For the purpose of interpreting American legislation, it may be noted that the concept of "country" in U.S. statutes is not confined to nations, but may be applied to other political entities, including a supranational community. Cf. Burnet v. Chicago Portrait Co. 285 U.S. 75-76 (1932).

Thus the problem of the international legal status of the EEC must be resolved by reference to the power which it possesses and not by abstract considerations as to its comparability to "a State".

2. INTERNATIONAL LAW PRINCIPLES OF JURISDICTION AND THE COMMUNITY ANTITRUST LEGISLATIVE JURISDICTION

6-5. In this section we shall consider the impact of principles of jurisdiction of international law (those principles have been generally described in 1-18 to 1-20) on the Community in relation to the extraterritorial application of the competition rules.

A. The Protective Principle of Jurisdiction

6-6. The Commission has only once mentioned the protective principle of jurisdiction (see explanation of that principle in 1-20), together with the concept of an effects doctrine, as a possible basis for jurisdiction.[10] But one could ask whether the Commission's view of the protective principle would coincide with the generally accepted meaning and purpose of that principle.[11] In fact the protective principle has never been the actual basis for the Community jurisdiction over aliens and their anticompetitive conduct abroad.

The protective principle is generally ranked as the basis of an auxiliary competence and has, in the context of the extraterritorial application of the law, to be interpreted very narrowly. In fact only those crimes which affect the most vital interests of a State, as defined and recognized in international law, give a State the right to claim extraterritorial jurisdiction to itself on the grounds of the protective

---

10. See the <u>I.C.I. Case</u> 629 (a quotation from the submission of the Commission appears in 2-68).

11. For an extensive elaboration of the meaning and operation of the protective principle in reference to antitrust cases see: I.L.A. <u>The Hague Conference</u> 232.

principle.[12] There is a considerable uniformity among States as to the types of offences which are punishable on the basis of the protective principle, e.g. counterfeiting or falsification of official documents, currency, immigration, etc.

The question of whether restraints of trade and competition are offences punishable by reference to the protective principle has been discussed on a number of occasions.

The European Advisory Committee, under the chairmanship of Lord McNair, which was appointed to make recommendations on the Draft Restatement of the Foreign Relations Law of the U.S., concluded on this point:

> The protective principle does not, in our opinion, ordinarily apply to the protection by a State of its economic policies, such as policies regarding the control of imports or restrictive trade practices. 13

The Committee stated in its report that it agreed with a similar conclusion by the American Law Institute.

In the International Law Association a Committee which examined the extraterritorial application of restrictive trade legislation concluded that, apart from circumstances of the most exceptional kind, the protective principle has no application as a basis of jurisdiction

---

12. See for example Sec. 33 of the Restatement of the Foreign Relations Law of the United States (1965)(hereinafter cited as "Restatement of the Foreign Relations Law") which adopts the protective principle "provided the conduct is generally recognized as a crime under the law of States that have reasonably developed systems". For an elaboration of this view see Riedweg (rapporteur) in I.L.A. Tokyo Conference 368.

13. See Final Report of European Advisory Committee on Tentative Draft No.2, Restatement of the Foreign Relations Law of the U.S. (Jurisdiction) March 3, p.15 et seq. (1961) Extracts from the report can be found in I.L.A. Tokyo Conference, 543.

in the context of antitrust legislation.[14]

B. The Principle of Nationality

6-7. Community case law has not indicated that the Community has based its jurisdiction on the principle of nationality in order to make the competition rules applicable to Community enterprises wherever they operate. It is obvious that the Community extraterritorial jurisdiction in antitrust matters, to the extent that it validly applies to the conduct of non-nationals, is based exclusively on a different principle from the principle of nationality; we, therefore, submit that to the extent that the Community extraterritorial jurisdiction applies to the similar conduct of nationals it has a valid basis on the same principle. If the threat against some vital interests of the Community is to be deterred, whether it comes form nationals or foreigners, nationality is not, logically, an appropriate connecting factor. Moreover, since the principle of nationality has not so far figured largely in the international antitrust cases[15] the Community approach, as described above, seems proper.[16]

C. The Principle of Territoriality

6-8. The application of the principle of territoriality as a basis of jurisdiction for the extraterritorial application of the Community competition rules may come under the scrutiny of international law in

---

14. See explanations to the report of the Committee by Hunter in I.L.A. The Hague Conference 233 (and examples thereof). See also I.L.A. Tokyo Conference 368; eventually a guideline along that line was adopted in the form of Art. 6 of the International Law Association's final resolution (see New York Conference 139).

15. See Mann"The Doctrine of Jurisdiction in International Law" 111 Recueil (1964-I) pp.97-98.

16. According to some views the use of the principle of nationality is essentially applicable to the group of offences which each State considers heinous only when they are committed by nationals, e.g. offences such as treason. See ibid. See also A. Acevedo, A Conflict of Criminal Laws 180, an unpublished Ph.D. thesis, The Senate House, University of London (1973).

two types of cases: (1) where the Community applies an economic unit theory; and (2) where the Community relies on an effects doctrine as a basis for its jurisdiction.

(1) Jurisdiction on the Basis of an Economic Unit Theory Under International Law

6-9. The method by which the behaviour of a subsidiary within the Common Market is attributed to its parent company has often been applied by the Community to assert its jurisdiction over NCES. See discussion in Section 1 of Chapter II. The question at issue here is whether a company incorporated in a foreign country becomes or does not become a "person within the territory", and is therefore within the jurisdiction, simply because it has a subsidiary company incorporated within the territory or has an agent there.

Mann criticizes the reasoning put forward by the Court of Justice in the I.C.I. Case, saying that it falls below the standard that is required to establish an economic unit for jurisdictional purposes.[17] See also 2-24. Allen joins that criticism of the I.C.I. Case over its formula of the economic unit theory while stating that similar faults can be observed in the American Alcoa Case (for details of the Alcoa Case and criticism of the judgment's failure to establish the economic unit theory see 5-42). He then adds:

> It is certainly not necessary to go deeper into the reasoning in the Alcoa Case, but the analogy raises the question of whether the fault of the disparity in applied theories may fall upon not only the courts, but also upon the unclarity or unadaptability of the territorial principles themselves. 18

---

17. Mann, supra note 1, at 48-50.

18. Allen, "The Development of European Community Antitrust Jurisdiction Over Alien Undertakings" 2 Legal Issues of European Integration 60 (1974).

The United Kingdom Government in its Aide Mémoire to the EEC Commission concerning the I.C.I. Case, indicated that the economic unit theory should not reach beyond the situation in which the subsidiary is actually an employee or agent of the parent company.[19]

The European Advisory Committee, under the chairmanship of Lord McNair, adopted the following approach to the question under consideration:

> It is difficult to lay down a rule on this type of case beyond saying that, if a State exercises jurisdiction over a person who, within the contemplation of international law, is not a 'person within the territory', then it violates international law even if, according to its own view, the person concerned is 'found within the jurisdiction'. [20]

Prior to the Barcelona Traction, Light and Power Co. Ltd. Case[21] in 1970, it was generally considered that international law did not have much to say as to when the corporate entity may be disregarded.[22] In the case Spain tried to maintain that Barcelona Traction, a Canadian holding company without an office, business or assets in Spain formed a single business unit with its subsidiaries in Spain and that such an "economic unit" justified the Spanish courts, inter alia, in assuming bankruptcy jurisdiction over the Canadian company. The International Court of Justice considered that lifting the veil for alleged violations of international law against a parent corporation's foreign subsidiary, in order to extend a State's right of diplomatic protection to the national State of the shareholders of the parent corporation, by the State utilizing bankruptcy procedures for purposes

19. See British Practice in International Law (1969) pp.58-59 (E. Lauterpacht ed.).
20. See extracts from the Committee's report in I.L.A., Tokyo Conference 542.
21. I.C.J. Reports (1970) p.1.
22. See Malawer, "International Law, European Community Law and the Rule of Reason" 8 J.W.T.L. 45 (1974).

of nationalization, was not authorized by international law. However, the International Court of Justice considered that lifting the corporate veil theory does have a role to play in international law: ".....the process of lifting the veil, being an exceptional one admitted by municipal law.....is equally admissible to play a role in international law."[23] Beyond holding that the corporate veil could not be lifted to enable the claim to be brought by Belgium on behalf of Belgian shareholders, the Court did not lay down general rules as to the lifting of the corporate veil.

The International Law Association, at the New York Conference in 1972, approved the following guideline concerning the application of the economic unit theory in antitrust cases:

> A State has jurisdiction to prescribe rules governing conduct originating outside its territory if and in so far as such conduct is implemented within its territory by an natural or legal person whose conduct can be attributed to the author of the conduct performed. 24

The question of establishing an economic unit is not concerned with the extraterritorial application of the laws, although that may be the ultimate objective of the attempt to exercise jurisdction. Here there is a dispute concrning not the legal principle but its application to the facts. It would therefore seem right to say that the question of jurisdiction over a foreign parent company through its subsidiary, in antitrust matters, which is based on a general principle of criminal law (Qui facit per alium facit per se), hence depends on proof that the subsidiary was acting on the instruction of the parent

---

23. Barcelona Traction Case, I.C.J. Reports (1970) 1, 40.
24. See I.L.A. New York Conference 139.

company. If sufficient rules for the creation of an economic unit are disregarded there will be an excess of jurisdiction from the point of view of international law, unless, of course, jurisdiction over the parent company can be based on some alternative ground recognized by international law.

(2) Jurisdiction on the Basis of an Effects Doctrine Under International Law

6-10. The Commission has stated on a few occasions that, in view of the limits imposed by international law on the exercise of extra-territorial jurisdiction, the effects within the Common Market of conduct abroad should be qualified. Qualified effects, according to the Commission's approach, are a constituent element of the offence, and are substantial, foreseeable and directly caused by the conduct of the accused. See 2-53 and 2-68 to 2-71. It needs to be stated at the outset of the following attempt to examine whether such a qualified effects doctrine is in line with the principle of territoriality of international law, that there is no unanimity among States on the question of how far a sovereign State may rightfully extend the reach of its penal and quasi-penal laws beyond the national territory on the basis of effects. No clear answers are available and, therefore, the main element to be studied here is controversial. Nevertheless, we shall attempt to identify some guiding principles of international law from a study of the structure of the Western legal order. The latter is based on the co-existence of many States side by side which have an equal right to claim mutual respect for their internal order.

(a) The Controversy Over an Effects Doctrine

6-11. It has already been explained in Chapter I that the problem with an effects doctrine, from the point of view of international law, is whether the extent to which the requirement of a "constituent element of the offence", occurring within the territory, can be applied in a context broader than the traditional one expressed by the objective territorial principle, and, in particular, whether it can be extended to antitrust offences which are indisputable *mala prohibita*. See 1-19. Effects have been mentioned by the Permanent Court of International Justice in the *Lotus Case* in its discussion of the limits of the territorial principle:

> .....it is certain that the courts of many countries, even of countries which have given their criminal legislation a strictly territorial character, interpret criminal law in the sense that offences the authors of which at the moment of commission are in the territory of another State, are nevertheless to be regarded as having been committed in the national territory if one of the constituent elements of the offence, and more especially its effects, have taken place there. 24a

However, the authority of the *Lotus Case* in the present context is limited, since the decision concerned only the prosecution of a common crime committed on the high seas against a national of the prosecuting State and not conduct in a foreign State where that foreign State had primary jurisdiction. All that the decision said beyond that issue of the general limitation of State jurisdiction was in our view *obiter dicta*.

6-12. An objection to the exercise of jurisdiction by the Community on the basis of an effects doctrine was reflected in the *Aide-Mémoire*

24a. The *Lotus Case* P.C.I.J. Ser. A., No.9, p.23 (1927).

which the Government of the United Kingdom submitted to the European Communities in October 1969.[25] A document, attached to the Aide-Mémoire contained a statement of principles according to which, in the view of the United Kingdom Government, jurisdiction may be exercised over foreign corporations in antitrust matters. The statement categorically rejected an effects doctrine as a basis for jurisdiction while emphasizing that the territorial principle justifies proceedings against foreigners and foreign companies only in respect of conduct which consists, wholly or partly, of some activity by them in the territory of the State claiming jurisdiction.

In the U.S. distinguished jurists felt themselves unable to support "an extension of the territorial principle" to an effects doctrine.[26] A number of foreign governments, foreign officials and even foreign courts strongly believed that the extraterritorial application of the U.S. antitrust laws, if based upon effects on U.S. trade, constituted a violation of international law and an infringement of the sovereignty of States, and protested to that effect. See 5-63.

Among the important opinions objecting to the application of an effects doctrine is that of Lord McNair's Committee which concluded that it is a travesty of the use of language to say that the resulting principle of an effects doctrine can still be referred to principles of territorial jurisdiction; such a further refinement and dilution of the territorial principle, the Committee stated, is a *reductio ad absurdum*.[27]

---

25. See *supra* note 19.

26. See for example the opinion expressed by the American Branch Committee of the I.L.A. in the *New York Conference* 112.

27. See Final Report of European Advisory Committee, *supra* note 13, at 35 (see extracts in I.L.A. *Tokyo Conference* 537-543 and *The Hague Confence* 230-238).

6-13. Writers who argue in favour of an effects doctrine as a basis for jurisdiction in antitrust cases stress that neither the traditional territorial principle nor the principles of nationality and protection suffice to cover every instance where the interests of a State are in jeopardy.[28] It has been argued that, because it is often difficult to localize restrictive trade practices for the purpose of the traditional territorial principle, a close analytical scrutiny of the actus reus of modern economic offences has necessitated a refinement of the statement of the territorial principle.[29]

6-14. Since the Commission has adopted a qualified effects doctrine it is necessary to examine that particular approach in view of the definition of the territorial principle in international law.

(b) Guidelines Approved by the International Law Association on the Applicable Principles of International Law in Antitrust Cases

6-15. A Committee of the International Law Association, which examined the extraterritorial application of restrictive trade legislation, including antitrust legislation, with special reference to the countries of the Common Market and the Atlantic Basin, reached agreement on the applicable principles of international law. Because of the importance of the Committee's conclusions for the assessment of a qualified effects doctrine under international law we propose to

---

28. For a general commentary on objections of strict territoriality see Miller "Extraterritorial Effects of Trade Regulation" 111 U.Pa.L.Rev. 1111 (1963); Brewster "Extraterritorial Effects of the U.S. Antitrust Laws; An Appraisal" 11 A.B.A., Antitrust Section Report 69 (1957); Jessup Transnational Law, ch. 2, (1956); Katzenbach "Conflicts on an Unruly Horse: Reciprocal Claims and Tolerance in Interstate and International Law" 65 Yale L.J. 1087 (1956).

29. See Hunter in I.L.A., The Hague Conference 227.

examine those conclusions in detail in the following paragraphs.

The Fifty-Sixth Conference of the International Law Association, held at New York in August 1972, received a report from the Committee on the principles of international law to be used as guidelines in the resolution of problems concerning the assessment and exercise of jurisdiction by States in connection with restrictive trade practices. After modifications the Conference approved the following guidelines:

Article 1.

The Rules which follow are concerned solely with the right of a State to prescribe and secure compliance with rules of law regulating conduct which has had or may have an anti-competitive effect within its territory if and to the extent that such rules are enforceable by penal, quasi-penal or administrative sanctions.

Article 2.

A State has jurisdiction to prescribe rules governing an act or acts occurring within its territory.

Article 3.

(1) A State has jurisdiction to prescribe rules governing the conduct of an alien outside its territory provided -
- (a) part of the conduct being a constituent element of the offence occurs within the territory and
- (b) acts or omissions occurring outside the territory are constituent elements of the same offence.

(2) Whereas municipal law is the sole authority for the purpose of ascertaining the constituent elements of a particular offence, international law retains a residual but overriding authority to specify what is or is not capable of being a constituent element for the purpose of determining jurisdictional competence.

(Article 4 concerns the economic unit theory and is cited in 6-9)

Article 5.

A State has jurisdiction to prescribe rules of law governing conduct that occurs outside its territory and causes an effect within its territory if:
- (a) the conduct and its effect are constituent elements of activity to which the rule applies,
- (b) the effect within the territory is substantial and
- (c) it occurs as a direct and primarily intended result of the conduct outside the territory.

(Article 6 concerns the protective principle and is summarized in 6-6; Article 7 concerns guidelines for the solution of conflicts with foreign law or jurisdiction and is cited in 6-34). 30

6-16. The guidelines above indicate that a State may punish conduct which commences within its territory and is consummated abroad, or which commences abroad and is consummated at home provided only that the conduct which occurs within its own territory is a constituent element of the offence.

Art. 3 extends the rule to cover omissions located abroad (e.g. boycotts and refusals to deal) so that the locus of an omission is the place where the act ought to have taken place. The article states in para. (2) that, although it is for the municipal law to specify the precise ingredients of the antitrust offence, including whether an alien is liable to punishment for his failure to act in a particular way, it cannot be exclusively for the municipal law to determine what acts ought to have taken place in its territory so as to confer jurisdiction upon its own courts according to international law. It must, as stated in para. (2) of Art. 3, in the final analysis be for international law to determine whether what has occurred within the territory is sufficient to justify the assumption of jurisdiction by the State. Art. 3, however, makes no reference to the distinction between an act occurring within a State's territory which would justify the assumption of prescriptive jurisdiction and mere economic effects and repercussions of acts occurring entirely abroad, even if they are stated in the municipal prescription to be constituent elements of the offence, which may or may not afford jurisdiction. This issue is reserved for Art. 5.

---

30. I.L.A. New York Conference 138-139.

Art. 5 is a definition of a qualified effects doctrine on the lines favoured by the EEC Commission and which is reflected also in Sec. 18(b) of the Restatement of the Foreign Relations Law of the United States (1965). The effects are qualified first in that their occurrence must be an integral part of the *actus reus* (a constituent element of the offence). The rule then attempts to introduce a more positive *nexus* between cause and effect by requiring that the effects be substantial, direct and an intended result of the conduct.

(c) The Meaning of the Qualifying Conditions of the Effects

Before considering whether a qualified effects doctrine is an extension of the principle of territoriality it is essential to elaborate more fully the meaning of the qualifying conditions and the probable circumstances for an actual application of a qualified effects doctrine.

(i) Effects as a Constituent Element of the Offence

6-17. The general meaning of the term "constituent element of the offence" in the context of the principles of jurisdiction of international law has already been explained in 1-19. This requirement, having a known legal meaning, implies, in the context of the qualified effects doctrine, that the effects of the form of conduct have been taken into account in law as such an element. The effects of antitrust offences are therefore legally significant consequences of the act; the law determines what the constituent elements of the offence are and the law may well establish that the economic effects of certain acts, even if the act took place abroad, are an essential element of the offence.

(ii) A Requirement for Substantial Effects

6-18. It is not clear from the report of the International Law Association what is the exact meaning of the requirement for "substantial effects". Some indications may be gained if one looks at the U.S. foreign commerce cases when the word "substantial" is used. This word did not then mean that an evaluation of the economic or business importance of the restraint's impact is required, but merely that the effects of the restraint must not be too slight or de minimis; the U.S. courts did not really try to measure the volume of effects.[31] Cf. 5-38. There is not as yet enough evidence in Community law to indicate whether the Community would follow the de minimis rule, which it has developed in domestic situations (see 3-6 and 3-17 to 3-19), when it intends to exercise jurisdiction on the basis of the qualified effects doctrine.

(iii) The Effects Must be Direct

6-19. "Directness" as a recognized legal term seems to have both the flexibility and the ambiguity of the "proximate cause" formula of tort law, which it closely resembles. The meaning of this term in the U.S., according to Rahl, is that this requirement is more a delegation of discretion to the judge than it is a self-contained test or measure - " a tool with which the court can catch cases obviously falling within the ambit of the law's policy while throwing out those which seem too far afield".[32] Community law in domestic situations is

31. See J. Rahl, Common Market and American Antitrust; Overlap and Conflict 62 (1970).

32. Rahl, ibid.

applicable either on the basis of direct or indirect effects (see 3-8). The nature of the effects is determined by generally accepted causation doctrines which have been developed in Community law (see 3-7 and 3-16). However, it may reasonably be expected, as in the American practice, that drawing the line between "direct" and "indirect" effects may not be easy.

(iv) The Effects Must be Intended

6-20. The requirement in the guidelines of the International Law Association that the effects be intended corresponds to Judge Hand's judgment in the Alcoa Case (see 5-43), but in the Restatement (Second) of the Foreign Relations Law of the United States (1965) it has been changed from mens rea to "direct and foreseeable result" (see 5-47). The American Bar Association, in the Supplement to the Attorney General's National Committee Report, concludes that the "intent" requirement of Alcoa and the "direct and foreseeable" test of the Restatement are "essentially identical, because of the customary antitrust doctrine that a general intent (as distinguished from specific intent) requirement is satisfied if the defendant engages in deliberate conduct which he 'should have known' would have forbidden effects".[33] See also 5-44. Community law does not require specific intent in antitrust cases but has developed tests in domestic situations to determine the actual degree of probability of the effects which are similar to the tests in the Restatement. See 3-7 and 3-16. Since those tests are fairly generally accepted it is expected that the Community will

33. ABA, Antitrust Section, Antitrust Developments in 1955-1968. Supp. to Atty. Gen. Nat. Comm. Antitrust Rep.; ch. II, 49 (1968) (hereinafter cited as "Supp. to Atty.Gen. Nat. Comm. Antitrust. Rep.")

follow the same tests of "foreseeability" which it uses in domestic situations when it applies the qualified effects doctrine.

In stressing the test of "foreseeability" both the U.S. and the Community avoid the difficult, if not untenable, position of basing jurisdiction on alien's state of mind. On the basis of the latter point objections were voiced in the International Law Association against an adoption of an "intent" requirement in the guidelines.[34]

(d) Conclusions on the Definition of a Qualified Effects Doctrine as an Extension of the Territorial Principle

6-21. Given the nature of the qualifying conditions of effects we may state that there are greater differences between the initiatory and terminatory forms of the territorial principle (see 1-18) than between the terminatory form and the qualified doctrine of effects. Moreover, what is characterized as "effect" may at the same time take the form of conduct while what may be termed "conduct" may turn out to be an effect. Therefore, it has often been stated by writers that if the anticompetitive effects of the form of conduct have been taken into account in law as a constituent element of the offence the objective territorial principle can be applied. For example, Fugate interprets Sec. 18(b) of the Restatement as a general statement of the objective territorial principle "although it may be noted that it has been criticized as being too vague and also as not sufficiently following the case law."[35]

---

34. See Jennings in I.L.A., Helsinki Conference 210.

35. W. Fugate, Foreign Commerce and Antitrust Laws 38 (2nd ed. 1973). See also K. Brewster, Antitrust and American Business Abroad 300 (1958).

6-22. A large part of the confusion in a search for a familiar jurisdictional solution for antitrust cases lies in the fact that those cases are in a way unique. The old analogies with traditional jurisdictional principles pertaining to strictly criminal behaviour often break down, but the failure may rest, in our view, in the analogies rather than in the principles. We submit that it may be correct tó say that the objective territorial principle will largely lead to the same result as of a qualified effects doctrine and that, therefore, the latter doctrine can be regarded as an extension of the territorial principle. However, we also propose that any labelling of this doctrine which resembles the traditional principles of jurisdiction should be avoided. What is required here is a generally acceptable criterion that could apply not only to criminal but equally to regulatory (and possibly civil) jurisdiction in antitrust cases. It is important to restate here that we are not so much seeking a classification of principles to be applied to jurisdictional problems as we are interested in guidelines which would be fair and just to both actor and injured. Moreover, we have to reckon with the possibility that suggestions of adopting a well-known principle that has a known connotation (even if modified) run the risk of being lost in a welter of arguments over competing principles.

6-23. We are still far from the day when the guidelines of the International Law Association, compiled at the expense of arduous work, will, in so far as they support a qualified effects doctrine, become the generally accepted body of rules of international law. However, what the guidelines have already achieved is that in the given field the uniform, or at least harmonized model of thinking of the jurisprudence of the Western world, extrapolated from legal practice and considerations of economic policy, has become more complete than before. Those guidelines are the legal archetype for what may be expected in municipal and international legislation, and of what to some extent is already being applied in practice with many variations of detail, through the application of municipal antitrust provisions to international business practices.

The policy of the Community authorities in applying the Community rules of competition in accordance with such principles add significant strength to the international movement towards a qualified effects doctrine. It may be said that an international custom is evolving subjecting international restrictive business practices to the domestic antitrust law where their effects take place, on the basis of such a doctrine.[36]

---

36. Cf. Kruithof "The Application of the Common Market Antitrust Provisions to International Restraints of Tradé" 2 C.M.L.Rev. 81 (1964).

3. JURISDICTIONAL LIMITATIONS UNDER INTERNATIONAL LAW AND COMMUNITY ANTITRUST LAW ENFORCEMENT JURISDICTION

6-24. Regarding the limits of State jurisdiction under international law, there is no essential distinction between the legal basis of legislative jurisdiction and of enforcement jurisdiction, because the one is a function of the other. If legislative jurisdiction is beyond lawful limits the consequent enforcement jurisdiction is unlawful.[37] Nevertheless, some writers have argued that the mere existence of legislative jurisdiction, without any attempt at enforcement, will not normally have to pass the test of international law.[38] In support of the latter opinion it is important to note that the bulk of antitrust regulation is in statutory form, and the enactment itself will generally contain no territorial limitation. On the basis of that approach, "judicial jurisdiction" (see definition of this term in 1-16) may be either "legislative" or "enforcement", depending on its function. The situation is, however, different where legislative jurisdiction so plainly implies the likelihood of enforcement that foreign States are entitled to challenge its presence on the statute book.[39]

A. Personal Jurisdiction and the Service of Process

6-25. The personal jurisdiction of courts and authorities depends upon their domestic law; in other words, it is regulated by municipal law and not by international law.[40] International law, however, places

---

37. Compare Restatement of the Foreign Relations Law, sec. 7(2). See also Brownlie, Principles of Public International Law 305 (2nd Ed. 1973); Huntter in I.L.A. The Hague Conference 222.
38. See Mann, supra note 15 at 14. Mann, nevertheless, states that this approach depends on the specific facts. See also De Arechanga, "International Law in the Past Third of a Century" 159 Recueil (1978-I) pp.276-277.
39. Cf. Mann, supra note 15, at 14.
40. See Schwartz "Applicability of National Law on Restraints of Competition to International Restraints of Competition" in Cartel and Monopoly in Modern Law, Vol. 2, pp.706 (1961).

limits upon the service of process abroad and requires standards of justice in the exercise of personal jurisdiction. Acts by courts or authorities which exceed those limits or standards will be in conflict with international law.[41]

6-26. As to the service of process abroad, there is a widespread practice of regulating by treaties (through consular officers or through the instrumentalities of the receiving State itself) performance of such official acts in the territory of another State. However, in the absence of foreign machinery or any rules in connection with the service of antitrust process, the service must be in accordance with customary international law. It would therefore seem that no State has any right at all to employ its own officials or other agents to effect on its behalf service of process or of other documents in another State.[42] What would then be the rule about service of process abroad by despatch through the post?

The practice with regard to the service of both the Commission decisions to commence proceedings and the Notices of Objections has been to send registered letters to the NCE abroad, and in case it was acting through a subsidiary within the Common Market to notify the subsidiary as well. (See 4-5 to 4-10). Applicants have raised the argument before the Court that such practice of despatch through the post is illegal. But the Court stated that if a despatch through the post is made with the ultimate aim that the defendant must be notified about the proceedings and be given a chance to be heard, there is nothing illegal in that practice. See 4-7. Mann points out that there

41. See ibid.

42. See Mann, supra note 15, at 132.

is only one qualification to that practice which requires that documents to be served by despatch have to contain merely a notification, as opposed to a command, and should not include a threat of penalties in the event of non-compliance.[43]

The service of process to the parent company through a subsidiary within the territory is a procedural method based on the principle of the economic unit theory which is equally valid for the application of substantive jurisdiction over foreign enterprises. See 6-9. Akehurst states that this method of service of process cannot, in any event, create a breach of international law, because there is no rule of international law subordinating the exercise of jurisidction to a requirement that the parent company itself carries on business in the State concerned.[44]

6-27. International law requires that for jurisdiction to be properly exercised the accused must be given an opportunity to be heard,[45] and

---

43. Ibid. Objections to service of process abroad by despatch through the post may, however, be found in the Hague Convention on the Law of Civil Procedure of 1954, which allows service through the post only where treaties so provide or where the receiving State raises no objection, and in Art. 6 of the Harvard Research in Judicial Assistance 33 Am.J.Int.L.Supp. 65 (1939). It is difficult, in our view, to find any conclusive guidance on that point in international law, apart from pointing out that there are examples of service of process abroad through the post in State practice, e.g. Germany (see 5-9). Guarding the standards of justice in these matters, as stated by the Court of Justice, is an indispensible requirement to that practice.

    It is important to point out here that where the service of the Commission's final decisions is concerned the Commission has also adopted the practice of despatch through the post (see 4-14 to 4-15) after first attempting service on parent companies through their subsidiaries within the Common Market (see 4-11 to 4-13).

44. The U.K. Government thinks otherwise (see Aide Mémoire to the EEC Commission, cited in British Practice in International Law, supra note 19), but Akehurst states that this is surely wrong (see "Jurisdiction in International Law" 46 Brit.Y.B.Int.L. (1975) p.209 in n.3).

45. See Brierly, The Law of Nations 278-281 (6th ed. 1963); Harvard Draft Convention on Jurisdiction with Respect to Crime 29 Am.J. Int.L.Supp. Art. 12 (pp.601-602)(1935).

that the judgment of the court should conform procedurally and substantively to minimum standards of justice.[46] The basis of service of process in all legal systems is, therefore, to make the defendant cognizant of the plaintiff's claim and that it may be an injustice to the defendant if the administrative authority or the court go into its merits without having taken the proper steps to acquaint him with the proceedings.[47] In the case of failure on the part of the organs charged with administering justice to aliens to conform to their international duties a State may be responsible for a denial of justice.[48] The Community's notions of justice concerning the service of process and the assumption of personal jurisdiction, as elaborated in 4-16 to 4-19, are therefore in accordance with the pertinent standards required by international law.

It is important to add here that as a matter of international law, provided that jurisdiction can be based on some valid ground, it cannot be defeated by the absence from the State of the defendant, individual or company, at the time when the proceedings are instituted, because, provided that the accused somehow receives notice of charge, there is no rule of international law against trials in absentia.[49]

B. The Reach of Discovery Orders of Foreign Located Documents

6-28. It is indisputable that the Community cannot make a discovery

---

46. Brierly, ibid.
47. See I. Baxter, Essays on Private Law: Foreign Law and Foreign Judgments 13 (1966).
48. See Jessup, Modern Law of Nations 104-105 (1950); Lissitzyn "The Meaning of the Term Denial of Justice in International Law" 30 Am.J.Int.L. 645-646 (1936).
49. See, for example, Council of Europe, Explanatory Report on the European Convention on the International Validity of Criminal Judgments (1970) pp.49 et seq. (to be found in I.L.R., vol. 38, p.133).

order and have it executed abroad; this would involve the exercise of police power in the territory of another State.[50] The Community, therefore, requires NCES under threat of penalties to provide it with documents necessary for its investigations even if the documents are located abroad. See 4-34 to 4-42. Although the existence of legal provisions in other countries may be an obstacle to the investigation or prosecution of restrictive business practices, the Community authorities are not powerless in all such cases to obtain documents located abroad. The way to accomplish this purpose, in spite of the conflicting foreign law, is still to issue such an order and oblige an enterprise before the Commission, or the Court, to go abroad and produce documents located there. See 4-52 to 4-53. The same practice is exercised by the American courts. See 5-57 to 5-60.

The difference in ordering the production of documents from abroad from ordering foreign enterprises to carry out other orders abroad, is that the first type of order which comes at the beginning of the trial is part of the jurisdiction to try the case; otherwise the judge would be unable to try the case properly.[51] Although this argument for the justification of the production of documents from abroad is generally correct, it should be noted that the objection in antitrust cases may be "that the documents are required for a preliminary investigation which ranges outside the permissible limits of extraterritorial jurisdiction, and attempts to subject aliens in respect of their doings even in their own countries....."[52]. Some

---

50. Cf. Riedweg (rapporteur) in I.L.A., Tokyo Conference 403.

51. See Akehurst, supra note 44, at 211 in n.2.

52. Jennings "Extraterritorial Jurisdiction and the United States Antitrust Laws" 33 Brit.Y.B.Int.L. (1957) p.171. See also Riedweg, supra note 50, at 409.

of the protests against the U.S. practice in matters of foreign discovery orders argue that international law forbids the U.S. to order foreigners to produce documents situated abroad; others maintain that the order for discovery is contrary to international law because the U.S. had no right to initiate the proceedings in the first place. Other protests rely on both of these arguments or alternate between them.

6-29. Mann, who considers that the American practice in ordering the production of documents from abroad goes much too far in some cases, submits that the true legal position as to the production of documents from abroad is as follows:

> Firstly, where the enforcing State proceeds against the local branch with a view to the production of documents relating to the affairs of the branch itself, the demand cannot be resisted merely on the ground that the documents are abroad or belong to a non-resident alien.....
>
> Secondly, if a non-resident alien appears as a claimant in the courts of the enforcing State, he must submit to the procedure of the courts to which he applies. An order for discovery which has properly been made and is not oppressive, cannot be resisted on the ground of the documents being abroad.
>
> Thirdly, in either of the above cases international law does not justify the refusal of discovery on the ground that according to the lex situs discovery is illegal.
>
> Fourthly, if discovery has been properly ordered but is not given by the non-resident alien, international law does not preclude the court from drawing appropriate inferences against him in accordance with the law of evidence or from making an order dismissing the claim or striking out the defence.
>
> Fifthly, where the enforcing State proceeds against the local branch with a view to the production of documents situate abroad and relating to the affairs or activities abroad of the head office of the non-resident alien, the demand would be lawful only if the enforcing State had legislative jurisdiction to regulate and, therefore, to enquire into those affairs and activities.....To the extent of such illegality the demand for discovery would be equally unlawful.
>
> Sixthly, it is a much more doubtful question what the law should be where the demand is made against the foreign branch

of a citizen resident in the enforcing State. Probably the branch should be treated as sufficiently independent to make the principles stated in the preceding paragraph applicable. 53

C. Orders Compelling Conduct by Aliens Abroad

6-30. An international custom allowing issuance of orders compelling conduct by aliens abroad does not appear to exist. On the contrary, such orders by the U.S. courts have produced numerous protests from other States. Cf. 5-63. The occurrence of diplomatic protests, and the fact that they have not been filed in all cases, might rather be due to the fact that the protesting States were not so much concerned about the assumption of jurisdiction as its exercise.[54]

Logically it seems that a State is precluded, a fortiori, from achieving its ends indirectly by having orders made in its own territory which are to take effect abroad and which thus assume a power equal to that of an order which the foreign country could, but refuses, to make.[55] However, the practice of the Community and the U.S. in response to that difficulty is that in many cases a prescription of a certain kind, which involves at least a modicum of action in foreign countries, can be completely effective without venturing outside the State's territorial boundaries for its enforcement.

6-31. The EEC Commission, while referring to a criminal sanction in the Dyestuffs Cases, i.e. fines, declared that they should not be confused with the stage of effective coercion; "that is to say, with

53. Mann, supra note 15, at 156-157.

54. Cf. Messen in I.L.A., New York Conference 122.

55. See Verzijl "The Controversy Regarding the So-Called Extraterritorial Effect of the American Antitrust Laws" 8 Nederlands Tijdschrift voor International Recht 12 (1961).

putting that declaration into effect and enforcing those fines by issuing injunctions or effecting confiscation" (see the full argument as set out in 4-59).

Verzijl suggests that there would seem to be no liability in international law for simple threats or attempts by courts to enforce abroad the internal legislation against restrictive practices. In order not to create an international responsibility for a State it is necessary that its judgments, which are intended to have extraterritorial effect, are in fact not carried out in any way which is contrary to the principles of international law governing the distribution and limitation of jurisdiction between States. So long as they remain on paper and are not followed by an actual assault on aliens beyond the limits permitted by international law, they remain under the doctrine of international nullities.[56]

The approach which distinguishes between "legislative jurisdiction" on the one hand, and "coercive jurisdiction" on the other hand, has often been stated in legal literature,[57] e.g. a preliminary report by the Legal Committee of the Council of Europe's Consultative Assembly.[58] This distinction carries the borderline of prohibited enforcement jurisdiction to the point where an action against aliens is actually taken.

---

56. Ibid. at 16. The doctrine of "international nullities" is explained in p.13.

57. See, for example, Lawrence "American Conception of Jurisdiction With Respect to Conflicts of Laws on Crime" 30 Transactions of the Grotius Society 184 (1944).

58. Report to the Consultative Assembly of the Council of Europe by the Legal Committee (de Grailly, rapporteur), The Extraterritorial Application of Antitrust Legislation, Doc.2123 at 8, 11-12, 14 (Jan. 25, 1966).

6-32. In the decisions given after the Dyestuffs Cases the Commission required NCES, under threat of sanctions, to do acts within the Common Market, although the enterprises to comply therewith had to take affirmative acts outside the Common Market (see for example 4-61). As to similar American practice see 5-52.

The question concerning the legality of such an order requiring the performance of acts abroad came under the consideration of the International Law Association's Committee on the extraterritorial application of restrictive trade legislation. The conclusions reached by the Committee on this point, as have been explained by Hunter, correspond to the very complex nature of the typical antitrust offences with the welter of remedies which may be available to the State to ensure compliance with its substantive rules or to reinstate the status quo ante. Hunter states that it is necessary first to characterize the pertinent prescription with a view to determining whether it is of a penal or quasi-penal nature; if they are, the State is prohibited from enforcing them.[59] The assertion that the State can be held liable for the commission of international delinquency against foreign States by unlawfully assailing their nationals depends, therefore, in the last resort, on the nature of the measures ordered by its authorities.[60] This view is further explained in the following paragraphs.

Where the sanctions which are to be invoked or applied are of the type traditionally employed by the criminal courts by way of

59. See I.L.A., The Hague Conference, 223.

60. See similar view by Verzijl, supra note 55, at 14; Metzger "The Restatement of the Foreign Relations Law of the United States; Bases and Conflicts of Jurisdiction" 41 N.Y.Un.L.Rev. 15 (1960).

enforcement (e.g. imprisonment, fines etc.) there is no difficulty in concluding that those enforcement measures would undoubtedly constitute an international delict, consisting in an inadmissible extension of criminal jurisdiction against foreign nationals. However, if the conduct required from the foreign enterprise is within a State's territory it is clear that in most cases prescriptions against the enterprise can be enforced within the territory. Such measures of enforcement could be, for example, the seizure of the assets of the enterprise which are within the territory of the State or the application of punitive measures through a subsidiary of the foreign enterprise or other interests doing business within the territory.

Where the sanctions are of a different nature, for example, denial of a licence or refusal to admit goods into the State, classifying such relief measures as administrative (and not as penal or quasi-penal) raises problems to which only tentative solutions can be advanced. The variants are so numerous and so diverse that it is not feasible to review them all. Nevertheless, the above-mentioned International Law Association Committee attempted to formulate a test regarding such administrative sanctions. If the use of an administrative sanction is essentially remedial and confined to acts committed within the jurisdiction (as determined by international law) there is no infringement of international law, but administrative measures which in effect seek to regulate economic activity within a foreign market are not justifiable.[61] This test involves the analysis of the administrative sanction as applied in each particular case with a view to determining the purpose underlying its use.

---

61. See Hunter, *supra* note 59, at 224.

These rules which define the limits of orders concerning conduct abroad have no direct application to such civil remedies as may be available to a plaintiff who alleges that he has suffered loss as the result of an antitrust offence. The rules of international law which come into play in this situation are entirely different from those operating in the context of criminal law. Attempts to formulate principles of international jurisdiction governing proper civil remedies would involve codification of the principles of private international law with particular reference to contract, tort and property rights.[62]

D. Foreign Law Barriers to the Reach of Extraterritorial Enforcement Orders

6-33. It has been observed above that certain orders of the Community may demand some activity to be carried out abroad. The problem of conflict with contradictory foreign laws relates most frequently to orders to produce or to disclose the contents of documents or other evidence located abroad at the investigation stage, but it may also be present with regard to final decisions and judgments. The pertinent rules of international law as to the production of documents were discussed in 6-28 and 6-29.

The practice of the Community in the incidents of conflict with foreign laws with regard to matters of substance (e.g. market behaviour), as distinguished from matters of procedure (e.g. provision of documents) has been explained in 4-78 to 4-80. The Commission is so far following the American approach and claiming powers over foreign

62. The necessity for a conflict of law approach to certain aspects of antitrust laws was recognised by the I.L.A. in the Buenos Aires Conference 402-403. It is very likely that such an approach will concentrate upon three issues: points of contact, applicable law and public policy, and endeavour finally to establish uniform rules on a regional basis.

enterprises right up to the point where the enterprise undergoes a conflict of obedience, and where the foreign law is permissive, the foreign enterprise must so use its own powers of choice to comply with the orders. For description of the American practice see 5-54 to 5-56.

6-34. Conflict with foreign laws may occur not only when a State requires conduct within the territory of another State which is manifestly unlawful under the law of the latter but also in the case of concurrent jurisdiction. Concurrent jurisdiction follows where there may be more than one State sufficiently interested in the conduct in question to regulate it and duly qualified under international law to make out at least a prima facie case for doing so. Concurrent jurisdiction does not, however, imply in every case that a conflict will necessarily exist between the various competing laws, although there may be a conflict on a certain particular issue either of law or policy between the two prescribing States.

Art. 14 of the Harvard Draft Convention proposes the following solution in respect of conflicts with foreign laws:

> In exercising jurisdiction under this Convention, no State shall prosecute or punish an alien for an act or omission which was required of that alien by the law of the place where the alien was at the time of the act or omission. [63]

The commentary to this article states that there are few precedents for it, either in national legislation, or in treaties, or in the resolutions of international bodies.[64]

The International Law Association has approved the following principles as guidelines for the solution of conflicts with foreign

---

63. Harvard Draft Convention, supra note 45 at 616.

64. Ibid.

laws or jurisdiction:

> In the event of there being a concurrent jurisdiction of two or more States so as to create a conflict with respect to the conduct of any person
> (a) no State shall require conduct within the territory of another State which is contrary to the law of the latter and
> (b) each State shall, in applying its own law to conduct in another State, pay due respect to the major interests and economic policies of such other State. 65

The Restatement of Conflict of Laws of the U.S. formerly stated the rule in that connection to be that a court may order any act to be carried out outside its territory provided the act is not contrary to the laws of the country in which it is to be performed. The present Restatement (Second) of Conflict of Laws omits this provision.[66] However, it adds a comment that "only in the most extreme situation will a person be ordered to do an act in a state which is contrary to that state's criminal law".

Some writers support the idea that it is contrary to international law to forbid an individual to behave in a way which is required by the law of the place where the act is performed;[67] a few writers extend this principle to acts which are merely permitted by the by the lex loci.[68] But, as Jennings indicates, a distinction between what a foreign law requires and what it permits is in many contexts a formal distinction; it is not sufficient that a local court should stop merely at the point where there is an actual collision with a court, or the legislation of the other country, for this is to put a liberal economic regime at a disadvantage and to put a premium upon

---

65. I.L.A., New York Conference 139-140.
66. Compare Restatement of Conflict of Laws s.94 (1934) with Restatement (Second) of Conflict of Laws s.53 (1971).
67. See, for example, Oppenheim International Law, vol. 1, pp.295-296 (8th ed., Lautherpacht, 1955).
68. For example see Manual of Public International Law 359-360 (Sørensen ed. 1968).

regimentation.[69] It is important to remember that extraterritorial jurisdiction, whether legislative or enforcement, must, in any event, stop short of interference by one State in the domestic affairs of another.[70] Exercising jurisdiction that would obstruct the economic policy of a foreign State would constitute an illegal abuse of rights if the State claiming jurisdiction has no legitimate interest in enforcing its own law and if the enforcement of its law would cause serious mischief in another State.[71]

The latter observation which refers to the "interest" of the State claiming jurisdiction, is in line with our proposal for the avoidance and the resolution of international conflicts in antitrust cases at the end of this chapter. See 6-48 to 6-51. Our proposal has to be seen in the light of the fact that international law has not evolved definite rules for priorities in concurrent jurisdiction,[72] and that the methods for resolving conflicts with foreign laws, as described above, are inadequate and are subject of dispute. Thus, for example, the guideline proposed by the International Law Association for the settlement of conflicts with foreign laws (see rule (a) above) would seem too rigid. This guideline could easily be abused by foreign States which enact general measures to counter legislation without protecting any legitimate interest. Indeed, the International Law Association has also proposed that courts will embark on a consideration of interests (see rule (b) above), but this proposal comes only second in priority. A similar suggestion for balancing interests has been made by the American Law Institute in item 2(b) of Sec. 40 of the

69. Jennings "General Course on the Principles of International Law" 121 Recueil (1967-II) pp.522-528.

70. Ibid. at 525; Brownlie, supra note 37 at 302.

71. See Jennings, supra note 52 at 151; Mann supra note 15 at 46.

72. Cf. Hunter in I.L.A., The Hague Conference 241.

Restatement of the Foreign Relations Law. However, in the U.S. the balancing of interests seems to be the first general principle involved, while the fact of conflict with foreign law is taken to mean that foreign legislation, penalizing compliance with the extraterritorial demands of other States, should be recognized only when its object is to protect fundamental principles of the national legal order. See application of that doctrine in the U.S. case law in 6-50.

E. The Defences of "Sovereign Immunity" and an "Act of State"

6-35. So long as the restrictive business practices take the form of direct foreign government action, those practices will not be touched by Community antitrust law. See 4-80. The defence of sovereign immunity and the principles governing the interpretation of governmental acts are well established in international law.[73] If, however, the government through legislative, administrative, or judicial action compels a private enterprise to participate in what amounts to a restraint of competition, international law does not seem to require recognition of such an "act of State" defence.[74] However, the Commission (and also the U.S. Department of Justice) generally recognize the defence of foreign government compulsion and they may consider it relevant in relation to activities in foreign markets. On the Commission's practice see 4-80.

---

73. General material on the defence of "sovereign immunity" can be found in Fawcett, "Trade and Finance in International Law" 123 Recueil (1968-I) 224-230; Kincaid, "Sovereign Immunity of Foreign State-Owned Corporation" 10 J.W.T.L. 110-128 (1976).

74. For example see § 39(1) of the Restatement (Second of the Foreign Relations Law of the United States (1965).

F. The Problem of Double Sanctions

6-36. One difficulty caused by orders conflicting with foreign laws, as well as by concurrent jurisdiction, is the hardship imposed on an enterprise that finds itself subject to contradictory rules of conduct. The practice of the Community with regard to offences which are also punished by antitrust laws of non-Member States runs counter to the principle non bis in idem. But there is no principle of international law equivalent to the latter municipal rule.[75] In accordance with tests similar to the one taken from domestic law the question as to which State shall punish can be dealt with by the forum State as a practical matter by application of the simple rules of fair play, incorporated in most legal systems.[76] However, we consider that it would now be desirable to incorporate the principle into an international convention.

---

75. It has, however, been argued by Seidl-Hohenveldern that the principle non bis in idem is also valid in international law and therefore he criticises the approach of the Court of Justice (see in the article: "Limits Imposed by International Law on the Application of Cartel Law" 5 The Int. Lawyer 289 (1971).

76. See Art. 13 of the Harvard Draft Convention, supra note 45; such a principle is incorporated upon an underlying concept of fairness and justice.

4. THE INTERNATIONAL APPROACH TO ANTITRUST MATTERS; PROBLEMS OF AN INTERNATIONAL CHARACTER AND PROPOSALS FOR THE AVOIDANCE AND THE RESOLUTION OF INTERNATIONAL CONFLICTS

> No time should be lost; the only way is to proceed into a new understanding of legal rules and legal sociology in the real sense of the word. Only after we agree on what is actually the present economic structure can we hope for economic control that will limit the public and private power in our economy. 77

A. The International Antitrust Problem

6-37. International law discussions which essentially concentrate critically on problems of the extraterritorial application of antitrust rules do not necessarily imply a negative judgment on the importance of the extraterritorial reach of the rules as a means of solving the disturbances caused by international restrictive business practices. It is rather the limited effectiveness of antitrust legislation in properly regulating restrictive business practices of international ramifications which is often a cause of concern to the international Community of States. The legal conflicts which are likely to occur, following the extraterritorial application of antitrust laws, have been considered above. The economic conflicts, which are often named the "international antitrust problem",[78] referred to in the introduction to this study (see 1-3 to 1-5), must now be considered more fully. Both the legal and economic conflicts illustrate the urgent need for an international approach to these issues.

---

77. H. Kronstein, The Law of International Cartels 482 (1973)

78. Cf. D. Swann, Competition and Consumer Protection 233 (1979).

(1) Exemptions for Restrictions in Foreign Trade

6-38. At the root of these problems is what could well be described as "the parochial character of restrictive trade legislation".[79] The point here is that, national laws, even to the extent that they address themselves to the matter of national export cartels, usually exempt them in some degree from the legal strictures which apply to restrictions affecting the domestic market.[80] This character of the legislation stems from the fact that despite the increasing economic interdependence of Western States, a State's economic well-being is still measured to a considerable extent by the relationship of its exports to its imports; "activities designed to increase one State's export at the expense of another State constitute beneficial conduct in the former State and a threat to the economic well-being of the latter State."[81]

There is an important gap in the Community's contribution in curbing international restrictive practices. Community law, as a general principle, does not attempt to prevent restrictions on export from the Community or restrictions applied by Community firms in non-Member States. The possibility remains open that firms may restrict their foreign trade provided they are careful to deprive their practices of restrictive impacts within the Common Market. Cf. 2-87. Following that approach the damage that business in the Common Market

79. See Riedweg (rapporteur) in I.L.A., Tokyo Conference 385.

80. For a general review of the legal position of national export cartels in the Member Countries of the OECD, see OECD, Report of the Committee of Experts on Restrictive Business Practices, Export Cartels (1974).

81. See Riedweg, supra note 79, at 386.

could thereby inflict upon other countries is greater than before the Common Market was established, because tendencies towards industrial concentration have developed within the Common Market and thus Community enterprises can maintain a common front in their exports to non-Member States more easily than before.

The Webb-Pomerence Act of the U.S. also provides a good example of an exemption for exports from the regime laid down under certain legislation, i.e. the Sherman Act.[82] See 5-30. As to the law in the U.K. see 5-13; German law is described in 5-4.

On the international arena mergers may also give rise to problems.[83] Vertical mergers in particular may have the effect of excluding the exports of developing countries. This problem has been studied by UNCTAD; for example, the would-be exporters to industrial countries among the less-developed countries are likely to need an affiliation with major international enterprises.[84] See also below in 6-39.

(2) The Case of the Developing Countries

6-39. A number of studies carried out by UNCTAD Secretariat in recent years and of the UNCTAD Export Group on Restrictive Business

---

82. There have been a number of reports and studies which have analyzed the nature and effects of these export associations and have considered the pros and cons of allowing them to exist. For example see Weiner and Parzych, "The Webb-Pomerence Export Trade Act; A United States Antitrust Exemption" 6 J.W.T.L. 119-127 (1972).
83. See Wertheimer "The International Firm and International Aspects of Policies in Mergers" in Monopolies, Mergers and Restrictive Practices (J. Heath ed., 1974); Kintor and Joelson, An International Antitrust Primer, ch.8 (1974).
84. UNCTAD, Restrictive Business Practices; Studies on the United Kingdom of GreatBritain and Northern Ireland, United States of America and Japan 29-33 (edited by D. Swann and D. Greer and UNCTAD Secretariat resp., 1973)(TD/B/390). See also UNCTAD, Proceedings of the United Nations Conference on Trade and Development, Third Session, (Santiago) 213-255 (1973).

Practices, as already mentioned above, have shown that a wide range and variety of restrictive practices are encountered by developing countries in their economic and trading relationships with the developed countries.[85] Developing countries need to accelerate their economic and technical growth to earn more external resources, to have greatly improved access to developed countries' markets especially for manufactured products, to obtain capital and technology on more economical and less restricted terms and, above all, to retain a fair degree of assurance and flexibility that they can pursue their social and economic goals and plans. The choices open to them are not easy. They are often obliged to choose foreign capital and technology at prices they regard as excessive and on conditions they regard as onerously restrictive or, if they do not accept these terms, they have to forego capital and technology.[86]

(3) The Problem of Multinational Enterprises

6-40. Multinational enterprises not only enjoy economies of scale and the possibility of international cross subsidisation, which is true of large diversified national groups, but may also have a number competitive advantages resulting from their transnational structure which are not based on efficiency.[87]

---

85. Of particular interest is the UNCTAD Report of the Ad Hoc Group of Experts, Restrictive Business Practices in Relations to the Trade and Development of Developing Countries (1973)(Doc.TD/B/C.2/119).

86. See Kirshnamurti "National and Supra-National Antitrust Legislation; Concerns, Aspirations and Requirements of the Developing Countries" in Cartel and Antitrust Law; Speeches of an International Conference 213-216 (Gettlieb Duttweilen Institute, Oct. 1973). See also OECD, Committee of Experts on Restrictive Business Practices, Restrictive Business Practices of Multinational Enterprises, secs. 13-43 (1977) (hereinafter cited "OECD, Restrictive Business Practices of Multinational Enterprises").

87. See ibid. sec. 36. However, the OECD Report also shows that such enterprises can produce substantial beneficial effects on national and international competition (see secs. 26-47). The literature on multinational corporations is voluminous and mostly listed in the recent Bibliography of Multinational Corporations and Foreign Direct Investment (to March 1978) by D. Browndorf & S. Riemer.

The UN Group of Eminent Persons, which reported in 1974 on problems caused by multinational enterprises,[88] pointed in particular to the following anticompetitive effects caused by such enterprises: (1) allocation of selling markets among subsidiaries, thus hampering the ability of some of them to export and thereby damaging the host country's foreign trade;[89] (2) using restrictive patent and know-how licence practices to restrict exports, to prevent host country acquisition of the benefits of the technology, and to restrict sources of supply of goods needed to practice the technology licensed; (3) using prices for the transfer of goods among the enterprise's subsidiaries which are artificial as compared with open market prices, and which may sometimes discriminate against, and sometimes for, given subsidiaries, with alleged anticompetitive consequences; and (4) making acquisitions and entering into joint ventures which may unbalance and sometimes threaten the survival of host country industries and markets.

An added difficulty in controlling multinational enterprises is caused by some characteristics of international corporate enterprises which have tended to deprive all governments of effective control of their activities by using the corporate system where it is possible to conceal the identity of the persons who own or effectively control a corporation and the de facto national allegiance of those persons. It is possible for an enterprise to change the number of its corporate personalities, the nature of their affiliation with one another, and the

---

88. United Nations Department of Economic and Social Affairs, The Impact of Multinational Corporations on Development and on International Relations, Report of the Group of Eminent Persons, 83-86 U.N. Doc. E/5500/Rev. 1ST/ESA/6 (1974).

89. As has already been explained (see generally Section 2 in Chapter II). the antitrust law of the Community does not, in general, cover intra-enterprise conspiracy. Where activities of multinational enterprises are entirely within the corporation, and there is no arrangement or injury with regard to third parties (or abuse of a dominant position) the Community rules of competition do not apply.

locus of nominal control without any changes in the underlying physical operations or actual control.[90]

The antitrust aspects of multinational enterprises are part of the whole multinational picture and are bound up in the relationships of multinational enterprises to the countries in which they operate.[91] Most countries adopt as a principle that the law of competition is of general application and make no distinction between the restrictive business practices of multinational and national enterprises. This, of course, does not mean that any present system of legislation is fully adequate to deal with all the restrictive business practices which are international in scope.

B. Possible Remedies and Proposals for Action

6-41. A wide range of proposals for possible remedies to the international antitrust problem have been put forward by writers and international committees: they include envisaging, among other things, the harmonization of laws,[92] the creation of new procedures to obtain more information about multinational enterprises at the national and international level,[93] the development of international consultation, conciliation and arbitration procedures,[94] the formulation of a voluntary code of good conduct (cf. 6-43) and standards of behaviour

90. See Edwards "The Internationality of Economic Interests" 111 U.Pa.L.Rev. 185 et seq. (1962).
91. Cf. Fugate, supra note 35 at sec. 12-13.
92. See Oliver "The Harmonization of Laws and the Development of Principles for the Resolution of Conflicts of Enforcement Jurisdiction as to Transnational Monopolistic and Restrictive Trade Practices" in I.L.A. Tokyo Conference 544.
93. See OECD, Restrictive Business Practices of Multinational Enterprises secs. 203-204.
94. See R. Baxter "Settlement of Disputes" in I.L.A., Tokyo Conference 200; a resolution to that effect was adopted by the Conference (see pp. 169-170).

or guidelines for enterprises and governments (see 6-42 and 6-44), and the creation of a binding international antitrust law and an international agency with powers of enforcement.[95]

Some of these remedies have already proved useful in solving or mitigating the problems identified before and might be acceptable to the Community.[96] In examining them it will be convenient to distinguish between possible action at the international level and possible action at Community level. There is no one measure to solve all problems, but the remedies considered below, taken together, might lead in this direction.

(1) Action at the International Level

(a) Activities Within International Organizations

(i) The United Nations

(1) UNCTAD

6-42. The UN Conference on Trade and Development (UNCTAD) has been engaged in a study of restrictive business practices in international trade, particularly with respect to the export interests of developing countries. It created a Group of Experts on Restrictive Business Practices and approved a report of that Group first at the meeting of

---

95. See H. Zwarensteyn, Some Aspects of the Extraterritorial Reach of the American Antitrust Laws 88-92 (1970).

96. For a general discussion of past efforts to control international restrictive business practices see Furnish "A Transnational Approach to Restrictive Business Practices" 4 The Int. Lawyer 318-351 (1970).

UNCTAD III in Chile, in 1972.[97] At present UNCTAD is engaged in formulating a draft outline for a code of conduct which will consist of guidelines addressed to governments and enterprises with regard to restrictive business practices and a code of conduct with the underlying aim of facilitating the transfer of technology.[98]

In UNCTAD the EEC has observer status, which means participation, without the right to vote, in sessions of the Conference, the Trade and Development Board, the subsidiary organs and working groups.[99]

The Commission of the EEC expressed its objections to some provisions of the draft outline for the code of conduct addressed to governments and enterprises which were submitted for consideration by the Third Ad Hoc Group of Experts on restrictive business practices to UNCTAD V.[100] Subsequent meetings of UNCTAD and a UN Conference in 1979 failed to resolve those substantial disagreements. Divergencies which exist between the attitudes of participants on the efforts to draft a code of conduct on transfer of technology are also still unresolved.[101]

---

97. See United Nations Conference on Trade and Development, 3rd Sess., Santiago, Chile, April 13, 1972, Agenda Item No. 14(d). See also TD/122, 22 Dec. 1971; TD/122/Supp.1, 7 Jan. 1972, and official records of Trade and Development Board, 8th Sess. annexes, agenda item 6(d), Doc.TD/B/C.2/54 (1969).
98. See UNCTAD Resolution 89(IV); see elaborations in Eighth Report on Competition Policy, points 48-49; Seventh Report on Competition Policy, points 72-73; Sixth Report on Competition Policy, points 43-44; Fifth Report on Competition Policy, point 18.
99. The EEC status is in accordance with Resolution 1995 (XIX) of the UN General Assembly, adopted 30 December 1964.
100 For details of the proposals for the code see Report of the Third Ad Hoc Group of Experts on Restrictive Business Practices, 6th Sess., April 17-27, (1979)(TD/250; TD/B/C.2/201; TD/B/C.2/AC.6/20). On the Commission's position see Communication of the Commission to the Council of 20 Sept. 1978, Doc. COM. (78) 447.
101 On substantial objections of the Commission see Communication of the Commission to the Council of 25 Sept. 1978, Doc. R/2421/78 (COMER 49).

(2) Centre on Multinational Enterprises

6-43. At the UN there is a Centre on Multinational Enterprises whose role is to back up the work of the General Assembly, the Economic and Social Council and an Inter-governmental Commission on Transnational Corporations, to collect and propagate information, to carry out research, and to organize and coordinate technical cooperation projects in the areas concerned.

The UN Commission on Transnational Corporations has adopted a recommendation for a programme of work for the Centre, the chief factor of which is the preparation of a code of conduct concerning transnational enterprises. The programme further lists the establishment of a comprehensive information system on the activities of transnational enterprises, research on the political, social and economic effects of their operations, and technical cooperation programmes to place developing countries on a stronger footing in their negotiations with such enterprises.

The EEC Commission takes an active part in the work of the Centre.[102]

(ii) OECD

6-44. A potentially useful forum for inter-governmental discussions on restrictive and monopolistic business practices is the Restrictive Business Practices Committee of the OECD. The OECD provides for

---

102. For more information on the EEC Commission's activity within this organ of the UN see replies to W.Q. 685/75 O.J. 1976 C 139/2, and W.Q.241/76 O.J. 1976 C 244/16.

discussion on a community basis of methods by which the Member Countries can achieve economic growth, increase economic and technical assistance to newly developed areas and contribute to the expansion of world trade.

The OECD recommendations of 5th October, 1967, established a voluntary procedure for the prior notification of antitrust investigations and proceedings by Member Countries when important interests of another Member Country are involved.[103] They also provide for the coordination of antitrust enforcement, cooperation in developing or applying mutually beneficial methods of dealing with international antitrust problems and exchange of information on antitrust matters. The OECD Recommendations of 3rd July, 1973, concern a consultation and conciliation procedure on restrictive business practices affecting international trade. That mechanism works by country to country consultations which, in case of failure, may by mutual agreement of the parties be followed by conciliation on the part of the Committee of Experts on Restrictive Business Practices. The parties would not be bound by the view of the latter.[104]

In June, 1976, the OECD published a declaration on international investment and multinational enterprises. In a series of recommendations of which one whole section is concerned specifically with restrictive business practices, the declaration established voluntary guidelines for multinational enterprises. The guidelines emphasized, as a matter of general policy, the responsibility of multinational enterprises to

103. OECD Doc. C(67) 53 Final of 10 Oct. 1967, reprinted in Markert, "Recent Developments in International Antitrust Cooperation" 13 Antitrust Bull. 370-372 (1968).

104. OECD, Recommendation of the Council Concerning A Consultation and Conciliation Procedure on Restrictive Business Practices Affecting International Trade, C(73) 99 (Final) December 1973.

comply with official competition rules and established policies of the countries in which they operate, and to be ready to consult and cooperate with national authorities responsible for competition issues and investigations (e.g. by providing information, subject to the safeguards normally applicable).[105] The application of these guidelines in practice is to be kept under review by OECD.

Following the publication of its report on restrictive business practices of multinational enterprises, in 1977, the Council of the OECD adopted a recommendation on 20th July, 1978, concerning action against business practices of this kind. The recommendation is addressed to the Governments of OECD Member Countries and sets two objectives:

(1) to adopt new or supplement existing measures on restrictive business practices, such as anticompetitive acquisitions and discriminatory pricing;

(2) to develop appropriate national rules to facilitate investigations and proper procedures where relevant information is located outside the national territory of the responsible authority, and the delivery of legal documents and the execution of decisions regarding enterprises located abroad. The recommendation recommends stronger international cooperation in this area.[106]

Following this recommendation, two new working parties have been set up to study which provisions of OECD Member Countries' national laws are most likely to retard the development of international

105. Cf. Sixth Report on Competition Policy, point 41.

106. See Eighth Report on Competition Policy, point 45.

cooperation.[107]

As regards relations between the EEC and the OECD it should be noted that, although the EEC is not a member of this organiszation, its status there is higher than that of an observer. The Commission takes part as of right in the work of the organization,[108] it participates in the Council - at ministerial level - without the right to vote, and it also participates in the work of the various committees, groups and meetings of experts.

(b) Separate Bilateral Arrangements

6-45. The EEC is party to various treaties with third countries which have considerably extended the territorial scope of the principles of undistorted competition. There are special provisions in these agreements containing rules ensuring that trade between the Community and those third countries should develop under conditions of competition which are not distorted by restrictive or improper practices. For an extensive discussion of these agreements see Section 3 in Chapter III

The U.S. concluded an agreement with the Federal Republic of Germany which came into force on 11th September, 1976.[109] The agreement stipulates which laws are covered by it and which are the competent authorities to apply the agreement and defines the scope and details of the undertaking entered into by the Contracting Parties to assist each other by exchanging information. It also contains provisions

107. See ibid.
108. See Supplementary Protocol No. 1 to the Convention on the OECD (14 December 1960).
109. Text of the Agreement of 23rd June, 1976, has been published in the Official Journal of the Federal Republic of Germany (BBGL II of 23.10.1976).

guaranteeing the confidential nature of information exchanged between the parties concerned. The information which the competent American Federal authorities will forward to their German counterparts could, for instance, refer to the activities of a private American company which are within the law in the U.S. but illegal under German law. The Commission of the EEC indicated that the agreement between Germany and the U.S. (the only one of that type between a Member State of the Community and a third State) will contribute to the implementation of the OECD recommendations on the voluntary supervision of multinational enterprises in as much as it is intended to encourage cooperation between antitrust authorities in dealing with restrictive practices affecting international trade.[110]

6.46. In addition to the various agreements mentioned above there are continual informal contacts between the EEC and third countries including the exchange of visits between antitrust authorities. The Directorate-General for Competition at the Commission of the EEC and the American Antitrust Authorities currently exchange, and have done so for several years, information on competition issues of mutual interest.[111] The Commission is developing its cooperation with the competition authorities of other non-Member States, which it considers essential if similar points of view on the measures to be taken to combat restrictive practices affecting international trade are to be reached. According to information which we received from officials of the Commission, a framework for informal biannual consultations has been established with Canada and Japan (in addition to the U.S.).[112]

---

110. See reply to W.Q. 434/76 O.J. 1976 C 294/24.
111. See in particular Commission's reply to W.Q. 653/77 O.J. 1979 C42.
112. Private interviews with Mr. Pappalardo, Head of Inspection and Studies Division at the Directorate-General for Competition, on 2nd October, 1979, and with Mr. F. Benyon, from the same Division on 3rdOctober, 1979.

The information which is made available at these occasions is strictly non-confidential, i.e. material which has either been published or information which has been given to a court and is not covered by rules of secrecy. At present the Commission does not consider that it will be possible to achieve agreements with third States for better cooperation in competition matters because of the possible objections by the Member States.

(2) Possible Remedies at Community Level

(a) The Introduction of Specific Measures

6-47. There are several measures which the Community is considering introducing in the competition system following recommendations of international organizations. For example, it is examining the OECD recommendations for States to consider how, and under what safeguards, to provide or allow disclosure of information relevant to the enforcement of antitrust laws and to competition policy purposes which at present may not be obtainable or transmissible to other States for legal reasons.[113] Another example, which is mainly the outcome of a Community initiative, is the proposal, currently under consideration, to introduce a special Community regulation dealing with multinational enterprises.[114]

(b) Conclusion: Proposal for a Balancing of Multistate Interests Approach

6-48. The nature of the present study does not lend itself to

---

113. See OECD, Restrictive Business Practices of Multinational Enterprises, secs. 203-204.
114. See Multinational Undertakings and Community Regulations (Commission Communication to the Council, 7 November 1973); O.J. C 114/28; Supplement 15/73 Bull. E C See also Second Report on Competition Policy, point 16.

general conclusions. But, having regard to the Community's own experience, discussed in detail in the study and the current needs of international society and international law, it may be appropriate to suggest a general, overall policy which the Community could adopt in relation to the extraterritorial reach of its rules of competition.

In addition to specific measures of cooperation and regulation, it would be possible for the Community to adopt an approach of a voluntary nature by which it would admit that the reach of Community competition rules is, inter alia, governed by interests which may not be purely domestic and by self-imposed rules for restraint. Such an approach, which could be named the "balancing of multistate interests", or the "balancing approach", has for its primary purpose the avoidance of legal and economic conflicts in the application of antitrust laws. In the long run, and if other States also develop similar approaches, we submit that the balancing of interests process, in conjunction with methods for the settlement of conflicts between States and for better international antitrust cooperation, will reduce the severity of antitrust problems on the international plane.

The balancing approach, already referred to in a narrower context (see 6-34), would not be used only in cases of concurrent jurisdiction or conflicts with foreign laws, although it is mostly in those instances where the approach is required, but also as an essential measure in directing the Community in the general exercise of its extraterritorial jurisdiction.

6-49. Support for a balancing approach can be found in the judgement of the International Court of Justice in the Barcelona Traction Case,[115]

---

115. I.C.J. Reports (1970) p.42.

which concerned the balancing of national interests in defining the nationality of a corporation. Of particular interest is the separate opinion of Judge Sir Gerald Fitzmaurice:

> It is true that under present conditions international law does not impose hard and fast rules on states delimiting spheres of national jurisdiction in such matters (and there are of course others, for instance, in the field of shipping "antitrust" legislation, etc.) but leaves to states a wide discretion in the matter. It does, however: (a) postulate the existence of limits, though in any given case it may be for the tribunal to indicate that these are with regard to the facts of that case; and (b) involve for every state an obligation to exercise moderation and restraint as to the extent of jurisdiction assumed by its courts in cases having a foreign element and to avoid undue encroachments on a jurisdiction more properly pertaining to, or more appropriately exercised by another state. 116

6-50. In the U.S. a balancing approach has been adopted in the Timberlane Case[117] where the Court of Appeals for the Ninth Circuit, in the context of an antitrust suit with international ramifications, formulated rules for the application of that approach. For the facts of this case see 5-51. The court declined the application of the recognized "direct and substantial effect" test for the assertion of jurisidction in this foreign commerce case and, instead, substituted a balancing approach incorporating multinational, as well as domestic, considerations.[118] The American court applied in fact a "jurisdictional rule of reason",[119] balancing the domestic factors and considerations of comity. It recommended that seven issues should be considered: conflicts with the law or policy of the foreign country; the nationality or domicile of the individuals; the situs of the business or corporations; the degree to which enforcement could be expected to

116. Ibid. at 103-106.

117. Timberlane Lumber Co. v. Bank of America, 549 F. 2d 597 (9th Cir. 1976).

118. Ibid. at 612.

119. For explanation of that rule see in Brewster (supra note 35, at 312 et seq.) who originally employed this phrase.

bring about compliance; the impact on the U.S. relative to the effects on other countries; the extent to which there was an intent to harm American commerce; the foreseeability of the result within the U.S. as compared to conduct elsewhere.[120]

Individual American scholars have also supported relativistic application of the antitrust laws by calling for a "conflict of laws" or "balancing" approach to the resolution of conflicts.[121] As indicated by Fugate, the Department of Justice and the courts now do weigh domestic interests and foreign policies, and the Department of Justice liaises on antitrust matters not only with the State Department but also with other governments.[122]

(i) The Proposed Operation of a Balancing Approach by the Community

6-51. The method of analysis which is proposed for a balancing approach is that employed by the private international lawyer who seeks to identify the "seat of the legal relationship". For example, the Anglo-American courts have increasingly abandoned mechanical rules for what in England is called the "proper law", that is, the law with which the legal event in question has, in all circumstances, the most substantial connection.

---

120. Even in an earlier case involving a Justice Department Grand Jury proceeding for obtaining documents from Germany, the Court of Appeals for the Second Circuit followed similar guidelines for consideration of interests. See In the matter of the Grand Jury Subpoena Addressed to First National City Bank 396 F. 2d. 897, 901-902 (2d Cir. 1968). Facts of the case are given in 5-59.
121. Note, "Extraterritorial Application of the Antitrust Laws: A Conflict of Laws Approach" 70 Yale L.J. 259 (1961); Trautman "A Study of the International Environment; The International Reach of American Regulatory Legislation Other Than the Sherman Act" in Brewster, supra note 35, at 312; Ongman "Be No Longer A Chaos; Constructing A Normative Theory of the Sherman Act's Extraterritorial Jurisdictional Scope" 71 Northw. U.L.Rev. 733 (1977); Stanford "The Application of the Sherman Act to Conduct Outside the United States; A View from Abroad" 11 Cornell Int.L.J. 209-210(1978).
122. Fugate, supra note 35, at sec. 15.1

A balancing approach therefore comes near to the theory of jurisdiction which rests on some genuine or effective link between the crime and the State of the forum as has been advocated by Mann. According to that theory a State has legislative jurisdiction if its contact with a given set of facts is so close, so substantial, so direct and so weighty that legislation in respect of them is in harmony with international law.[123] However, a distinction between the balancing approach and that theory has to be observed. The areas in which we are concerned with the balancing approach are where the Community (or other States) will search for an appropriate law rather for an adequate jurisdictional basis. The balancing approach is concerned with the question whether the Community (or other States) already having legislative jurisdiction should apply the respective law. Therefore, not only factors supporting legislative jurisdiction, but other factors as well, may be relevant in answering that question.[124]

In this study we have indicated that the Commission has accepted a jurisdictional model of thinking, i.e. a qualified effects doctrine, which indicates the contour of its jurisdictional competence under international law. We propose that instead of trying to insist on principles of jurisdiction by a somewhat artificial concept, we should broaden the general area of jurisdiction in accordance with the

---

123. See Mann, supra note 15, at 49.

124. The balancing approach poses the question of the scope of considerations which are essentially matters of degree and involve a multitude of changing factual circumstances. For example see factors mentioned in Brewster, supra note 35, at 446; compare Restatement (Second) of Conflict of Laws § 6 (1971) with Restatement (Second) of the Foreign Relations Law of the U.S. at § 40 (1965). An examination of interests to be taken into account in various circumstances is given by A. Von Mehren and D. Trautman in The Law of Multistate Problems; Cases and Materials on Conflict of Laws, ch. III (1965).

competition policy, and then devote our efforts to reduce possible conflicts with other jurisdictions by a balancing approach. This would do two things. First, we would recognize that other States have interests which are affected by the anticompetitive conduct. Secondly, we could tailor principles to avoid conflict with other jurisdictions in a way which would entail a contextual analysis of the various interests involved.

The determination of the limit of the extraterritorial reach of the antitrust rules should not therefore be confined to ascertaining only whether the principles of international law, in any way, restrict a conclusively presumed authorization in the Treaty of the application of the rules extraterritorially. Instead it would appear more appropriat for the Community initially to address itself to the question of its competition policy, as based on the rules, and the weighing of the relevant interests involved. Once the Community decided that the rules authorized an extraterritorial reach then, and only then, would it consider whether principles of international law in any way limit the application of the rules.

The main problem with the qualified effects doctrine is that it spends too much time defining the basis of jurisdiction within the territory and not enough time analysing and balancing various interests involved in the extraterritorial application of the antitrust laws. The qualified effects test, by focussing solely on the domestic impact of antitrust violations, heightens the risk of conflict with foreign States. Strict implementation of such an effects doctrine could result in an unfavourable impact on the conduct of the Community's foreign relations.

A flexible evaluation of a wide range of domestic and international factors will, instead, enable the Community to decline jurisdiction in cases in which adjudication would hinder the implementation of foreign policy by the EEC. Thus the introduction of a balancing of interests approach will involve an increased degree of sophistication and complexity of analysis by the Community.

GPSR Compliance

The European Union's (EU) General Product Safety Regulation (GPSR) is a set of rules that requires consumer products to be safe and our obligations to ensure this.

If you have any concerns about our products, you can contact us on ProductSafety@springernature.com

In case Publisher is established outside the EU, the EU authorized representative is:

Springer Nature Customer Service Center GmbH
Europaplatz 3
69115 Heidelberg, Germany

Batch number: 10824476

Printed by Printforce, the Netherlands